**HUMAN RESOURCE
DIRECTOR'S HANDBOOK**

HUMAN RESOURCE DIRECTOR'S HANDBOOK

Mary F. Cook

Prentice-Hall, Inc.
Englewood Cliffs, N.J.

Prentice-Hall International, Inc., *London*
Prentice-Hall of Australia, Pty. Ltd., *Sydney*
Prentice-Hall Canada Inc., *Toronto*
Prentice-Hall of India Private Ltd., *New Delhi*
Prentice-Hall of Japan, Inc., *Tokyo*
Prentice-Hall of Southeast Asia Pte. Ltd., *Singapore*
Whitehall Books, Ltd., Wellington, *New Zealand*
Editora Prentice-Hall do Brasil, Ltda., *Rio de Janeiro*

Library of Congress Cataloging in Publication Data

Cook, Mary F.
   Human resource director's handbook.

   Includes index.
   1. Personnel management—Handbooks, manuals, etc.
I. Title.
HF5549.C724   1984   658.3   83-17810
ISBN 0-13-445859-1

Printed in the United States of America.

ACKNOWLEDGMENTS

A special "thank you" to Ruth Spanarella, for her help and support in the preparation of the manuscript. It was a tedious job, and her efforts and good humor were considerable. Thanks to my husband, Fred Cook, and my daughter, Erin Haley, who were most supportive during the year it took to write the book. Thanks also to the many contributors to the book, each of whom is acknowledged in the chapter where their contribution appears, and to the president of Rocky Mountain Energy Company, James C. Wilson, who gave me encouragement that enabled me to proceed while working full-time in my capacity as Director of Employee Relations, a very active and challenging position.

WHAT THIS BOOK WILL DO FOR YOU

Organizations that invest heavily in the human resource function expect it to be successful and to pay its way by contributing to the economic success of the organization.

This book delivers more than 150 tested ideas, procedures, and examples for successfully managing a cost-effective human resource function. It's full of practical, comprehensive, and effective guidance and advice, written in plain language, in a simple format for quick and easy reference. There is no "theory" in this book; it's full of practical ideas and programs that have been used by other human resource directors in other organizations. Detailed information on major aspects of the human resource department are indexed for convenient reference and are illustrated with numerous tables and graphs.

Whether you call it the Personnel Department, the Human Resource Department, or the Employee Relations Department makes little difference; the function's basic purpose is to manage the human resource effectively; and to help you do that, ideas and techniques are provided that will work in any company, large or small. Key areas of the field are covered, from ideas for recruiting today's more independent workers and complying with various regulations, including a policy and procedure for handling sexual harassment issues, to designing and implementing competitive compensation programs. The book also reviews special programs that are necessary to attract and retain today's more physically active, entitlement-oriented work force.

Each chapter in the book contains special checklists and tips to help you focus your attention on techniques that will make you more successful; and case examples are provided to highlight problem-solving techniques used by other human resource directors. The specific information necessary to achieve a successful, cost-effective human resource function in today's fast-changing business organization—any organization, private or public—is included in this book.

HOW THIS BOOK IS ORGANIZED

The *Human Resource Director's Handbook* is organized into twelve chapters, each representing a key area of the human resource function and showing how each of these areas should affect the organization's business plan and profitability. Whether the organization is private or public, large or small, the ideas and techniques outlined in each chapter will work successfully with only simple modifications.

Each chapter includes case examples and tips for managing the situations described. For example, chapter 1 includes a checklist of human resource department responsibilities and a method for ensuring successful implementation of all human resource programs that are needed.

The first chapter tells what is expected of the human resource function and what it takes to be successful in most organizations. It also arrays a variety of structure options for organizing the department reviews budgets, staffing levels, and other human resource activities. This chapter also emphasizes the fact that the human resource function cannot be managed in a vacuum, and key human resource interfaces are identified.

The other eleven chapters actually review in depth the human resource responsibilities and programs that any organization should have in place in order to be successful. These chapters also cover federal regulations and other internal and external pressures working on the human resource function, and they tell you how to deal with them effectively.

An alphabetical index is provided at the end of the book for easy reference when a specific question arises and you need a fast answer.

HOW TO USE THIS HANDBOOK

Each chapter addresses itself to a specific area of the human resource function. If you have a problem in compensation, just turn to chapter 4 and review it for references. If the problem is salary compression, turn to the index at the back of the book. Look for the term "Compression" and the page number. A graph shows what salary compression is, and there is an explanation of a program one company used to address the problem successfully. The pros and cons of the program also are given in detail.

If you are concerned, for example, that you do not have a policy on sexual harassment, and you need one, turn again to the index, look up "Sexual Harassment," go to the page number indicated, and you will find a policy, the pros and cons of having such a policy, and the procedures to follow if you receive a complaint from an employee.

This book covers in detail several aspects of personnel management that are not well covered in other books, including tips on handling human resource relationships, outside influences affecting employers, and the issues of employee motivation, corporate social responsibility, and issues management.

Laws are changing. Courts have begun to rule that employees may be able to recover substantial sums for wrongful discipline or discharge; it is more important than ever to have good business procedures in these areas. These timely subjects are reviewed in detail, and solutions to many problems can be found quickly in this book.

Mary F. Cook

Table of Contents

HUMAN RESOURCE
DIRECTOR'S HANDBOOK

CHAPTER 1

The Human Resource Function:
Catalyst for Excellence

The traditional personnel function has its roots in the administration of routine activities needed to carry on the processes of planning, organizing, staffing, and managing groups of employees.

Because of the number of laws and regulations emanating from the social unrest of the 1960s, the personnel function grew rapidly to include the programs needed to comply with regulations in the areas of Equal Employment Opportunity, Affirmative Action, Occupational Safety and Health, and Workers' Compensation, to name a few.

This era of the new worker, the self-fulfillment seeker, and corporate social conscience has brought a new responsibility to the personnel professional. This is perhaps the greatest change in the personnel function that has occurred in the last decade. It's the quantum leap from the personnel function as the management of a routine set of processes to a varied function that is now more human-resource-oriented—addressing the needs of the employees it serves as well as the needs of the organization. While personnel administration responsibilities focus mainly on routine recordkeeping, regulatory compliance, and procedural and administrative aspects of the business, the overall human resource function also embraces the people-related, motivational, and human resource development aspects of the business.

Today, more companies are beginning to give employees the same priority that they give their capital investment. The human resource is the crucial ingredient that makes everything else work.

The new work ethic is beginning to take its toll, however, with companies that are frustrated when people refuse to relocate because they like where they are.

There's also frustration on the part of workers at benefit programs tailored to the family of the 1950s and 1960s, where the man worked and the woman stayed home to raise the children. More women work outside the home today, and there is a need for benefits like flexitime and child care. More companies are beginning to understand these needs and to take positive action.

As companies begin to understand that they face a critical productivity challenge with this new worker, and as government regulation increases, the role of the human resource director is strengthened. Experienced human resource professionals now command top dollar. Executives at the 250 largest American companies average more than $100,000 a year in salary, and some receive bonuses. This new human resource executive focuses more sharply on profits and knows how to analyze a profit-and-loss statement and a balance sheet. The capital structure of the organization, its financial strength, market position, human resource strength and productivity, are all factors that will determine the future of the company; and human resource professionals are looking at their companies in dimensions that encompass the whole spectrum, not just the human resource element.

This new, more successful human resource director has learned to marry the many human resource systems to the organization's business objectives in order to positively affect the bottom-line economic goals of the company and the overall career goals of the work force.

This new trend toward total human resource management allows the human resource director to contribute more directly and quantitatively to an organization's profitability.

1.1   THE HUMAN RESOURCE DEPARTMENT

This new recognition that the human resource is a key element in company success has evolved in part because organizations have had to react to six important needs:

1. The need to maximize the return on the investment of hiring, relocating, and training new employees.
2. The need either to "grow" or to attract from outside the organization broadly skilled managers for the top levels of the organization in order to ensure outstanding executive succession.
3. The need to provide creative, enthusiastic contributions to productivity in an era of rising labor costs and business competition.
4. The need to retain a work force that has a self-fulfillment and entitlement attitude regarding their jobs, their pay, their benefits, and their personal challenge.
5. The need to provide equal employment and promotional opportunity to special-interest groups, women, minorities, and the handicapped.
6. The need to respond to increasing government regulation and intervention in the decision-making process in areas of employment, health, safety, and retirement.

It is necessary to respond to all of these items and still maximize profits. The two lists that follow detail some of the key elements that both management and human resource people feel are essential to the success of the organization and to the success of the human resource function.

Twelve Elements Management Expects of the Human Resource Function

1. To provide expertise and leadership to ensure that the right numbers of people are in the right jobs at the right time.
2. To assist management in creating an organizational climate that enhances employee effectiveness.
3. To be creative human resource problem-solvers.
4. To ensure that employees at all levels are being compensated competitively at their location and in their industry.
5. To ensure that employees have the benefit programs they need and that the programs are administered effectively.
6. To provide training and development programs to ensure that employees are effective in their current jobs and to prepare them for bigger assignments.
7. To develop and maintain a credible reputation inside the organization as well as in the community and the human resource profession; to develop an effective human resource staff.
8. To provide leadership and commitment to affirmative action in the employment of women, minorities, and the handicapped; to maximize potential and minimize dislocations.
9. To maintain employee recordkeeping and administrative responsibilities effectively; to comply with all local, state, and federal regulations.
10. To provide expertise and programs in the areas of employee health and safety.
11. To maintain positive labor relations; to provide leadership in a union-free environment, or managerial effectiveness in a union environment.
12. To take a proactive rather than reactive stand on issues that will affect the organization in the coming years.

Nine Items a Survey of Top Human Resource Executives Picked as Being the Most Important to the Success of a Human Resource Director

1. Know your management people. Know what they expect of you and your function, not what you *think* they expect. Be absolutely sure.
2. Know what your budget is for providing human resource services, what you can spend and how many people management expects you to have on your staff to provide the services they need and want.
3. Keep in close personal contact with management, the people who have the power over your function. Really communicate. Don't just think you know what they expect of you.
4. Be impeccable in everything you do. Know all you can about your function, hire people who are experts in their discipline. Eliminate mistakes. Do things ethically and with class.
5. Be ready to give top management what they need when they need it. Be prepared to get the job done quickly; never make excuses.
6. Be enthusiastic and optimistic about the company, the future, and your function; this is essential to maintaining a motivated staff and your own credibility.

7. Look at the big picture. Develop your perceptual skills. Stop to think about how what you do and how you do it will affect others' responses to you and the outcome of any endeavor.

8. Work at developing good relationships at all levels of the organization and across all functional groups. You can't do anything in any organization without help.

9. Never be self-serving, but find subtle ways to gain visibility for your function and your staff; not yourself, particularly, but the job that is being done. Be sure that your management knows the value of your staff and their work.

1.2   A CHECKLIST OF HUMAN RESOURCE RESPONSIBILITIES

During the 1981 budget year, a survey conducted by the Bureau of National Affairs showed that personnel department activities cost employers approximately $433 for every employee on the payroll.[1] That would amount to $437,448 for a company with 1,000 employees. In addition, recruiting and relocation costs necessary to hire new professional employees have soared into the thousands of dollars. One company estimates their average relocation cost at $35,000 per employee when buy-out of an old home and assistance in getting into a new home are needed.

An effective human resource function will pay its way in savings from recruiting and employment efforts and compensation and benefits programs that attract and retain good workers, and by providing fully trained and highly motivated employees at all levels of the organization.

Most human resource managers feel that if they provide the elements of a successful full-service human resource program shown in the checklist (figure 1–1), the function will more than pay its way in positive contributions to the economic results of the organization.

Look over the checklist. Make a special list of the Bs and Ds and priortize them on a "worst-first" basis for immediate action. Each of the items listed in the checklist is covered more fully in chapters that follow.

IMPORTANT TIP:

The first time you go through this process, you may want to do it yourself. Decide what elements of the program you feel you need to make your organization most successful.

However, it is important that you also have your management do the same thing. If you don't, you may find later that you were off doing the things you thought were important when your management was wondering why you never got to items *they* thought were important.

---

[1] Reprinted by permission of *ASPA–BNA Survey,* copyright 1981 by the Bureau of National Affairs, Inc., Washington, D.C.

FIGURE 1-1

Checklist of Human Resource Department Responsibilities

Check appropriate box: A = Already have it. B = Don't have it; do need it. C = Don't need it. D = Have it, but needs revision.	A	B	C	D
Human Resource Planning and Organizational Development				
Recruiting, Selection, Employment, New Employee Orientation				
Compensation, Benefits Programs				
Human Resource Development				
Affimative Action and Equal Employment Opportunity				
Personnel Policies and Procedures				
Communications Programs				
Health and Safety Programs				
Labor Relations				
Federal Regulations, Procedures, and Administration Recordkeeping				
Employee Counseling and Special Programs				

1.3 PERSONNEL PRACTICES—1,108 COMPANIES SURVEYED BY THE CONFERENCE BOARD HIGHLIGHT KEY PERSONNEL PRACTICES

A survey of selected personnel policies was completed by the Conference Board.[2] Some of the highlights of the companies' practices were as follows:

- Almost 45 percent of the companies have written policies regarding the privacy of personnel records.
- More than 85 percent provide employee access to records containing personal information about themselves.
- More than half require an employee's permission before disclosing personal information other than work location, term of employment, and last position held.

---

[2] "Personnel Practices I: Recruitment, Placement, Training, Communication," *Information Bulletin no. 89,* The Conference Board, 845 Third Avenue, New York, New York 10022, 1981.

- Most companies fill nonexempt positions through unsolicited applications and their exempt positions through ads in general newspapers.
- Almost all of the companies check applicants' work references.
- More than half of the companies hire some of their retirees on a part-time basis.
- Job posting is used for production job openings in three out of four companies; office and clerical openings in three out of five; and professional and lower-level managerial positions in less than half of the survey group.
- Performance appraisals are used by 95 percent of the participants for exempt and nonexempt white-collar workers. About 75 percent use performance appraisals for blue-collar workers, mainly to assess performance during the probationary period.
- About two-thirds of the respondents make company financial reports available to employees.
- Suggestion award programs were found in one-third of the companies.
- About 85 percent of the participants maintain onsite training or education programs.
- Tuition aid plans are provided for full-time white-collar workers, exempt and nonexempt, by 90 percent of the respondents, and to full-time nonexempt blue-collar workers by almost 80 percent of the survey group.
- The average participation rate in tuition aid plans by eligible employees stands at 5 percent for white-collar and 3 percent for blue-collar groups.

1.4   HOW YOU CAN SAVE BIG DOLLARS IN JUST TWO KEY AREAS BY INSTALLING A FULL-SERVICE HUMAN RESOURCE FUNCTION

Organizations must pay competitive wages and provide benefits competitive with other organizations in their field if they want to attract and retain the qualified and motivated work force they need to achieve their business objectives.

In order to implement compensation and benefits programs, organizations require professionals with expertise and know-how in these fields. A full-service human resource department includes such compensation and benefits expertise.

Case in Point: A young, fast-growing energy company began losing experienced geology and engineering personnel they badly needed. The managers began to conduct exit interviews and found that people were leaving basically for higher salaries. Employees liked the company and felt the future was bright, but they couldn't turn down significant salary increases.

The company did not have a human resource department. There was one person who interviewed and hired people, but that was the total human resource function. The company lost twelve people before they decided to hire a human resource manager and to concentrate on upgrading their compensation and benefits programs.

1.5   APPROXIMATE COSTS TO THE COMPANY FOR REPLACING TWELVE TECHNICAL EMPLOYEES

Recruiting Costs

> Eight of the employees came through search firms, one was recruited by an employee, and three came through classified advertising

- *Advertising* . . . . $ 3,100.00
- *Search firms*
  (8 applicants × average salary of $30,000 × 30% placement fee) 72,000.00
- *Interviewing costs*
  (Recruiter's salary of $28,000 per year or $13.46 per hour × 2,080, typical number of hours worked in a year) (4 hours interviewing × 12 applicants) 646.08
- *Department manager's salary for interviewing*
  ($50,000 per year or $24.03 per hour × 2,080, typical number of hours worked in a year) (5 hours of interviewing × 12 applicants) 1,441.80
- *Travel expenses to bring applicants in for interviews* 2,600.00

Employment Costs

- *Relocation*
  Six required full relocation benefits, including help selling old home and assistance in purchasing new home. (6 × $15,000, average cost) 90,000.00

  Two required assistance only in purchasing new home. (2 × $7,000, average cost) 14,000.00

  Eight required move of household items. (8 × average move of $5,000) 40,000.00

New Employee Orientation

- $150 per employee (12 × $150) . . . . $ 1,800.00

Training

- The costs of new employee training and break-in costs were not calculated.   —

  Approximate Cost of Replacing Twelve Employees $225,587.88

    The cost of a qualified human resource manager with professional expertise in the areas of compensation, benefits, recruiting, training, and Equal Employment Opportunity is approximately $40,000 to $50,000 per year, depending on the industry and the area of the country in which the company is located.

No one can guarantee that hiring a qualified human resource manager will eliminate the high cost of turnover in all situations, but a human resource manager who ensures competitive wages and benefits, appropriate motivation through training and development, and fair and equitable treatment of all employees, must affect the economic results of the organization positively.

EEO Case in Point: Another high cost area where a Denver company lost big dollars because it didn't have the human resource expertise it needed was in the critical area of EEO and affirmative action.

A manager fired a female minority employee for absenteeism. The manager failed, through lack of knowledge and experience in the EEO field, to keep adequate absentee records of all employees and, further, did not check to see if he was treating all employees in his department in the same way. In fact, he had a white male in his group who had a similar absentee record, and he did not fire him.

The company was committed to affirmative action, but it didn't have the professional expertise in the human resource area to train department managers and to acquaint them with EEO regulations.

An experienced human resource manager would audit the absentee records of all employees to ensure equal treatment. In addition, an internal procedure that provided guidance to managers in handling human resource problems could have prevented the dismissal, which occurred without appropriate progressive warnings and discussion.

The Company Hired a Human Resource Manager after the Civil Rights Charges Were Filed

Following is a summary of the actions filed against the company and the costs expended:

State Civil Rights charge filed:
- Charge received and read by the following executives:
  CEO (½ hour at salary of $48.07/hour) $24.03
  Vice-President Administration (½ hour at salary of
  $33.65/hour)   16.83
  Attorney (½ hour at salary of $28.85/hour)   14.43
  Human Resource Manager (½ hour at salary of
  $19.23/hour)   9.61
- Attorney briefs CEO for ½ hour   38.46
- Interrogatories received and read by Vice-President
  Administration and Human Resource Manager (1
  hour)   52.88
- Interrogatories reviewed by Attorney (1 hour)   28.85
- Human Resource Manager reviews interrogatories
  with the Department Manager (1 hour)   43.27
- Human Resource Manager completes interrogatories
  (4 hours)   76.92
- Human Resource Manager reviews interrogatories
  with Vice-President, Administration and Attorney (1
  hour)   81.73

- Secretary types answers, makes copies, and mails material (8 hours) — 69.20
- State Civil Rights Commission hearing attended by Department Manager, Human Resource Manager, and Attorney (2 hours) — 144.24
- Company loses case—fact-finding results issued
- EEOC institutes charges
- EEOC charges reviewed by the following executives:
  - CEO — $24.03
  - Vice-President Administration — 16.83
  - Attorney — 14.43
  - Human Resource Manager (½ hour each) — 9.61
- Attorney briefs CEO, Vice-President Administration and Human Resource Manager (1 hour) — 100.95
- Human Resource Manager reviews EEO charges with Department Manager (½ hour) — 21.63
- Interrogatories received and completed by Human Resource Manager (4 hours) — 76.92
- Completed interrogatories reviewed and approved by Vice-President Administration and Attorney (1 hour) — 62.50
- Secretary types, copies, and mails all material (8 hours) — 69.20
- EEOC fact-finding conference attended by Human Resource Manager, Attorney, and Department Manager (3 hours) — 216.36
- Travel costs minimal because hearing was held in Denver, and all parties lived in Denver
  - Travel costs — 86.00
  - Food — 250.50
- EEOC asks for a conciliation meeting—company agrees and meeting attended by Department Manager, Human Resource Manager, and Attorney (4 hours) — $288.48
- Company agrees to put employee back to work — _____

Total Costs in Salaries and Expenses for Preliminary Investigation and Subsequent Meetings — $1,837.89

Corporate Salaries

	per year
CEO	$100,000
Vice President Administration	70,000
Attorney	60,000
Department Manager	50,000
Human Resource Manager	40,000
Secretary	18,000

The hourly cost of each individual was arrived at by dividing the annual salary by 2,080 hours, a typical number of hours worked in a twelve-month period.

1.6   THE NATURE OF THE HUMAN RESOURCE JOB

The human resource job cannot be accomplished in a vacuum. The nature of the job is always changing, vulnerable to a variety of situations, and almost constantly redefined by both internal and external forces. The external forces—economic, technological, political, and social—also are constantly changing.

The ongoing success of the human resource department frequently depends on the responses of the department to the forces constantly working on it.

The human resource manager must be a business manager as well as a human resource manager. There are six factors in any organization that the human resource manager must understand:

1. The structure of the organization
2. The personality and style of the organization
3. The purpose of the organization
4. The tasks involved in the functioning of the organization
5. The technology of the organization
6. The people who perform the tasks

The basic premise in business seems to be that the manager's primary task is to make decisions solely about his or her own department. We all know, however, that in any management situation or environment there are hundreds of interrelated factors, and the critical question for the manager is which of those factors is most important in its effect on the success of the human resource function.

There is a distinct interrelationship between internal and external forces. In order to be successful, the human resource manager must be able to evaluate all the factors, study their dimensions, and understand their interrelationships. No one factor is unaffected by the others.

The matrix in figure 1–2 shows major internal and external human resource interfaces.

HUMAN RESOURCE DIRECTOR'S TIP:

The importance of good ongoing personal relations with all of these groups cannot be overstated, no matter what level or how often the interface occurs. *Never fail* to consider seriously the future impact of what you say or do.

Remember the purchasing agent you brushed off six months ago? This month, that purchasing agent is in charge of purchasing a $2-million piece of equipment from one of your subsidiaries.

Remember the secretary you snubbed a year ago? This year, she's working for the president of your company.

How about the attorney you failed to give a courtesy interview to several months ago? Today, she's in charge of compliance reviews for the OFCCP.

FIGURE 1–2

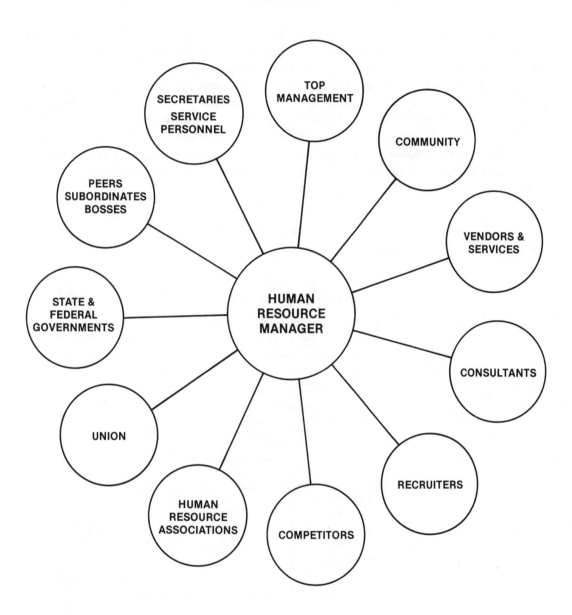

KEY HUMAN RESOURCE INTERFACES

Your personal business style and the kindness you show to others—taking time to explain what you are doing and why—will pay big dividends in your human resource interfaces. It also will go a long way toward building credibility in your company and in the community where you work.

1.7   HUMAN RESOURCE DEPARTMENT STRUCTURE

Many textbooks and books on personnel administration go into great depth about why organizations are structured the way they are. Instead of reviewing the line-and-staff concept, the hierarchy/pyramid concept, and the standard theories of personnel management structure, this chapter covers personnel and industrial relations (PAIR) positions and survey data on salaries of human resource people at most professional salaried levels. The survey data are drawn from the 1981 ASPA/Hansen Salary Survey completed by the American Society for Personnel Administration. The chart in figure 1–3 shows Pair unit model A, and the one in figure 1–4 shows Pair unit model B. The two models reflect medium and large size company organizations and salaries.

FIGURE 1–3

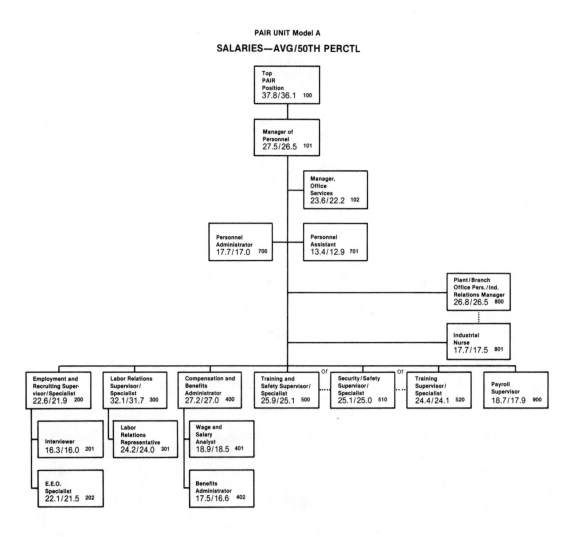

PAIR UNIT Model A

SALARIES—AVG/50TH PERCTL

FIGURE 1-4

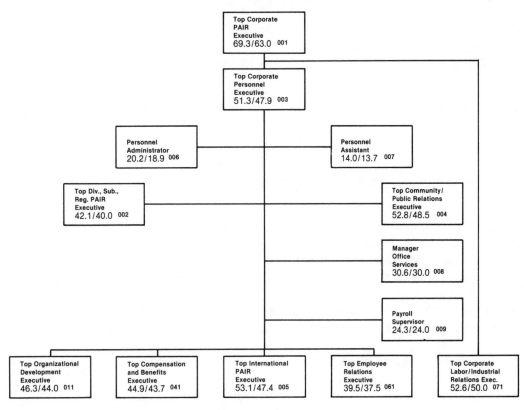

PAIR UNIT Model B

SALARIES—AVG/50TH PERCTL

Personnel and Industrial Relations Salary Survey

In a comprehensive salary survey of personnel and industrial relations, the American Society for Personnel Administration and A. S. Hansen, Inc., have analyzed 1981 compensation data from more than 2,600 PAIR units, involving over 19,000 individual employees.[3] The ASPA/Hansen Salary Survey covers salary levels for two organizational forms, the first for larger PAIR units (those having twenty or more positions) and the second for smaller PAIR units (those having nineteen or fewer positions).

The survey can be used to test current compensation levels against prevailing competitive salaries. When using the survey findings to test your own compensation levels, ASPA stresses, it is critical to:

- Match your positions to survey positions based on position content rather than title, making sure that comparisons actually reflect the relationships among, and responsibilities of, positions within your own organization.

---

[3] "Personnel and Industrial Relations Salary Survey," American Society for Personnel Administration, 30 Park Drive, Berea, Ohio 44017. With the A. S. Hansen Company.

- Recognize that not all of the functions described in the survey positions have to be performed by the employee whose job is being compared in order for there to be a valid position match.

The survey includes salary data for PAIR positions:

- On a nationwide basis, with an analysis of the relationship compensation levels have to gross sales and employment.
- For a group of selected cities where sufficient data were reported by participants.

A copy of the survey can be ordered from the American Society for Personnel Administration, 30 Park Drive, Berea, Ohio 44017. The cost of the survey is $95.00 for participants, and $140.00 for nonparticipants.

1.8   PERSONNEL DEPARTMENT ACTIVITIES

In the 1981 ASPA and the Bureau of National Affairs annual survey entitled "Personnel Activities, Budgets, and Staffs," there are forty-six activities listed. Respondents were asked whether the cost of the activity was budgeted solely to personnel or shared by other departments. For activities not clearly budgeted and for companies with no separate personnel budgets (30 percent of the total sample), respondents were asked to consider the items in terms of overall responsibility for the activity. The table shown in figure 1–5 lists the forty-six activities and assignments of responsibility.

Personnel Department Budgets

On the basis of annual cost per employee on the payroll, the 1981 expenditure on personnel activities is a median of $433 per employee.

The median size of the personnel budget for all companies reported in the ASPA/Hansen survey was 2.5 percent of the total company payroll. See figure 1–6.

Personnel Staffing Ratios

According to the Bureau of National Affairs, staffing ratios for 1981 for companies they survey average one personnel employee for each 100 people on the payroll. This varies with added responsibility, or conversely with less responsibility. Some human resource functions include other related groups, such as office services, security, and facilities. See figure 1–7.

Human resource department budgets and staffing ratios must fit the needs of the organization. The president of one company insists on several sophisticated programs that he feels are necessary to the success of his company and has therefore approved a much larger staff than most organizations would feel was necessary.

It's very important to know what your management expects of your function and what size staff and budget they will approve in order to get that job done effectively.

FIGURE 1-5

Activities Handled by Personnel Departments

Activity	Percentage of All Companies (503)			
	Extent of Personnel Department's Responsibility			No Such Activity at Company/Facility
	All	Some	None	
Personnel records/reports	94	5	*	—
Personnel research	85	3	*	11
Insurance benefits administration	84	13	3	—
Unemployment compensation administration	83	12	4	1
EEO compliance/affirmative action	78	20	1	*
Wage/salary administration	76	22	*	*
Worker's compensation administration	73	19	8	*
Tuition aid/scholarships	70	12	8	11
Job evaluation	66	29	2	3
Health/medical services	65	14	9	12
Retirement preparation programs	64	15	4	17
Preemployment testing	64	10	1	25
Vacation/leave processing	62	29	8	*
Induction/orientation	59	39	2	—
Promotion/transfer/separation processing	57	41	2	—
Counseling/employee assistance programs	57	26	2	15
Pension/profit-sharing plan administration	55	30	8	7
College recruiting	54	17	2	26
Recreation/social/recognition programs	53	32	8	7
Recruiting/interviewing/hiring	52	47	*	*
Attitude surveys	52	12	2	34
Union/labor relations	50	17	2	31
Complaint/disciplinary procedures	48	50	1	*
Relocation services administration	47	19	5	29
Supervisory training	43	44	9	3

33

FIGURE 1-5 (cont'd)

Activities Handled by Personnel Departments

Activity	Percentage of All Companies (503)			
	Extent of Personnel Department's Responsibility			No Such Activity at Company/Facility
	All	Some	None	
Employee communications/publications	40	34	19	7
Executive compensation administration	39	32	23	6
Human resource planning	38	48	4	10
Safety programs/OSHA compliance	38	39	20	3
Management development	34	49	9	8
Food services	32	8	34	26
Performance evaluation, nonmanagement	29	55	13	3
Community relations/fund drives	28	37	29	5
Suggestion systems	28	17	12	43
Thrift/savings plan administration	26	17	6	51
Security/plant protection	25	14	53	8
Organization development	22	50	13	15
Management appraisal/MBO	19	46	15	20
Stock plan administration	19	14	8	58
Skill training, nonmanagement	15	48	30	7
Public relations	13	30	52	5
Administrative services (mail, PBX, phone, messengers, etc.)	13	12	73	2
Payroll processing	10	26	63	1
Travel/transportation services administration	9	24	46	21
Library	9	6	48	37
Maintenance/janitorial services	6	8	81	5

*Less than 1 percent.

34

Personnel Department Budgets: 1980 and 1981

FIGURE 1-6

	Range				
	Low	First Quartile	Median	Third Quartile	High
			(Dollars per year)		
Total Budget: 1980					
All Companies (300)	$17,830	$172,500	$419,255	$1,012,384	$52,883,354
By Industry					
Manufacturing (140)	17,830	210,000	463,580	983,500	32,763,000
Nonmanufacturing (83)	42,277	220,000	624,996	1,460,666	52,883,354
Finance (42)	69,618	207,000	472,325	1,084,000	5,425,000
Nonbusiness (77)	28,000	115,000	258,000	488,109	8,500,000
Health Care (34)	67,000	115,000	159,897	439,607	8,500,000
By Size					
Up to 250 employees (17)	17,830	63,000	96,480	115,000	454,000
250–499 employees (50)	27,000	88,500	179,000	463,580	1,910,000
500–999 employees (74)	58,251	134,595	272,862	435,601	2,325,920
1,000–2,499 employees (86)	106,960	276,808	538,000	1,012,384	10,030,492
2,500 or more employees (73)	129,000	794,350	1,500,000	2,800,000	52,883,354
Total Budget: 1981					
All Companies (305)	22,050	200,420	437,448	1,114,136	48,414,057
By Industry					
Manufacturing (144)	22,050	250,000	438,400	964,299	37,700,000
Nonmanufacturing (85)	46,320	300,000	740,500	1,530,886	48,414,057
Finance (43)	77,200	215,760	608,760	1,194,698	6,000,000
Nonbusiness (76)	30,000	122,758	290,150	504,000	7,950,000
Health Care (34)	71,500	146,165	245,000	504,000	7,950,000
By Size					
Up to 250 employees (19)	22,050	80,000	100,300	130,788	438,400
250–499 employees (52)	30,000	100,210	250,000	400,000	1,900,000
500–999 employees (73)	41,015	167,520	336,200	470,000	2,060,000
1,000–2,499 employees (90)	110,767	310,000	574,000	1,119,000	11,568,224
2,500 or more employees (71)	145,000	817,072	1,600,000	3,292,000	48,414,057

Personnel Department Budgets: 1980 and 1981

FIGURE 1-6 (cont'd).

		Range		
Low	First Quartile	Median	Third Quartile	High
Cost per Employee: 1980				
All Companies (292)				
29	200	385	619	5,600
By Industry				
Manufacturing (137)				
86	300	451	716	5,600
Nonmanufacturing (80)				
29	260	436	687	4,942
Finance (41)				
43	290	444	687	1,505
Nonbusiness (75)				
39	127	177	303	2,537
Health Care (32)				
51	116	147	228	2,537
By Size				
Up to 250 employees (17)				
117	354	544	622	2,873
250–499 employees (48)				
86	278	425	1,116	5,600
500–999 employees (73)				
75	199	372	545	2,326
1,000–2,499 employees (84)				
70	179	355	593	4,089
2,500 or more employees (70)				
29	145	359	577	4,942
Cost per Employee: 1981				
All Companies (300)				
32	232	433	690	5,600
By Industry				
Manufacturing (142)				
86	317	500	821	5,600
Nonmanufacturing (84)				
32	298	503	723	4,778
Finance (43)				
52	312	478	690	1,898
Nonbusiness (74)				
49	140	202	326	2,373
Health Care (32)				
86	127	180	257	2,373
By Size				
Up to 250 employees (19)				
145	404	604	839	2,775
250–499 employees (51)				
92	315	550	1,204	5,600
500–999 employees (72)				
51	217	415	591	2,354
1,000–2,499 employees (89)				
66	215	404	690	4,716
2,500 or more employees (69)				
32	168	382	608	4,778

Note: Figures in parentheses indicate the number of companies in each category providing figures.

FIGURE 1-7

Personnel Staff Ratios

	Number of Persons on Personnel Staff per 100 Employees on Company Payroll				
	Low	First Quartile	Median	Third Quartile	High
Professional/Technical Staff					
All Companies (491)	0.03	0.4	0.5	0.8	9.1
By Industry					
Manufacturing (257)	0.05	0.4	0.5	0.8	9.1
Nonmanufacturing (130)	0.03	0.4	0.6	0.9	3.7
Finance (69)	0.15	0.5	0.6	0.9	2.1
Nonbusiness (104)	0.06	0.3	0.4	0.7	8.3
Health Care (44)	0.14	0.3	0.3	0.5	1.1
By Size					
Up to 250 employees (69)	0.24	0.5	0.7	1.2	9.1
250–499 employees (92)	0.17	0.4	0.6	0.8	4.0
500–999 employees (117)	0.12	0.4	0.5	0.7	2.9
1,000–2,499 employees (122)	0.09	0.3	0.5	0.7	2.0
2,500 or more employees (91)	0.03	0.3	0.4	0.6	1.7
Total Personnel Staff					
All Companies (493)	0.05	0.7	1.0	1.4	13.6
By Industry					
Manufacturing (257)	0.08	0.7	1.0	1.4	13.6
Nonmanufacturing (132)	0.05	0.8	1.2	1.6	4.5
Finance (69)	0.30	0.9	1.2	1.8	3.2
Nonbusiness (104)	0.17	0.5	0.8	1.2	10.8
Health Care (44)	0.35	0.5	0.6	0.9	1.8
By Size					
Up to 250 employees (70)	0.50	1.1	1.5	2.3	13.6
250–499 employees (92)	0.26	0.8	1.1	1.4	7.9
500–999 employees (118)	0.25	0.7	0.9	1.2	3.5
1,000–2,499 employees (122)	0.18	0.6	0.9	1.3	3.2
2,500 or more employees (91)	0.05	0.5	0.8	1.2	2.9

Note: Figures in parentheses indicate the number of companies in each category providing data.

Through participation in an energy-related compensation survey for the last three years, one Denver organization reports that energy companies pay approximately 20 percent higher salaries than are reported in the ASPA/Hansen survey for general industry.

It's important to validate wage and salary data in your particular area of the country to ensure that your compensation programs are competitive for your industry and your geographical area.

HUMAN RESOURCE DIRECTOR'S TIP:

Charge departments back for services provided by the human resource department. Work with the accounting manager to define a plan whereby the costs of recruiting, relocation, training, temporary help, and other key expenses can be charged back to the user department. Compensation and benefits are normally charged to the user department, and other key expense items also can be treated in that manner.

1.9   THE HUMAN RESOURCE DIRECTOR'S ORGANIZATIONAL EFFECTIVENESS

People's effectiveness in an organization frequently stems from their personal style and their beliefs about management theory. Many times a manager's style has developed through years of association with an organization that had a specific management style. The style may have been one of Douglas McGregor's classic theories.

According to McGregor, the theory X manager thinks that people need authority and coercion to motivate them, that people normally avoid work and must be told what to do and when to do it.

The theory Y manager thinks that people are self-directed and will discipline themselves to the tasks that need to be done. People respond better to challenge in their jobs than they do to authority.

Theories are just that—theories. However, they do help us spot management and organizational styles; and if we are aware of them and understand how to work with them, we will be far more successful in the human resource function.

The Most Common and Generally Accepted Theories of Personal Effectiveness

	Effective	*Ineffective*
Chris Argyris	Authentic	Autocratic
Warren Bennis	Democracy	Bureaucracy
Frederick Herzberg	Challenging	Comfort
Rensis Likert	Participative/consultive	Exploitive/authoritative
Douglas McGregor	Theory Y (people are self-directed	Theory X (people need coercion)
Abraham Maslow	Self-actualization	Lower need for self-actualization
William Glasser	Coping with reality	Avoiding reality

Even though the words and theories may differ, they define conditions that inhibit or enhance the individual's effectiveness in an organization.

Every human resource director should understand the theories of personal effectiveness. Understanding the theories will not lead to change in behavior, but they do lead to an awareness of managerial behavior.

Because management style at the top of the organization tends to set the pace and creates a particular environment in the organization, it is important for the human resource director to identify and understand that style in order to be able to pass that knowledge on to other executives and employees.

The success of the organization, and the success of individuals working in that organization, frequently will depend on the two styles of personal and organizational effectiveness meshing and working well together.

John D. Rockefeller once said that more millionaires came out of the executive ranks of the Standard Oil Company when John D. Rockefeller Sr. personally managed that organization than from any other corporation before or since. One reason is found in a remark made by Rockefeller: "The ability to deal with people is as purchasable a commodity as sugar or coffee, and I pay more for that ability than for any other under the sun."

Rockefeller was tremendously successful in choosing associates who combined executive strength with the ability to deal effectively with people.

I asked the president of one company what qualities he looks for in a human resource director, and he listed them as follows:

1. The ability to get along well with others, establishing smooth working relationships.
2. Decisiveness, having guts to fight for what he or she believes in.
3. Maturity of mind and poise when dealing with others and when the going gets rough.
4. Creative imagination, fresh thinking, good, fresh, workable ideas.
5. Knowledge and effectiveness in the human resource discipline.
6. Proactive rather than reactive attitude.
7. A good sense of timing.

The Credibility and Professionalism of the Human Resource Director

Have you ever heard someone say, "Don't go to the personnel department—they won't do anything"? Or, "Don't talk to the human resource director; the word will get back to your boss, and you'll be on the list"? If those comments are frequent and not just an occasional remark from a disgruntled employee, the human resource department has a credibility problem.

To build credibility in any organization, the human resource director has to be ethical, honest, and discreet; must get things done, get answers to problems, and manage problems in a proactive style. However, the director must also be successful in reacting to problems in an effective, quiet way in order to gain the respect of employees at all levels of the organization.

In my interviews with several top executives, there seemed to be a general consensus. "Quiet," "maturity," "good timing," "realism about organizations and how they work" were some of the things I heard most frequently.

All the executives I talked to said that what they look for in their top human resource executive is a mature business mind.

1.10 SIX CHARACTERISTICS EXECUTIVES LOOK FOR IN A HUMAN RESOURCE DIRECTOR

1. *A realistic view.* This means an understanding of how organizations work. Problems in organizations are the norm. When everything goes right and falls into place at the right time, that is the exception.
2. *An organizational sense.* It's the politics of how things get done in organizations. It's the idea that if you do this for me, I'll do that for you. It's organizational synergy. Machiavelli said that the political process is a vital part of human organizations. You can't get away from it. The political process controls who gets what, and how—in world government, in local government, and in every work place.
3. *Self-management.* Directors shouldn't have to be told how to spend their time. The sign of a mature mind is that the person is a good manager of time and is a self-starter.
4. *Poise under fire.* Human resource directors frequently come under fire from many groups—top management, employees, the federal government, and other managers who don't get the person they want for a job as soon as they think they should. The mature mind handles problems quietly and efficiently, with a minimum of organizational disruption.
5. *The ability to keep a confidence.* One executive said that he deliberately leaked confidential information and checked back later to see if it was shared with others.
6. *Creative thinking.* Creative problem solving. Most executives I talked to mentioned this as one of the key qualities they looked for, especially in the human resource executive. People problems are frequently the toughest ones to resolve. You can recognize a creative business mind by watching the reaction when a problem is thrown at the person. The average person resists problems or change. The creative person welcomes change and adversity as a challenge and uses ingenuity and imagination to solve problems.

1.11 HUMAN RESOURCE ISSUES MANAGEMENT

The human resource director has a new responsibility, that of issues manager in the human resource arena—staying on top of issues as they emerge in order to avoid additional legislation.

The following are issues that may affect the human resource function in the coming years:

The new work ethic	Productivity
Changing employee values	Robotics
Worker democracy	Plant closings
Union participation in management	Income assistance
Retirement income	Social Security benefits
Pension funding liability	Day-care benefit
Employee benefits choice	Equal Rights Amendment
EEO	Equal rights for women

Skilled labor shortage in the 1990s	Tuition tax credit
Illegal aliens	Privacy
Retraining the unemployed	Low opinion of business by public
35-hour work week	Social performance reporting
Compressed work week	Freedom of Information Act
Increased use of flexitime	Confidentiality
OSHA reform	Computer/communications links
Walsh-Healy Act	Plant renewal

Volunteerism
Corporate executive responsibility
Corporate governance
Corporate disclosure

- Entire job categories may become obsolete.
- Worker retraining will be necessary.
- Telecommunications will advance to the point where more people will be able to work at home.
- The work force will undergo significant demographic changes. Fifty percent of the labor force will be 25 to 44 years of age.
- Seventy percent of employable women will be working by 1990.
- There will be a new stronger emphasis on health and wellness.

1.12 ADDITIONAL WAYS TO GROW PERSONALLY AND GAIN CREDIBILITY IN THE HUMAN RESOURCE FIELD

The successful human resource director continues to learn and grow professionally, to be out in front of trends and change in order to gain or extend professional credibility. How can you do this?

1. Join associations and be active.
2. Write and speak in your field.
3. Act as a mentor to your staff and others.
4. Assist members of your staff in gaining recognition. Give credit honestly and openly.
5. Be active in the community and with civic groups. Assume social responsibility.
6. Learn as much as you can about at least one aspect of the human resource function. Become *the* expert on that subject, at least in your particular part of the country.
7. Donate some time once or twice a year to helping those less fortunate. For example, hold a class on interviewing for people entering the job market for the first time or reentering the market.
8. Develop a healthy sense of perspective about yourself and your job. Don't take it all too seriously.
9. Read in your field. Keep up to date. Here are pertinent publications:

Personnel Administrator
30 Park Drive
Berea, Ohio 44017

Personnel Management
1231 25th Street, N.W.
Washington, D.C. 20037

Personnel Policies and Practices
Bank Administration Institute
303 South Northwest Highway
Park Ridge, Illinois 60068

Personnel Psychology
P.O. Box 6965
College Station
Durham, North Carolina 27708

President's Personnel Letter
Executive Reports Corporation
Englewood Cliffs, New Jersey 07632

Public Personnel Management
1313 East 60th Street
Chicago, Illinois 60637

Recruiting Trends
20 North Wacker Drive
Chicago, Illinois 60606

Training
731 Hennepin Avenue
Minneapolis, Minnesota 55403

Training and Development Journal
P.O. Box 5307
Madison, Wisconsin 53705

Women in Business
9100 Ward Parkway
Kansas City, Missouri 64114

Working Woman
600 Madison Avenue
New York, New York 10022

*Publications of the United States
Department of Labor*
Washington, D.C. 20402

CHAPTER 2

Planning Human Resource Requirements

A good human resource plan ensures that an organization has the right people at the right place at the right time, and that the people are trained, qualified, and motivated to perform the work that is essential to the success of the organization.

The success of human resource planning is measured by whether the organization has the personnel it requires when they are needed. These concerns are both quantitative and qualitative, and human resource planning should benefit both the organization and the employees.

Five Ways a Good Human Resource Plan Can Affect Company Profits

1. A human resource plan helps ensure that the organization has the people it needs when it needs them. Economic losses occur when an organization has vacancies in critical positions.

2. A human resource plan allows lead time for training and development or for recruiting to fill jobs from outside the organization.

3. The human resource plan provides inventories of people for jobs, identifies backups and cross-training needs.

4. The plan identifies external elements and makes assumptions that will affect the organization now and in the future. Without a human resource plan, many organizations don't take the time to think about the plan for external events and the impacts of technology, social, and environmental concerns.

5. A plan provides impetus for succession planning, which is critical to any organization. If a crisis were to wipe out several key management people, and there was no provision for successors to move in and provide leadership, the organization could experience immediate and long-term economic loss.

HUMAN RESOURCE DIRECTOR'S TIP:

Your point of view about human resource planning is important. Human resource planning is certainly nothing to take lightly. It is the *key factor* in the achievement of the organization's economic goals. *It is not a primary objective*! If you try to sell human resource planning to management and measure the success or failure of the plan by the sophistication of the process or by the accuracy of the forecasts, you may be shot down. What you need is a simple but effective way to project manpower needs. When business plans change, the human resource plan must also change; therefore, a good plan is in a constant state of revision, just as corporate business plans are constantly revised.

2.1   ELEVEN QUESTIONS AND ANSWERS ON HUMAN RESOURCE PLANNING

Q: Why does an organization need human resource planning?

A: Organizations spend a great deal of time planning for equipment, new technology, and systems, but not as much time planning for people. A frequent reason for the failure of long-range business plans is the lack of serious human resource planning. For example, if you plan to purchase an expensive piece of equipment and you don't have the people trained to run it when it is delivered, you may lose thousands of dollars in productivity while the equipment sits idle. Magnify this example by the hundreds of other examples you can think of, and the impact to the economic results of your organization could be substantial.

Q: How about timing? When does an organization need a full-blown human resource plan?

A: Every organization needs some type of human resource plan. It may only be a short one- or two-page document for a small company, but there should be an effort in every company to determine personnel needs for the current year and at least three years out. It takes at least two or three years to get people trained in current jobs and ready to move up when the opportunity arises. It can also take as long as six to twelve months to recruit a technical or managerial employee.

Q: How does a human resource plan make an organization more successful?

A: An effective human resource plan ensures that staffing requirements are identified far enough in advance so that people can be trained and ready to fill the positions when they are available. A company that has the foresight to plan staffing needs in advance is bound to be more successful than the company that merely reacts to changing needs. The manpower plan should be tied directly to carrying out the organization's corporate strategies and business goals.

Q: How can a human resource plan affect company profits?

A: A company must have the people it needs when they are needed, or the company's production will suffer. For example, the sales department has a goal of selling 5 million widgets. A subgoal is to train or recruit two more sales representatives to join the sales staff. If the people are not hired and trained, the sales objective can't be met. Tie the plan to specific corporate goals.

Q: How long does it take to produce an effective human resource plan?

A: A good rule of thumb is six months. See figure 2–1. Specific items that might be needed in order to complete a project, the people needed, and an approximate time frame for each item appear in figures 2–2 and 2–3.

Q: How far in the future should the plan go?

A: The human resource plan should tie in to the organization's long-range plans. Frequently, however, the long-range plans go out five years, and that is too long to project staffing needs effectively. A typical human resource plan covers a three-year period. Anything beyond that is not realistic because of the rapid change that goes on in any organization today.

FIGURE 2-1.

MINIMUM TIME TO DEVELOP A HUMAN RESOURCE PLAN

	6 months	
Internal/External Analysis		Data Collection. Preplanning.
Missions/Objectives		Review and reach common understanding of organization's Human Resource strengths, weaknesses, opportunities, and risks.
Strategies/Action Plans		Design action plans and tasks and develop manpower inventory. Formulate strategies.
Review/Approve		Review of action plans by management. Modify.
Implement Plan/Control		Implement action plans and control mechanisms.
Yearly Plan Review		Review plans yearly and update.

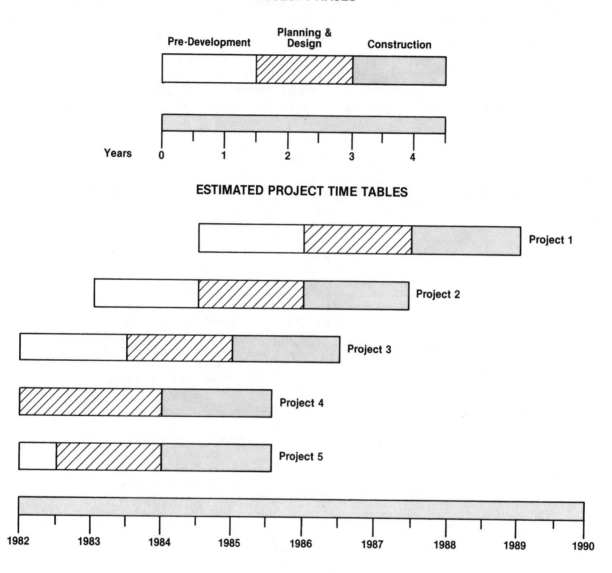

FIGURE 2-2.

PROJECT PHASES

ESTIMATED PROJECT TIME TABLES

Q: Who in the organization should be responsible for the human resource plan?

A: Managers at all levels of the organization must accept responsibility for human resource planning. Managers are responsible for planning, organizing, directing, and controlling all the activities in the organization for which they have responsibility. Generally, however, the human resource or personnel department has responsibili-

FIGURE 2-3.

PROJECT PERSONNEL REQUIRED TO COMPLETE TASKS FOR NEW PROJECTS

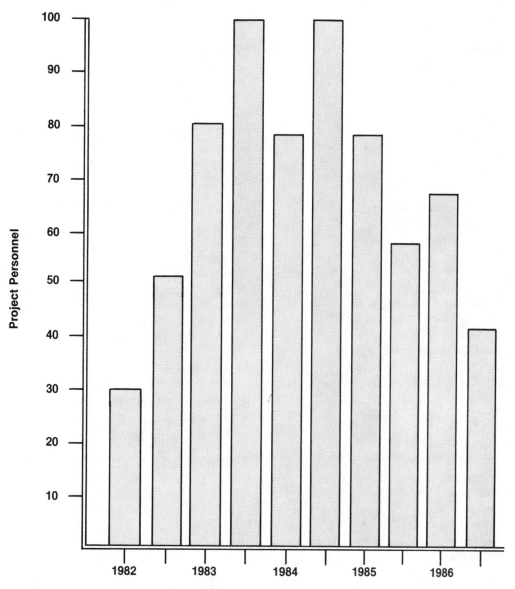

ty for pulling the information together from the operating managers and implementing the final human resource plan.

Q: What are some of the key issues to consider in human resource planning?

A: Following are some planning issues, listed in alphabetical order:

Planning Issues

Human Issues	*Technical Issues*
Benefits	Action plan
Budget	Annual plan review
Commitment	Assumptions
Communications	Audits
Comparison with competitors	Automation
Compensation	Competition
Consultants	Components of the plan
Contracts	Control program
Corporate environment/style	Data analysis
Employment agencies	Data gathering
Equal Employment Opportunity	Employee assessment
Human resource inventory	External analysis
Human resource planning	Impact analysis
Line/staff relationships	Internal analysis
Management development	Inventories
Morale	Locations
Objectives	Long-range plan
Obsolescence	Manpower forecast
Organizational development	Manpower inventory
Performance appraisal	Performance analysis
Personnel policies	Productivity analysis
Position descriptions	Objectives
Productivity	Operating plan
Promotion policies	Organizational effectiveness
Recruiting	Strategies (to meet objectives)
Safety	Technology
Security	Trends
Staffing plans	Work-force analysis
Succession planning	Work methods
Supervisory training	
Teamwork	
Testing	
Training	
Turnover	
Union concerns	

Q: How can you show visually the need for personnel over an established time span?

A: Let's say you have five specific projects that must be completed over the next several years. One way to describe needs in a time span graphically is to use bar charts (figures 2–2 and 2–3).

Q: What are the key elements of a human resource plan?

A: The first and most important element is the identification of the organizational objectives. Until the organization's objectives have been quantified and set on paper, a full-scale human resource plan isn't practical. A format for setting organizational objectives in a workable plan appears in figure 2–4. The key elements of the hu-

FIGURE 2-4.

XYZ CORPORATION   1982 OPERATING PLAN

Key Tasks	Responsibility	Completion Date	Comments

man resource plan are the human resource inventory, the forecast, the objectives, and the program that is defined as a result of reviewing the first three items. The final three items of key importance are the human resource control plan, the review process, and the succession plan. The chart in figure 2–5 gives a better idea of the elements that comprise a good human resource plan.

Q: How do you establish what programs are needed in an organization in order to make human resource planning effective?

A: Put together a needs-analysis matrix in order to establish priority areas that need attention and specific programs assigned. See figure 2–6.

HUMAN RESOURCE MANAGER'S TIP:

Leader Responsibilities. Let a winner lead the way. Pick a person in the human resource department who has a reputation for getting things done. Then let that person:

1. Design the human resource inventory system.
2. Work with managers throughout the company in completing a human resource inventory.
3. Produce the internal work-force analysis.
4. Produce the first draft of the human resource forecast for management review.
5. Work with managers to complete individual development plans and a succession plan for the organization.
6. Design and promote an annual organization review system.

Results are the answer to the success of the plan.

FIGURE 2-5.

HUMAN RESOURCE PLANNING PROCESS

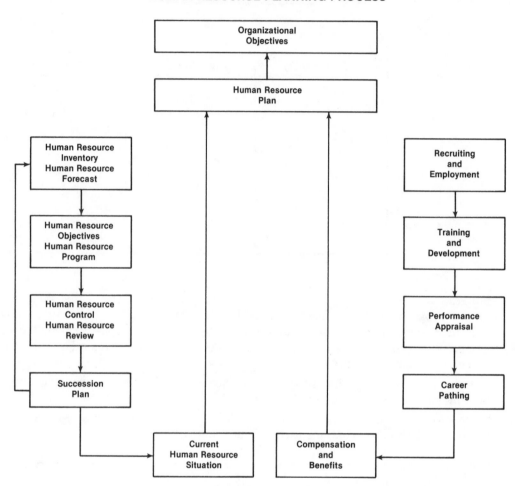

2.2 KEY ELEMENTS OF A HUMAN RESOURCE PLAN

Organization Plan. The human resource plan must be formulated using the assumptions and objectives of the organization's business plans. If the organization doesn't have a formal plan, key organizational objectives must be identified. For example, if the organization's objective is to produce $60 million in income during the next twelve months, the organizational plan would include specific projects or actions for accomplishing that economic objective and the human resource plan would identify the numbers and types of people needed and the timing in order to accomplish the plan.

Situation Audit. Many elements can affect your organization. The situation audit should be an attempt to itemize all those elements that can or will affect your organization over the next three years. Classify these elements. Key classifications might be

FIGURE 2-6.

<u>NEEDS ANALYSIS STRATEGY MATRIX</u>

Conclusions Drawn from Internal Analysis. Human Resource needs reflect as follows:	Areas where effort needed								
	Training & Development	Labor	Compensation	Human Resource Forecasting	Management Development	Organization Development	Management Systems	Recruiting	Other
(Examples Only)									
1. Growing manpower needs	x			x	x				
2. Lack of management depth and success plans					x				
3. High turnover	x							x	
4. Need career pathing					x	x	x		
5. Compensation problems			x						x (further studies required)
6. Need new performance evaluation system	x		x						
7. Improve communications, etc.						x			

This matrix is used to establish the priority areas for needed programs and to develop the Human Resources Plan strategy.

(1) outside influences, such as the community, stockholders, customers, creditors, technology influences; (2) inside interests, such as employees, performance of the organization and its workers, adequacy of facilities. It is important to establish a data base through the situation audit that includes past performance, current situation, forecasts, opportunities and threats, organization strengths and weaknesses, and any other items you feel will have an impact on the human resource plan.

Work-force Analysis. The internal work-force analysis provides a common understanding of strengths and weaknesses and analyzes the present situation. The internal work-force analysis should answer the following questions:

1. How many people do we have who can potentially staff positions identified by the forecast of human resource needs?
2. How difficult will it be to recruit skilled people from outside the organization to fill forecasted positions if we cannot fill all of the positions from inside the company?
3. If the numbers and types of people needed cannot be found either inside or outside the organization, to what extent will the organizational plan and the human resource plan have to be altered?
4. Which skill requirements identified in the forecast can be met by training and development? Which cannot be met through training and development? Are the necessary training programs now available in-house? Will we have to go to the outside for the training programs we need? What kind of lead time are we looking at?

Through systematic evaluation of these questions and answers, the human resource plan can be formulated and implemented.

Human Resource Inventory. This is an inventory of all of the people on the payroll, their skills, abilities, experience, education, jobs they've held, and their performance levels. The inventory is a critical look at the present work force. It becomes the major data base and is the profile from which the human resource plan is developed. See figure 2–7.

Human Resource Forecast. Following the internal work-force analysis, the future human resource requirements can be forecast through a projection of trends in the economy, developments in your industry, and an estimate based on the organization's future plans. This forecast projects present staffing into the future and compares it with the forecast of requirements to determine the adequacy of the current human resource capability. See figure 2–8.

2.3 LABOR MARKET ASSESSMENT

While plans are being made to identify and prepare current employees for possible promotion or transfer, a labor market assessment should be made. Following are some of the initial steps that can be taken to make a valid labor market assessment:

FIGURE 2-7.

HUMAN RESOURCE INVENTORY AND ESTIMATED ANNUAL COST

Department _____

Date _____ 19 __ through _____ 19 __

Name	Title	Performance	Experience	Education	Skills	Jobs Held	Cross-Trained	Estimated Annual Cost		
								Salary Cost	Benefit Cost	Total

FIGURE 2-8.

HUMAN RESOURCE FORECAST SUMMARY AND ESTIMATED ANNUAL COST

C = Current Staff
F = Forecast Staff

Date _____ 19 __ through _____ 19 __

DEPARTMENT		MANAGERS	PRO-FESSIONALS	TECHNICIANS	CLERICAL	Estimated Annual		ESTIMATED TOTAL COST
						SALARY COST	BENEFIT COST	
	C							
	F							
	C							
	F							
	C							
	F							
	C							
	F							
	C							
	F							
	C							
	F							
TOTALS	C							
	F							

1. Identify the best employment source by type of position.
2. Review the position's starting salary against current area practice to ensure that your job will pay competitively in the marketplace.
3. Complete research that gives you a good indication of the availability of qualified people.
4. Prepare some estimate of time that will be needed to fill the position once the recruiting begins.
5. Identify those positions for which relocation is a probability. Establish a relocation policy and procedure.
6. Identify positions for which your management is willing to pay search fees, relocation costs, and so on.

Figure 2–9 provides a schematic of the work-force and labor market assessment process.

FIGURE 2-9.

SCHEMATIC OF WORKFORCE AND LABOR MARKET ASSESSMENT PROCESS

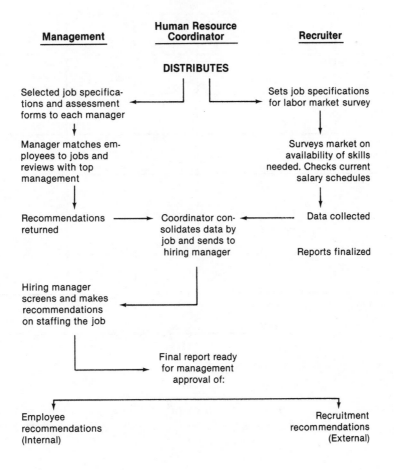

Recruitment Plans

After the work-force and labor market assessment have been completed, the first attempt at a recruitment plan can be initiated. Figure 2–10 provides a sample Human Resource Recruitment Control Sheet.

FIGURE 2-10.

<u>HUMAN RESOURCE RECRUITING CONTROL SHEET</u>

Department   Date _____ through _____

Job Title	No. of Jobs to Be Filled	Date Needed	To Be Recruited	To Be Trained	To Be Filled from Within	Date to Be Filled
TOTAL NEEDED						

2.4 EXTERNAL ANALYSIS

The external analysis is a review of legislative, social, economic, competitive, and technological trends and the company's assumptions about those trends and how likely any one of them is to affect the company. The external analysis includes planned responses to meet those impacts and is a part of the total human resource planning process. Forms for completing an external analysis appear in figures 2–11 through 2–15.

FIGURE 2-11.

<u>EXTERNAL ANALYSIS</u>

LEGISLATION			
Current Conditions and Future Trends	Assumptions	Organizational Impact	Action Program

FIGURE 2-12.

<u>EXTERNAL ANALYSIS</u>

SOCIAL			
Current Conditions and Future Trends	Assumptions	Organizational Impact	Action Program

FIGURE 2-13.

<u>EXTERNAL ANALYSIS</u>

ECONOMIC			
Current Conditions and Future Trends	Assumptions	Organizational Impact	Action Program

FIGURE 2-14.

<u>EXTERNAL ANALYSIS</u>

TECHNOLOGY			
Current Conditions and Future Trends	Assumptions	Organizational Impact	Action Program
Specific technology affecting the industry to increase or decrease need for people.			

2.5   MEASURING LABOR PRODUCTIVITY

There are simple measures of productivity, such as pieces assembled, number of units sold, number of people hired, number of units produced, and so on. Basically, what is needed is an analysis of labor productivity and a plan for using the data

FIGURE 2-15.

<u>EXTERNAL ANALYSIS</u>

COMPETITION			
Current Conditions and Future Trends	Assumptions	Organizational Impact	Action Program

obtained to estimate future staffing needs. Following are five areas where productivity objectives can be set and employee morale can be positively affected:

1. Identify areas where specific objectives can be set. Work with employees to set objectives.
2. Break key objectives into major result areas.
3. Break objectives into routine or innovative objectives.
4. Develop performance indicators for each key result area.
5. Involve employees. Participation in goal setting is important. Professional employees want to have some say in setting the objectives by which they will be measured.

Five Ways to Measure the Productivity of Professional Workers

The simpler measures of output, such as units produced or sold, are not the only measures of productivity. They are the easiest measures. We often hear the comment that the productivity of professional workers cannot be measured; however, that statement is not true. Productivity of professional workers can be measured by the results expected.

1. Measure the quantity or quality of assistance to the organization. Decide whether the person's advice leads to some improvement.
2. Measure the number of innovative ideas and programs the person initiates.
3. Measure the employee's problem-solving skills. Develop a three-step process consisting of problem identification, an action plan, and implementation of the plan.
4. Develop a process for measuring quantity and quality of output.
5. For special projects, measure number, completion time, and quality.

2.6   CRITICAL STEPS IN HUMAN RESOURCE PLANNING

Step 1.   Preparation of data base for human resource planning. The data base is a current work-force analysis. Prepare a human resource inventory for each department that is to be included in the forecast and the plan for that particular area. Include a measure of productivity (number of projects, amount of sales, etc.). Identify the types and numbers of people to be included in the forecast.

Step 2.   Analyze all data included in step 1. Then, review past economic objectives, productivity, and actual staffing; review current trends and projected future demands and prepare a preliminary human resource forecast.

Step 3.   Working with each department, review external concerns such as new technology or social and environmental issues. Make assumptions regarding the future and the impact of these changes on the forecast.

Step 4.   Prepare the forecast for review and approval.

Step 5.   Translate forecast numbers into position specifications. Write job descriptions. Evaluate jobs. Set salary ranges.

Step 6.   Prepare cost estimates that include numbers of people, recruitment costs, relocation costs, and the costs of salaries, benefits, space, equipment, training, and other miscellaneous items.

Step 7.   Review current employees against projected positions. Employees who do not meet job specifications on forecast positions are screened out.

Step 8.   Prepare a labor market assessment.

After these eight steps are completed, top management will have the following opportunities:

1. *Accept* the forecast and proceed with implementation of the plan.
2. *Adjust* the forecast as needed to meet the organization's objectives. Then, authorize the next step in the process.
3. *Reject* the forecast and recycle through the process.

2.7   HUMAN RESOURCE SUCCESSION PLAN

Succession planning should be done for at least five levels of the organization—president, vice-president, director, manager, and supervisor. It should be done eventually for all levels, but the significant dislocation that can be suffered within the organization if someone leaves would be at these higher levels, and it is best to start with these positions. It is also at these levels that development frequently takes place in preparation for promotion, and development here can take a great deal of time, so advance planning is necessary.

Q: What is succession planning?

A: Succession planning is basically a procedure for identifying the person who could replace a vice-president, manager, or other key person in the organization; and, further, identifying what additional development that backup person needs to be ready to fill the higher position.

Succession planning requires much thought on the part of the president and key executives. Individual performance appraisals are necessary, and in order to devote significant personal thought to the effort, some do their succession planning offsite. There are basically three key elements to the succession plan:

1. *The succession planning statement.* This is basically a mission statement that sets out the objectives that the organization wishes to accomplish through succession planning.
2. *The succession planning backup summary.* The summary lists the key positions, and the backup personnel are identified.
3. *Individual development plans.* After successors have been identified, individual development plans must be carried out.

Succession Plan Backup Summary

It is important for top management to prepare a key position backup summary for the succession plan. When the key positions have been listed and their backup personnel identified, the individual development plans can be formalized on each of the backup personnel. See figure 2–16.

FIGURE 2-16.

SUCCESSION PLAN BACKUP SUMMARY

							Comments
Key Position	Dept.	Yrs. in Co.	Yrs. in Position	Performance Level	Current Salary	Salary Range Min. Mid. Max.	
Name	Location						

BACKUPS

Key Position	Dept.	Yrs. in Co.	Yrs. in Position	Performance Level	Current Salary	Salary Range Min. Mid. Max.	
Name	Location						

FIGURE 2-16 (cont'd)

Key Position	Dept.	Yrs. in Co.	Yrs. in Position	Performance Level	Current Salary	Salary Range Min. Mid. Max.	
Name	Location						

The forms shown in figures 2–16 and 2–17 are merely suggested formats. To be successful, the succession plan should be simple and flexible enough to meet the requirements of the organization.

Individual Development Plans

The human resource planning process is integrated with individual development, through performance appraisals, establishing career paths, and training and development. Appraisals of potential also may determine the possibility of an individual taking on more responsibility. The plan should be integrated with a program to move people through the organization as they gain skills and experience.

Figure 2–17 may be used in structuring individual development plans.

Indicate the individual's name in the space for "Employee," your name as "Manager," and the current date. Under "Present Job," indicate the position now held. Under "Potential Job," there are three alternatives—an existing specific job you think is most likely to be the next assignment, a hypothetical job that could be created and that is likely to be the assignment, or a statement of the kinds of additional responsibilities the individual is likely to assume.

The sections entitled "Knowledge" and "Skills" are intended to be triggers to your thought process in identifying development needs. Blank spaces are indicated under both for other items that may occur to you. Put an X after those items where the employee is fully adequate, and XX by those items where development is needed. If development is indicated in the present job, the development needs should be listed specifically and communicated to the employee as soon as possible.

If development for a potential job is indicated, it should be listed and communicated to the employee. In addition, employees should be asked to identify needs they feel they have in specific areas.

The lower half of the form is intended to be the basis for an individual development plan. Checked items from above will be converted into a specific training and experience need. For example, you may check "Technical" under "Knowledge for the Present Job." If the present job is Manager of XYZ Department, the specific training need might be indicated as a better knowledge of managerial communication. The second half of the form indicates "How to Accomplish." You might check "School," filling in the appropriate course and university. You also might check "Assignment

FIGURE 2-17.

INDIVIDUAL DEVELOPMENT PLAN

_____   Date _____
Employee

_____
Manager
                                Present Job:
                                1. _____
                                Potential Job:
                                2. _____

Knowledge	1	2	Skills	1	2
Technical Business	___	___	Managerial	___	___
General Business	___	___	Technical	___	___
Knowledge of the			Leadership	___	___
Organization	___	___	Problem Solving	___	___
Company Policy	___	___	Decision Making	___	___
Company Procedures	___	___	Administrative	___	___
_____	___	___	Communication		
_____	___	___	Oral	___	___
_____	___	___	Written	___	___
			Organization	___	___
			Planning	___	___
			Precision	___	___
X = fully adequate			Motivation	___	___
XX = needs development			Handling Stress	___	___
			Sensitivity to People	___	___
			Interpersonal Skills	___	___
			_____	___	___
			_____	___	___

Training or Experience Need	√	How to Accomplish	Date to Be Accomplished
	___	School _____	_____
	___	Seminar _____	_____
_____	___	Assignment Shadowing ___	_____
	___	Months Experience in _____	
		_____ Position	_____
_____	___	Temporary Assignment as ___	
		_____	_____
	___	Special Emphasis on _____	
		_____	_____
	___	_____	_____

Shadowing" and fill in the manager's name. "Date to Be Accomplished" is a key item in completion of the form. If there are more than two training or experience needs to be planned for, additional forms can be used.

2.8 ORGANIZATIONAL DEVELOPMENT

More organizations are getting into full-blown organizational development programs in order to ensure achievement of specific organizational objectives. Some of these objectives can be classified as follows:

1. Identify the organization's philosophy and business style, and communicate it effectively to all employees.
2. Improve the organization's ability to adapt to its environment, including the ability of managers to understand organizational problems and their effectiveness in consistently reaching effective solutions.
3. Improve internal behavior patterns, including such things as interpersonal and intergroup effectiveness, the level of trust and support, openness of communication, and participation in the planning of organization strategy and human resource development.
4. Improve organizational performance, and measure performance by such items as profitability, turnover, and innovation.

Many companies are attempting to develop new forms of organization and management style. The need is to learn to fit together the values and needs of employees to the objectives of the organization.

The needs of organizations must blend with the desires of the new work force, which wants a management style that's best described as participative and includes a downward shift of decision making lower in the organization.

Organization Variables
- Structure
- Technology
- Personality
- Objectives
- Tasks
- Human resources
- Business climate

The theme of organizational development today is team building. Team-building training runs the gamut from T-group, or sensitivity training, through managerial games, exercises, and role playing. No matter what techniques are used, team building aims at improving the ability of members of the team to work effectively with one another to accomplish a common business objective.

Another change strategy or technique used by many organizations quite effectively is MBO, management by objectives. There is some feeling that MBO is a specific change strategy to be used in the initial stages of an overall organizational development effort. MBO is a widely accepted management planning and control technique that even our most traditional manager accepts as realistic and work-related.

Management by objectives is also an effective way to tie personal goals to company goals. Employees want to see how personal efforts affect the bottom-line economic results of the organization.

Effects of the Information Age on Organizational Development

As the telecommunications age descends on us, the organizational development (OD) function will change also. The OD intervention will take place more frequently in front of a terminal for live long-distance consultations at remote locations.

Who Manages the Organizational Development Function?

An organizational development person may be added to the human resource manager's staff, or the services of an outside OD consultant can be used. Some factors to look at are:

1. Number of people in the organization
2. Speed of growth and internal change
3. Seriousness of organizational problems
4. Employee climate
5. Organizational structure
6. Personality and environment of top management and their commitment to change

Human resource planning, succession planning, and organizational development are all important elements of the organization's overall business plan. All plans should be simple, flexible, and in a constant state of change.

Peter Drucker said, "Perfect balance in a business exists only on the organization chart. A living business is always in a state of imbalance, growing here and shrinking there, overdoing one thing and neglecting another."

CHAPTER 3

Recruiting, Selection, and Employment Programs

One of the main jobs of management is to affect positively the bottom-line economics of the organization through the effective use of its people. It follows that, in order to accomplish that objective, we must hire the right people. We have a tremendous responsibility to recruit and hire the people who will be most effective in their jobs, ones who will stay with the organization in order to achieve a positive return on investment in training and development.

One of the functions of human resource directors is to look constantly for new and better ways to perform our functions. We often hear the phrase, "There is a new type of worker today." That's a valid statement, and the old methods of recruiting and employment won't attract the people we want to attract. So what do we do to turn the human resource function into a "with-it" function that hits the right market?

Some Ideas in Action

Recruiting Literature: Design recruiting ads and literature to attract today's worker. People today are concerned with the quality of work life, self-fulfillment, participative management. The class and style of ads and other recruiting literature is a barometer of the organization's philosophy and commitment to employee concerns.

Advertising: Only certain jobs today are filled through help-wanted ads. They are basically technical, service and clerical, white- and blue-collar jobs. The exception to this might be professional jobs advertised in your local paper or the *Wall Street Journal,* or a high-level position that warrants an expensive box ad on the financial page of your local paper. These ads are usually "blind" ads that list a box number for replies and don't show the company name.

Television Advertising: TV ads have become more popular and are used more frequently now by large companies as demand for skilled employees has accelerated. The main consideration here, naturally, is the cost. Local commercial spots can cost as little as $100, depending on the market, while national 60-second spots can cost hundreds of thousands of dollars. The key here is to identify accurately the audience you wish to reach before you spend the money.

Recruiting Sources: Keep track of sources when you hire people, in order to identify the best recruiting sources for each job. Eliminate those sources that are not providing the best candidates, and gear up the ones that are. Trim your recruiting activities and spend the money where it brings the best return.

HUMAN RESOURCE MANAGER'S TIP:

When recruiting hard-to-fill jobs: Flexibility is the answer. Be open-minded regarding working hours, job-sharing, and other alternative working conditions. Gear company procedures to workers' needs.

3.1 EFFECTIVE METHODS OF FILLING OPEN POSITIONS

The matrix in figure 3-1 shows the most effective methods of filling most open positions.

FIGURE 3-1.

Most Effective Ways to Fill Jobs	Managers and Executives	Professionals	Technical, including Data Processing	Administrative, Accounting, etc.	Clerical	Laborers and Service Workers
Ads in local newspapers		x	x	x	x	x
Ads on TV and radio						
Employment agencies	x	x	x	x	x	
Executive search firms	x					
College campus recruiting		x		x		
Employee referrals		x	x	x	x	x
State Job Service					x	x
Walk-in applicants, unsolicited résumés					x	x
Note: There are times when one of the above methods of filling a job would work better than another, but over a long period the ones checked should prove most effective.						

3.2 WRITING RECRUITING ADS AND LITERATURE THAT GET RESULTS

A certain percentage of jobs will be filled by help-wanted ads and recruiting literature, but so many ads are sterile and boring. There is no way to know exactly how effective advertising is, even if you keep records of applicants who respond to your ads. Here are some ideas to keep in mind when running ads:

- People are attracted by class. If you can afford it, use display ads. Be sure the ads reflect the company personality.
- Use a clean-cut type style and graphics.
- The first few words need pizazz to hook the reader and appeal to the people you want to attract. They should be printed in large type.
- For the headline, be sure your ad is placed under the appropriate job classification.
- Use your company logo if you have one.

Here is a checklist of items you may wish to include in an ad:

What you're looking for
- List specific skills.
- List work experience required.
- State whether or not relocation is necessary.
- State educational requirements.
- Indicate whether job does or does not require regular travel.
- Say whether you will or will not train.

Benefits
- Full-paid medical insurance
- Full-paid life insurance
- Full-paid dental insurance
- Thrift plan
- Disability pay
- Pension
- Service awards
- Health programs
- Company cafeteria
- Tuition refund program
- Social activities
- Flexitime
- Company van pools
- Internal job-posting system for promotional opportunities

Pay
- High pay for experienced people
- Salary plus commission
- Overtime pay for hourly workers
- Bonus

Where to apply
- Address
- Phone number
- Interviewing hours
- Résumés accepted

EEOC and AAP
- "We are an Equal Employment Opportunity Employer (M/F/H/VV)"

Blind ads
- If you want to keep the fact that you're hiring confidential, you may wish to run a blind ad. However, many people will not answer a blind ad, and your responses may be curtailed.

No matter what kind of ad you run, be sure to give each applicant a courteous reply.

Recruiting Tip

A policy for placement of help-wanted ads will eliminate conflict over who should place the ads and the ad content. The following policy is used by one company to avoid such conflict.

Help-Wanted Advertising Policy
The human resource department will be responsible for coordination and placement of all employment advertising. It is the responsibility of the human resource department to:
- Determine most appropriate media to be used.
- Determine advertisement content with input from the hiring manager.
- Ensure that all recruitment advertising is in accordance with applicable state and federal laws, including Equal Employment Opportunity regulations.
- Ensure that advertisements present a positive image of the company.

The form shown in figure 3-2 may be used when placing ads (see page 70).

3.3 DESIGNING RECRUITING LITERATURE THAT TARGETS TODAY'S WORKER

Very little time seems to be spent on developing recruiting materials, and yet today's workers—who are seeking new horizons, who are concerned with the quality of work life, management commitment to participative management, and proactive leanings on social issues—are more inclined to read recruiting literature *before* they show serious interest in a company. They look for literature that sets out a company's philosophy and style.

The degree of sophistication displayed in recruiting literature many times serves as a barometer of management's philosophy and commitment to employee develop-

FIGURE 3-2.

ADVERTISING REQUEST FORM

Position: _____ Salary: _____

Location of position: _____

Paper to be run in: _____

_____

Dates to be run: _____

Body of ad: _____

_____

_____

_____

_____

Job requirements: _____

_____

Experience required: _____

_____

Reply to: _____

_____

_____

Telephone: _____

Person to contact: _____

We are an Equal Employment Opportunity Employer M/F/H/VV

---

ment. People today are also more adept at distinguishing between meaningful information and public relations rhetoric.

Your recruiting literature must have a finished selling value for all levels of people, and it's important to review the overall strategy and the goals you wish to achieve through use of the literature. See figure 3–3 for a sample recruiting brochure matrix. Figure 3–4 presents a classified ad that appeals to the new worker—the self-fulfillment seeker.

FIGURE 3-3.

RECRUITING BROCHURE MATRIX

Creativity	Brainstorm Type of format Amt. of data to include Market Cost Colors Corporate restrictions, if any	Interview managers Identify jobs to highlight Research Concept
Management Review Process	Send to management for review	Make needed changes
Production	Write copy Take photos Design format Design layout	Copy review and approval Photo layout and approval Preliminary composition Prepare final mockup Solicit printing bids
Distribution	Send to management Send to all employees	Send to schools and colleges Send to recruiting services

HUMAN RESOURCE MANAGER'S TIP:

If you have leftover photos, use them in slide shows and employee newsletters to capitalize on expenditures.

3.4 ELEVEN IDEAS FOR ATTRACTING CAPABLE PEOPLE

1. Use job-sharing as a technique to attract clerical and technical people to your company. Two part-time clerical or data processing people can do one job. You meet the needs of the person who can only work part-time, and you have two people who are trained on the same job.
2. Use odd-hour scheduling to attract clerical, technical, or service and blue-collar workers, and even students. People working full-time jobs elsewhere who need extra work will be attracted to odd-hour scheduling. If they see how enlightened your management is in providing for employees' needs, they may be attracted to work for you full-time.
3. Allow professional and clerical workers, such as writers, typists, data processing people who have a home computer, draftspersons, and others who can work just as well from home as from your office, to work at home and bring

FIGURE 3-4.

"Ideal" is exactly the word for our location, about midway between Boulder and Denver

the work in at scheduled times. You can pay by the hour by asking them to keep time cards; you can pay a salary; or in some cases you can pay them as independent contractors. Adapt the method of payment to the individual and the company needs. As long as payment complies with all necessary regulations, you can be flexible.

4. Use retired workers for special projects. Whether they retired from your company or another company, if they have needed skills and abilities, they can do special projects at home or in your office. Use the local Over 40 employment

service of your State Employment Office, or use your own retired workers. There's a distinct possibility that a critical worker shortage lies just over the horizon. Slowly but surely, the baby boom of the late 1940s and 1950s will work its way through the labor force. Pretty soon, not enough young workers will be entering the bottom end of the ladder. This will put pressure on employers to consider what would have been unthinkable a few years ago: hiring back older workers from retirement.

"You can see it happening already in the defense industry," says a House Committee on Aging staffer. He points to Lockheed, which sent out offers to some 4,000 of its retired employees with special skills (machinists, metal workers, etc.). The company got back 2,000 replies, and 1,000 or so were affirmative. "Yes, I would like to come back to work," was the enthusiastic answer. And it's little wonder. With inflation eating up pension paychecks, workers learned that they could go back to work and get 20 percent more than their younger colleagues. They would get no special benefits, but they would continue to receive their company pension. To make this intricate deal work according to company and pension-plan bylaws, a contracting company actually hires back the Lockheed workers and then rents them to the company. This way, pension and benefit rules can be side-stepped.

5. Create an ad hoc committee in-house with engineers, accountants, and the same types of people you are trying to hire. They can help you come up with new ideas for recruiting. They also can add a networking element with a variety of professional associations.

6. More than 50 percent of the women in the country today work outside the home. By 1990, it's predicted that 70 percent of women will do so. Be sure your ads and recruiting literature appeal to women. Ask women currently on staff for new recruiting ideas.

7. Set up a hotline for people who might be interested in a job with your company to call in and get information about specific jobs. Keep one hotline open during evening hours for people who work.

8. In every company there are people who, if given the chance to learn a new skill, could do so in a very short period of time. Can a data clerk learn a job one or two levels above the current assignment? Can a secretary learn a job as a report writer or a project coordinator? Can an order clerk learn new skills and become a warehouse or purchasing supervisor? Are you being creative and thoughtful in looking inside your own company for talent? An investment in training might bring a better return than recruiting costs. Look for tradeoffs.

9. Consider organizational change as an alternative staffing method. If you cannot hire a specific person, consider an alternative move. *Case Example*: One company had two managers in its data processing organization—one manager for business systems and one manager for technical mineral systems. They lost the mineral systems manager and could not replace that person immediately with another qualified individual. A discussion about organizational alternatives brought excellent results. They reorganized the data processing function. The manager of business systems had a good general background and knowledge of the mineral systems function, had a great deal of credibility with both groups, and was an excellent manager. When they were unable to find an experienced mineral systems manager, they decided to reorganize by putting

both groups under the business systems manager and beefing up the technical mineral systems group by adding a geologist with a degree in data processing. The reorganization proved to be a good move and resulted in a more productive department.

10. The *Wall Street Journal* recently reported that some companies have started paying middle managers hiring bonuses. Upfront bonuses, a perk once reserved for senior executives, has become a way to attract middle management. The perk helps combat inflation while not upsetting established compensation levels. The bonuses range from 8 percent to 25 percent of a manager's first-year salary. They seem particularly popular in New York, Texas, and Louisiana. With all of the substantial pluses, there are, however, certain negatives on the front-end bonus. Unless deferred in some way, it has no holding power. Once paid, the candidate is free to walk away. No matter how large the bonus may appear, its impact on a candidate's financial well-being is soon dissipated. In fact, because this amount is taxed at no less than 50 percent, even a very substantial bonus has only a brief impact on the lifestyle of most executives. Some companies also pay bonuses to employees who refer applicants. The bonus is awarded if the person is hired and stays for a certain period of time, usually three to six months.

11. Make an effort to recruit and employ handicapped workers. Forward-thinking companies like Control Data allow workers like technical writers to work at home while receiving employee benefits. There are more than 35 million Americans with some form of mental or physical handicap. The Xerox Corporation has an excellent program for employing disabled workers, and AT&T has developed a program to train managers of disabled people.

3.5   WAYS TO SCREEN IN HANDICAPPED WORKERS

Here are some ways to "screen in" qualified handicapped people:

• Ensure that job requirements don't "screen out" disabled workers.
• Ensure that training programs include handicapped workers.
• Provide car or van pools for disabled workers or consider subsidizing a van pool.
• Ensure that your employment office is accessible to the handicapped, and that receptionists are trained in dealing with handicapped applicants.

Interviewing the Handicapped Applicant

The objective of any employment interview is to match an applicant's qualifications with the requirements of the job. Handicapped applicants are the same as any other applicants and don't require any special interviewing knowledge or skill. Look at the handicapped applicant as a person with abilities, strengths, and weaknesses, just like any other applicant.

Some Do's and Don'ts

• Handicapped people enjoy being treated normally. Don't avoid humorous situations that may occur.

- Don't tell the applicants you admire their courage. Don't sympathize with their problems—they don't want sympathy.
- Do maintain eye contact. Speak directly to the applicant, even if he or she is accompanied by another person.
- Do offer assistance if you see it's needed, but don't be oversolicitous.
- If you have trouble communicating, do ask the applicant how you can best communicate and understand answers to your questions.

3.6 FIVE-STEP METHOD FOR SETTING UP EFFECTIVE RECRUITING PROCEDURES

All organizations have ways of doing things. Procedures save time. They contribute to the overall corporate objectives, and guidelines free managers to take action.

Step 1. Identify the need for the job, and ensure that proper approvals have been obtained.

Step 2. Identify the procedures you think you need, including procedures for approval of positions, requisition procedures, and procedures on the use of employment agencies and advertising.

Step 3. Draft the procedures. Be straightforward and use common terminology; don't use legalese or stilted phrases.

Step 4. Review the procedures with managers who will have to interpret and use them. Let those managers have input and ownership if they will have to live with the policies.

Step 5. Publish the procedures and distribute them to everyone who has a part in the recruiting process. See that secretaries have access to the procedures. Many times the secretary is the one who initiates the recruiting process for the boss.

3.7 KEY RECRUITING PROCEDURES

Advertising Procedures. The human resource department should be assigned to coordinate and place ads to ensure compliance with federal regulations and also to ensure accuracy and appropriateness of the ad. Ads either have class or they don't. The ones without class won't draw a good response. The human resource coordinator should provide uniform guidelines for style and content.

Employment Procedures. Employment procedures need to reflect support and compliance with the Fair Employment Practices and the Equal Employment Opportunity laws. These procedures set out the company's policy with regard to interviewing, testing, preemployment physicals, hiring procedures, orientations, use of employment agencies, and any other element of the recruiting process.

Equal Employment Opportunity Procedures. This policy establishes the company's commitment to Equal Employment Opportunity for qualified individuals. It should be in every policy manual, and the scope of the policy should include both employees who might be applying internally for jobs and applicants from outside the company.

Although responsibility for carrying out the letter of the policy rests with the human resource department, the commitment and daily practice must be understood and carried out by all managers and supervisors.

Open Position Listing Policy. In order to maintain a high level of morale within the organization, the company should provide a method for employees to apply for open positions for which they feel qualified. Let employees apply for open positions, provide forms for application, and set some guidelines. Let all permanent employees who have passed the probationary period and are not under disciplinary action apply for open positions. Most companies post the jobs on a bulletin board provided for that purpose.

3.8 WORKING WITH SEARCH FIRMS AND EMPLOYMENT AGENCIES

There is such a proliferation of companies in the recruiting business that a general guideline for use of such agencies is in order.

The company we talked to insists on a 90-day placement guarantee from any organization they work with. Most companies feel good enough about their placements to accept a short-term guarantee.

There are firms in business today that are not as reliable as they should be. They practice such shady policies as "churning," which is the practice of placing a candidate (usually a person who has hard-to-find skills) and then recruiting that same person into another company several months later, thus collecting two placement fees. Another questionable practice is to parade a succession of poor candidates through for interviews to make a mediocre candidate look good by comparison, thus wasting everyone's time.

Here are a few questions you might ask about an employment agency or search firm *before* you commit to using them:

1. Question the background and professionalism of the people you will be working with. Ask for a résumé if you have doubts about credentials and experience.
2. Have a meeting with the person away from your offices—maybe over lunch, where the person will be less formal and "on guard"—and observe his or her interpersonal skills and what he or she says about other clients. Then ask yourself if this is the type of person you want representing your company.
3. Can you communicate with the person? Is there good chemistry?
4. How well does the person know your industry and the positions you will have to fill?
5. Does the recruiter ask the right questions and have the right insights?
6. What personal attributes come across? Honesty, commitment, professional standards?
7. What is the firm's current work level? Will they have the appropriate time to devote to your company?

3.9 HOW JOB-POSTING SYSTEMS WORK

A few years ago, it was unthinkable to post open positions in a nonunion salaried environment. But over the past few years, with Equal Employment Opportunity, the need for companies to maximize their human resources and increasing concern for individual career progression, job posting has become quite common.

How One Company's Job-Posting System Works

Eligibility

- All permanent employees who have completed their probationary period are eligible to use the open position listing policy in order to request consideration for a position that would constitute a growth opportunity.
- Employees who have been promoted or transferred, or who have changed jobs for any reason, must wait a six-month period before applying for a different position.

Policy

- A list of open positions will be communicated to all employees in all facilities. Notices will include information on job title, salary grade, department, supervisor's name and title, location, brief description of the job content, qualifications, and instructions concerning whether or not candidates will be expected to demonstrate their skills during the interview process.
- Basic job qualifications and experience needed to fill the job will be listed on the sheet. Employees should consult with the human resource department if there are questions concerning the promotional opportunities associated with the job.
- Open position lists will remain on bulletin boards for five working days.
- Forms for use in requesting consideration for an open position may be obtained from the human resource department.
- The human resource department will review requests to substantiate the employee's qualifications for the position.
- The hiring manager will review requests for employees inside the company before going outside the company to fill the position.
- It is the responsibility of the employees to notify their managers of their intent to interview for an open position.
- The hiring manager makes the final decision when filling the position; however, the guidelines for filling any open position are based on the employees' ability, qualifications, experience, background, and the skills they possess that will allow them to carry out the job successfully. It is the responsibility of the hiring manager to notify the previous manager of the intent to hire the employee.
- Employees who are aware of a pending opening, and who will be on vacation when the opening occurs, may leave a request with the human resource department for consideration.
- It is the manager's responsibility to ensure that the human resource department has notified all internal applicants that they did or did not get the job before general announcement by the manager of the person who did get the job.

- "Blanket" applications will not be accepted. Employees should apply each time a position they are interested in becomes available.
- Since preselection often occurs, employees should be planning for their career growth by scheduling time with potential managers before posting, to become acquainted with them, and to secure developmental information to be used in acquiring appropriate skills for future consideration.
- There are occasions when jobs will not be listed. Two such examples might be (1) when a job can be filled best by natural progression or is a logical career path for an employee, and (2) when a job is created to provide a development opportunity for a specific high-performance employee.
- In keeping with this policy, managers are encouraged to work with employees in career development in order to assist them in pursuing upward movement in a particular career path or job ladder.

What the Human Resource Department Does

- Reviews applications for open positions, and checks to see if applicants meet minimum time-on-the-job requirements.
- Reviews background material of applicants with hiring manager. Hiring manager selects the employees qualified for interviews.
- Notifies all applicants who will not be interviewed, and gives them the reasons why.
- Provides counseling to applicants who will not be interviewed.
- Answers questions from interviewed candidates concerning selection, if the interviewing extends beyond the normal three-week period.

What the Manager Does

- Selects employees to be interviewed for the position.
- Contacts employees selected and arranges for interviews.
- Screens interviewed applicants (may contact previous manager for reference).
- Decides who is the best-qualified candidate.
- Informs the human resource department of the selection and provides reasons for rejecting unsuccessful applicants.
- Notifies the successful applicant and his or her current manager.
- Arranges release dates with the current manager (normally two weeks).
- Completes application forms in full, at the bottom of the form, and answers all appropriate question blocks as necessary.
- Notifies the unsuccessful candidates, advising them of reasons for rejection.
- Makes sure that the interview process does not extend more than three weeks beyond the date the notice comes off the bulletin board.

Some Pros and Cons of Posting Open Positions

Pros
- Fewer employees look for new jobs or transfers because they find suitable jobs through the posting system.
- The program makes upward mobility easier.
- It creates better morale by making employees aware of open positions.
- Employees have more control over career progression.

- It assists with affirmative action programs.
- It affords better use of the human resources.

Cons
- The program lengthens the process of filling jobs.
- It creates a chain reaction, and more jobs have to be filled.
- Employees who don't get jobs require counseling and may become disgruntled.

3.10 A TYPICAL SELECTION PROGRAM—SEVEN STEPS TO SUCCESSFUL SELECTION

The recruiting and selection process takes a lot of time, and most of us spend too much time interviewing applicants who are not qualified. We need to work smart at attracting the right people. Following are seven steps to consider adding to your selection process:

Step 1. Much time is spent interviewing applicants for jobs when the position's specifications and the actual requirements of the job are not clear. Many times even hiring managers haven't defined the job clearly in their own minds. Job responsibilities are frequently blown out of proportion, resulting in too high an expectation of the job on the part of the person hired. To avoid a lengthy, costly recruiting process and a poor selection decision, it is important to know the precise job specifications, including daily interfaces, ability to commit to the company, interpersonal skills, and levels of sophistication and experience.

Step 2. A brief discussion with the hiring manager could save hours of interviewing time later. It's important to understand what the manager wants in the person to be hired. What are the person's obvious objectives and "hidden agendas"?

Step 3. Identify the best recruiting source for the open position. The interviewing process will be successful only if you are able to attract the most qualified candidates for the job. The chart in figure 3–1 shows some of the most successful recruiting sources for the jobs identified. You frequently have to try several sources until you're successful at attracting the best candidates for the job.

Step 4. Use an assessment approach to reviewing applicants and choosing the top candidates. Assess the following qualities:

- Technical skills
- Academic credentials
- Credentials for the position
- Experience in the field
- Past successes
- "Can do" qualities
- "Will do" qualities
- Past promotions
- Attitudes
- Interpersonal skills
- Knowledge of your business

Step 5. Check the applicant's credentials, employment references, academic credentials, and so on.

Step 6. Conduct a thorough selection interview. Cover such items as education, work experience, the "can do" qualities of the applicant; watch for good listening skills, speaking and interpersonal skills. Determine the applicant's technical expertise by asking open-ended questions about job assignments. Encourage open discussion by putting the applicant at ease at the beginning of the interview.

Step 7. After you have put together a complete file of information on your top three candidates, the hiring manager must make a decision based on the data collected. I recommend using a form to evaluate the top candidates initially. A form tends to make you more objective about the data gathered. Ask yourself which candidate best fits the job specifications and the internal environment of the department and the company.

3.11   USING THE RÉSUMÉ WHEN INTERVIEWING

Top Executives Tell How to Dig Deeper in a Résumé's Three Key Areas[1]

Make the right decision when hiring by applying the tactics for reading résumés that other top managers tell us work for them.

The first "rule" suggested by our panel is to pay little or no attention to a résumé without a cover letter. Their next hint is to look for tipoffs that an applicant may be a high achiever.

Educational history: The executives we spoke to feel that a college degree in and of itself doesn't mean much. They look for a good performance at a demanding college. They also look for a listing of major areas of study and how these areas relate to job requirements. Supplemental education, such as attendance at conferences or special training programs, is a plus. But Jack Reston, president of an Alabama company, offers this advice:

> "I look for some rhyme or reason behind the education the applicant has taken. Do courses, for instance, follow a progression that shows interest in the area I have a job opening for? Or does it look like the applicant has just been browsing; especially, has he done it on a former employer's educational expense reimbursement plan?"

Work experience: Most executives watch for unexplained gaps and shifts in position that don't reflect substantial advancement. Louis Ravelman, the owner of a California firm, looks for this:

> "I give high marks to a résumé that describes in clear, simple language the applicant's past job duties."

According to Ravelman, he prefers to read "supervised four press operators in producing radial tires" to "had responsibility for implementation of management decisions/objectives in production area." Reason:

> "The applicant has thought far enough to realize that what I—or anyone—will need are hard, precise facts on which to base a hiring decision."

---

[1] *The President's Personnel Letter*, Executive Reports Corporation, Englewood Cliffs, New Jersey 07632.

A Minnesota president suggests that the facts in a résumé may not be as crucial as its presentation. Look at the frills, too:

"The grammar, punctuation, spelling—even the typing and layout—of a résumé say something about its author. So does its conciseness or, at the other end of the scale, its comprehensiveness. If the job's such that a missed detail could be disproportionately costly, I don't want someone who paints in broad strokes. On the other hand, if the job requires communicating with employees, customers, or what have you, I'll interview someone who submits a 'bare bones' résumé. The applicant may be relying on his conversational skills during the interview to carry the day—and that's the skill I'm interested in."

Career objectives: Most executives look for statements of career goals that are (1) realistic, and (2) relevant to the job that's open. But Ravelman offers this caution:

"In my experience, applicants' stated career goals are often too much on target. Everyone's goals are flexible enough to include exactly the type of position they're applying for. So, though I want the company's goals and an employee's to be compatible, I don't look for a close match."

Look for long-range goals that seem overambitious for the size of your company. Provided that the objective seems realistic for the individual, Ravelman will call the applicant in and try to sell him or her on the benefits of working for his firm.

Using a Résumé as a Blueprint for the Interview

You can get valuable information during an interview by using the applicant's résumé, and the questions it raises, as a guide. Here are some of the questions to ask:

- Why are there unexplained gaps in the applicant's educational history? What did the applicant accomplish during these gaps?
- Why did the applicant shift educational aims?
- Why are there gaps in the applicant's employment history?
- Why has the applicant changed jobs so frequently?
- Why is employment history inconsistent with educational background? Have the applicant's interests changed, or is he or she just biding time?
- Why doesn't the applicant's supplemental education seem targeted or appropriate to the job opening?
- Why is the applicant switching careers?
- What are the applicant's nonwork commitments?

3.12   WATCH FOR RÉSUMÉ FALSIFICATIONS

The *Wall Street Journal* reported in a story by John Andrew entitled "Résumé Liars Are Abundant, Experts Assert," that falsification of credentials is a familiar phenomenon.[2]

The director of personnel for Lockheed Corporation in Burbank, California, estimates that a fifth of the applications sent to Lockheed are in error in some fashion. A Harvard University registrar says she gets two or three calls a week about job appli-

---

[2] John Andrew, "Résumé Liars Are Abundant," *The Wall Street Journal*, April 24, 1981.

cants who claim to have attended the university but aren't in the records. Stanford University says it gets a like number of queries. Doctorates and Masters degrees in business are the degrees most commonly faked, a Stanford official says.

Most firms these days make a prospective employee sign a statement affirming that the application is accurate and stating that the person can be fired if misrepresention occurs.

3.13 INTERVIEWING

Interviewing today is a whole new process. Many of today's applicants are as aware of the interviewing process as the company interviewer. Smart applicants are well prepared for the interview, and it is tough to elicit the data you need to make a wise hiring decision.

Because interviewing has become such a widely practiced skill, there is a need for human resource people to learn and apply new techniques constantly.

Principles of a Good Selection Interview

- Really know the job. A quick review of the job description won't do.
- Understand what the hiring manager is looking for.
- Learn about the applicant in advance. Do your homework.
- Plan the interview in order to come away with the information you need.
- Establish a comfortable conversational style to build rapport.
- Use plain language, and reveal aspects of yourself in order to give as well as get information.
- Maintain objectivity about the applicant as the interview progresses.
- Remain flexible, and guide the conversation from general to specific and from harmless to sensitive areas.
- Listen. Concentrate on what the applicant is saying. Show empathy and respond appropriately.
- Structure the interview so that you use a variety of questioning techniques. Use more open-ended questions, rather than questions that can be answered "yes" or "no."
- Don't ask questions that could be considered discriminatory.
- Give information during the interview. There should be a psychological one-to-one exchange.
- Use silence to obtain more information. If the applicant seems to run out of things to say, let the silence build up for a few minutes. The applicant probably will offer more information.
- If there are statements you'd like the applicant to expand on, repeat them in another way. This is called "echoing" and is an effective information-gathering technique.
- Watch for the "halo" effect, where an interviewer permits one or two favorable traits, such as a good appearance or ability to speak, to bias judgment favorably on other entirely unrelated traits. The halo effect can work in reverse, biasing the interviewer unfavorably because of one or two bad impressions.

- Don't talk too much. Respect the applicant's need. Exchange information.
- Show energy and enthusiasm. A stiff, formal interviewer will turn off most applicants.
- Don't try to give advice or counsel in a selection interview.
- Follow up hunches and unusual statements. If the applicant says, "I don't get along with certain kinds of people," you want to find out who those kinds of people are.
- Maintain control of the interview.
- Close the interview in a reasonable period of time. Close on a positive note, but don't lead an applicant on or promise anything you can't deliver.
- As soon as the interview is over, write down the facts and your impressions of the interview.

3.14 FIVE TYPES OF INTERVIEWS

Patterned Interview

The patterned interview is designed to cover specific areas and to identify personal strengths and weaknesses. It provides specific, systematic answers regarding an applicant's qualifications and experience. The patterned interview provides a guide for interpreting information for judging what the applicant can do; however, the classic patterned interview is too structured to appeal to today's more sophisticated applicant; and in order to keep from turning an applicant off to the company, it's best to try a more informal style that can still elicit the information needed to make a good hiring decision.

Conversational Interview

The conversational interview is an unplanned, rather haphazard discussion-style interview that puts an applicant at ease but does not provide comprehensive information and is not an objective type of interview. The conversational interview may appeal to some, but more times than not it leaves the interviewer without all the information needed to make the right choice of applicants.

Comprehensive Interview

The most widely used and successful interview technique with today's applicants is a combination of the informal conversational style and the more formal patterned style. It's most commonly referred to as the comprehensive interview.

The comprehensive interview follows a definite plan, but the interviewer deviates from the plan to pursue important details and shows respect for the applicant. This style of interview encourages the applicant to share in the process and to obtain needed information. It is a participative approach that encourages discussion.

Stress Interview

Stress questions are becoming more popular in executive interviews. Stress questions are usually asked on a subject that is foreign to the subject under discussion. For example:

An applicant may be discussing abilities in a particular area, and the next question the interviewer asks suddenly changes to an entirely different subject. Like, "What is your favorite magazine?" A man might respond by naming *Playboy*. A more prudent reply would be *Business Week*, but the sudden switch might confuse the applicant.

A woman might respond by saying "*Ms.*" which could brand her a feminist and would not be a prudent answer in an interview for a conservative organization. *Time* or *Business Week* would be a better response.

A conversational or comprehensive interview may suddenly include a stress question to see how the applicant responds.

Group Interview

Another type of interview we're beginning to see used more frequently is the group interview. One large bank in the West uses group interviews of peers in the same department for all applicants for professional, supervisory, and management level positions. The Vice-President of Human Resources feels that a group of peers can collectively render a more objective decision. I don't agree. Somehow, peer group decisions used in employment interviews never seem as objective as they could be, simply because peers may tend to view the applicant as competition.

3.15 SIX INTERVIEWING STRATEGIES YOU CAN USE TO HIRE TOP PERSONNEL[3]

There's a way to put top achievers on your payroll and cut your company's turnover at the same time. Make the most of job interviews. Pinpoint in advance those qualifications necessary for the job you're filling. And make sure the interview focuses on how the job applicant will fit the bill.

Here are some effective techniques many company presidents use to boost the odds that the person they hire today will become tomorrow's top asset:

1. Do some comparison shopping before you sit down with an applicant. Pull a few résumés of some of your successful employees to see how the applicant's experience stacks. You'll have a clearer idea of which qualifications point to success in that particular job.

2. Get a second opinion. Involve your supervisors to see what their ideas are. They'll have a different perspective to add. Send the applicant's résumé to the supervisor and ask if he or she would hire this person. And find out the reason why the supervisor would or wouldn't hire the prospect. When you send the résumé to the supervisor, don't indicate any preference or dissatisfaction. If you do, the supervisor will most likely just second your opinion.

3. Test their involvement. This is especially important when an executive position is at stake. Check on the applicant's powers of observation. Let's say the prospect has worked for a company manufacturing corrugated boxes. Ask him or her to explain the production process and cost-cutting procedures used by that

---

[3] *The President's Personnel Letter.*

company. Then ask what changes the prospect initiated. A detailed answer with suggestions for good changes indicates a get-ahead person. An answer merely describing the operation suggests an employee who is happier as a follower.

4. Keep the spotlight on the candidate. Try to avoid the trap of talking about what naturally interests you—your own business. Tell a candidate just enough about your company so he or she can relate any personal or work experience to your company's operations. Here's a Michigan manufacturer's idea:

"I'll ask a purchasing agent how he or she would help us find the right suppliers for plastics. Hopefully, the applicant will then ask what we use plastics for. Then, I'll explain our production of circuit boards—a large part of the business."

The spotlight is on the candidate's ideas, even while the executive tells about the company. Usually, applicants learn as much about the company as you do about them—all in a give-and-take conversation.

5. Fit the applicant to the job. Conduct the interview according to the position the applicant is seeking. An Illinois publisher, when interviewing an advertising copywriter, for instance, does this:

"I ask applicants to tell me about their cars. Usually, they give me the model and year. Then I tell them I'm in the market for a used car. I'd like to hear them give me a sales pitch. I can often tell whether the applicants have sales—and advertising—talents by the way they develop the pitch."

6. Look for "take charge" qualities. In particular, look for salespeople who are aggressive. Move the applicant's chair about four feet away from your desk before the interview. Then, observe what happens when the applicant comes into the office. The person to look for is the one who moves the chair closer to you. This person is aggressive. He or she doesn't feel that just because the chair was far away from the desk, it should stay there. This type of person will pursue a sale even after an initial turndown.

3.16 HOW TO ASK THREE TOUGH INTERVIEW QUESTIONS WITHOUT ASKING FOR TROUBLE[4]

Is there a way to stay clear of EEO problems when you have to ask "sensitive" questions during a job interview? Let's examine some situations that require careful interviewing techniques to avoid trouble.

1. *Child care.* You are considering hiring a woman for a position that will entail considerable overtime on short notice. You know from your conversation that this applicant has a young child at home.

Wrong way: "Will the irregular hours you may have to work interfere with your taking care of your child? Can we depend on you?" Recent rulings view such a query as discriminatory, since it is normally asked only of women.

Right way: "Can you work overtime on a consistent basis? Are you aware that this job requires late-night work with short advance notice?" Even here, you

---

[4] *The President's Personnel Letter.*

must keep in mind that if the question is asked only of one sex or if it is only applicable to one sex, then you might be asking for trouble.

2. *Travel.* In another situation, you are considering a married woman for a position that requires extensive travel. You have doubts about whether she could handle being away from home several nights a week, and whether her husband would approve.

Wrong way: "Are you sure your husband won't mind your being on the road so often?" Whatever your reservations, you must operate under the assumption that the applicant is aware of the travel requirements, is willing to make the "sacrifice," and does not need her husband's approval to take the job.

Right way: "Do you know there is a considerable amount of travel involved?" Clearly spell out the amount of travel needed. You may suggest that the candidate think over her decision carefully. But place the responsibility where it belongs: on the applicant, not her husband.

3. *Arrest record.* Before hiring an applicant for a cashier's position, you want to know if the person is trustworthy. You are especially interested in information concerning a criminal background.

Wrong way: "Have you ever been arrested or convicted of any crime?" You may not inquire into the arrest records of job applicants. Nor may you ask about "any" convictions.

Right way: "Have you ever been convicted of theft or embezzlement?" You cannot go on a fishing expedition when it comes to asking about a criminal record. Be specific. Ask only about convictions that would affect the person's fitness for the job you have open.

3.17 HANDLING PROBLEM APPLICANTS, QUESTIONING TECHNIQUES, SAMPLE QUESTIONS

Part of the control problem of an interview is handling problem applicants—the talkative, the glib, the egomaniacs, the point-dodgers, the evaders, and the interviewers.

The talkative applicant goes off on a tangent:

Interviewer: "John, what special assignments did you perform for your boss?"
Applicant: "I purchased office supplies and equipment such as mining equipment, company card, etc. I bought furniture for our offices. It was walnut-grained and was especially functional because you could choose the pieces you wanted, etc., etc., etc."

If this interview is to come to a succesful conclusion before nightfall, the interviewer will have to assume control. This can be done by frequent interruptions with key questions. When the applicant digresses, the interviewer waits for him to pause for breath, and then asks a specific question to bring him back on the track.

The glib applicant is so well prepared for the interview that he or she knows all the answers to your questions before they are asked. This applicant is often a superficial candidate, with knowledge of the language of the job, but not the experience or know-how to perform. To determine if the applicant is as good as he or she sounds, ask more probing questions. Probe deeper into the specifications of the job: "How did you accomplish specific aspects of the work?" "What was the result of your approach to this?" "What did it cost? How much profit ensued?"

The ego applicant may start the interview with the statement, "I'm the man for the job." When questioned about specifics, he or she may say; "I've just been offered a job with your competitor." He or she may evade questions by bragging about "accomplishments" which are usually vague and in conflict with each other. A great deal of conflicting information usually comes out of this interview, and this applicant is usually not worth considering seriously.

The point evader operates this way:

Interviewer: "On what type and dollar level purchase did you have the authority to make final decision?"
Applicant: "I know a great deal about tires."
Interviewer: "Did you buy all the tires for your firm?"
Applicant: "I recommended which lines to buy."
Interviewer: "Who actually made the deal?"
Applicant: "My boss."

The interviewer is the applicant who tries to turn the situation around and tries to interview *you*:

Interviewer: "Can you give me some details of your duties in your current job?"
Applicant: "I'd be glad to, but first tell me about your opening."

This will probably lead nowhere. A better response might be:

Interviewer: "I appreciate your interest in our position, but first I would like to know more about you. If you meet the qualifications, we can discuss the job further."

3.18 QUESTIONING TECHNIQUES

To obtain the necessary answers from an applicant, good questioning techniques must be used. These include the following:

1. *Unstructured question.* This cannot be answered by a "yes" or a "no" and will enable the applicant to speak openly and help the interviewer to better obtain the underlying reason for particular views on the part of the applicant. Questions beginning with "who," "what," "when," "where," "why," and "how" will elicit an unstructured answer.
2. *Structured question.* This places the applicant in a position to answer with either a "yes" or a "no." An elaborate answer is not necessarily given:
   Q. Did you like your last job?
   A. Yes.
3. *Unstructured question combined with structured question.* A structured question may be followed by an unstructured question to help clarify the applicant's feelings, pinpoint a particular fact, or obtain additional information.
   Q. Did you like your last job?
   A. Yes.

Q. What in particular did you like?

A. Well, . . .

4. *Use of silence.* A brief pause between questions allows the applicant more time to elaborate on an answer if he or she desires.

5. *Reflective feeling.* This is an interpretation by the interviewer of the applicant's statement in terms of content and feelings. Phrases beginning with "It seems that" or "It sounds like" reflect feelings.

6. *Active listening.* This means repetition or restatement by the interviewer of what the applicant has said, usually in the form of a question. The applicant is then aware of the interviewer's interest.

Q. What did you think of your previous employer?

A. He was all right, but a bit overbearing.

Q. Overbearing?

A. Well, he . . .

7. *Assertions of understanding.* These neutral phrases will place the applicant in a position to elaborate on his or her answer. These phrases might include "I understand," "Uh-huh," or "Yes, I see," and so on.

3.19   UNSTRUCTURED (OPEN-ENDED) QUESTIONS

1. Tell me about . . .
2. Would you tell me about . . . ?
3. I'd be interested in knowing . . .
4. How did you feel about . . . ?
5. Would you explain . . . ?
6. I'm not certain I understand . . .
7. Would you explain that in more detail?
8. What do you mean by that?
9. Tell me more about . . .
10. Perhaps you could clarify . . .
11. What was there about . . . that appealed to you?
12. Has there been any opportunity to . . . ?

3.20   SAMPLE QUESTIONS

1. I'd like to discuss your technical experience. Tell me about your experience in the technical area.
2. What were your major responsibilities in your last job?
3. In your last job, what duties did you spend most of your time on?
4. How did you feel about the progress you made with your last company?
5. In what ways do you feel your past job developed you to take on greater responsibility?
6. What are some of the reasons you had for leaving your last job?
7. What were some of the things you particularly liked about your last job?
8. Most jobs have pluses and minuses. What are some of the minuses in your last job?
9. Did you consider your progress on the job representative of your ability? Why?

10. What are some of the things your boss did that you particularly liked or disliked?
11. How did your manager rate your job performance?
12. What did your manager feel you did particularly well? What were major criticisms of your work? How do you feel about these criticisms?
13. What kind of people do you like working with? What kind of people do you find most difficult to work with?
14. What are some of the things in a job that are important to you? Why?
15. What are some of the things you would like to avoid in a job? Why?
16. How do you feel your last company treated its employees?

3.21 QUESTIONS INAPPROPRIATE TO ASK CANDIDATES FOR EMPLOYMENT

Questions seeking the following information are illegal and cannot be asked of an applicant before he or she is hired:

1. Date of birth
2. Maiden name
3. Previous married name
4. Marital status
5. Name of spouse
6. Spouse's occupation and length of time on the job
7. Spouse's place of employment
8. Number of children and their ages
9. Arrest record
10. Convictions may be asked about, but you cannot refuse employment because they were convicted, unless it is a bona fide job qualification
11. If child care has been arranged for the children
12. Reasons that would prevent an applicant from maintaining employment
13. Ancestry
14. National origin (color)
15. Age
16. Sex
17. Religion
18. Affiliations with Communist party, or a union
19. Garnishment of wages

It should be kept in mind that much of the above is the type of information necessary for personnel records and employee benefit programs once the individual is employed. However, the information is obtained *after* employment, and therefore can have no bearing on the employment decision.

3.22 EMPLOYMENT TESTING

There are many pros and cons of testing. The main guideline, however, is that tests must be job-related and given to all applicants for the job for which the test applies. You cannot give a test to some applicants and not to others. Uniformity is the key.

The EEOC has adopted six testing guidelines to help employers establish objective standards for selection, screening, and promotion of workers:

1. Job descriptions should be examined and their critical requirements established before tests are selected for screening applicants.

2. Tests used should be developed by reputable psychologists. Such tests should be administered by professionally qualified personnel who have had training in occupational testing in an industrial setting.

3. Rigidly inflexible minimum scores should be reexamined in light of the considerable research under way on differential selection.

4. Test scores must be considered as only one source of information and must be combined with other available information on performance, such as motivation, leadership, organizational experience, self-sufficiency, and dependability.

5. Tests should be validated within the setting where they will be used. Validation should be for as many separate groups as possible in preference to one large heterogeneous group.

6. It may be advisable for employers who deal with applicants from culturally deprived backgrounds to offer retests to candidates who are unsuccessful on their first test, since these people are less familiar with the testing situation and may not do as well as they are able.

3.23   AUDIO PRESENTATIONS

The Bureau of National Affairs is offering seven 90-minute audio cassettes that discuss the federal government's new approaches to testing and fair employment practices.

Taped during a recent Washington conference, the cassettes' topics include the employer's view as espoused by the American Bar Association and the U.S. Chamber of Commerce; recent developments in the compliance and enforcement field; recent developments in the field of industrial and personnel psychology; the future direction of federal government emphasis in contractor compliance; recent developments in minority recruiting, analysis of labor markets, and determination of adverse impact; false premises underlying the 1978 Uniform Guidelines on Employee Selection Procedures; and personnel and public policy implications.

The tapes are available from BNA Education Systems, Suite S–602, 1231 25th Street, N.W., Washington, D.C. 20037.

3.24   LIE DETECTOR TESTS

A growing number of companies are using polygraph tests as part of their personnel programs, according to a study of 400 large U.S. corporations. While the American Civil Liberties Union and the AFL–CIO oppose polygraph tests as an infringement of personal liberties, some personnel departments in states where such lie detector activities are legal are insisting on using them in preemployment screening.

The heaviest users of polygraphs are retailers and commercial banks, according to John A. Belt and Peter B. Holden of Wichita State University, who conducted a survey.[5] Half of the companies studied in these categories use polygraphs, compared to only 12 percent of industrial companies, 25 percent of transportation companies, 4 percent of life insurance companies, and 20 percent of all firms in the sample.

Companies using polygraphs cited three major purposes: verifying job applications (34.5 percent), with one in ten administering tests to all applicants; periodic checks of honesty (also 34.5 percent); and investigation of specific thefts and irregularities (89.5 percent).

However, in seventeen jurisdictions—Alaska, California, Connecticut, the District of Columbia, Hawaii, Idaho, Maine, Maryland, Massachusetts, Michigan, Minnesota, Montana, Nebraska, New Jersey, Oregon, Rhode Island, and Washington—employers are prohibited from requiring workers or prospective workers to take lie detector tests as a condition of obtaining or continuing employment.

In Massachusetts, an employer that requires an employee or job applicant to take a lie detector test may be fined up to $200, and in the District of Columbia employers that violate a similar law may be subject to civil liability to the person who took the test. Employers in Virginia are barred from requiring prospective employees to answer polygraph questions about their sexual activities, unless such conduct has resulted in a conviction for the applicant.

Employers in Pennsylvania and California must obtain the written consent of an employee before administering psychological stress evaluators or voice stress examinations, respectively. Under a new Wisconsin law, employers are prohibited from using a polygraph, voice stress analysis, psychological stress evaluator, or similar devices to test an employee's honesty. However, the law does permit the use of an instrument or device to verify truthfulness or to detect deception, but only with the employee's written consent.

In other states, however, there are no provisions against lie detector tests, and some employers still use them as part of their employment process.

Some people feel lie detector tests are an unwarranted invasion of privacy. The tests have definitely become an emotional issue.

3.25 PREEMPLOYMENT REFERENCE CHECKING

Because of privacy concerns and other social pressures, American business seems to have swung from overchecking to nonchecking in preemployment investigations. Businesses are in a vulnerable position today. U.S. Department of Commerce statistics show that 30 percent of all business failures result from employees' dishonest acts; internal theft occurs at a rate fifteen times higher than external theft; embezzlement causes an annual loss of more than $4 million; employee pilferage costs business from $5 billion to $10 billion annually.

Good reference checking and employee screening and selection procedures are a must in any business. Include in the process checks on former job experience and per-

---

[5] John A. Belt and Peter B. Holden, "Polygraph Usage Among Major U.S. Corporations," copyright February 1978. Reprinted with permission of *Personnel Journal*, Costa Mesa, California. All rights reserved.

formance, schools attended and school performance, physical and mental health as it would apply to the position, public records, litigations, Workers' Compensation claims, possible conflicts of interest, and so on.

The value of background information on a prospective employee is obvious, but many employers mistakenly believe that the traditional methods of screening and selection are not permissible under the law. This is not true. Many employers have eliminated reference checking, not because of legal restrictions, but because of fear of a lawsuit. There is no absolute protection against being sued, unless the employer eliminates personnel selection altogether; but that's obviously not a smart move, either.

What Are the Laws?

Title VII of the Civil Rights Act of 1964, as amended by the 1972 Equal Employment Opportunity Act (EEOA), applies most directly to reference checking. The Age Discrimination Act of 1967 and the Rehabilitation Act of 1973 preclude discrimination based on age and disability. It is illegal to use applicant information if it has an adverse impact on groups of individuals protected by the law, unless it can be shown to be a business necessity, or unless there is no less discriminatory selection procedure readily available. Although limitations apply, these restrictions do not prohibit the use of background investigations.

The uniform guideline on employee selection, adopted in 1978 by the Equal Employment Opportunity Commission, the Civil Service Commission, and the Department of Labor, specify that no specific personnel selection procedure is prohibited, including reference checking, preemployment investigations, and tests, and any selection procedure must meet the requirements of all applicable laws. The procedure must be relevant to a specific position. Any selection procedure that discriminates against applicants on the basis of race, sex, religion, and so on, is prohibited. Employees can, however, seek information about applicants and interpret and use the information during the selection process.

A Preemployment Checklist

With regard to reference checking, the bottom line is making sure the criteria used in reaching employment decisions are pertinent but not discriminatory. Ask yourself these questions:

1. Are you being consistent? Are you sure job standards are applied evenly in all job classifications? If an item is grounds for denying a job to one applicant, it should be the same for any other applicant.
2. Do you use a telephone interview checklist? Using a standard format will keep you from digressing into areas not relevant to the job.
3. Is data relevant? Be sure information used for employment decisions is job-related. Eliminate unnecessary requirements, such as unusually tough physical or educational requirements.
4. Are you keeping written documentation? Be prepared to back up your hire or no-hire decision with written proof verifying that the decision was based on relevant information.
5. Are you using the Fair Credit Reporting Act? If an applicant is not hired because of information contained in a preemployment report, the applicant must be notified and the reporting agency must disclose the contents of its report to the applicant.

For further guidelines on preemployment reference checking, see the Prentice-Hall Legal Service or check with your legal counsel.

3.26 MORE ON CHECKING AN APPLICANT'S REFERENCES

Ninety percent of all hiring mistakes can be prevented through proper reference checking procedures, according to Norman D. Sanders.[6] Yet reference checking seldom constitutes the one-third of the hiring process (together with screening and interviewing) he feels it should. The reason: Many employers don't make adequate reference checks because they are difficult.

Here are some of the major problems in reference checking, along with Sanders's suggestions for overcoming them.

1. Because of the possibility of litigation, many organizations have adopted strict policies against giving more than rudimentary reference data. So there's often a problem in obtaining any references at all from previous employers. Get written authorization from the candidate to contact his or her former (or present) employer. This can sometimes encourage that employer to talk more freely with you.

2. Many of the references furnished by candidates themselves can be described as "setups" (someone who has been carefully "programmed" to respond the way the candidate wishes). Often, there is a personal relationship between the candidate and the person given as a reference, which makes for a built-in bias in the candidate's favor. Try to find out whether there's a family relationship, a long-standing friendship, or an outside business relationship involved. If there is, discount the reference accordingly.

3. An employee who does give a reference can be subject to an "I want to be a good guy" impulse. Here, perhaps, in its worst case, the person giving the reference may have terminated the candidate for outlandish behavior or lack of performance, but doesn't want to stand in his or her way. Telephone the person giving the reference, and get as many specifics as you can about how well the candidate has performed. Even the reference's tone of voice may indicate he or she is simply trying to "be a good guy."

See figure 3–5 for a telephone reference check, and figure 3–6 for a written reference check.

3.27 REFERENCE CHECKING GUIDELINES

These guidelines can be useful in culling out priority items you wish to check:

- Did the person achieve the objectives of the job?
- How were the candidate's working relationships?
- Can you confirm the achievements claimed by the candidate?
- What kind of job would you recommend the candidate for?
- Under what conditions can the candidate work best?
- Did the candidate have any problems?
- Would you rehire the candidate?
- Would you recommend the candidate for this job? (Describe the requirements of the job.)

[6] Norman D. Sanders, "President's Guide to Attracting and Developing Top-Caliber Employees," Executive Reports Corporation, Englewood Cliffs, New Jersey 07632.

FIGURE 3-5.

<u>TELEPHONE REFERENCE CHECK</u>

Applicant's Name: Position Applied For:
(last, first, middle initial)

_____   _____

Name of Person Contacted: Title and Department:
(last, first, middle initial)

_____   _____

Company: _____   Telephone No.: _____

Employment Dates: from _____ to _____
Leaving position: _____ Leaving Salary: $ _____
Reason(s) for leaving: _____
_____

Eligible for rehire: Yes ( ) No ( ) If no, state reason(s): _____
_____

Major duties:

Ability to plan, organize, and control:
Ability to work with others:
Interpersonal skills:

Supervisory or managerial ability/potential:

No. of people supervised: _____ How long? _____
Able to select, motivate, discipline: _____
Evaluation of supervisory/managerial potential: _____
_____

Ability to work with others: _____

Strong points: _____
_____

Weak points: _____
_____

Attendance: Good ( )   Average ( )   Poor ( )   State reason:
_____

Were there any personal reasons that affected job performance?
_____

What is your overall evaluation of applicant? _____
_____

Comments: _____
_____
_____

Human Resource Coordinator

_____   Date _____

FIGURE 3-6.

<u>WRITTEN REFERENCE CHECK</u>

(Date) _____

Atlas Energy Company
10 Brown Deer Drive
Denver, Colorado 80020

Attention: (Human Resource Manager)

The person identified is being considered for employment with our company and has signed a statement authorizing this verification and investigation. We shall appreciate a statement of your opinions and experiences with this person as outlined below. Your reply will be considered confidential.

Name of applicant: _____

Soc. Sec. no.: _____

Dates of last employment: _____

Position last held: _____

Final rate of pay: $ _____

   Is the above information correct? Yes ( ) No ( )

   If not, please make corrections.

Reason for leaving your employ: _____

_____

Eligible for rehire? Yes ( ) No ( ) If not, why?

_____

Your further comments on any personal or professional strengths and weaknesses will be appreciated.

_____

_____

(signed)

(title)

3.28 RELOCATION POLICY

A majority of companies who ask employees or newly hired people to relocate pay their relocation costs, including the cost of selling their old homes and buying new ones. Various relocation policies include, but are not limited to, the following benefits:

- Paid moving expenses
- A month's salary to cover incidental expenses
- Mortgage interest differentials
- Cost-of-living differentials
- Relocation taxation policies
- Up-front bonuses to move

In recent years, executives have become more resistant to relocation. Runzheimer and Company, a management consulting firm based in Rochester, Wisconsin, estimates that as many as 80 percent of employees refused the first transfer assignment they were offered last year. Likeliest to say "no" are executives between 25 and 45 years of age who define their personal goals in terms of lifestyle rather than life's work.

According to an article in *Fortune* magazine on June 16, 1980, in order to lessen the financial sting of relocation, hundreds of companies are liberalizing their relocation policies to include mortgage differential payments, cost-of-living differentials, and up-front bonuses. Particularly valuable employees are likely to get other perks if they relocate. A hefty increase in salary and a bonus are not unusual.

New relocation benefits add up to higher and higher costs for companies. Homequity Company reports that the cost to the corporation for an average employee move increased 48 percent in 1979, from $20,500 to $30,300. Westinghouse figures that its domestic moves cost an average of $40,000. Since the company transfers about 1,000 people a year, that's a total of some $40 million, or around 12 percent of their 1979 pretax profits.

The tremendous increase in costs is making many organizations look hard at the people they hire and transfer.

The current rule of thumb is that it will cost a corporation one year of an employee's salary to relocate the person.

The Employee Relocation Council, a nonprofit Washington-based association, recently completed a study based on a survey of 350 employees from ten companies who had experienced job-related relocations.[7] Among the issues explored in the study are the reasons some workers are more willing to relocate than others, factors that contribute to easier and more successful moves, and the effects of a mobile lifestyle on workers and their families.

Measuring Mobility

Contrary to commonly held assumptions, the study says, an employee's rejection of a transfer does not mean the worker is totally unwilling to move again in the future.

---

[7] "The Effect of Job Transfer on Employees and Their Families," Employee Relocation Council, 1627 K Street, N.W., Washington, D.C. 20006; and principal researcher, Jeanne M. Brett, Northwestern University, Evanston, Illinois.

Similarly, the fact that an employee recently has completed a move "does not mean that he will reject a new opportunity to move and advance his career." The study points out that 54 percent of the surveyed employees who had accepted a transfer offer said that they would relocate again if the move meant a better job, while 61 percent of those who had turned down a transfer during the previous year also said they would be willing to move for a better position. In other areas, the study shows that younger workers are more willing to move than older employees, that employees in sales and marketing functions are more willing to relocate than other types of workers, and that spouses who are willing to move had experienced few difficulties with previous relocations and, if employed, were not committed to their own jobs.

Among the factors that made transfers easier were: the move was anticipated, the relocation involved "only moderate change in terms of level or function," the employees were "well informed about the scope of the new job," workers felt that they had most of the skills necessary to perform the new job well, and employees experienced a feeling of success "in at least one aspect of the new job within the first month." Also helping to facilitate the transfer process were: the degree to which a spouse's opinions were considered in the employee's decision to transfer, the ease with which the family adapted to the new locale, and the family's ability to cope with the cost-of-living changes in the new location.

Relocation Recommendations

The study offers a number of relocation recommendations to employers, as well as employees. Corporations are advised to:

- *Give "first-choice" workers the opportunity to transfer:* Management should not assume that certain employees automatically will refuse a transfer offer. If the most qualified employee is not offered the job, both the organization and the worker stand to lose.

- *Emphasize how the transfer fits into an employee's career progression:* While it is easy for management "to see how the company's personnel needs are being met by the transfer," the study notes, it isn't always clear to employees how the move will further their careers.

- *Make the new job challenging:* "The most important factor stimulating an employee to accept a job transfer is the challenge of the new job," the study maintains. In cases where the transfer involves a lateral move, companies should investigate job enrichment possibilities or stress the advancement potential of the new position.

- *Don't "dead-end" employees who reject relocations:* Many employees feel that refusing a transfer could damage their careers, the study notes. In companies that explicitly state that transfer refusals won't result in dead-ending, employees have a greater feeling of control over their careers.

- *Assist spouses with job-placement help at the new location:* Companies can assist working spouses by providing them with job contacts in the new area, job-search counseling services, help with preparing résumés, and information about the local labor markets.

Among the recommendations for transferring workers and their families are:

- Employees should evaluate the kinds of demands that their job places on them and their families.

- Spouses of employees who relocate frequently should try to select "complementary" careers.
- Parents in a "mobile" family should try to encourage positive attitudes toward moving in their children and help the children acquire social skills that will ease their adaptation to a new environment.

3.29   HUMAN RESOURCE FORMS—APPLICATION

The application form gives you most of the information you need to make a determination of an applicant's qualifications for the open position. Applications must comply with all federal regulations. An application revised and approved by the Mountain States Employers Council in Denver, Colorado, is shown in figure 3–7.[8]

3.30   PERSONNEL REQUISITIONS

The guidelines presented in figure 3–8 are provided by one company for the acquisition of personnel.

The basic purpose of the personnel requisition is to explain the reasons for a job vacancy and to establish the existence of a bona fide job opening in the company. The personnel requisition should be completed in the following cases and for the following reasons:

New position or revised position

1. To indicate if the job opening is the result of a newly created position that has been budgeted and approved.
2. To verify that the position has been evaluated and assigned an appropriate salary range.
3. To verify that a bona fide job exists so that it may be recorded in order to meet EEO reporting requirements.
4. To authorize expenditure of money by the human resource department in recruiting to fill the position.

Replacement position

1. To indicate the opening is the result of an employee being terminated, transferred, or promoted.
2. To verify by the correct coding that the job opening is a replacement position.
3. To verify an open position for EEO purposes. Promotions, transfers, and new hires all must be recorded in order to meet EEO reporting requirements.

These are merely sample guidelines and should be amended to fit each individual organization's needs.

3.31   HUMAN RESOURCE FORMS—APPLICANT APPRAISAL FORM

The time to evaluate an applicant is immediately after the interview. Figure 3–9 shows an applicant appraisal form used by the Rocky Mountain Energy Company, Broomfield, Colorado.

---

[8] Mountain States Employers Council, 1790 Logan Street, Denver, Colorado 80201.

FIGURE 3-7.

An Equal Opportunity Employer — Male/Female

We do not discriminate on the basis of race, religion, national origin, color, sex, age, or handicap. It is our intention that all applicants be given equal opportunity and that selection decisions are based on job-related factors.

APPLICATION FOR EMPLOYMENT

instructions

Each question should be fully and accurately answered. No action can be taken on this application until all questions have been answered. Use blank paper if you do not have enough room on this application blank. **PLEASE PRINT**, except for signature on back of Application. All information you give on this application will be held in strict confidence.

personal data

Job Applied For _____ Today's Date _____
Are you seeking: Full-time ☐ Part-time ☐ Temporary or Summer ☐ employment?

When are you available for employment? _____

| Last Name | First Name | Middle Name | Telephone Number |

| Present Street Address | City | State | Zip Code |

Answer the appropriate question checked below:
☐ Are you between 18 and 70 years of age? . . . . Yes ☐ No ☐

☐ Date of Birth _____ (for jobs with minimum age requirements)
If you are applying for a job with minimum age requirements, you may be required to submit proof of age.
Social Security Number _____ Are you a citizen of the United States or do you
have a valid work permit? . . . . Yes ☐ No ☐

military

Military Status: Active Duty Service From _____ to _____
Branch of Service _____
Service Duties _____
Are you a member of a Reserve organization? . . . . Yes ☐ No ☐

general

Were you ever employed here? . . . . Yes ☐ No ☐ When? _____
Have you ever applied here before? . . . . Yes ☐ No ☐ When? _____
Have you ever been convicted of any law violation (except a minor traffic violation)? . . . . Yes ☐ No ☐

If yes, give particulars _____
Have you missed any work during the past six months? . . . . Yes ☐ No ☐

If yes, how much? _____
Are you now or do you expect to be engaged in any other business or employment? . . . . Yes ☐ No ☐

If yes, please explain _____
Of what clubs, organizations, civic or other groups have you been a member in the last five years? (List offices held.) (Exclude any labor organizations or any organizations the name and character of which indicate race, color, religion, sex, age, national origin or ancestry of its members.) _____

For Driving Jobs Only: Do you have a valid drivers license? . . . . Yes ☐ No ☐

Drivers License Number _____

education

Name, Address and Location of School	Highest Grade Completed	Did You Graduate?	Date of Leaving
High School:			
College or University:			
College Major: _____ Degree: _____			

Additional Educational and/or Vocational or Technical Training Information:

Name, Address and Location of School	Courses Taken	Courses Completed	Date of Leaving

health

Do you have any physical limitations which would adversely effect performance of the job
for which you are applying? . . . . Yes ☐ No ☐
If yes, please explain _____
Would you take a physical examination, if required? . . . . Yes ☐ No ☐

MSEC 1.1a
9/80

FIGURE 3-7 (cont'd)

references

Give three references, not relatives or former employers.

Name	Address	Phone	Occupation

work history

List names of employers in consecutive order with present or last employer listed first. Account for all periods of time including military service and any periods of unemployment. If self-employed, give firm name and supply business references.
PLEASE GIVE MONTH AND YEAR.

Name of Present or Last Employer	Employed	Pay	Title and Duties	Reason for Leaving	Name of Last Supervisor
	From	Start			
Address					
City, State, Zip Code	To	Final			
Telephone					
Name of Employer	Employed	Pay	Title and Duties	Reason for Leaving	Name of Last Supervisor
	From	Start			
Address					
City, State, Zip Code	To	Final			
Telephone					
Name of Employer	Employed	Pay	Title and Duties	Reason for Leaving	Name of Last Supervisor
	From	Start			
Address					
City, State, Zip Code	To	Final			
Telephone					
Name of Employer	Employed	Pay	Title and Duties	Reason for Leaving	Name of Last Supervisor
	From	Start			
Address					
City, State, Zip Code	To	Final			
Telephone					

Is any additional information relative to change of name, use of assumed name, or nickname necessary to enable us to check your work
record? . . . . Yes ☐   No ☐
Are you presently employed? . . . . Yes ☐   No ☐
          If yes, may we contact your present employer? . . . . Yes ☐   No ☐

special skills

If you are an experienced operator of any business machines or equipment, please list _____

_____

If you are an experienced operator of any plant machines or equipment, please list _____

_____

Do you type? . . . . Yes ☐   No ☐   Words Per Minute _____
Do you take shorthand? . . . . Yes ☐   No ☐   Words Per Minute _____
Do you have any other skills you wish to mention? _____

investigative consumer report

In making this application for employment, it is understood that an investigation may be made whereby information is obtained through personal interviews with your neighbors, friends and others with whom you are acquainted. This inquiry includes information as to your character, general reputation, personal characteristics and mode of living. You have the right to make a written request within a reasonable period of time for complete and accurate disclosure of additional information concerning the nature and scope of this investigation.

affidavit

I certify that the answers given by me to the foregoing questions and statements are true and correct without consequential omissions of any kind whatsoever. I agree that the company shall not be liable in any respect if my employment is terminated because of falsity of statements, answers or omissions made by me in this questionnaire. I also authorize the companies, schools or persons named above to give any information regarding my employment, character and qualifications. I hereby release said companies, schools or persons from all liability for any damage for issuing this information. I certify that all statements and answers to questions about my health are true and were made by me without any reservations. I expressly waive all provisions of law prohibiting any physician, person, hospital or other institution that has or may hereafter attend or furnish me with treatment from disclosing to the company any knowledge or information thereby acquired. I understand that any misleading or incorrect statements may render this application void, and if employed, would be cause for termination.

                                                              Signature_____Date_____

company use only

Do Not Write Below This Line

Disposition_____   Date Employed _____ Starting Rate_____per_____
Job Classification_____   Department _____ Clock No. _____
Interviewed by_____   Interviewer's remarks and recommendations _____

_____

_____

Application information checked by: Name _____Date_____

FIGURE 3-8.

PERSONNEL REQUISITION - (Please Type This Form)

JOB TITLE			RANGE	SHIFT		REQUISITION NUMBER
						CURRENT DATE

☐ REPLACEMENT	☐ NEW POSITION	☐ EXEMPT ☐ NON-EXEMPT	DEPT. — LOCATION		DATE NEEDED

NAME OF VACATING EMPLOYEE — REGULAR / TEMPORARY / PART TIME

REASON FOR VACANCY OR NEW POSITION — SKILLS REQUIRED

EDUCATION OR EQUIVALENT EXPERIENCE

PRINCIPAL ACCOUNTIBILITIES (In Order of Importance)

1.   5.

2.   6.   ADDITIONAL JOB OR AD INFO

3.   7.

4.   8.

SCHEDULE INTERVIEWS THRU (Name and Extension) — ORIGINATOR OR SUPERVISOR

NEW ORGANIZATION CHART ATTACHED

MANAGER'S SIGNATURE — V P OR OTHER SIGNATURE — PRESIDENT'S SIGNATURE

PERSONNEL USE ONLY

POSITION FILLED BY	START DATE	RANGE	SALARY	MS

101

FIGURE 3-9.

APPLICANT APPRAISAL FORM

Current Opening

Position _____   Name of Applicant _____   Yes ____ No ____

This rating form will become a part of the candidate's permanent record which will be made available to governmental compliance agencies upon request.

DO NOT FILL OUT IN PRESENCE OF APPLICANT Consider the overview of the candidate in all categories below and comment on each rating in Section V.	Outstanding	Above Average	Below Average	Average	Inadequate
I. EXPERIENCE—How does previous experience relate to current position opening? Consider communications and other skills such as knowledge, information and technical competence based on previous training.					
II. CAPABILITY—Verbal ability, judgement, analytical, logical, decisive, resourceful, imaginative.					
III. EDUCATION/SKILLS—Degrees(s), professional licenses, registrations, certifications, data processing, languages and equipment.					
IV. GOALS AND AMBITION—Initiative, persistence, drive, goals are well defined (as they relate to predicting success on the job).					

V.   OTHER FACTORS—Geographical preference, management potential, current salary, etc.

_____

_____

_____

_____

Comments: _____

_____

_____

_____

For Additional Comments Use Back

Overall Appraisal:

    Outstanding _____ Above Average _____ Average _____ Below Average _____ Unacceptable _____

Recommend employment for current position opening: Yes _____ No _____

Future Consideration: Yes _____ No _____ If Yes, for _____
                                            Position Title

Recommendation Based Upon: Resume/Application Review ☐   Interview ☐   Telephone Contact ☐

_____   _____
     Signature of Interviewer   Date Completed

3.32 HUMAN RESOURCE FORMS—FILLED POSITION SUMMARY

After the interview, when impressions are fresh in your mind, it's a good idea to complete a summary of key thoughts regarding the applicant.

A filled-position form also allows you to keep track of which applicants applied for each specific requisition, for EEO recordkeeping requirements. Figure 3–10 is a sample filled position summary form, also used by the Rocky Mountain Energy, Broomfield, Colorado.

3.33 KEY LAWS AND RECORD-RETENTION REQUIREMENTS PERTAINING TO THE EMPLOYMENT FUNCTION

There are a vast number of local, state, and federal laws, government regulations, federal guidelines, executive orders, and court decisions affecting the employment and utilization of women and minorities. As a result of all these regulations, human resource managers must be thoroughly informed. The matrix in figure 3–11 lists key federal regulations covering the employment process and the recordkeeping requirements that pertain to those regulations.

3.34 DECISION AND IMPLEMENTATION

The final decision must match the whole person with the whole job. This requires a thorough analysis of both the person and the job; then, an intelligent decision can be made as to how well they will fit together.

To understand the job, it's necessary not only to review the formal job description, but also to identify a feeling for the manager and work group to which the prospective employee will be assigned. A personality match is important.

To evaluate the person, you must analyze all the data collected on the individual: résumé, application form, reference checks, interview materials, and so on.

Weigh all the facts and feelings gleaned from the personal interview, and try to come to a sound conclusion. Up to this point, the selection system will have helped gather data in a systematic fashion, but how this data is evaluated depends upon the judgment of the human resource manager. The ultimate decision—whether or not to hire the person—depends not only on the individual and the organization, but upon all the environmental factors. Other factors include such items as government regulations or the affirmative action program, and should be taken into account when making employment decisions. Final decisions are generally made with two factors in mind: the applicant's qualifications for the current job opening, and his or her potential for future promotion. The best decisions are generally those that match an applicant to a specific position. Looking into the future and trying to determine what a person's potential may be five years from now is risky. Nevertheless, it may have an important bearing on the employment decision.

FIGURE 3-10.
FILLED POSITION SUMMARY

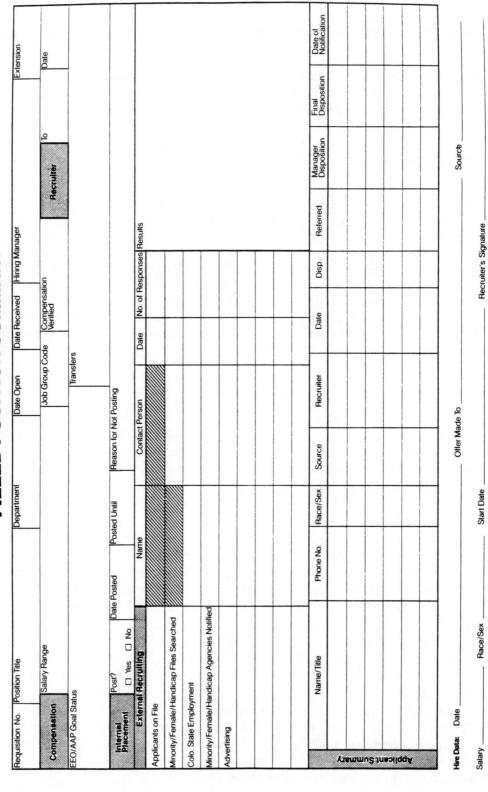

104

FIGURE 3-11.

RECORDKEEPING REQUIREMENTS
SELECTED FEDERAL LAWS PERTAINING TO THE EMPLOYMENT FUNCTION

Statute	Covers	Records-Retention Requirements
The Equal Employment Opportunity Act of 1972, including Title VII of the Civil Rights Act of 1964	Job discrimination based on race, color, religion, sex, or national origin for all private employers of fifteen or more people	Any personnel or employment record kept by employer, including application forms and records having to do with hiring, promotion, demotion, transfer, layoff, termination, rates of pay, other terms of compensation, and selection for training or apprenticeship.
	Educational institutions both private and public	Personnel records relevant to charges of discrimination or action brought against employer, including, for example, records relating to charging party and to all other employees holding similar positions, application forms or test papers completed by unsuccessful applicants, and by all other candidates for same position.
	State and local governments	
	Private and public employment agencies	
	Labor unions with fifteen or more members	Those required to file apprenticeship reports shall maintain (1) chronological list of names and addresses of all applicants, dates of application, sex, and minority group identification, or (2) file of written applications containing same information.
	Joint labor-management committees for apprenticeship and training	

FIGURE 3-11 (cont'd)

Statute	Covers	Records-Retention-Requirements
Age Discrimination Act of 1967	Job discrimination based on age 40 to 65 years	Payroll records containing each employee's name, address, date of birth, occupation, rate of pay, and compensation earned per week.
	Employers of twenty-five or more employees and engaged in interstate commerce	Personnel records relating to (1) job applications, résumés, or other replies to job advertisements, including records pertaining to failure to hire; (2) promotion, demotion, transfer, selection for training, layoff, recall, or discharge; (3) job orders submitted to employment agency or union; (4) test papers in connection with employer-administered aptitude or other employment tests; (5) physical examination results; (6) job advertisements or notices to employees regarding openings, promotions, training programs, or opportunities for overtime work.
		Employee benefit plans, written seniority or merit rating systems.

For further information pertaining to federal laws, see the Prentice-Hall Legal Service.

"Can Do" versus "Will Do" Characteristics

"Can do" qualities show a person's intelligence, education, training, experience, skills, aptitudes, and so forth. But the "will do" characteristics—drive, determination, stability, maturity, and so on—are what determine whether or not the person will put these basic abilities to good use.

An employer is interested in hiring an "achiever," a person who performs and gets work done through others. What the person will do in the future is best determined by what has been done in the past. Hence, the emphasis in this manual has been placed on work history in particular and achievement in general.

The emphasis on "will do" characteristics is based on the following premise:

Actual behavior is largely determined by a person's habits or character traits, such as initiative, perseverance, and so on. These traits develop early in life and become so conditioned that they seldom change.

Most people feel that if you look at past behavior, future behavior can be predicted realistically.

The interview and reference checks provide the basic data on "will do" characteristics, and the interview also measures the "can do" qualities. Taken together, they provide a good picture of the whole person.

3.35 NEW EMPLOYEE ORIENTATION PROGRAM

An effective orientation program makes a positive and lasting impression and could have a significant impact on a new employee's success or failure during the first few weeks on the job.

Orientation programs should be designed specifically for the company that will use them. By customizing the program, you match company needs and employee needs.

There are two levels of orientation—general company procedures and departmental procedures. The human resource department and the new employee's supervisor must share orientation responsibilities.

One part of new employee orientation that is frequently overlooked is the company's personality and style, traditions, customs, norms, standards of conduct, organizational chain of command, and so on. There is also an overall company philosophy. In order for a new employee to be successful, it's imperative that he or she understand the overall environment in which he or she must operate.

Provide an orientation package for each new employee. The package might include the following:

- A company organization chart and department functions
- Map of the facility
- Key terms unique to the industry and company
- Copy of policy handbook and other company pamphlets
- Copy of company operating plan
- List of company holidays
- Benefits book
- Copy of compensation policies

- Copies of performance evaluation forms, dates, and procedures
- Copies of other required forms (supply requisitions, expense reimbursement, etc.)
- List of on-the-job training opportunities and career ladders
- Detailed outline of emergency and accident-prevention procedures
- Sample copy of each important company publication, including employee newsletters
- Telephone numbers and locations of key personnel and operations
- Safety requirements, accident procedures

An employee who understands the organization's history, products, scope of operation, economic goals, and future prospects will identify more readily with the entire organization and should develop a sense of belonging more quickly than an employee who is left to search out needed information on his or her own.

3.36   SEVEN EMPLOYMENT PROCEDURES THAT GET NEW EMPLOYEES UP TO SPEED QUICKLY

1. Give a two-part new employee orientation.

   a. First day on the job.

   b. Thirty days after hire: go over benefits and more in-depth review of policies and procedures.

2. Provide a review of the company personality and style and how things get done.

3. Assign a buddy or mentor to help the new employee through the first few weeks on the job.

4. Take the new employees' pictures and print them in the company newsletter so others will know who the new employees are and where they work.

5. If a new employee is in supervision or management, get the person into the company training programs as soon as possible to learn about:

   a. Performance appraisals

   b. Budgeting

   c. Planning and how the company uses MBO or similar management techniques

   d. Human resource policies and procedures

   e. Administrative policies and procedures

6. Ensure that no matter what level the person is at in the organization, meaningful assignments are made immediately to challenge the new employee.

7. Follow up with new hires 30 to 60 days after hire, to ensure that the person is doing well and is happy on the job.

3.37   ANALYZING AND COMPUTING THE IMPACT RATIO OF HIRES TO APPLICANTS FROM GUIDELINES PROVIDED BY THE OFCCP

Each new administration in Washington brings a different slant toward EEO and affirmative action. No matter what the emphasis may be, however, business will not go back to earlier positions of discrimination in hiring and promotion of women and minorities. Discrimination of any group is socially unacceptable and, further, it's not good business.

It's a good idea to analyze the ratio of hires to applicants in order to know what liabilities you may have built into your hiring practices.

The Office of Federal Contract Compliance Programs (OFCCP) and the Equal Employment Opportunity Commission (EEOC) mandate an annual impact analysis between hire and applicant rates in the *Uniform Guidelines on Employee Selection*.[9] In order to complete this analysis, divide hires by applicants for each job group or major job classification, and for each racial, sex, or ethnic, group constituting 2 percent or more of the population of the relevant labor area. The racial or sex group with the highest rate is considered as the favored group against which all others are compared.

The test of adverse impact is determined by dividing the rate for each racial or sex group by that of the favored group to see if the lower rate is 80 percent or more of the favored group's rate. Any lower variance is indicative of adverse impact, according to the guidelines. If the hire rate for males is 50 percent and that for females is 30 percent, adverse impact would be indicated as 30 divided by 50, or 60 percent.

This analysis may unfairly represent the actual situation in your company if you loosely define criteria in accounting for applicants and hires. Adverse impact may lead to allegations of an "affected class" with back-pay implications and may be used against the company in establishing a case of discrimination. For these reasons, it's a good idea to be cautious in designing an applicant intake system and in defining the applicants you will count as new hires.

The following ideas may not apply to all companies but you might consider them when analyzing current procedures in defining applicants and new hires:

1. Do not accept applications unless you actually have positions open.

2. It's a good idea to establish an information process that allows job-seekers to become aware of the nature of the work and working conditions before completing an application. This results in applicants doing self-evaluation before becoming statistics for which the company is accountable. The hotline idea is one way to do this.

3. Accept applications on specific days and at certain times of the day.

4. Ensure that employees transferred from other locations or returning from layoff or leaves of absence are not counted as new hires.

5. If certain high-level positions are not recruited through the human resource department, be sure accurate data are maintained.

6. It's a good idea to maintain applications on an active status for only 60 to 90 days. This requires an effective communications process but offers some defensive advantages if the applicant hire ratio is challenged by regulatory agencies.

7. Require applicants to apply for specific positions. Don't allow them to state "any" or "open." You can make defensible judgments on applicants only when their backgrounds are compared to specific job requirements.

8. Keep detailed records on applicant disposition in order to eliminate applicants who voluntarily withdraw or who do not respond to follow-up. Records also should identify applicants who fail to meet minimum qualifications for an open position.

---

[9] *Uniform Guidelines on Employee Selection*, Department of Labor, Office of Federal Contract Compliance Program, 41

IMPORTANT POINT:

The objective of this particular type of recordkeeping is to ensure that the analysis between hires and applicants is fair, objective, and representative of the actual applicant flow rather than being biased by deficiencies in recordkeeping or in the applicant intake system.

It's a good idea to review any program with your EEO attorney or advisor.

3.38 HOW TO FIGURE RECRUITING AND SELECTION COSTS

The cost-to-hire is probably one of the most difficult indices to develop because there are both tangible and intangible cost factors. There are two categories to be concerned with: those that are measurable or tangible, and those that are immeasurable or intangible. Factors that are immeasurable can create as significant an impact upon the efficiency and organization of the corporation as the measurable costs.

Tangible costs include such items as:

- Advertising
- Employment agency fees
- Publications used in recruiting
- Medical examinations for selection
- Security, credit, and reference checks
- Personnel department overhead (office space, personnel staff compensation, etc.)
- Telephone calls
- Stationery and other paperwork
- Interviewing costs
- Relocation costs
- Data processing costs
- Related clerical costs
- Other recruitment costs
- Testing equipment and material costs

Intangible costs include such items as:

- Disorientation of the department
- Disruption of morale
- Increase in employee complaints
- Reduced management efficiency
- Reduced morale
- Generally lower productivity
- The stimulation of additional turnover
- Overhiring in order to maintain an average work force

Some items we might include as intangible on closer examination might be determined to be tangible costs. Depending on the industry, they might include more on-the-job accidents, higher scrap rates, additional overtime, larger human resource staff in order to handle replacement needs, and so on. See figure 3-12 for a sample cost-to-hire computation.

FIGURE 3–12

XYZ COMPANY
SAMPLE COST-TO-HIRE COMPUTATION

Search and Selection

Advertising	$ 1,884.00
Employee handbooks	248.60
Medical examinations	525.00
Security, credit, reference checks	1,350.00
Personnel department overhead	27,393.11
Interviewing costs	1,847.80
Relocation	40,000.00
Telephone	436.00
Subtotal	$73,484.51

Assignment and Placement

Personnel department overhead	$12,898.85
Administrative expenses	706.00
Follow-up telephone calls	172.00
Stationery and other paperwork (incl. data processing forms)	1,263.00
New employee orientation costs	1,505.00
Subtotal	$16,544.85

Training

Training department overhead	$27,129.00
Follow-up telephone calls	272.00
Makeup pay during training period	20,400.00
Subtotal	$47,801.00

Retention

Publications (Christmas/birthday cards, employee newsletters)	$ 2,830.00
Professional expenses	4,500.00
Increased benefits	14,856.00
Personnel department overhead	12,898.85
Miscellaneous costs	3,165.50
Subtotal	$38,250.35

Terminations

Outplacement fees	$ 4,000.00
Follow-up telephone calls	72.00
Stationery and other paperwork	1,126.00
Lost production	23,828.00
Subtotal	$29,026.00

SUMMARY ANALYSIS—COST TO HIRE

It cost XYZ Company:

$73,674.51 to find and relocate people
16,544.85 to assign and place them
47,801.00 to train them
38,250.35 to retain them
29,026.00 to terminate them

HUMAN RESOURCE DIRECTOR'S TIP:

Further study in your company will give you a good indication of your costs to hire. This computation is merely a sample. You may want to take the computation further and divide the costs by the number of people employed in a given period. Some companies divide costs by hourly and salaried hires because of a significant difference in hiring and relocating salaried people.

3.39 HOW TO SAVE BIG DOLLARS BY USING TEMPORARY HELP TO FILL SHORT-TERM STAFFING NEEDS

The third fastest growing industry in the country today, according to the National Association of Temporary Services, is the temporary help industry. Industry figures show that more than 90 percent of American business and practically all of the Fortune 500 companies currently use temporary help on a regular basis. An estimated 2 percent of the entire work force works temporary, and that number is expected to triple in ten years.

According to Ted K. Cobb, president of "TOPS" (Temporary Office Personnel Service in Denver, Colorado, and San Diego, California), temporary help fills two key needs:[10]

1. The need of most organizations for a readily available work force for short, temporary periods
2. The need of many experienced, skilled people to work, but not on a permanent full-time basis.

Overstaffing is a significant hidden cost in many organizations. Companies should staff for normal workloads rather than peak periods. A permanent staff that is lean can be supplemented with temporaries to handle special projects, unexpected absences, or seasonal workloads, and temporaries can cut the costs of excessive overtime.

3.40 EIGHT CREATIVE USES FOR TEMPORARY HELP THAT CAN LOWER PAYROLL COSTS 10

1. Placing employees on the payroll of a temporary help service during their probationary period can minimize a company's unemployment compensation rates.
2. Temporary help teams are a new service offered by some agencies. Teams of word processors, data processors, sales people, and so on, can staff a whole department until permanent staffing is arranged.
3. Mandatory retirement policies can cause an organization to lose valuable employees at a time when a particular project is crucial to the business plan. A temporary help service can assist by transferring the person to their payroll and ease the pressures on both the company and the employee.
4. Before a company recruits a permanent employee for a new position, a temporary worker can be used to determine if a valid position really exists.

---

[10] Ted K. Cobb, president, TOPS Temporary Personnel Service, Denver, Colorado, and San Diego, California.

5. Using temporary help for one-time demands involves a special project such as product sampling, assembling an annual report, taking or doing the extensions on inventory, or a data processing conversion program, where a team of persons can go in for a short term and complete the project.

6. Smoother transitions can be delivered when temporary workers are used during office or plant relocation as job vacancies occur.

7. Temporaries can fill crucial spots until a hiring freeze is lifted.

8. Sometimes exactly the right applicant comes along, but it takes a week or more to process the paperwork for authorization to hire the person. During this delay, the prospect may consider another attractive offer. If a manager can place the applicant on the job, but on a temporary service firm's payroll immediately, the problem of losing the applicant may be averted.

If you are in the process of choosing a temporary help service, Ted Cobb offers six questions you should ask in order to make a good decision:

1. How long has the temorary help service been in business? (It takes a fair amount of time to develop a backlog of well-trained, experienced personnel.)

2. What recruiting methods and screening procedures are used in hiring temporary employees?

3. What kinds of training programs are there for temporaries, particularly in the more specialized areas such as word processing? (Dig for detailed information.)

4. What sort of insurance or bonding coverage is carried for the protection of the company in case of loss?

5. What are the billing rates for various job classifications?

6. What is the policy on transferring a temporary employee to the client company's payroll?

Some advance planning before the temporary arrives will save time and get the work flowing as quickly as possible. Here's a checklist of seven items to help you get organized before the temporary arrives:

1. A list of the basic duties and responsibilities for the position, including a list of work priorities.

2. A summary of company procedures, work hours, lunch periods, parking areas, and so on.

3. A calendar of important events that will affect the temporary person.

4. A current list or file of frequently used names, titles, telephone numbers, and addresses.

5. Directions on how mail is to be handled and how additional supplies may be secured.

6. An index to office files, indicating any that are to be locked at the close of the day.

7. A set of samples of regularly prepared reports and forms that will be used.

CHAPTER 4

Designing a Wage and Salary Program Tailored to Your Particular Organization

Organizations go to great expense and effort to implement strategic plans for the future, and more companies are beginning to tie the compensation of their key people to the organization's long-range plans. This one item may be the most significant compensation issue of the 1980s and 1990s.

For years, compensation programs have been confined to narrow, inflexible guidelines and policies that ignore the fact that different people have different needs. I'm not suggesting that we can have a different salary program for each individual—only that by being more open to new and innovative compensation ideas, we will be more likely to hold our top performers.

For example, a few years ago, no one considered the lump-sum salary increase. Today, it's gaining wider acceptance in many industries. (See chapter 9.)

Just as organizations must alter their thinking and become more flexible in recruiting and employment of the top performers, we must also become more creative and flexible in our approach to compensation. In the 1980s, effective compensation programs will have to be bold and innovative in approach, and timely and flexible in their ongoing management processes.

4.1 PREPARING A SALARY PROGRAM THAT FITS THE CHANGING NEEDS OF YOUR ORGANIZATION

Consider the following organizational issues as you prepare your salary data:

1. Review the business objectives of the organization and the long-range plans. Put them in writing in a succinct form, and be sure they are communicated to all employees.
2. Tie each executive's and each manager's accountabilities to the business plan. Communicate the fact that compensation will be competitive in your industry and your location, but emphasize individual accountabilities.
3. Design the organization structure in a way that allows management to carry

out the business objectives in an orderly, effective manner. Push authority to act and accountability down to manager levels to enhance productivity. The structure may be designed around major functions, products, or geographical areas. If the organization has been structured along functional lines but is growing very fast and adding new products, a product line organization may be a good approach.

4. Each group or function should be assigned to an organizational unit. The assignments should be the ones normally found together, like accounting assigned to the finance function. Make sure the assignments are made in view of the capabilities of the management staff.

5. The simpler the organization structure and the fewer organizational components, the easier and less costly the salary program is to design and implement.

6. The number of levels of authority should be kept to a minimum if you have the ability to influence this factor. Each added management level lengthens the chain of authority and adds considerably to payroll.

7. The span of control, the number of people reporting to one individual, should not exceed the number that individual can effectively coordinate. There are no standards, but most executives feel that no more than six positions can be managed effectively by one person.

8. As much as it is possible to do so, position titles and designations of organizational components should be standardized to eliminate the need for hundreds of titles and hundreds of evaluations.

9. Look at expected growth and recruiting needs of your organization, the competitive factors, and also at your industry and your location. What will it take to hire and retain the work force you need to achieve your business plans?

There are ways to check whether or not your salary program is meeting the needs of your organization. The most common way is to track turnover and to perform exit interviews on all terminating employees. If salaries are not adequate, that fact will begin to show up in the data.

> **HUMAN RESOURCE DIRECTOR'S TIP:**
>
> If you are evaluating a current salary program that needs to be revised, look at the total program. Don't try to put a bandage on the trouble spots—you'll only solve problems temporarily. Look at the whole program. Review internal equities, salary structures, compa-ratios, and external competitiveness in each job class.

4.2 ADMINISTERING AN EFFECTIVE SALARY PROGRAM

Inflation has brought the subject of pay up-front with almost everyone who works. Making a living and supporting a family are increasingly tough subjects. Companies are under constant pressure to pay what other organizations in their industry and location are paying. If you don't pay competitively, people will walk across the street for a higher paycheck. If your salary program is competitive, it will allow you to:

- *Hire qualified people.* The salary a job pays and the perks attached to a position are probably the most important elements in an applicant's decision to take a job.
- *Retain a full staff.* The salary a job pays is one of the most important elements in keeping people. People will usually stay with a company if they are paid competitively.
- *Motivate your people.* A good merit pay system, coupled with a performance appraisal program, will motivate people. Again, the merit increase must be competitive in your industry and location, and it must be earned. Some companies are going to unscheduled merit pay increases in order to emphasize that the raise is in recognition of good performance.
- *Experience lower turnover.* If pay is perceived as being too low and noncompetitive, unless the company is in an area of high unemployment, the employee will most likely quit or, at the very least, the employee will be demotivated and less productive.

It's important to have a flexible and timely orientation to salary administration. Designing a salary program that fits your organization needs today is fine, but you can't walk off smugly and think that the same program will be effective in six months or one year. There's a new work ethic, and organizations today find it tougher to attract and retain a highly technical, professional work force. Even during periods of high unemployment, people with key skills and top track records will migrate for more money, more opportunity to achieve, more paid time off, and so on.

If your salary program pays attention only to one or two items, and those items are not the ones your key people are looking for, you won't achieve your goal of attracting and retaining a productive work force.

4.3   PAY TERMINOLOGY, DEFINITIONS, AND PURPOSES

Automatic pay increases/general adjustments. Some organizations have automatic pay increases at specified intervals. These organizations have a fixed-rate type of pay structure. This results in employees in certain job classifications with the same number of years of service to the organization making the same salary. This is typical of the civil service.

Base-rate structure. An organization that has no type of compensation other than pay shows only a base pay structure. If there are additional forms of compensation, they may be reflected in total compensation. Many companies pay bonuses at certain levels, and it's important when making external comparisons through surveys to be sure you compare base pay to base pay, and that the bonuses and other perks are listed separately.

Benchmark jobs. When using a point method of measuring jobs, evaluations of a selected group of representative jobs help to clarify various factors and establish a framework for evaluating and comparing jobs throughout the organization. If you are installing a job evaluation system from scratch, establishing benchmark jobs saves time, effort, and cost by providing points of comparison throughout the organization. Benchmark jobs should be easy to define, noncontroversial, and representative of the organization in general.

Bonus. A bonus can be most anything other than base pay or perks. Most bonuses are cash, usually determined at the end of the fiscal year after profit-and-loss statements are completed. Other bonus payments might be in the form of company stock, stock options, and so on.

Call-back pay. This is hourly pay guaranteed for a certain minimum number of hours when an hourly worker is called to work at a time other than the ordinary shift.

Call-in pay. This is hourly pay guaranteed for a specified number of hours if the worker is called to work on a day that is not an ordinary workday.

Career ladders. These are successive promotional steps in an occupational or professional area that allow movement up through the organization. There is normally at least a 15 percent increase in pay between each step.

Career planning. Job descriptions and performance appraisals form the basis for planned career development in most organizations, and include identifying needed skills and abilities for higher level jobs and scheduling the training needed to prepare for those jobs.

Centralized vs. decentralized compensation program. A centralized salary program is designed, implemented, and administered at the corporate level. A centralized compensation program is less complex, easier, and less costly to administer in one location. The main characteristic is its uniformity throughout the organization—it can address the diverse needs of separate groups, but it has the same overall guidelines. A centralized compensation effort provides more control over internal equity and uniform administration. A company that has union contracts may decentralize hourly pay. Hourly pay administration will follow union contract provisions and can follow administrative guidelines without regard for the type of company organization.

Compa-ratio. When you talk about compa-ratio, you simply mean a person's current salary as a percentage of the midpoint of their salary range.

Compensation survey. Companies that wish to compare their salary ranges and actual pay practices participate in compensation surveys. The surveys include companies in their industry and their location. It is important to compare actual benchmark jobs—apples to apples, so to speak—when using the data of any survey. When participating in a compensation survey, it's a good idea to have a third party collect the data and produce the survey so that raw data are not exchanged. There might be antitrust implications.

Compression. Compression is the narrowing of pay differentials between employees who should be paid at varying levels. Three of the most common situations where compression can occur are:

- Subordinate vs. supervisor
- New hire vs. senior employee
- Superior performer vs. average performer

The obvious problems associated with inequities caused by salary compression are poor morale and performance, unwillingness to accept promotions, and higher turnover.

COLA. An increase based on measure of cost of living (nationally) used in union contracts.

Cost-of-living allowances or geographic differentials. Some corporations pay cost-of-living allowances to employees they ask to relocate to areas of this country or overseas where the cost of living is significantly higher than the cost of living at their current location.

Deferred compensation plan. This is compensation awarded to an employee, but payment is deferred to a later date. Deferred compensation is usually in the form of cash or stock. Some plans require purchase by the employee and might be (1) employee savings plans, (2) stock purchase plans, and (3) stock options. Some plans that do not require purchase by the employee are (1) stock bonuses, (2) profit-sharing plans, and (3) deferred cash compensation. Deferred compensation plans are desirable because of their tax advantages.

Equity. There are two main kinds of equity—internal and external. The perceptions that employees have of equity are so variable they are difficult to define. Equity seems to exist as an individual perception that is influenced by a variety of factors, a perceived sense of rewards. Equity is seen by most people as the balance between output and the pay received for the job done. It is also a perception that persons are paid fairly within their work group, their total organization, and externally compared to other companies in the same industry.

Exempt employees. Exempt employees are salaried and hold managerial, supervisory, administrative, professional, or sales positions. They are exempt from the overtime provisions of the Fair Labor Standards Act.

Guide charts. The guide chart profile method of job evaluation was developed by Edward N. Hay Associates to provide a systematic, easily administered approach to evaluating jobs at all levels in all organizations. The evaluations may form the basis for pay comparisons.

Two principles are fundamental to the guide chart method:

1. A thorough understanding of the content of the job to be measured.
2. The direct comparison of one job with another job to determine relative value.

Three job elements are reviewed:

1. *Know-how* is the amount of knowledge and skills needed for satisfactory job performance.
2. *Problem solving* is the amount of original thinking required by the job for analyzing, evaluating, reasoning, and arriving at an effective conclusion.
3. *Accountability* is the responsibility for actions and for the consequences of those actions, usually expressed in dollar figures.

Incentives. Incentives are frequently part of an executive's total compensation package. Incentives may include such items as added compensation, commissions, bonus plans, prizes, awards, stock options, and profit sharing, to name a few.

Management by objectives. In 1943, Peter Drucker coined a new phrase, "Management by Objectives," as a new approach to performance appraisal.[1] In his book, *The Practice of Management*, Drucker said:

> "Business performance requires that each job be directed toward the objectives of the whole business, and in particular each manager's job must be focused on the success of the whole. The performance that is expected of the manager must be derived from the performance goals of the business; the results must be measured by the contribution they make to the success of the enterprise."

Maturity curve data. Maturity curve data are a comparison of pay levels with years of experience. We traditionally look at technical people like scientists and engineers in relation to the number of years since their Bachelor's degree. This kind of analysis is a normal characteristic of most engineering salary surveys. Maturity curve data are not normally found in other salary surveys, but are available from professional organizations.

Merit increases. A merit increase system rewards employees for job performance and ties job performance to the percentage increase in pay.

Nonexempt employees. Nonexempt employees are hourly paid people who hold white- or blue-collar jobs and are paid overtime for working more than 40 hours in a week. The tests that determine whether a job is exempt or nonexempt are set out in the Fair Labor Standards Act.

Report-in pay. This is hourly pay guaranteed when work is called off because of something like bad weather or machine breakdown.

Salary budget. The human resource manager normally prepares a budget for the organization's pay increases. Personnel and payroll policies and the company's total financial philosophy are taken into account. The formal budget is normally established after a survey of the external competitive situation and a review of the company's resources and financial condition.

TRASOP and ESOP. The 1975 Tax Reduction Act provided a 10 percent tax credit for capital investment with an additional 1 percent tax credit available to companies using that 1 percent to establish an employee stock ownership plan. An Employee Stock Ownership Plan (ESOP) is a special form of employee benefit plan that is primarily for the purpose of providing participating employees with stock in their company. The additional investment credit for contributions to a Tax Reduction Act Employer Stock Ownership Plan ("TRASOP") terminated with respect to qualified investments made after December 31, 1982. Beginning January 1, 1983, a credit based on payroll (a "payroll-based" ESOP) will replace the additional investment credit and will allow an income tax credit to employers limited to a prescribed percentage of the compensation of all employees under the plan. The percentages would be 0.50 percent in 1983, 0.75 percent in 1984, and 1.00 percent in 1985 and thereafter. No credit would be allowed if more than one-third of the employer's contributions for the year are allocated to the group consisting of officers, 10 percent shareholders, and highly compensated. "Highly compensated" is defined as those earning more than twice the defined contribution plan limit under ERISA (in 1981, this would have been $41,500 × 2, or $83,000).

---

[1] P. R. Drucker, *The Practice of Management*, New York: Harper and Row, 1954.

4.4 HOW TO SAVE BIG MONEY WHEN DESIGNING A NEW SALARY PROGRAM OR REVISING AN ESTABLISHED PROGRAM

* Design an organization that is tightly structured with a minimum of management levels, one that includes only the numbers of people needed to get the job done effectively.
* Eliminate jobs and titles such as "assistant to" and other "gofer"-type jobs. If the job is needed, it should have full authority to act.

The two companies represented in figures 4–1 and 4–2 are similar in products, structure, and net worth, but one is spending $440,000 more per year on management payroll because of added management levels. If the key levels of management such as President, Vice-President, Director, or General Manager, and Manager, are effective in their jobs, levels of "assistant to" jobs shouldn't be needed.

4.5 QUESTIONS AND ANSWERS ON CURRENT COMPENSATION TOPICS

Q: What are the key elements of a successful compensation program?

A: External competitiveness, internal equity, pay for performance, the ability to be flexible and innovative in pay approaches, and an effective employee communication program.

Q: How does an organization keep up with the constantly rising expectations of the work force? More pay, more benefits, shorter work weeks, etc.?

A: Organizations could handle big increases in pay and continuing increases in benefits when cheap energy, significant advances in technology, low inflation rates, and little foreign competition were the order of the day, but now that these influences have nearly all turned around, organizations do not have the big pie to split with employees, and a new era is dawning where both employees and organizations will have to identify new ways to relate to expectations. The way to do this is to look at total compensation versus just pay. Look at benefits also. Here are some compensation and benefit ideas that organizations are using to attract and retain people:

* Lump-sum increases
* More time off with pay
* More perks like company cars and stock programs, like TRASOPs and ESOPs
* Giving management employees and other professionals a "piece of the action"
* Deferred compensation
* Incentives
* Day-care
* Dental, vision, and legal insurance
* Job-sharing
* Flexitime or four-day work weeks

Complicated programs like TRASOPs and ESOPs require competent consultants for design and implementation.

FIGURE 4-1.

COMPANY A—$80 MILLION YEARLY NET INCOME

President ($200,000 per year)
　　Assistant to the President ($50,000 per year)

Executive Vice-President ($150,000 per year)

Senior Vice-President ($120,000 per year)

Vice-President Marketing and Sales ($100,000)	Vice-President Operations ($110,000)	Vice-President Engineering ($100,000)	Vice-President Finance ($90,000)

Vice-President Human Resources ($80,000)　　　　　Vice-President Administration ($60,000)

Assistant Vice-President Marketing and Sales ($60,000)　　　　　Assistant Vice-President Operations ($70,000)

Director Human Resources ($50,000)　　　　Director Finance and Accounting ($60,00)

General Manager Operations ($70,000)　　　　　General Manager Engineering ($70,000)

Assistant General Manager Western Operations ($65,000)　　　　　Assistant General Manager Eastern Operations ($65,000)

Manager Compensation and Benefits ($40,000)	Manager Employment and Affirmative Action ($47,000)	Manager Accounting ($42,000)	Manager Operations ($47,000)
Manager Engineering (Mechanical) ($48,000)	Manager Engineering (Civil) ($48,000)	Manager Tax and Treasury ($40,000)	Manager Facilities and Office Services ($38,000)

TOTAL MANAGEMENT SALARIES:　　$1,920,000

I polled more than thirty compensation managers in the energy industry, and all reflected on the current escalation in compensation. Salaries at all levels seem to be going out of sight. On the other hand, talk to compensation managers in the auto

---

FIGURE 4-2.

COMPANY B—$93 MILLION YEARLY NET INCOME

President ($210,000 per year)

Executive Vice-President ($140,000 per year)

Vice-President Marketing and Sales ($120,000)	Vice-President Operations ($110,000)	Vice-President Engineering and Technical Sales ($90,000)

Vice-President Finance, Accounting, and Purchasing ($90,000)	Vice-President Human Resources and Administration ($75,000)

General Manager Operations ($68,000)	Director Finance and Accounting ($60,000)	Director Marketing and Sales ($72,000)	Director Employee Relations ($65,000)

Manager Western Operations ($55,000)	Manager Eastern Operations ($55,000)	Manager Engineering ($50,000)	Manager Technical Service ($42,000)

Manager Accounting and Tax ($45,000)	Manager Human Resources ($43,000)	Manager Market Research ($38,000)	Manager Purchasing and Administration ($52,000)

TOTAL MANAGEMENT SALARIES: $1,480,000

---

industry, and they tell you employees are willing to forego increases to keep their jobs. The pendulum swings, and where it's going from here, no one knows. The answer to this question lies in the area of tailoring programs specifically to the organization, keeping the organization as lean as possible, while maintaining a competitive position in your particular industry. Success in the compensation field in the 1980s will depend on the manager's ability to be flexible, creative, and open-minded to change and innovative techniques.

Q: How do you handle the question of inflation and your salary program?

A: Most companies have not found a workable way to deal with inflation in their merit budgets. We've just hoped inflation would go away. The real question here may be a more serious one, however, assuming inflation won't go away, but continue at a rate of, say, 10 percent; and if your corporation is lucky and increasing in earnings at 15 percent per year, you are still only holding your own or achieving a 5 percent upward movement. When using competitive market surveys, pay increases from inflation tend to be rolled in so that market rate will actually reflect the impacted inflation. I'm convinced organizations will have to look for ways to address inflation aside from "pay for performance" or merit budgets. The average company may not be able to address inflation but instead find ways to cut expenses, including cutting executive bonuses in order to fund a merit budget that allows the organization to maintain a "stay-even" pay policy as opposed to an "external competitiveness at all costs" policy. Some companies are moving to provide more perks in the way of added benefits such as child day-care, more say in work schedules (flexitime or four 10-hour days), or company cars, instead of higher pay, which keeps putting the employee in a higher tax bracket anyway. Human resource managers will have to come up with new ideas and innovations in pay and benefits in order to meet the challenge of competitive compensation in the 1980s.

Q: Why don't promotions come faster, and why aren't there more in our organization?

A: Most organizations are structured in pyramidal shapes—there are too many middle managers and top executives in their late twenties, thirties, and forties who will be there for another 10 or 20 years, thus slowing promotional opportunities for a bright, young, well-educated work force.

Q: What is the best method of job evaluation for a company that has a large percentage of professional, technical, and managerial personnel?

A: There are so many ways to evaluate jobs. You need to understand the organization, its needs and goals, and its personality. Probably the most objective evaluation method is the Hay Guide Chart Profile Method, designed many years ago by Edward N. Hay and Associates of Philadelphia, Pennsylvania. Hundreds of medium and large companies in the United States today use the Hay job evaluation method. Implementing the Hay system facilitates job correlation when using and participating in salary surveys. There are other proprietary systems used by consultants such as Towers, Perrin, Forster, and Crosby.

Q: What is the major function of the compensation manager?

A: The position of compensation manager is a fairly new one in most organizations. As regulations become more complex and companies grow in size and diversity, the compensation function becomes more important to the success of an organization's plans. There are eight main responsibilities in the compensation function:

1. Planning and control of compensation and merit budgets.
2. Policy and procedure development.
3. Maintaining internal equity.
4. Maintaining external competitiveness.
5. Wage and salary recordkeeping, policy control, and administrative responsibilities.
6. Advisory and counseling responsibilities related to recruiting, promotions, and organization restructuring.
7. Establishing and maintaining a valid system of job evaluation.
8. Establishing an effective program for communication of compensation programs.

4.6   JOB DESCRIPTIONS AND JOB EVALUATIONS—HOW TO CHOOSE THE BEST SYSTEM FOR YOUR ORGANIZATION AND HOW TO DESIGN A SIMPLE BUT EFFECTIVE PROGRAM

Job descriptions and effective job evaluations are the underpinnings of a good compensation program. A small company might be able to get by with a hit-and-miss, case-by-case type of system, but once you start to grow, a complete system should be designed to fit the needs of your particular organization.

The job description is the single most important document to the compensation program. Howard Smith, Director of Personnel Services for Amstar Corporation, addressed a seminar on job descriptions and job evaluations given by the New York Chamber of Commerce and Industry.[2] Smith advised his audience to approach the task of writing job descriptions in a logical, organized manner and to ask themselves three questions before beginning to prepare job descriptions:

1. How are the job descriptions to be used?
2. What kind do we want?
3. Are we capable of maintaining and updating the job description file?

The one-day seminar covered the practical and legal aspects of job descriptions and job evaluations. Here are the highlights of the seminar:

The uses of job descriptions. How the job description is to be used should determine the kind you want. Job descriptions can be used in many ways, from placement and training to labor relations and salary surveying. Attitudes toward job descriptions are changing, however, and many experts believe it's best to tailor job descriptions to one or two basic uses. Many personnel professionals believe that job descriptions should be primarily designed for compensation and legal defense purposes only. For these purposes, job descriptions should be designed to compare jobs internally, to price jobs in salary surveys by comparing internal and external positions, and to explain to others or defend the company against violations of the Equal Pay Act, Title VII of the Civil Rights Act, Age Discrimination in Employment Act, and the Rehabilitation Act.

Writing job descriptions with an eye toward legal defense is important, Smith said, because "when a charge of wrongdoing is filed against your company, poorly written job descriptions too often support the allegations of the aggrieved employee or inspecting governmental agency."

Preparing job descriptions. The first step in preparing your job descriptions is the collection of data. This should be done systematically, by gathering important facts about the job. There are four key data elements: skill requirements, effort, responsibility, and working conditions.

In order to include all of the key data elements, Smith recommended a seven-point data collection process:

1. *Principal job duties and responsibilities.* Determine and record any function that takes up 5 percent or more of the employee's time.
2. *Output.* Determine what results are expected by the job, quantitative and qualitative.

---

[2] Howard Smith, *Compensation,* Englewood Cliffs, N.J.: Prentice-Hall, Inc., October 5, 1979.

3. *Reporting relationships.* Determine all reporting relationships, upward and downward. Include an accurate and current organizational chart.
4. *Skill requirements.* Determine all skill, ability, or training requirements, including formal education (degree), specialized training (certification), specialized skills (licensing), and amount of experience.
5. *Effort.* Include the physical and mental effort required to perform the job.
6. *Responsibilities.* Determine and record in detail how much independent judgment is allowed and used, the impact of the job on the organization, whether the job has responsibility for the supervision of others, and whether it has responsibility for policy design and administration.
7. *Working conditions.* Include any unpleasant or dangerous working conditions, travel required (determine percentage of time), or abnormal working times or workdays.

Methods of collecting data. There are several methods available to the job analyst collecting the key data elements for job descriptions. Interviews are often conducted on a one-to-one basis with the job incumbent. This method produces high-quality data but is very expensive. It's most suitable for collecting data on senior management jobs. Direct observation also produces high-quality data. But it's time-consuming and methods-oriented, slanted to the incumbent's way of doing things. This method is recommended for use with short-cycle, production-type jobs.

The fastest and least expensive method of data collection is the questionnaire. It's also considered the best general-purpose method. Smith recommended, if possible, having the entire group of employees that hold the job fill out the questionnaire at the same time. This gives a fuller picture of how the job is performed and doesn't damage morale by singling out employees to be surveyed.

When the data collection is completed, and you begin to write the job descriptions, remember to:

- Keep in mind the primary use of the job description (compensation, legal defense).
- Make sure all personnel-shop jargon is removed.
- Review the description in light of legal requirements.

Job descriptions and the law. To help make sure job descriptions won't run afoul of the law, remember to focus on job content, not the incumbent. Keep your descriptions up to date with periodic review. Do an immediate follow-up when job duties change. Keep your records accurate. Don't include unreasonable requirements or expectations. Some specific tips are as follows:

- Make sure your job descriptions don't include such phrases as, "This job requires a young, aggressive . . . " or, "A training position for a recent college graduate." Such statements in your job descriptions could get you into trouble under the Age Discrimination in Employment Act.
- Keep educational and experience requirements job-related. The EEOC considers such requirements to be employment "tests," and they are subject to the uniform guidelines on testing. Requirements that aren't job-related can get you into trouble under Title VII of the Civil Rights Act.
- Make sure your job descriptions' references to health requirements, working conditions, and effort are proper and accurate. Job descriptions that don't fully

explain physical activities won't help you if you're charged with violating the Rehabilitation Act.

- When developing your wage and salary programs, use only complete and accurate descriptions of job content. When the content of two or more jobs is similar, grade and range should be similar.

4.7   THE THREE MOST COMMON METHODS OF JOB EVALUATION

1. The *classification method* of job evaluation is used by most civil service systems. Before the jobs are evaluated, a decision is made as to the number of pay grades that are needed, and then job descriptions are written for each class of jobs in the structure.
2. The *ranking method* of job evaluation is one of the easier methods. A list of jobs to be evaluated is established, and the jobs are then ranked in relation to each other on an overall basis. The overall judgment is made on the value of each job in relation to all other jobs on the list. This method works best in smaller companies.
3. The *point method* of job evaluation reviews three or four job factors that are common to all the jobs being evaluated and then rates each job in relation to each factor on a numerical scale. Points are given for each factor, looking at the degree to which the job possesses each factor. There are usually four or five factors reviewed. They might be education, know-how, safety, responsibility for budgeted dollars, management skills, and so on. The points are added, and a total point factor is assigned for each job. Jobs are then related to each other on the basis of the total point scores, and total points can be related to wage and salary ranges. To arrive at a salary range, points usually apply to a dollar formula, which will place the job at a particular place on a salary policy line. For example:
Job points = 500
Policy line formula = $50 per point + $10,000
Multiply through, and you get a salary range midpoint of $35,000 for a job worth 500 points.
If the measured worth of a job fits an established job grade schedule, a range of point totals (e.g., 401 to 500 points) could be assigned a specific salary grade (e.g., a grade 12 in a 20-grade system).

4.8   MAKING JOB EVALUATION SIMPLE BUT EFFECTIVE

There seems to be a trend today of hiring qualified compensation people and implementing your own salary programs in-house. One area, however, where we do see outside consultants used most in human resource management is the area of job evaluation. Consultants in this area are expensive, but there are good reasons for considering an outside expert:

- Trial and error is an expensive way to attempt to install a salary program. The errors can cost more than the consultant.

- The consultant can devote full time to the project, and if there are time constraints this is a real plus.
- Top management's commitment is essential to the successful installation of a job evaluation program, and executives may be more amenable to an outside expert with prestige in the field.
- You can utilize the expert to the fullest in the job evaluation process by seeing that your staff is trained as the installation is implemented.
- The consultant should provide an operating guide for use of the system, and cooperation between your staff and the consultant can ensure that the program and the guide are tailored specifically to your company.

The fact that the consultant is an impartial third party should aid the installation. One of the foremost consultants in the job evaluation field today is Edward N. Hay Associates of Philadelphia, Pennsylvania.[3] They install the Hay Guide Chart Profile method of job evaluation, which is a popular method in many larger organizations throughout the country. There are many other proprietary systems available.

4.9 THE HAY GUIDE CHART PROFILE METHOD OF JOB EVALUATION

The two key elements for measuring job content under the Hay Guide Chart method are (1) a thorough understanding of the content of the job to be measured, and (2) the comparison of one job with another in order to determine the relative value.

It's almost impossible to measure an entire job against another entire job, so elements that are present in all jobs are measured. These elements are:

- *Know-how.* The sum total of all knowledge and skills, however acquired, needed for satisfactory job performance.
- *Problem solving.* The amount of original, self-starting thinking required by the job for analyzing, evaluating, creating, reasoning, and arriving at conclusions.
- *Accountability.* The person's responsibility for actions and for the consequences of those actions.

The most important aspect of the Hay job evaluation method is understanding the job. This understanding usually comes from the job description, so it's important that the job description be current and complete, and capture the total essence of the job—what it's expected to accomplish, why it's needed, what results are to be achieved, and so on.

Whether you use the Hay job evaluation or another system of your own design, there are several essential elements to consider.

4.10 ESSENTIAL ELEMENTS OF JOB EVALUATION

Job evaluation (JE) is a systematic method for comparing jobs in an organization to determine a reasonable and effective order or hierarchy. A good job evaluation program will give you an accurate measure of differences in accountabilities and duties of

---

[3] Edward N. Hay Associates, Philadelphia, Pennsylvania.

the jobs in your company so that reasonable salary differentials can be made between them.

Performance is irrelevant to JE. Job evaluation is not meant to judge the performance of the employee being observed. Its purpose is to measure *what* is done, not *how well* one particular person performs.

The goal of JE is to offer a solution to the basic management problem of pay inequity. When employees feel there is no logical connection between their compensation and their jobs, dissatisfaction and poor performance can easily result. Job evaluation works on the premise that a basic pattern controls the wage relationships between jobs in every company. JE helps you discover what that pattern is and produces an *explainable* system for comparing the relative worth of similar or widely differing jobs—routine, observable jobs with easily defined tasks, as well as jobs requiring the performance of nonobservable, highly cognitive tasks.

The following are important goals and benefits of a sound job evaluation program as reported by Prentice-Hall in their *Compensation Service*:[4]

- To simplify and make rational the relatively chaotic wage structure likely to result from chance, custom, and individual biases; to eliminate favoritism and discrimination.
- To justify existing pay rates and relationships between jobs (internal equity).
- To provide a factual guideline for judging the relevance of job applicants' backgrounds to available jobs.
- To aid performance review. (Only by knowing what the job consists of can the quality of performance be measured.)
- To attract and hold capable employees by setting pay in line with rates for comparable jobs in other firms (external equity).
- To provide work incentives and boost morale. (Only by studying jobs can you recognize superior performance.)
- For unionized firms, to provide a rational basis for setting negotiated rates.
- For nonunionized firms, to remove a common cause of low morale and dissatisfaction when employees perceive an inequity exists. If there is a perception of inequity, it might encourage unionization drives.
- To safeguard a company's prerogative to grant salary increases during periods of government wage control (incomes policy).
- To develop a policy of equal pay for equal work consistent with federal law.

How can you determine whether your firm is in sufficient need of a JE plan to justify a large commitment in capital and manpower? Here are some rules of thumb that may help you decide:

- *How large is your company?* If your CEO can't have personal knowledge of all the jobs in the organization, salary decisions must be delegated to others. Job evaluation will keep these decisions objective, consistent, and justifiable. Many JE experts feel that the critical point is somewhere between 500 and 1,000 employees. However, many smaller offices and manufacturing firms install programs covering only 50 or 100 people. It depends on the complexity of the organization and the jobs.

---

[4] *Compensation,* October 5, 1979.

- *How fast is your firm growing?* Regardless of size, you may need a JE plan because of your company's growth or expansion. If former organizational patterns, recruiting techniques, or pay practices are no longer applicable, a JE program can provide a flexible system in which to grow.
- *Are you having a recruiting or turnover problem?* If you find your company is attracting low-quality job applicants or losing many employees, your pay rates may be to blame. Inconsistencies in pay, both internally (among jobs in your organization) and externally (when compared with your competitors), may be the culprits.
- *How is employee morale?* Even if recruiting or turnover problems haven't materialized, productivity and costs can be adversely affected if employees are dissatisfied with existing pay relationships.

If your answers to these questions indicate that you need a formal program, your next step is to make all of the top decision-makers in your organization share your awareness.

The decision to undertake a job evaluation program must be arrived at by the top operating officers of the firm without undue sales pressure from you, and with full knowledge of all that is involved. The initiator of the program, whether a personnel executive or some other manager, should never try to minimize the costs of the JE program. A lack of honesty at this stage can undermine the program later. The plan will cost money, it will take managers and staff away from their normal duties, and it will interfere with the operating routine of the workers. To indicate otherwise, either directly or indirectly, in an effort to sell the program is unwise. The decision to install a JE program must be made with the full knowledge by all concerned that there will be inconveniences. The job of the initiator is to show that the benefits of the plan will far outweigh any temporary annoyances. The formation of a top management committee to approve the establishment of the JE plan can be of great help in gaining acceptance of the concept. Participation in the plan should begin at this level and continue downward to the lowest levels of the organization.

If your company has a compensation specialist, he or she can be invaluable in the early stages of the plan. The compensation department will be intimately involved with the plan and can offer strong support to the claim that the plan will be soundly administered after its installation.

HUMAN RESOURCE DIRECTOR'S TIP:

Be sure your job evaluation program is tailored to your industry. Some industry associations, such as the Administrative Management Society, Willow Grove, Pennsylvania 19090; the National Metal Trades Association, Rutherford, New Jersey 07070; and Life Office Management Association, 100 Park Avenue, New York, New York 10017, have developed job evaluation plans for their particular industries.

There are many good books on job evaluation, including the Prentice-Hall *Compensation* publication, which is published monthly; the American Society for Personnel Administration (ASPA) Handbook, and volume II, *Motivation and Commitment*, published by the Bureau of National Affairs, Inc., Washington, D.C. 20037.

4.11.   ESTABLISHING CAREER LADDERS TO FACILITATE UPWARD MOVEMENT AND REWARD GOOD PERFORMERS

The influx into business of a whole generation of well-educated, career-oriented, self-fulfillment-motivated men and women, particularly between the ages of twenty-five and thirty-five, is beginning to demand opportunities for professional growth and advancement that traditional hierarchical organizations often fail to provide. Historically, promotional opportunities have been limited to progressions from individual contributor-type positions up to supervisory slots and then into management. This still happens, of course, but in a company with a stable organizational structure promotions for many younger professionals will be limited to waiting for someone to leave or retire.

One method of providing these opportunities for career growth and advancement in organizations is the development of formal career ladders for different professional or occupational areas in which the concept of a job is expanded into the identifiable steps of a career. This allows employees to see and plan for a future in the company. From management's point of view, development of logical progressive steps in job scope and responsibility can form the basis for succession planning. Promotion from within is often less expensive and more effective than going outside the company for needed professional talent.

Following are some answers to frequently asked questions about career ladders and guidelines for developing them, provided by Laura A. Wallace, senior compensation analyst at Rocky Mountain Energy Company in Denver, Colorado.[5]

4.12   WHAT ARE CAREER LADDERS?

Career ladders are logical, incremental steps in a job progression within an established functional discipline. Often they start with an entry-level slot where a minimum of education or substituted years of practical experience can be easily identified, and step upward to a level of "senior" or fully experienced professional.

Career ladder steps are standards of what is typically done at different experience levels within an occupation. These levels can be applied to groups of employees working in the same occupation.

Progressive career ladder steps will have correspondingly higher salary ranges or grades, which allows a monetary reward, along with the status reward and recognition of a promotion.

4.13   WHY DEVELOP CAREER LADDERS?

Career development. Career ladders provide and communicate opportunities for employees to grow in knowledge and job responsibilities and to be equitably compensated for this occupational development.

---

[5] "Career Ladders and Guidelines for Developing Them," Laura A. Wallace, Senior Compensation Analyst, Rocky Mountain Energy, 10 Longs Peak Drive, Broomfield, Colorado 80020.

Promotions. Within specific professional or occupational areas, career ladders provide guidelines for supervisors and managers as to when it is appropriate to promote individuals who remain individual contributors, based on their service with the company, job experience, and ability to perform.

Career counseling. Career ladders provide assistance to supervisors in the form of a career blueprint in response to employees' questions: "Where can I go in this company?" "What will be expected of me for promotion?" "What kind of experience and education do I need to move up?"

Salary administration. Career ladders identify equitable salary ranges or grades for standard accountabilities to ensure fairness in pay policy and practice for individuals in similar jobs.

Recruiting. They set standards in terms of knowledge, education, and experience for both internal transfers and outside candidates. These standards allow the flexibility to hire and fairly compensate a new employee at a number of different job levels, depending on the availability of candidates having varying levels of experience.

Succession planning. Career ladders define logical progressive steps in job responsibilities and experience with which management can plan for the development of employees for future management responsibility.

Case Example: A Company Without Career Ladders

As a company's employee population grows, problems arise that could be alleviated by career ladders. The following case study shows how these problems can get out of hand.

> The ABC Company is a fast-growing, high-technology company making great strides in the data processing equipment industry. In less than ten years the company has grown from 200 employees to 10,000 employees. Although the company has a policy of promotion from within, they have no established career ladders and no standard guidelines for work experience or knowledge on which to base promotions. Because the company is growing so fast, management's emphasis in the personnel function has centered on recruiting rather than development and grooming of current employees.
>
> They have found that there is consistent turnover in professional ranks, particularly with financial analysts, computer programmers, and younger engineers. The exit interviews show that the professionals who have left were unhappy with being passed over for higher-level jobs in their areas. The better jobs were being given to new recruits from outside the company.
>
> Management finally has focused attention on a centralized evaluation of companywide compensation and promotional practices, and it has found that there are significant differences in pay levels and titles for the same type of professional jobs in different divisions of the company. These kinds of internal pay inequities for similar jobs have caused discontent among employees and have placed the company in the position of receiving potentially legitimate charges of discriminatory employment and pay practices.
>
> The compensation manager has formed a task force of his compensation people to prepare a career ladder program to address these internal inequities and to provide promotional opportunities for current employees.

The How-To of Career Ladders

There are probably functional areas in your company where a number of professional employees are doing essentially the same kind of work. The accounting department, engineering, and data processing are all good examples. If you can identify any such occupational or professional areas with a number of individual contributor incumbents, this is a good place to start in the development of a career ladder.

There are a number of effective approaches to get started, using information that should be readily available. Depending on the methods and systems already in place, one of these approaches may work. Some creativity helps when tailoring the program to your company.

Job Evaluation Systems. Whether you use a simple job-ranking system, a factor evaluation method, or one of the more sophisticated proprietary systems such as Hay, you will have some method in place to measure the "worth" of jobs.

1. Gather together all of the job descriptions or task summaries that have been written for a particular occupational area, such as data processing. Many of these job descriptions will have been ranked or evaluated already. If not, look at the experience and/or educational requirements for the various jobs, the kinds of tasks performed and their level of complexity, the authority to make recommendations or decisions, and so on.
2. Rank these different aspects of your jobs in a logical progression from the least to the heaviest. Then, using your evaluation system, develop some measure of worth for the different levels of jobs to give them an overall ranking. There may be gaps in the progression based on the existing jobs. Extrapolate and fill in gaps, using your knowledge of what would be done logically at progressive levels of experience.
3. Meet with a manager to whom a number of these professionals report, and check out the accuracy of ranking and typical years of experience or education needed to perform at these various levels. You will come up with something like the summary in figure 4–3 for computer programmers developed for a large systems and data processing department.

The computer programmer career ladder was designed to fit into other already established career ladders in the business systems and data processing departments. Transferable knowledge and skills had been identified so that both lateral and promotional moves could be made by employees from the computer operations function into the programming and systems analysis function. At the levels above the horizontal line in the figure 4–4, the step could be made to professional salaried exempt positions from hourly nonexempt positions. The schematic illustrates these interconnecting career ladders.

In assigning salary ranges or grades to career ladder levels, it is advantageous to set up steps for promotion that are already within your established salary administration policy. If a normal promotion would be a 15 percent increase in salary, then the difference between the ranges for successive career ladder steps should be a minimum of 10 percent and a maximum of 20 percent.

FIGURE 4–3.

SAMPLE

CAREER LADDER COMPANY
for
COMPUTER PROGRAMMERS

Step 1   Programmer Technician   (salary range or grade)

Under close supervision, performs coding, documents programs, prepares test data, executes program tests, assists in the analysis of program malfunctions, and performs other programming tasks required to develop and maintain computer systems. Provides limited assistance in program design. (Typically, Associate degree in Computer Science or two years of computer operation experience, including scheduling, JCL, data control, and knowledge of COBOL.)

Step 2   Programmer   (salary range or grade)

Under general supervision, participates in analysis and design of computer programs and performs coding and other programming tasks required to develop and maintain computer systems. (Typically, B.S. in Computer Science with no experience, or nondegreed with two years of direct programming experience. Requires knowledge of COBOL and JCL.)

Step 3   Analyst/Programmer   (salary range or grade)

Performs analysis, program design, coding, and other programming required to produce reports and computations or maintain information files. Works with systems analysts in defining pertinent specifications for information requirements and operational needs. (Typically degreed with one year of experience, or nondegreed with three to four years of direct programming experience.)

Step 4   Senior Programmer   (salary range or grade)

Performs technical development of new computer programs and maintenance of operational programs in the identification and solution of company programming problems. Works with systems analysts in design of effective program applications, and participates in specific project organization and scheduling. (Typically degreed with three to five years of experience, or nondegreed with six to seven years of direct programming experience.)

Salary Survey Benchmarks. If you have an established human resource function, you probably participate in a number of different salary surveys. The more sophisticated surveys will have short job description summaries for matching different levels of jobs in an occupational area, such as junior engineer, engineer, and senior engineer. Taking these benchmark descriptions as a starting point, you can adapt or expand the descrip-

FIGURE 4–4

**BUSINESS SYSTEMS AND DATA PROCESSING
CAREER LADDERS**

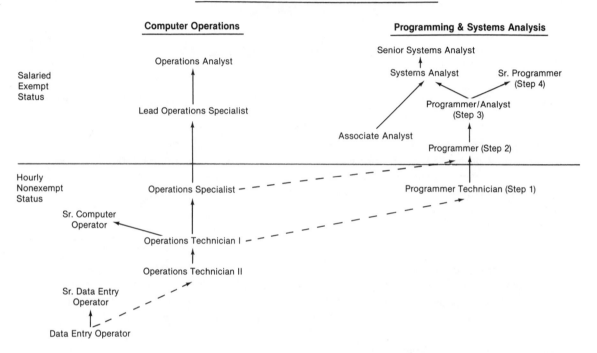

tion of job-related criteria to fit the needs of your company's jobs. You may find that three levels, as in the previous example for engineering jobs, are not enough.

There may be a need for a lower step to act as a crossover slot from nonexempt to exempt positions. This was the case in the computer programmer career ladder example. Or, your incumbent population may be comprised mostly of fully experienced professionals, so that a step above "senior" would be useful. Salary survey benchmarks also will provide you with a key to assigning appropriate salary ranges or grades.

Questions to Ask Yourself

1. What is the percentage difference between the survey's salaries for an entry-level position and a journeyman-level position?
2. Do your salary administration policies allow that much of a promotion, or should there be smaller steps?

Maturity Curves. A method to determine typical benchmark steps, or to check the logic and validity of the career ladder structure you have already developed, is to look at maturity curve data for an occupational area. Maturity data will be an array of years of experience (or years since degree) with corresponding average salaries. Typically, the more experience, the higher the pay. Many of the more comprehensive salary surveys will publish this data, or they may be available through professional organizations that do independent salary research.

Questions to Ask Yourself

1. In looking at your maturity data, identify where the significant jumps in compensation occur: at three years, at five years, at ten years, or more often?
2. How far apart in percentage terms are the salaries from year to year of experience?
3. How does this information correspond with the education and experience guidelines you have set up for your career ladder steps? Are your salary ranges or grades in line?

4.14 HOW TO IMPLEMENT YOUR CAREER LADDERS

Once you have developed career ladders for at least two or three of the occupational areas where there are significant numbers of employees, lay the groundwork for adoption and implementation. You have probably already gained the enthusiastic support of the managers to whom these employees report, if you have shared your ideas and solicited their input. You may want to detail potential costs.

Determining the Costs. Some Questions to Ask Yourself. Look at the education and experience of current incumbents in the occupations for which you have developed career ladders. Look at their current salaries, given the stated experience guidelines. At what step would each be on the career ladder? Are their current salaries consistent with the stated salary ranges or grades? If they are too low, how much would it cost to promote or bring them into the appropriate range? Are they too high? Will this limit potential salary increases in the future? Overall, would inserting current incumbents into the career ladder structure cause internal inequity problems or resolve existing ones?

Seeking Approval. In most organizations, any new policy related to salary administration will require discussion and approval up through the ranks of senior management. But the first step will be to inform the first-line and middle managers who will use the career ladders. Set up a meeting with all managers who might possibly have such incumbents reporting to them to explain how the career ladder can be used, how salary increases and promotional guidelines will be administered, and so on. Find out if they can think of problems you haven't yet considered, and try to resolve them.

Once you have gained the backing of the users, you can present your proposal for adoption of the career ladders to senior management. If the costs of the implementation are a key consideration, have suggestions ready for a phased approach (maybe just one career ladder this year to see how it works), or a plan to implement the career ladders in conjunction with next year's salary program in order to minimize immediate additional salary costs.

After approval by senior management, materials should be prepared to inform incumbents, managers, and other company employees of the adoption of the career ladders. The career ladder summaries can be printed and included in career planning guides and distributed to managers for use in career counseling. Your company's basic policy regarding confidentiality of job information and salaries will dictate how much specific information can be disseminated.

HUMAN RESOURCE DIRECTOR'S TIP:

There are some potential pitfalls in developing and implementing career ladders:

1. Always obtain management approval before communicating plans for career ladders to the employees affected. Should implementation of plans be delayed or approval denied, the expectations of employees will not be disappointed.
2. Once career ladders are implemented, it is essential that managers and supervisors be trained in understanding and using the promotional guidelines. As a means of maintaining internal equity among employees in the same professional area, career ladder guidelines must be applied fairly and consistently.

4.15   JOB ANALYSIS AND THE UNIFORM GUIDELINES ON EMPLOYEE SELECTION PROCEDURES

Employers subject to the requirements of the job analysis under the Uniform Guidelines on Employee Selection Procedures according to C. Paul Sparks, with Exxon Company, writing in *Compensation,* Prentice-Hall's monthly service, pay special attention to job analyses as a key element in the justification of any selection procedure, especially if actual selection reflects an adverse impact on any race, sex, or ethnic group.[6] Following are the guidelines:

"Any measure, combination of measures, or procedure used as a basis for any employment decision. Selection procedures include the full range of assessment techniques, from traditional paper and pencil tests, performance tests, training programs, or probationary periods and physical, educational, and work experience requirements through informal or casual interviews and unscored application forms."

Where a selection procedure has a differential impact, its continued use may be justified only by a showing of *job-relatedness* or *business necessity.* Federal EEO enforcement agencies generally require demonstration of job-relatedness through a formal study that shows validity for the selection procedure. The guidelines specify the collection of information about the job, generally in the form of job analysis, as one of numerous conditions for an acceptable validity study.

The ASPA published *A Professional and Legal Analysis of the Uniform Guidelines on Employee Selection Procedures* that was adopted by the EEOC effective in September 1978.

Under section 14, Technical Standards, subtitle C2, Job Analysis for Content Validity, the guidelines emphasize a task-oriented job analysis of observable behavior. Because companies have had problems justifying and/or transferring criterion-related validity, a specific situation approach is probably the best answer. Associations like the ASPA can be helpful in providing guidelines on job analysis.

---

[6] *Job Analysis Under the Uniform Guidelines,* C. Paul Sparks, Exxon Company, Houston, Texas; *Compensation,* October 5, 1979.

4.16 THERE ARE RESEARCHED SYSTEMS OF JOB ANALYSIS— YOU DON'T HAVE TO REINVENT THE WHEEL!

Current systems for conducting a job analysis generally fall into two broad categories: (1) systems that provide a standardized set of descriptors and are programmed to provide output in quantitative terms that can be compared with a data base established by a compendium of research studies, and (2) methods that require origination of job elements, task inventories, or other descriptors, but with the analysis programmed to provide results according to a prescribed matrix. Some of the best known of each type are listed below. Publications should be available under Psychology or Job Analysis in most libraries.

- *The Position Analysis Questionnaire (PAQ)* is a standardized instrument developed by Ernest J. McCormick and his associates at the Occupational Research Center, Department of Psychological Sciences, Purdue University, West Lafayette, Indiana. Dr. McCormick and two of his principal research associates have founded an organization called PAQ Services, Inc., to provide data processing and to conduct further research on the instrument.
- *The Occupation Analysis Inventory (OAI)* is a standardized instrument developed by Joseph W. Cunningham and his associates at the Center for Occupation Education, North Carolina State University, Raleigh, North Carolina.
- *The Skills and Attributes Inventory (SAI)* is a standardized instrument developed by Melany E. Baehr and her associates at the Industrial Relations Center, University of Chicago, Chicago, Illinois.
- *Functional Job Analysis* is a method attributed principally to Sidney A. Fine and his associates at the W. E. Upjohn Institute for Employment Research, Kalamazoo, Michigan. The results are exemplified in the *Dictionary of Occupational Titles,* published by the U.S. Department of Labor.
- *Job Element Method* was developed principally by Ernest Primoff at the U.S. Civil Service Commission. The method is the foundation for the "J coefficient," whereby job elements are translated directly into selection characteristics.
- *Health Services Mobility Study Method (HSMS)* was developed by Eleanor Gilpatrick of Hunter College and the Research Foundation, City University of New York, under contract to the U.S. Department of Labor. Originally envisaged as a means of providing upward mobility for nonprofessionals in hospital settings, the end product is a carefully integrated system for any setting.
- *Air Force Comprehensive Occupational Data Analysis Program (CODAP)* was developed by Raymond E. Christal and his associates at the Personnel Research Division, Air Force Human Resources Laboratory, Lackland Air Force Base, Texas. Organizations outside the Air Force are beginning to use the system.

4.17 WHY HAVE A PERFORMANCE APPRAISAL?

The performance appraisal provides management with a unique opportunity to tie the employee's accountabilities and achievements to the company's objectives and strategic plans.

If you design your performance appraisal form around the major accountabilities of the job rather than the minute tasks and personality traits that appear on most performance appraisal forms, you will maximize a significant motivational opportunity.

The key to making performance appraisals effective but painless is for managers to meet with their subordinates at the beginning of each year to discuss the subordinates' accountabilities and to agree on the subordinates' goals and objectives for the coming year. Once agreement is reached, managers have a responsibility to monitor progress during the year to make sure that subordinates are on track and to coach and assist subordinates in achieving their goals. Coaching should be a daily occurrence.

At the end of the year when the performance appraisal is due, it has been done through the year, and the actual sit-down appraisal—filling out the forms and discussing the subordinate's performance for the year—is easy and painless. You have been discussing it as you went along. There should be no surprises. This three-part motivational plan includes:

1. Agreement at the beginning of the year on accountabilities and objectives.
2. Review of accountability achievement and timing throughout the year.
3. Completion of performance appraisal.

Figure 4–5 is a performance appraisal form used by one Colorado company. It's based on accountabilities and specific goals and assignments. (Figure 4–5 appears on pages 140–145.)

HUMAN RESOURCE DIRECTOR'S TIP:

Train managers to treat performance appraisal as a unique opportunity to coach and develop subordinates and to tie individual goals and objectives to the organization's business plans. The new worker wants to feel a sense of self-fulfillment and to make a contribution. A workshop for managers on coaching and developing subordinates would be a good place to start.

4.18   DESIGNING AN EFFECTIVE PARTICIPATIVE PERFORMANCE APPRAISAL PROGRAM

An effective performance appraisal program can help a company achieve corporate goals through the active management of the human resource. To be effective, though, the program must be accepted by management and by all employees; it must be participative in order to be successful with the contemporary worker.

The program should also tie performance and development of the employee together. The form should provide a place to identify development needs in the current job and for the next job when the time is right to start preparing the employee for promotion.

More specifically, the program must:

1. Identify and communicate corporate goals to all employees. The manager should do this with each individual during the appraisal.
2. Identify the employee's current accountabilities and then establish clear, realis-

tic, and challenging objectives for every employee.

3. During the appraisal, tie the employee's objectives and accountabilities to the corporate objectives. Show how the employee's contribution will help the organization achieve its business plans.
4. Provide coaching and counseling in order to assist every employee in using his or her talents and capabilities to the fullest in performing the current job and in preparing for greater responsibility.
5. Be a successful tool for compensation administration.

A Program One Company Used to Gain Full Acceptance on the Part of Managers and Employees

The Phoenix Equipment Company wanted to install a new performance appraisal program that would be accepted by all employees. Top executives discussed the need for communicating the program at all levels of the company and the need to gain full commitment to the program in order for it to be successful.

The human resource director put together a task force of six employees from all levels of the organization. The task force decided that discussion groups involving all employees would gain needed visibility for the program and would involve everyone in the company in the new program. (There were 473 employees in the company.)

The task force agreed on a list of subjects for the discussion groups. Their criteria for choosing the subjects were:

1. Why does our company need a performance appraisal program?
2. How can employees successfully affect the company's business plans?
3. Can performance appraisals lead to promotion?
4. Can performance appraisals lead to better employee–boss relations?
5. Does pay for performance improve productivity?
6. What skills are needed in order to give or to receive a performance appraisal? Some skills might be: coaching, counseling, and learning to give feedback.

The discussion groups met once a week for twelve weeks, from 4:00 P.M. to 6:00 P.M., with supper served after each meeting. The top executives led the discussion groups and hosted the supper. The company gave one hour with pay and the employee gave one hour of personal time.

The program not only introduced all employees to the performance appraisal system, but it also gained insight and commitment to the need for such a program. And as executives, managers, and employees discussed performance appraisal with one another, a new sense of commitment and awareness of personal values and needs became apparent. The suggestions and ideas from discussion groups became the base for the program.

The key to painless performance appraisal is mutual goal setting at the beginning of each year and ongoing coaching throughout the year. At the end of the year, when the performance appraisal is due, it's really a matter of tallying up the results of already-agreed-upon objectives.

FIGURE 4-5.

Confidential

EMPLOYEE ACCOUNTABILITY & ACHIEVEMENT

_____

Incumbent _____

Position _____

Date _____

ACCOUNTABILITIES/OBJECTIVES
(Identify each accountability described in the job description)

1 _____

_____

_____

_____

Related Annual Objectives

_____

_____

_____

_____

_____

2 _____

_____

_____

_____

_____

_____

_____

_____

3 _____

_____

_____

_____

_____

_____

_____

_____

4 _____

_____

_____

_____

_____

_____

_____

_____

5 _____

_____

_____

_____

_____

_____

_____

_____

ACCOUNTABILITIES╱OBJECTIVES
(Identify each accountability described in the job description)

6 _____

_____

_____

Related Annual Objectives

_____

_____

_____

_____

7 _____

_____

_____

_____

_____

_____

_____

8 _____

_____

_____

_____

_____

_____

_____

9 **Administrative and/or Service Responsibilities**—Accountable for the proper and timely completion of the administrative responsibilities associated with the position, e.g., purchase orders, expense reports, performance appraisals, demonstrated support of EEO policies, achievement of affirmative action goals, and/or for providing support services to other departments.

10 **Project Management Responsibilities**—Accountable for the accomplishment of assigned tasks associated with project management.

ACCOUNTABILITY ACHIEVEMENT
(Explain results achieved in relation to each accountability)

PERFORMANCE RATING

1 _____

2 _____

3 _____

4 _____

5 _____

ACCOUNTABILITY ACHIEVEMENT
(Explain results achieved in relation to each accountability)

PERFORMANCE RATING

6 _____

_____

_____   _____

_____

_____   _____

_____

_____   _____

7 _____

_____

_____   _____

_____

_____   _____

_____

_____   _____

8 _____

_____

_____   _____

_____

_____   _____

_____

_____   _____

9

Reviewing Dept.	Performance (check one)					Comments
	DNM	MM	FM	S	O	

10

Project Title	Performance (check one)					Comments	Project Manager Providing Input
	DNM	MM	FM	S	O		

Overall Performance Rating (Check only one)

☐ Outstanding
☐ Superior
☐ Fully Meets Job Requirements
☐ Meets Minimum Job Requirements
☐ Does Not Meet Job Requirements

Comment upon the individual's potential for development in this position or other positions in the department or company.

Development Needs

Actions To Be Taken	Responsibility	Date To Be Initiated

Supervisor Comments or Recommendations

Employee Comments

Evaluated By	Title	Date
Reviewed By	Title	Date
Employee's Signature (Does not necessarily indicate concurrence)	Title	Date

54.134 (10–81)

4.19   WAGE AND SALARY SURVEYS—HOW TO USE THEM—HOW TO START ONE OF YOUR OWN

You can have the most sophisticated compensation program there is, but if you don't pay competitively and keep your eye on the market, your pay could fall below prevailing salaries in your industry, and you could lose people. You can find out what other companies are paying by participating in a salary survey. There are several ways to obtain survey data:

1. Participate in a survey group in your industry. Contact your industry association.
2. Participate in the American Compensation Association survey.[7] If you have responsibility for compensation, it would be to your advantage to join the ACA. The data you'll receive and the contacts you'll make will be invaluable.
3. If you use a consultant like Edward N. Hay Associates to install your job evaluation program, you can obtain the Hay All-Industry Salary Survey.
4. Other consultants like Towers, Perrin, Forster, and Crosby also provide salary surveys.
5. Create your own survey by forming a survey group.

Whatever methods you use to gather survey data, you should get two sets of figures: base rates and salary structures set for each job, and average base-rate salaries earned by employees currently holding the jobs.

Jobs and pay relationships are changing continually. Information you gather today won't be accurate next year. To be most useful, salary surveys should be continually reviewed and revised. Your other concern must be with the jobs themselves: are they truly comparable to jobs in your company? Titles alone aren't guarantees. Detailed job descriptions will increase your chances of getting market information that's valid and reliable as well as up to date.

The Prentice-Hall *Compensation Service* provides the following guidelines for making your own survey:[8]

Why make your own survey? Published surveys can be valuable inputs to your pay decisions, but they're not the answer to all your survey problems. You need facts and figures from companies in your own recruiting area. Chances are you'll have to do a survey yourself sooner or later, and you'll have to train one or two staffers to work with you.

Preliminary considerations. The first and most important consideration in planning a survey is to determine its purpose: will the data be used to establish a new salary program, to assess your competitive position, to verify your hunch that excessive turnover may be caused by low pay, to get data on which you can base your position in collective bargaining sessions, or for other reasons? Once the specific purpose is identified, you'll need to make some key determinations as listed below.

- *Compensation information required.* You'll need information on basic compensation (wages) and supplemental compensation (benefits). In obtaining basic wage information, the base salary or base rate should be used. The base rate is the

---

[7] American Compensation Association, P.O. Box 1176, Scottsdale, Arizona 85252.
[8] "How to Make a Wage Survey," *Compensation.*

compensation paid before deduction of taxes or the addition of premiums, overtime, bonuses, shift differentials, and so on.

- *Define wage rates.* Wage rates can be expressed as hourly, weekly, or monthly rates for hourly or clerical employees. Choose the method of payment that coincides with the majority of the rates you'll be surveying. (This eliminates the need for having to make time-consuming conversions.) Although a work week of 40 hours is normal for reporting wages or salaries, be sure to get the standard work week from each firm you survey. (You will have to make conversions to allow for firms working a 35-hour, 37½-hour, or other work week.)
- *Collect benefits information.* Because supplemental compensation may have a direct effect on wages, you should collect this information to provide a more complete picture of total compensation paid. (Bear in mind that a company with a large benefits package may not pay as high a direct wage as a company with a smaller benefits package, but the total compensation package may be the same in both cases.)

Select jobs. The validity of a wage survey depends largely on the selection of survey jobs. They must satisfy both employees and management that the survey and its findings are credible.

Obviously, every job in an organization cannot be included in a wage survey. The usual practice is to select twenty or thirty key jobs. These jobs should range from the lowest to the highest paid in the group being surveyed. They should also meet these standards:

- Many rather than a few employees should be engaged in them.
- Many rather than a few organizations should have such jobs.
- The jobs should be clearly identifiable.
- The jobs should bear a distinct relation to other jobs with reference to difficulty.
- The jobs should be well known to management and labor leaders.
- In many instances, the jobs should be those customarily involved in collective bargaining.

Jobs that meet these requirements are called benchmarks and are value-setters for all other jobs in your company. Some typical benchmark jobs are secretary, keypunch operator, janitor, and maintenance machinist.

Select companies. Your choice of companies to survey is critical. The companies you choose must contribute to the purpose of the survey. In many labor markets, almost any wage hypothesis can be proven by carefully selecting the companies to be surveyed. Of course, the results then are misleading, meaningless, and dishonest. For valid results, choose participants on the basis of questions such as:

- Does the company really compete with us in the labor market? Do our employees ever go looking for jobs with this company? Have we hired employees away from them?
- Are the company's operations comparable to ours (not products or services, but the managerial, administrative, or physical demands made on employees)?
- Do we have enough jobs in common to make the survey practical?
- Does the company have a reasonably sound wage and salary program?

One of the most perplexing survey problems is the up-and-coming employer whose wage and salary data are unorganized or who has no personnel person with whom to compare data. The critical issue for inclusion in a survey is whether or not the company is competing with you for labor. If the answer is yes, the company should be included. Give these newcomers extra time to gather their data, and offer some tips on collecting the data efficiently. Only in this way can they be counted on to supply accurate and reliable data.

Industry, area, and size considerations. For each position, there is a labor market. The companies you choose must sample that market, whatever it may be.

- *Industry.* Frequently, pay practices are unique to a given industry or group of industries. Certain jobs exist only in particular industries—such as the needle trades, publishing, or retailing. In such a case, your sample will be limited to firms in your industry.
- *Area.* Lower-level jobs are local concerns. A typist, secretary, or clerk will not relocate for a better job in another town or city. So if you are surveying these jobs, your labor market is composed of only your own geographic area. Rates in other parts of the state or country need not concern you. If you are surveying higher-level executive or professional jobs, your survey area will be much wider—regional or national. This group of employees frequently will relocate if salaries are substantially higher in another area of the country.
- *Size.* Organization size also affects your survey. Large employers (measured in terms of sales or work force) frequently pay better and provide a wider variety of benefits than smaller companies. If you want a truly representative sample of your competitors in the labor market, you should include employers of all sizes. You can always take size into account when evaluating the results.

Choose survey method. A wage survey may be conducted by interview, mail, telephone, conference, or a combination of these.

- *Direct Interview.* This is the best technique because it permits the most accurate descriptions of job content. It's also the most expensive and time-consuming, because you have to visit each company to be surveyed. But if you want to establish a sound wage and salary survey, the extra time and money are justified by the superior results obtained. The interview method is particularly important when you're conducting an original survey. It allows you to verify job comparability, ensures that the right people will give you the information, and offers an opportunity to clear up questions. Follow-up surveys can be made on the telephone or through the mail if the foundation of the survey is solid.
- *Telephone survey.* In this method, all survey information is obtained directly by phone. Telephone surveys are the quickest and most inexpensive. They're normally used for conducting surveys for a limited number of positions. They have several disadvantages: firms surveyed may release incorrect information because they lack time for research; your call may be directed to the wrong person and result in lost time, incorrect data, or even unauthorized release of information; firms may not release information to a voice over the telephone. If you must use the telephone survey method, plan your questions in advance to eliminate some of these disadvantages.
- *Conference method.* This technique brings together representatives from all participating companies at one time and place. As many as twenty-five firms can exchange data at one session, with savings in time and effort. Each participant

conducts his or her own survey at a single meeting by recording only data that are pertinent for his or her company.

- *Using a consultant.* If you feel that the demands of doing your own survey are too great, you can still have data tailored specifically to your needs by hiring a consultant to do the survey for you. The consultant will do most of the work—help pick benchmark jobs, help choose companies, prepare the questionnaires. You'll get a professionally conducted, analyzed, and interpreted survey. The disadvantage is obviously the cost, which may be difficult to justify.

After your preliminary planning steps and the selection of your survey method, you're ready to begin direct preparation for conducting the survey. Here's what's involved.

Prepare job descriptions. By now you've selected the jobs you want to survey. Review the job descriptions involved to make sure they're complete and up to date. Then, prepare a brief job description for use in the survey. One paragraph of operational job description should be sufficient.

Develop questionnaires. The questionnaires used for collecting wage and salary information should be designed so that they are easy to answer and so that information in them may be quickly and easily tabulated and analyzed. Two separate questionnaires are commonly used:

- A short questionnaire for collecting basic wage data about each job covered by the survey. (A separate questionnaire is completed for each covered job by each cooperating organization.)
- A lengthy questionnaire about the wage and salary policies and practices of the company as a whole. (Only one questionnaire about wage and salary policies is filled out by each respondent organization.)

The individual job questionnaires should request basic information, such as number of employees on the job, base rates paid, minimum and maximum rate range of each job. Also, request other benefit, policy, or practice information that's needed to reflect the total compensation package.

- Ask for individual base rates of all employees in the jobs surveyed, rather than averages, so you can spot abnormal rate distributions. Also, offers actually made sometimes tell more than the established rate for the position. (Employers may tell you their "normal" in-hire rate for a position but in practice consistently will hire people above or below this level.)
- Be specific but brief. One of the biggest pitfalls in conducting a survey is to ask for too much information. Completing the survey then becomes such a huge task that firms can't devote the time and attention necessary to provide accurate data, or they don't bother to complete it at all.

The questionnaires should be developed to make it easy to obtain information and to permit tabulation of the data as quickly and easily as possible. For example, within broad groupings, such as production and maintenance or office and clerical jobs, group specific survey jobs by job families. In the policy, practice, and benefit area, ask questions that require a specific short answer, such as "yes," "no," "$1000 a month," and so on. (They're easier for you to tabulate than questions such as, "Describe your firm's vacation policy.")

Assure firms contacted that you will treat all of their information confidentially and that you won't identify them directly with the information they provide. (A common practice is to assign each company a code identification, such as A, B, C, D, and so on. You then can include all individual company data without divulging any identities.) If you intend to list the names of participating companies, get permission from each in advance.

HUMAN RESOURCE DIRECTOR'S TIP:

The checklist (figure 4–6) of some cover letter and questionnaire items will help you in the development of your survey questionnaire. The list isn't intended to be all-inclusive, nor is it necessary to include all of the items listed.

Pros and cons: using outside surveys vs. doing it yourself. Using surveys you've purchased or participated in has many advantages: they're relatively inexpensive, involve only supplying your own data and interpreting survey results, and usually have a large number of participants. In addition, purchased surveys are professionally conducted and summarized.

They also have a great many disadvantages: you can't choose key jobs, questions, or companies; you can't identify individual companies; you can't weight the data according to the importance to you of the individual participants; and you may have to resummarize the data so that they meet your company requirements.

But conducting your own survey is time-consuming, you have to contact each prospective respondent (and you can expect many to refuse to participate for one reason or another), it's difficult to get a statistically sound sample size, you have to compute and summarize the data for all participants, and you have to distribute the results.

What it comes down to is a tradeoff between getting exactly what you want and getting results quickly, easily, and cheaply. If you absolutely demand personalized information, a do-it-yourself survey is your only answer. (Of course, you can pay a consultant to run the survey for you.)

If, on the other hand, you feel that participating in another company's survey or buying one designed for a work force similar to yours is adequate, you can save yourself a lot of time and expense. The choice is yours.

4.20 CHECKLIST FOR PREPARING THE COMPANY'S YEARLY SALARY PROGRAM AND MERIT BUDGET

1. Identify each unit of the organization that will require a separate salary program and merit budget. For example, you may have the corporate headquarters people, salaried and hourly employees at outlying locations, and scientific or special technical people at a research facility. Each of these groups requires a separate survey and separate salary program, and the specific jobs must be correlated with the jobs in the survey in order to ensure that you are comparing apples with apples.

FIGURE 4-6.

SURVEY QUESTIONNAIRE CHECKLIST

Cover Letter
>
> Purpose of survey.
> Request for participation.
> Date survey information is to be returned.
> Confidential treatment of information.
> Copy of survey results will be provided when completed.

Survey

A. General:
>
> Surveyed company's name, address, and phone number.
> Name and title of individual furnishing data.
> Principal product, service, or type of industry.
> Sales volume.
> Number of plants or locations.
> Number of employees.
> Union affiliation, if any.
> Date of wage and salary information.
> Number of hours in normal work week.
> General instructions.

B. Compensation practices:
>
> Type of merit increase program, frequency of increases, amounts.
> Length of vacations.
> Number of holidays.
> Overtime rates; special incentives.
> Cost-of-living or general increase policy.
> Life insurance.
> Health and welfare insurance.
> Dental insurance.
> Pensions: profit sharing.
> Bonus plans.
> Productivity incentives.

C. Wage and salary rates:
>
> Salary ranges, minimums and maximums.
> In-hire rates.
> Individual rates or averages for the job class.

D. Job descriptions of positions surveyed.

2. Then look at the company's competitive position for each separate group by reviewing appropriate compensation surveys.
3. Review the Bureau of Labor Statistics cost-of-living changes for the past year.
4. Review the organizational changes that have taken place during the past year to see what jobs have changed, what relationships between jobs have been altered, and how the wage structure should change as a result.
5. Look at your local industry practice, especially if the wage surveys you use are national surveys.
6. Review grade, step, or career ladder adjustments.
7. Set merit adjustments based on performance levels and compa-ratio in salary range.

In order to motivate and retain a wide range of employees at all levels of the organization, the salary program and merit budget must be competitive, must reward performance, and must be perceived by all employees as competitive and equitable. In addition, the salary program must be flexible enough to fulfill the needs of each individual in the company.

As you prepare the program and discuss compensation with management, decide what portion of the increase you plan to give will be for the cost of living and what portion is for merit. It's important for each manager to communicate the differences in order for the employee to understand that at least a portion of the increase is for performance on the job.

Companies are looking for new ways to reward performance. One company uses a variable merit pay plan. This plan provides an award for outstanding performance. It's a one-time cash award that doesn't increase base pay.

If the appraisal indicates that an employee's performance is unacceptable, the employee does not receive an increase. Special coaching may be in order. If improvement is not seen within a specific period of time, the person may be terminated. If the employee's performance is fully adequate, the employee will receive the cost-of-living increase.

4.21 HOW ONE COMPANY USED A VARIABLE MERIT PAY PLAN TO MOTIVATE THEIR PEOPLE

The Merritt Company wanted to increase productivity and decided to try a variable merit pay plan in order to tie pay to performance. The following table was used:

Type of Increase	*Variable Merit Pay Plan* *Based on Performance*			
	Unacceptable	Fully Adequate	Superior	Outstanding
Cost-of-Living	No (0%)	Yes (7%)*	Yes (7%)*	Yes (7%)*
Merit Award	No (0%)	Yes (3%)	Yes (5%)	Yes (7%)
Performance Bonus	No (0%)	No (0%)	No (0%)	Yes (5%–8%)

*Assumes a 7 percent economic factor or cost of living for that year.

If an employee's performance is superior, the employee gets the cost-of-living increase and the merit increase. If performance is outstanding, the employee gets the cost-of-living increase, the merit increase, and the performance bonus.

The amount of each award is based on the company's financial condition, profits, increases in the cost of living, and local and regional salary surveys of similar companies.

4.22 QUESTIONS FREQUENTLY ASKED REGARDING SALARY COMPRESSION

Q: What is salary compression?

A: Salary compression is the narrowing of pay differentials between job levels.

Q: What are some of the jobs where compression occurs?

A: Compression occurs between:
- Subordinates and supervisors
- Recent college graduates and long-time employees
- Office employees and assembly-line or shop employees
- New hires and senior employees
- Superior performers and average performers
- Nonunion and union employees
- Middle and top management
- Plant and office supervisors
- Hourly workers and piece workers

Compression also may occur because of job transfer.

Q: What are the main problems with compression?

A: Poor morale, poor performance, high turnover, and people being unwilling to accept promotions and added responsibility because the pay is about the same.

Q: Does compression occur when there is a lot of overtime?

A: Yes. Compression caused by overtime is very common in the automobile, utilities, mining, and oil industries.

Q: What are some of the best solutions to overtime compression?

A: Naturally, the best solution is to control the overtime, but that may not be possible. Some companies maintain a constant pay differential between their top hourly workers and their first-line supervisors, usually somewhere between 10 percent and 15 percent. It's an automatic increase programmed into the system. When the top hourly employee reaches a pay level equal to that of his or her supervisor, the supervisor's pay accelerates by the percentage differential that is agreed upon. When the compression is a result of overtime, some companies pay overtime to their supervisors as well as their hourly people in order to maintain a differential. Other companies add responsibilities to the supervisor's job and reevaluate the job upward to a level that ensures an equitable differential.

Q: How do you address the compression issue in managerial and executive ranks?

A: Some companies use bonuses and other perks. Performance bonuses are fairly common. Some companies have a specific merit pay program of, say, 10 percent for the general population and an extra percentage for special equity situations. For example, regular merit increase of 10 percent plus an additional 3 percent to 5 percent may be applied to the merit percent when necessary, because of internal equity or special performance.

Q: What other general guidelines would you recommend for compression problems?

A: Most companies like to pay for performance, so when performance is satisfactory to superior, companies just bite the bullet and provide special salary adjustments to employees affected by salary compression.

It is the responsibility of the compensation manager and/or the human resource director to ensure that there are timely checks and balances to highlight compression problems. If you have compression and don't react quickly to address it, you have a situation ripe for poor morale and union organization activity.

Case Example

Here's a plan Richard Bell, compensation manager for Rocky Mountain Energy Company, designed to address hourly compression caused by an overtime situation. The company determined that compression was the result of overtime that was regularly scheduled.[9] Employees in one department worked a 45-hour schedule, another department worked 42 hours, and all others worked a normal 40-hour week. These schedules could be changed by the general manager as conditions dictated. Foremen might also be transferred to another part of the operation or to another location where overtime requirements or hourly rates might be different. The concern in developing the recommendation was flexibility.

After considering the various options, the company determined that it was important for maximum flexibility to establish all hourly–supervisor relationships on base pay. Overtime would be addressed separately.

With this approach, the salary ranges for foremen in different departments can be the same. This maintains the integrity of the salary structure. Foremen in both high and low overtime areas can have similar base salaries with differences based on performance. In terms of base, they are paid in the proper relationship with engineers, accountants, and so on.

The remaining part of the solution involved the method of making the supervisor whole for the overtime compensation received by hourly employees.

In this regard, the company felt that the only concern should be overtime associated with an established work schedule. This encourages supervisors to keep unscheduled overtime to a minimum. Since an equitable pay differential was established using base pay relationships, foremen were given a monthly pay adjustment that equated to the actual scheduled overtime payments of the highest paid hourly employee that could be assigned to them. The successive level of supervision, up to superintendent, also received an adjustment, although the amount was reduced in direct proportion to the relative position in the salary structure. (See figure 4–7.)

Following this logic for a variety of possible schedules, a chart was prepared and given to management (see figure 4–8). With this approach, the size of the adjustments could be changed to accommodate modified schedules.

Once the program was implemented, it was easy to maintain. For normal merit

---

[9] "Timely Checks and Balances to Highlight Compression Problems," Richard T. Bell, Manager, Compensation and Benefits, Rocky Mountain Energy, 10 Longs Peak Drive, Broomfield, Colorado 80020.

FIGURE 4-7.

Mine Monthly Adjustment Schedule

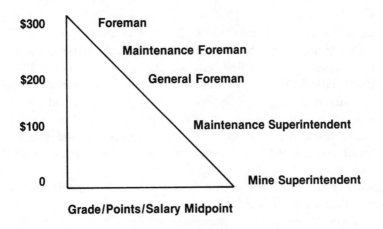

Grade/Points/Salary Midpoint

FIGURE 4-8.

MONTHLY SALARY ADJUSTMENT FOR EXTENDED SCHEDULES*

Salary Grade	SUBORDINATES SCHEDULED WEEKLY HOURS									
	41	42	43	44	45	46	47	48	49	50
I	$56	$112	$168	$224	$281	$337	$393	$449	$505	$561
II	47	94	140	187	234	281	328	374	421	468
III	42	83	125	166	208	250	291	332	374	416
IV	37	73	110	147	183	220	256	293	330	366
V	32	63	95	126	158	190	221	253	284	316
VI	27	53	80	107	134	160	187	214	240	267
VII	22	44	65	87	109	131	153	174	196	218
VIII	17	34	50	67	84	101	118	134	151	168
IX	12	24	36	48	59	71	83	95	107	119
X	9	19	28	37	47	56	66	75	84	94

* For supervisors only. The schedule refers to the hours assigned to a supervisor's subordinates. It is expected that department F will be 45 hours; department C will be 42 hours; and the maintenance department will be 40 hours.

increases, the standard procedures and current budgets could apply. The adjustment schedule was updated whenever the hourly rates changed.

4.23 EQUAL PAY FOR COMPARABLE WORTH AND PAY DISCRIMINATION ISSUES

At a meeting sponsored by the Equal Employment Advisory Council in Washington, D.C., in 1982, speakers told attendees that two of the key EEO issues of the

1980s would be sexual harassment and the hotly debated issue of equal pay for comparable worth.

The Bureau of National Affairs has published a special report entitled *The Comparable Worth Issue*, which provides a comprehensive review. According to Eleanor Holmes Norton, former chair of EEOC, comparable worth is the "most difficult issue ever" to fall under Title VII of the Civil Rights Act of 1964.[10]

The key issue seems to be the Supreme Court ruling in the *County of Washington* v. *Gunther*. The Supreme Court ruled that women bringing sex-based wage discrimination claims under Title VII are not required to satisfy the equal work standards of the Equal Pay Act. Even though the Supreme Court has not ruled on the comparable worth theory, the *Gunther* case has already generated some significant legal decisions, and most experts think the case will produce extensive federal court litigation. The comparable worth issue is the last major unresolved issue in equal employment opportunity law.

The catalyst of the tremendous comparable worth movement of the 1980s is obviously the huge influx of women into the job market. Women realize that they are concentrated in several low-paying occupations and job categories, and a new consciousness of wages for those occupations as compared to similar male occupations has risen significantly.

The market forces of supply and demand haven't raised women's wages. Norton says that "market forces have not worked to correct shortages there the way they work to correct shortages in, say, engineering." If there is an engineering shortage, wages immediately will begin to reflect that shortage, whereas, while wages have been affected somewhat for nurses, it is not nearly what the nursing shortage should allow. "Market forces are highly imperfect when they act upon female job categories," says Norton.

Enlightened human resource managers will attempt to equalize wages where unwarranted differentials exist. The whole comparable worth issue is significant and far-reaching, and it must be addressed, looking at the realities of our free enterprise system.

The unions have had all kinds of settlements that have amounted to comparable worth settlements. More companies are looking at men's and women's salaries for various jobs and trying voluntarily to remedy obvious disparities.

Case Example

The city of Colorado Springs, Colorado, without prodding from a union, decided to raise the wages of its women workers up to within 80 percent of men's wages. Women didn't press the issue. The city was sympathetic to the issue of pay inequity and decided to correct that inequity on its own.

Combatting the Sex-Based Wage Discrimination Claim

Employers should examine wage practices to minimize possible liability for intentional discrimination and be ready to prove compliance with Title VII in the event that they are hit with a sex discrimination suit. The Supreme Court's recent ruling in *County of Washington* v. *Gunther* is worth reviewing.

---

[10] Eleanor Holmes Norton, "The Comparable Worth Issue," Bureau of National Affairs, Washington, D.C.

In *Gunther*, the Court held that wage discrimination claims that ordinarily would be precluded under the Equal Pay Act's requirement of equal work could be pursued under Title VII. Employers, the Court ruled, could be held liable for "intentional wage discrimination" even where the jobs performed by women are not substantially equal to those performed by men. Noting that "prompt action" to correct intentional discrimination may completely avoid back pay liability. Employers should take the following steps:

Eliminate sex-segregated jobs. The concentration of women in traditionally female jobs is the reason for virtually all wage discrimination claims of a class nature. An employer's conscious decision to desegregate traditionally male and female jobs would be protected from claims of reverse discrimination by EEOC's affirmative action guidelines.

Review job evaluations and market data. Most large employers have used job evaluations to set wage rates, and the evaluation systems used may provide employees with grounds for arguing that the systems were based on intentional discrimination. Consider the following questions when reviewing the wage-setting process:

1. Was the job evaluation free of factors that might have carried sex discrimination?
2. Did the evaluation process result in different jobs, some of which are predominantly held by women, receiving similar total scores? As evidence of intentional discrimination, employees may cite the existence of certain jobs that have been rated the same for internal analytical purposes but are compensated differently. To avoid such potential problems, employers should examine the total evaluation process to ensure that such pay differences are attributable to factors other than sex.
3. How was the internal ranking of jobs meshed with market rate considerations? To achieve internal equity and a good fit in the labor market, a job evaluation system relies on an internal ranking of jobs and a wage survey that compares the organization's pay scale to those in the appropriate labor market. When the internal equity analysis is conducted, if women's jobs are devalued the result may be cited as evidence of intentional discrimination. The argument of intentional discrimination may be less persuasive if market rate considerations are incorporated before the internal equity analysis evaluation takes place.

Minimize liability under the Equal Pay Act (EPA). An employer's exposure to liability in an EPA action has increased as a result of the *Gunther* decision. In the future, an EPA suit may be coupled with a Title VII suit on behalf of women in other "female" jobs who are claiming that their pay rates are related to that of the EPA complainants. Thus, a violation of the EPA with respect to one group of workers may serve as the basis for a claim of intentional discrimination by other groups.

Issue a formal policy statement. Employers would be well advised to publish a formal policy statement as part of the job evaluation review process, emphasizing the company's position on wage discrimination issues.

Determine any current effects of past discrimination. Wage discrimination complainants have sought to prove that, in the past, one employer had deliberately devalued "women's" jobs because of sex and that this devaluation could be traced into the present. To counter the risk posed by such claims, an employer should review the history of wage rates to determine if any period of overt discrimination existed and if the wage relationships established during that period still exist. If the discriminatory relationships persist, the employer should determine whether they can be justified on grounds other than sex.

Comparable Worth Special Report

"The Comparable Worth Issue," a Bureau of National Affairs special report that analyzes what former EEOC chair Norton calls one of the most difficult issues ever to arise under Title VII law, is included with a recent issue of *Federal Employment Practices Summary*.

The report analyzes the impact of the Supreme Court's *Gunther* ruling, which left the door open for future lawsuits based on the comparable worth doctrine, and includes an analysis of significant court cases decided since *Gunther*. The report also examines the federal government's role in the comparable worth issue, including cases awaiting EEOC action, and discusses state legislative activities. Included is a series of interviews with representatives of women's groups, academic and labor organizations, and management officials, who outline their views on comparable worth developments in the 1980s.

4.24 MANAGING EXECUTIVE COMPENSATION

Top executive compensation continues to set all-time highs. Total cash compensation (salary plus bonus) continues to increase at a 10 percent to 13 percent rate. Median total cash compensation reached $616,570 in 1982. Throughout the 1980s, executive compensation, particularly bonuses, should play an important role in corporate efforts both to increase productivity and to marry compensation to achievement of corporate economic goals.

At the current time, many bonus programs aren't functioning as valid incentive plans because profits are declining and bonuses are still being paid. The 1981 Hay Executive Compensation Comparison Survey showed that in 83 percent of the industrial companies tracked, total cash compensation (salary plus bonus) increased in spite of the fact that there was a 6 percent drop in median corporate net income. At top levels of corporations, much of the executive income that is billed as being linked to performance is really fixed. With passage of the Economic Recovery Tax Act of 1981, corporate incentive systems probably will change significantly to take advantage of the incentive stock option. Many organizations already have modified their programs involving deferred compensation and other benefits.

The best idea for human resource managers is to watch the regulations as they come down, especially from the Treasury Department, and tailor their programs to the needs of their organizations and their executives. Be more selective in your approaches. Do what makes sense in your industry and in your location.

Executives in the $50,000 to $60,000 bracket are the ones that will feel the most need for tax relief of some kind. Companies will need to look for new incentives that relieve some of the pressure of high inflation and tax-bracket creep. Smaller incentive bonuses may be showing up more, as well as other benefits and perks.

As executive salaries and bonuses accelerate and tax liabilities also increase, more organizations are looking at deferred compensation plans. Approximately 40 to 45 percent of the Fortune 500 industrial companies are permitting optional deferrals.

Income Deferral

More companies are beginning to consider deferring income for highly paid professionals and executives. Most of the companies that do allow income deferrals include both salary and bonus, and they do pay some type of interest on the deferred income.

Because deferred amounts are not included in the executive's current compensation, other benefits that are tied to compensation, such as life insurance, thrift plan, profit-sharing programs, and long-term disability coverage, are reduced by the amount deferred.

Interest is usually paid on the deferred amount, so with interest credited on the pretax amount, the executive can earn a great deal more. Current taxation can be avoided if the executive elects to defer income *before* it is earned.

The executive is not taxed on deferred amounts or interest payments until received, and payments received after retirement ordinarily won't be subject to FICA or FUTA tax and will not reduce Social Security benefits. Payments are subject to income tax withholding, however.

Organizations need to consider how they want to handle deferrals. Most organizations expense deferrals for book purposes when earned. Interest also should be expensed for book purposes when credited to the deferred compensation account. Deferred payments are deductible for tax purposes only when paid.

There are some disclosure requirements. Any deferral arrangement must be reported to the Department of Labor under ERISA, and income deferral arrangements must be disclosed in the proxy statement.

Executive and middle-management compensation programs need to be tailored to the specific organization, its current needs and challenges. The key for the 1980s is that programs, in order to be competitive, must be unique to the individual company.

Case Example: A small high-technology company based in a high-growth area faced the problem of retaining its management team, which included top people in the computer industry. Three of the company's key executives left to start their own company. The recruiting nightmare and the cost of relocation, especially housing, became a key issue. The company's normal salary program, while competitive in its industry, did not provide a method to pay a premium for people in the discipline, nor did the relocation policy address the need for added incentives to get people to move.

An innovative compensation program was designed to help the company retain its highly technical management and professional group and to attract new people. The program included:

- Widening the salary ranges to allow more freedom to hire people at competitive levels.
- Increasing the merit budget to allow executives to give larger increases to retain a competitive edge in the area.
- Introducing a restricted stock plan.
- Instituting a money purchase plan whereby managers and executives could put a part of their before-tax salary into bank certificates of deposit.
- Enhancing the company's relocation program by adding an MIDA (mortgage interest differential adjustment). The MIDA provided relocated employees with a payment to offset some of the costs incurred by higher interest payments. The MIDA was based on the following formula:

The new annual interest rate, if at least two percentage points greater than the old, minus the old interest rate multiplied by the old or new mortgage balance (whichever is less), multiplied by 3. This amount is payable in a lump sum.

In order to be eligible for the MIDA, the relocated employee had to put the full equity from the old home into the purchase of the new home. If an employee owned a home, but did not have an outstanding mortgage, the MIDA formula used 9 percent as the old mortgage rate and applied it to the new mortgage balance. An example of how the MIDA worked is illustrated as follows:

New interest rate	11.5%
Less: Old interest rate	−8.5%
Difference	3.0%
New mortgage balance (assuming it was less than the old balance)	$60,000
	× 3%
	$ 1,800
	× 3
MIDA =	$ 5,400

> NOTE: The MIDA formula would have to be changed to fit the situation, the times, and the location if used by another organization.

If a relocated employee had to close on his or her new home before the sale of the old home, the company provided a short-term temporary equity loan.

By implementing an already competitive compensation and benefit package with these few changes, this company was able to retain its technical and managerial staff and recruit new key executives into the company.

Executive Incentive Bonus

Many companies consider executive incentive bonus plans in order to retain their top-level personnel. Most bonus programs tend to be rather complicated, and companies need attorneys and tax experts to draw them up.

Case Example: The Redding Company manufactures a line of positioning arms and industrial robots and has an annual sales volume of $163 million. The company was formed through a merger of a highly profitable company with sales of $60 million and a second company, less profitable, with annual sales of $103 million. Because of the merger, there was a need to combine many of the key executive and managerial positions, and some jobs were eliminated.

The merger and resulting changes, and the elimination of many jobs, have resulted in personality problems, conflicts in management style, and an increase in operating costs, turnover, and poor morale in the work force.

The president and the chairman of the new company feel that an incentive bonus for top management could be keyed to improvement in invested capital and better use of manpower and technology. They feel that the bonus also could motivate top executives to work harmoniously to resolve their differences.

The bonus fund could be set up to give the top two or three executives a higher bonus than the next level, or one fund could be set up for all executives with varying percentages to be paid based on the level of the position.

A formula must be established for creation of the incentive fund from which the bonuses can be paid. The formula should be set looking at the profits of the organization and the desires of the key executives and board of directors. The one way to establish a fund might be to set aside 5 percent of net earnings before taxes in excess of 10 percent of net capital. The bonus might be distributed in the following manner:

Position	Percent of Bonus
Chairman of the Board	19
President	18
Senior Vice-President	14
Vice-President, Operations	10
Vice-President, Engineering	9
Vice-President, Marketing	9
Vice-President, Finance and Accounting	8
Vice-President, Human Resources	7
Controller	6

Requirements for earning the yearly bonus could be based on performance as determined by (1) increase in sales and revenues, (2) increase in productivity of operations, and (3) decrease in turnover.

An attorney should draw up a formal management incentive plan. If the company is publicly held, the plan should be submitted to the stockholders for approval.

Using Stock to Compensate Executives

During the past several years, the use of stock as part of an executive's compensation package has become more popular. Richard M. Davies, consultant with A. S. Hansen, Inc., a compensation and benefits consulting organization, provides the following explanation of stock plans:

Executive stock plans fall into two broad categories: those under which income is taxed as a capital gain (incentive stock options), and those under which income is subject to ordinary income taxation (nonqualified options). In recent years, the incentive stock option and nonqualified stock option have become the most frequently used type of executive stock program.[11]

Nonqualified Stock Option. An executive is granted the option to buy company stock for a specific number of years at a price that is set at the time the option is granted. The executive may receive multiple grants, and there is no requirement that the options be exercised in any particular sequence. As time passes from the date of grant and the price of the stock increases, the individual may buy the stock or exercise the option. The example below demonstrates the transaction:

1. Option is granted for 500 shares at $10.00 per share.
2. Two years later the market price of the stock is $18.00 per share.
3. The executive decides to exercise the option and purchase 200 shares.
4. When the price of the stock two years later is at $24.00 per share, the individual sells 200 shares.
5. The individual's marginal tax rate is 50 percent.

Steps of Transaction:

1.   200   shares
    ×$10
    $2,000   cost to executive for 200 shares

2.   200   shares
    ×$18
    $3,600   value of shares at time of exercise

3. $3,600
    −2,000
    $1,600   gain to executive as a result of option exercise (This amount will be taxed immediately as ordinary income, irrespective of whether the shares are held or sold. Maximum tax could be as high as $800

4.   200   —50 percent.)
    ×$24
    $4,800   value of shares at time of sale

5. $4,800
    −3,600
    $1,200   amount of taxable income at time of stock sale (Remember, tax was already paid on the difference between the exercise and the grant price.)

6. $1,200
    ×0.2
    $240   tax at long-term capital gains rate

7. $2,000   purchase price
    800   tax at ordinary income rate
    +240   tax at long-term capital gains rate
    $3,040   cost of transaction

8. $4,800
    −3,040
    $1,760   net gain to executive

[11] Richard M. Davies, Consultant, A. S. Hansen, Inc., 2330 Energy Center, 717 Seventeenth Street, Denver, Colorado 80202.

The disadvantage of the nonqualified option to the executive is that he or she has to have the necessary cash to exercise the option and that the gain that results from the exercise is immediately taxable as ordinary income.

Incentive Stock Option. The incentive stock option (ISO) was created in 1981 by the Economic Recovery Tax Act. ISOs receive more favorable tax treatment than nonqualified stock options, but the administration of them is more restrictive. Incentive stock options may be granted for periods up to ten years. They must be exercised, however, in the same sequence in which they were granted. An example of an ISO transaction follows:

1. Option is granted for 500 shares at $10.00 per share.
2. Two years later the market price of the stock is $18.00 per share.
3. The executive exercises the option and purchases 200 shares.
4. When the price of the stock two years later is at $24.00 per share, the individual sells 200 shares.

Steps of Transaction:

1. $\begin{array}{r} 200 \\ \times \$10 \\ \hline \$2,000 \end{array}$ shares

    cost to executive for 200 shares

2. $\begin{array}{r} 200 \\ \times \$18 \\ \hline \$3,600 \end{array}$ shares

    value of shares at time of exercise

3. $\begin{array}{r} \$3,600 \\ -2,000 \\ \hline \$1,600 \end{array}$

    gain to executive as a result of transaction. There is no tax at time of exercise

4. $\begin{array}{r} 200 \\ \times \$24 \\ \hline \$4,800 \end{array}$

    value of shares at time of sale

5. $\begin{array}{r} \$4,800 \\ -2,000 \\ \hline \$2,800 \end{array}$

    gain before tax on transaction

6. $\begin{array}{r} \$2,800 \\ \times 0.2 \\ \hline \$\ 560 \end{array}$ capital gains tax rate

    tax on entire transaction

7. $\begin{array}{r} \$2,000 \\ +560 \\ \hline \$2,560 \end{array}$

    cost of transaction

8. $\begin{array}{r} \$4,800 \\ -2,560 \\ \hline \$2,240 \end{array}$

    net gain on transaction

The above examples demonstrate how two stock option plans might work. In reviewing stock option principles, the human resource executive should review accounting and securities rules that apply to the adoption and administration of option programs.

It's a good idea to look at total executive compensation and to take a systems approach to your programs.

Key Actions to Take When Reviewing Executive Compensation

- Determine what your organization's pay and benefit policies will be in relation to the market you are in.
- Assess the competitiveness of base salary, bonuses, and perks of your executives compared to those of executives of your competition.
- Analyze your competition's bonus levels against their profitability as well as your own organization's bonus and profitability.
- Look at deferred compensation to help your executives with income tax considerations. Be sure to review the cost-effectiveness of deferred compensation.
- Plan an integrated systems approach to executive compensation by linking base salary, bonus levels, short-term and long-term incentives, and other perks and benefits.

The CEO is the key to competitive, creative, individualized executive compensation. The CEO is in a position to override excessive concern about "how other companies handle it." The CEO, backed by the board, can insist on a compensation program that rewards executives, and an effective program can be successfully implemented. He also can ensure that executive compensation is tied to the company's business plans and reinforces the strategic direction of the organization.

Which Industries Are Paying the Highest Compensation?

Washington Report

Top Managers Paid Most in Drug, Oil, Broadcasting Firms

Top executives receive the highest compensation in bonus-paying companies in the petroleum, broadcasting and pharmaceuticals industries, a new study shows.

Segal Associates, a New York-based consulting firm, surveyed companies ranging in size from $100 million in annual sales to more than $50 billion. It compared the salaries and bonuses of the five highest paid executives in each for 1979 and 1980.

Among bonus-paying companies — 74 percent of the total — the average bonus was $70,300. The average salary was $159,800, slightly more than at non-bonus paying companies.

The lowest salaries in bonus-paying companies were in the furniture, jewelry and musical instruments businesses.

For non-bonus companies, the highest paying jobs were in financial, mining, crude oil and retail industries, and the lowest were in furniture, food and textiles.

Most of the executives surveyed have single-company careers of long duration. The average age is 57, and the average years of service is 21.

A more limited study of the country's largest corporations was made by Towers, Perrin, Forster & Crosby, management consultants. It compared compensation of the five top executives in the 100 largest industrial corporations with those in the "bottom 100" companies. The bottom 100 are those ranked from 400th to 500th in size.

**MONDAY
FEBRUARY 8
1982**

CHAPTER 5

Benefits Administration

In the past decade or so, government intervention into the employee benefits arena has been unprecedented. Inflation and rising health-care costs are additional problems that organizations must deal with when administering their benefits programs.

In a 1980 employee benefits survey published by the Economic Policy Division of the U.S. Chamber of Commerce, employee benefits varied widely among the 922 reporting companies, ranging from less than 18 percent to more than 65 percent of payroll, and from less than $2,400 to more than $9,500 yearly per employee. The average payment in 1979 was 36.6 percent of payroll, and in 1980 the average payment rose to 37.1 percent of payroll.[1]

The human resource director has had to become more knowledgeable about benefits administration and benefits. Consultants have flourished in an atmosphere of continued regulation and inflation.

5.1 KEY ISSUES THAT HAVE HAD AN IMPACT ON THE ADMINISTRATIVE COST OF BENEFITS IN RECENT YEARS

- The Employee Income Security Act (ERISA) passed by Congress in 1974.
- Litigation over coverage of pregnancy as a disability, leading to the Pregnancy Disability Act of 1978. Pregnancy now establishes eligibility for benefits on equal terms with other disabilities. Both a company's health insurance plan and short-term disability income plans are affected. Before the new law was enacted, approximately 60 percent of the established short-term disability plans had no provision for pregnancy benefits.
- Amendments to the Age Discrimination In Employment Act (ADEA) in 1978. Because the act extended the mandatory retirement age from 65 to 70, coverage of most benefits was extended by five years.
- The Health Maintenance Organizations (HMO) Act enacted in 1973. There are more than 120 qualified HMOs throughout the country and most companies make employees aware of the HMO option.
- Current rates of inflation.
- Increased cost of new health and medical technology.

---

[1] "1980 Employee Benefits Survey," published by U.S. Chamber of Commerce.

As benefits costs continue to go up, personnel managers will have to look for innovative ways to provide new benefits and to alter current programs to fit the needs of their particular work force.

Installing a benefit program is a seven-step process. The personnel manager should:

1. Review the benefits currently in place.
2. Assess their adequacy.
3. Review the cost of each benefit.
4. Conduct an employee survey to identify benefit needs and desires of the work force.
5. Ensure compliance of the benefit programs with federal regulations, including sex and age discrimination legislation.
6. Have a benefits consultant review the programs to ensure compliance and to provide advice regarding cost-effectiveness.
7. Install needed programs and communicate their purpose to employees.

5.2   BASIC BENEFITS FURNISHED BY MOST COMPANIES

Medical Coverage

Most companies provide a base medical–hospital–surgical plan and a supplemental major medical plan for employees and their dependents. Most base benefit plans include the following:

- Surgical charges are fully reimbursed at "reasonable and customary" rates, except in some states where fee schedules are in place.
- Most companies pay full charges for a semiprivate room.
- Most companies pay all costs for up to four months of hospitalization.

The normal major medical plan includes:

- $100 deductible.
- Coinsurance, where 80 percent is paid by the company and 20 percent by the employee.
- Maximum major medical benefits of $250,000.

Most plans today also cover mental illness and treatment for drug or alcohol addiction, normally only at a 60 percent level.

Most companies pay the total cost of medical coverage for the employee while the employee pays for dependent coverage.

> TRENDS:
>
> To add dental and vision insurance and cover prescription drugs.

Pension Plans

Most medium-sized and larger companies provide a fully paid pension plan to all employees. Inflation is one of the most serious concerns of employees, and most companies are maintaining parity with inflation before retirement and making other adjustments from time to time as inflation accelerates. Vesting for pension plans occurs after ten years of service.

Most companies also have some type of capital accumulation plan such as a thrift plan or savings plan. Employees contribute an amount up to six percent of their income, and the company matches that amount 50 cents on the dollar. Some companies are increasing their matching amount. Most companies now use a Social Security offset.

TRENDS:

Some companies are becoming more liberal with vesting requirements.

Life and Accident Insurance

Most companies provide death benefits and accidental death and dismemberment insurance. The typical life insurance plan is based on a formula that is twice the annual salary or a percentage of the annual salary, and some companies provide an additional amount if the employee elects to pay a portion of the cost. For example:

- Company provides $50,000, free to employee.
- Employee takes an additional $50,000, employee pays premium.
- Company provides additional $50,000, free to employee.

Accidental death and dismemberment insurance is provided by most organizations and is company-paid. Many companies also provide a portion, usually one-third, of the employee's preretirement life insurance, to be continued at company expense.

TRENDS:

The trend has been to provide added life insurance coverage at the employee's expense, and many companies add a third level at company expense as the example above shows. Added income benefits for survivors and spouses' pension provisions are also more common now.

Disability

Long-term disability benefits are normally 60 percent of base pay reduced by any other benefit such as Social Security or unemployment. Long-term disability benefits usually start after twelve to twenty-six weeks of total disability or at such time as the company's short-term disability benefits run out.

TRENDS:

More companies are moving to a rehabilitation clause in their long-term disability benefit to curb accelerating costs. A rehabilitation clause might read as follows:

"The company at its discretion may require disabled employees to join a rehabilitation program that will be paid for by the company and is intended to improve the employee's condition and allow the employee to return to the work force in some productive role. If an employee is requested to enter a rehabilitation program, he or she must do so in order to continue receiving long-term disability pay."

More than 1,400 postal employees who formerly received Workers' Compensation benefits for job-related disabilities resumed their jobs under a special rehabilitation program established in 1979 by the U.S. Postal Service and the Department of Labor. The program has enabled the Postal Service to trim compensation costs by nearly $17 million a year.

Severance Pay

Not all companies have a severance pay policy, but many do. The pay is usually determined by a formula based on years of service, with a restriction or maximum limit; for example, two weeks severance for each year with the company, to a maximum of twenty-six weeks.

Some companies limit severance pay to salaried or management employees only, but most companies today feel that their severance pay policy should be available to all employees.

Time Off with Pay

Most companies give employees paid vacations, holidays, and time off to take care of family and civic responsibilities.

Vacations. These are normally two weeks after one year, three weeks after five years, and four weeks after ten years. Some companies require fifteen years of service before giving four weeks of vacation.

Holidays. Ten to eleven paid holidays seem to be standard today. Holidays are:
New Year's Day
President's Day
Good Friday
Memorial Day
Independence Day
Labor Day

Thanksgiving Day
Day after Thanksgiving
Christmas Day

One or two floating holidays are given by many companies. The day before Christmas is usually given as one of the floating holidays.

Most companies give up to three days of leave for an employee to attend the funeral of a member of his or her immediate family. Paid time off for voting and for some civic responsibilities is also a common benefit.

OTHER BENEFIT TRENDS:

Trends are toward flexible benefits to allow an employee a choice of benefits based on individual need, and more companies seem to be leaning toward flexible work schedules.

5.3 WHAT WILL BE THE FASTEST-GROWING BENEFITS IN THE 1980s AND 1990s?

A U.S. Chamber of Commerce expert was quoted in the August 3, 1982, issue of *Washington Report* as saying that the changing nature of America's work force will soon dictate changed patterns of employee benefits.

Day-care for children of working mothers will be the fastest-growing new benefit, with flexible working hours a close second. Half of the women in America are working outside the home now, and it's been projected that 60 percent of the women in America will be doing so by 1990.

In 1981, Congress changed the tax law to provide incentives for employers to become more active in providing day-care for children of employees.

The number of women working outside the home will have a significant impact on benefit programs in the next decade.

5.4 SAVE YOUR COMPANY MONEY BY PERFORMING A BENEFIT NEEDS ANALYSIS

If you are thinking of improving your benefits, or if you just want to know if your benefits are competitive, it's a good idea to analyze your work force to ensure that you are currently providing the benefits package that the majority of your workers need and want. Most benefit packages provide excellent coverage for the typical middle-aged male worker with a wife and children. The package includes good medical coverage, disability insurance, life insurance, a pension plan, vacations, and usually a capital appreciation plan of some kind.

The problem is that there is no longer any such thing as a typical employee. That so-called typical male employee with a family now makes up only about 15 percent of the work force. Today's workers come from diverse backgrounds and a variety of situations and responsibilities, and they have diverse benefit needs.

One of the most obvious changes in recent years is the number of women working outside the home. Other social trends reflect higher divorce rates, later marriages, lower birth rates, and longer life expectancy. There is no typical employee, and for this reason some companies have moved to flexible benefit plans that allow individual employees to choose the benefits they need. Some companies also feel that the flexible benefit approach will save them money.

Meidinger, Inc., a consulting firm based in Louisville, Kentucky, published a breakdown of employed people (shown in figure 5–1) in their December 1981 newsletter, *Update*.[2]

FIGURE 5-1.

EMPLOYED PEOPLE

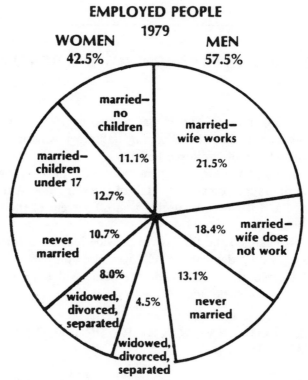

This diverse work force has far different benefits needs from those of the work force of the 1970s.

By identifying the age of your work force, you can better understand their needs.

Young people want more "cash now" benefits like medical and dental insurance and tuition refund programs. Older workers look for longer-term benefits, such as pensions and life insurance. If you have a predominantly young work force, you may lean toward more short-term cash benefits. If you have a mixed work force, you may want

---

[2] "Breakdown of Employed People," *Update*, December 1981. Meidinger, Inc., Louisville, Kentucky.

to consider a flexible benefit program. In order to keep pace with employee needs, some companies have increased employee contributions to benefits costs.

Figure 5–2 is an age demographic chart for the XYZ Company. You may want to do a chart for your particular work force in order to identify the age demographics in your organization.

5.5 ASK EMPLOYEES ABOUT THEIR BENEFIT PREFERENCES IN A BENEFIT QUESTIONNAIRE

The obvious question here is how to design benefits programs that match the needs and preferences of your employees.

If your current programs are not meeting your needs, you may want to ask employees to complete a questionnaire identifying the benefits they would choose if they had the option.

Ask employees to provide answers for the questionnaire shown in figure 5–3. It's a good idea to survey employees periodically to ensure that the benefit programs are continuing to meet the needs of your work force.

5.6 QUESTIONS AND ANSWERS REGARDING EMPLOYEE BENEFITS

Q. Who is usually responsible for managing employee benefits?

A. Every organization seems to have its own method of assigning benefits responsibility, depending on the specific benefit. Following are the most common assignments:

Benefit	*Responsibility*
Medical insurance	Compensation manager
Dental insurance	Compensation manager
Vision insurance	Compensation manager
Life insurance	Compensation manager
Workers' Compensation	Medical or safety manager
Unemployment compensation	Payroll supervisor
Group insurance (not medical)	Insurance manager
Pension plan	Treasurer, vice-president of finance, and/or vice-president of personnel
Profit sharing	Compensation manager
Relocation	Employment manager
Tuition refund	Manager of management development
Fitness program	Health and safety manager

Q. What are key issues in the employee benefit field today?

A. Cost is, of course, a key issue. With benefits costing 37 cents for every payroll dollar spent, companies are looking for ways to hold down the costs.

Another significant issue is the need for flexibility in choosing benefits, identifying the needs of individual employees.

FIGURE 5-2.

AGE DEMOGRAPHICS
XYZ COMPANY
July 1, 1982

EXEMPT EMPLOYEES				NONEXEMPT EMPLOYEES				HOURLY EMPLOYEES				COMPANY		
Age	#	%		Age	#	%		Age	#	%		Age	#	%
21–25	6	1.9		21–25	32	18.0		21–25	47	22.8		21–25	85	12.1
26–30	59	18.4		26–30	41	23.0		26–30	52	25.2		26–30	152	21.6
31–35	100	31.2		31–35	23	12.9		31–35	36	17.5		31–35	159	22.6
36–40	65	20.3		36–40	34	19.1		36–40	35	17.0		36–40	134	19.0
41–45	27	8.4		41–45	16	9.0		41–45	12	5.8		41–45	55	7.8
46–50	25	7.8		46–50	12	6.7		46–50	11	5.3		46–50	48	6.8
51–55	23	7.2		51–55	11	6.2		51–55	5	2.4		51–55	39	5.5
56–60	13	4.1		56–60	2	1.1		56–60	5	2.4		56–60	20	2.8
61–	2	0.6		61–	7	3.9		61–	3	1.5		61–	12	1.7

Mean Age 37.5

Mean Age 35.4

Mean Age 33.2

Mean Age 35.7

EXEMPT EMPLOYEES
26–40 = 69.6% (224 ÷ 320)

NONEXEMPT EMPLOYEES
26–40 = 55.0% (98 ÷ 178)

HOURLY EMPLOYEES
26–40 = 59.7% (123 ÷ 206)

COMPANY
26–40 = 63.2% (445 ÷ 704)

FIGURE 5-3.

<u>BENEFITS QUESTIONAIRE</u>

Please answer the following questions regarding your benefit program.

List current benefits. (This will show you whether or not employees actually know what benefits they currently have.)	Would you be willing to contribute a portion of the cost of new or improved benefits? Yes ____ No ____ How well do you understand your current benefits?
List current benefits you feel need improvement.	How efficient do you feel the current claims-processing effort is?
List benefits you would pick if you had the option. Why?	If you had to choose, would you rather have a salary increase or an increase in benefits? What is the most important benefit to you and your family?

In an article entitled "What We Can Learn from Japanese Management," published by *Harvard Business Review* in March–April 1971, Peter Drucker said:

Underlying our entire approach to benefits—with management and union in complete agreement, for once—is the asinine notion that the work force is homogeneous in its needs and wants. As a result, we spend fabulous amounts of money on benefits which have little meaning for large groups of employees and leave unsatisfied the genuine needs of other, equally substantial groups. This is a major reason why our benefit plans have produced so little employee satisfaction and psychological security.

Another emerging issue is that Social Security and pension plans no longer guarantee a comfortable retirement, and workers are looking for more tax-sheltered savings programs.

Younger workers highly value personal time and are looking for more time off with pay. Increases in flexible work schedules and four-day work weeks are becoming more prevalent.

The effects of dual-career marriages are beginning to make themselves felt in tangible ways. Companies are beginning to offer transferred employees job-finding services for spouses through their own employment departments.

Capital accumulation plans have been a trend in the 1980s. Most larger companies sponsor thrift plans, ESOPS, or PAYSOPS.

The Economic Recovery Tax Act of 1981 provides some new benefits options:

- *IRAs.* Employees may make tax-deductible contributions to Individual Retirement Accounts (IRAs) even if they participate in qualified employer-sponsored retirement plans. The new law also permits employees to make tax-deductible voluntary contributions to employer-sponsored retirement programs, if the plans agree to accept such contributions. Beginning on January 1, 1982, employees were able to make tax-deductible contributions of up to 100 percent of their pay, or $2,000 per year, whichever is less, to an IRA or to their employer's pension, profit-sharing, or savings plans. IRAs also may be established for a nonworking spouse, in which case the maximum is increased from $2,000 to $2,250 per year. In addition to IRAs and employer-sponsored retirement plans, employees can make tax-deductible contributions to tax-sheltered annuities and government plans.
- *ISOs.* The incentive stock option basically gives an executive the right to pay today's market price for a block of shares in the company at a future time. The market price could be higher by the time the option is exercised, but no tax is due until the shares are sold. The employee has to hold the stock for one year to qualify for capital gains tax, instead of the former three years. ISOs are a good recruiting tool, and many companies are moving ahead with ISO plans.

There are other issues emerging in the compensation and benefits areas, and those issues are covered elsewhere in this book.

Q. Are there any new benefits besides IRAs and ISOs?

A. The *New York Times* on February 21, 1982, and the *Wall Street Journal* on January 25, 1982, both touted a new idea in tax-sheltered programs. The *Times* called it the hottest new development in employee benefits. It's the salary reduction plan (SRP): employees can defer as much as 15 percent of salary, sometimes more, by putting the money into a company savings or profit-sharing plan, in contrast, for example, to an IRA, where an employee can put only $2,000 per year away tax-free. Under the salary reduction plan, you don't get a direct tax deduction for contributing as you do with an IRA, but the amount deferred isn't part of your current taxable income. In addition, when the money comes out of the corporate plan at retirement, it gets a more favorable tax treatment. Some companies are concerned about putting in an SRP because of antidiscrimination rules. They fear that if they put in a plan, it might not qualify if many lower-paid workers can't afford to participate. The plan must meet an annual test that basically says that the highest paid one-third of all employees can't defer more than the other two-thirds. There isn't much of any way to know in advance whether or not the plan will qualify.

Example:

If the average contribution of the lower paid two-thirds of employees is:	The limit on the contribution of the highest paid one-third is:
1%–2%	2½ times the lower paid
3%–6%	3% times the lower paid
more than 6%	1½ times more

One company that is happy with their salary reduction plan is Honeywell. Half of their employee population was enrolled in their plan during 1981. More companies will establish salary reduction plans as Social Security taxes increase.

Q. What might be a reasonable list of benefits and costs to an organization for a typical benefit program?

A. The Stanfield Company provides an example of benefits costs for one year to a 32-year-old man with a wife, one child, and a salary of $35,000 per year.

Benefit	Employer Cost	Employee Cost if Purchased
Tuition toward Executive MBA	$12,500	$12,500
10% Profit Sharing	3,500	3,500
Three Weeks Vacation	2,019	2,019
Pension Plan	2,525	3,280
Health Insurance	1,227	1,563
Yearly Physical Exam	160	250
Dental Insurance	670	not available
Disability Insurance	226	594
Term Life Insurance	475	892
11 Paid Holidays	1,480	—
Totals	$24,782	$24,598

NOTE: Sick leave and Social Security taxes are not included in these figures.

Q. What are "cafeteria" benefits?

A. Fred Dalton is a 30-year-old systems analyst for a computer software company. His wife works, and her employer provides an excellent medical program for the whole family, so Fred skips extra medical coverage and takes added life insurance instead.

Jane Cook is a personnel manager. She skimps on medical and life insurance in order to increase her employer's contributions to a capital accumulation plan, hoping to borrow against her plan to buy a condominium.

Companies who have "cafeteria" benefit plans provide employees with a package of basic benefits and optional benefits. Most basic plans include some medical coverage, life insurance, vacations, pensions, and some disability pay. In most cafeteria plans, employees use credits to choose other benefits, such as dental or vision insurance, day-care, more vacation time, more life insurance, or higher company payments to pensions.

Cafeteria, or flexible benefit, plans are great in most cases, but there are some problems associated with them, as there are with any benefit plan:

- With most plans, employees can adjust their benefit packages once a year, and that requires a lot of additional bookkeeping and administrative hassle.
- In order to offer a flexible benefit program, companies have to scale back their existing benefit programs, which can alienate employees.
- Many personnel people feel that the administrative costs associated with flexible benefit programs are high.

Some key pluses are:

- Companies that have installed cafeteria-style benefit plans have found that turnover decreases.
- Flexible benefits are a good recruiting tool.
- Changes in tax laws have made cafeteria plans more attractive.
- The plans give an illusion that the company is providing more benefits without increasing costs. As companies find it difficult to keep up with high wage increases brought on by inflation, they are looking for other forms of compensation.
- A variety of benefits to choose from at different stages in a person's life seems to make good business and economic sense.

Q. Current retirement benefits seem to be in long-term financial trouble. What are the critical elements at work here?

A. Aging of the work force and a longer life expectancy have resulted in a higher percentage of the population reaching the normal retirement age of 65. In addition, the birth rate has been dropping steadily, so that when the huge postwar baby-boom generation starts retiring in the year 2010, there will be far fewer workers financing retirement benefits.

Inflation has been a significant factor. Federal retirement programs provide for benefit increases for retired workers, and questions are being raised by younger federal workers who are asked to pay increased Social Security costs in order to protect retired workers from inflation, when they themselves do not receive wage increases that keep up with inflation.

Private pensions are most often fixed at retirement, and inflation has adversely affected the income that retirees receive from private pension plans. Some corporations have increased benefits, but many have not. There is another subject, too long to discuss here, of unfunded private pension liabilities. The entire question of pension benefits must be studied seriously, and new strategies for the future must be forthcoming soon. Most personnel professionals believe in an assured minimum level of retirement income for all workers and their families, providing social equity for all groups of workers while at the same time helping workers to maximize personal savings through various corporate capital accumulation plans. Private retirement plans should encourage retirement income that includes Social Security, employer pensions, and greater personal savings plans, if that's possible in these financially restrictive times.

Q. What information about benefits must employees receive on a regular basis?

A. There is an obligation to comply with ERISA reporting requirements, but because organizations spend so much on employee benefits, it seems only practical to communicate information regarding the programs and their cost to workers.

The Employee Retirement Income Security Act of 1974 (ERISA) partially satisfies the goals of labor unions, consumerists, human rights advocates, and employers by reporting to employees information on pension and welfare plans. The requirements for routinely distributing summary plan descriptions and summary annual reports to active employees and statements of entitlements to terminating vested employees are generally reasonable and satisfy most groups of workers who want current benefit information.

A significant new trend in regular benefits communication is the use of personalized annual benefits statements. Most large companies with comprehensive data processing capability can now produce their own reports, using either customized or purchased software. Smaller companies can choose from a number of outside consulting firms that produce these reports on a contract basis. Information about benefits also can be communicated through company newsletters, bulletins, and payroll inserts.

Q. I've heard about self-funding. Why should a company self-fund?

A. The big reason could be money. Self-funding is utilized by some companies to:

- Eliminate prepayment for liabilities that haven't occurred.
- Reduce the internal retention costs of the plan.
- Reintroduce the plan's reserves into corporate cash flow or other interest-earning investment programs.

Q. What is the difference between self-insurance and self-funding?

A. The term "self-insurance" implies that any plan that is self-insured has unlimited liabilities. Conversely, "self-funding" means that a plan is operated under an annual aggregate deductible, through which the employer only pays losses as they occur up to the limit of an annual aggregate "stop-loss" insurance policy. Use of the stop-loss policy clearly limits the liability of the insured corporation in any one year, while allowing the employer to defer payment of any dollars until payment is actually due.

Q. Are there many companies that self-insure instead of self-fund?

A. Yes, but self-funding is generally recommended under a stop-loss policy to insure against possible claims exposure above the expected losses. Additionally, the cost of stop-loss is small enough to justify the expense. Most stop-loss carriers require that an independent administrative firm provide the claims administration on a third-party basis. When the third party is used, the cost of the stop-loss is greatly reduced.

Q. How is stop-loss applied?

A. If, for example, you now pay an annual premium averaging $650 per employee to provide health-care benefits, then you should purchase insurance that would limit the company's liability to $650 a year per employee or some higher figure. Insurance covering the first $650 of health claims isn't needed, since up to this point all you need are administration services.

Q. Is self-funding of group health care similar in principle to self-funding of Workers' Compensation?

A. Yes, in at least two areas:

- The company's liability is limited through utilization of the stop-loss policy, limiting the maximum dollars the program can cost each year.
- The employer no longer prepays premiums or reserves, thereby retaining those dollars in cash flow until payable as losses.

If you are interested in self-funding, you need experts in insurance, benefits, and tax areas to advise on the pros and cons of self-funding for your particular company.

Case Example

Comparison of Insured vs. Self-Insured Trust Fund
January 1–December 31, 1981

	Insurance Company	(Self-Insured) Present Operation
Total contributions	$364,100.00	$364,100.00
Interest on savings accounts	11,342.00*	19,573.08
Misc. income (claims refunds)	35.00	35.00
Total claims	185,766.91	185,766.91
Increase in claims reserve	69,765.06	69,765.06
Trust expenses	16,801.38**	20,699.03***
Insurance company retention	29,492.00	
Increase in unallocated reserve	73,651.65	107,477.08
Surplus at beginning of period	352,491.93	352,491.93
Surplus at 12/31/81	426,143.58	459,969.01
	Savings =	$ 33,825.43

 * Could vary slightly.

** Assuming some claims and claims reserve on both plans. The retention is an interpolation of bid showing increase of claims and premiums as they actually were, not as a bid. As a result, they could vary slightly.

*** Difference is increased consulting and legal fees.

Q. Social Security taxes are continuing to go up. At the current rate of increase, what will be the taxable wage base by 1987?

A. The Social Security taxable wage base will be up to $46,800 by 1987. The following are year-by-year estimates, projections from the government. They are useful for budget planning and for estimating pension contributions. Note the big jump in 1985:

Year	Wage Base	Employers and Employees		Self-Employed	
		Tax Rate (%)	Maximum	Tax Rate (%)	Maximum
1982	$32,400	6.70	$2,171	9.35	$3,029
1983	35,100	6.70	2,352	9.35	3,282
1984	37,800	6.70	2,533	9.35	3,534
1985	40,500	7.05	2,855	9.90	4,010
1986	43,800	7.15	3,132	10.00	4,380
1987	46,800	7.15	3,346	10.00	4,680

Q. What is the regulation on Social Security taxation of sick pay?

A. The first six months of sick pay become subject to FICA, effective January 1, 1982. The IRS has published regulations that include disability payments; any sickness or accident payment, except Workers' Compensation payments; third-party payments made under certain contracts that were terminated before March 1, 1982; and payments attributable to employee contributions.

Q. Are there concerns to be aware of regarding benefits and EEO?

A. Yes. For the third time a New York judge has struck down a retirement system that uses sex-designated actuarial tables. The courts say that retirement programs based on equal contributions but providing larger annuities to male retirees than to female retirees are unlawful.

Courts have explained that while Title VII does not refer specifically to the business of insurance, its prohibition against sex discrimination in compensation covers retirement benefits.

In addition, pregnancy must be treated as a disability. Congress enacted Public Law 95–555 in 1978. This is an amendment to Title VII of the Civil Rights Act, and the key provisions are:

- Women disabled because of pregnancy must, for benefit purposes (including leave, disability income, and medical benefits), be treated on exactly the same basis as those employees who are disabled by sickness or accident.
- Increased costs for contributory plans may be apportioned between employers and employees.
- Employers must provide comparable medical coverage for abortion only if the abortion is to protect the mother's life. The bill might be interpreted as requiring comparable disability income benefits for any abortion. Also, employers must provide comparable coverage for any medical complications arising from an abortion.

Q. What is an HMO?

A. In 1973, Congress passed the Health Maintenance Organization Act with emphasis on preventive medicine. An HMO provides medical service either directly with its own staff or by contracting for medical services in exchange for a predetermined, prepaid fee.

Q. In recent years, some HMOs have gone under. What can employers do if their HMO is sick? Are there any tips on choosing an HMO?

A. The best action is to file a complaint with the Department of Health and Human Services against the HMO. You can request that the Department demand financial improvement on the part of the HMO or take legal action and revoke the federal qualification.

The HMO act requires, among other things, that each federally qualified HMO have a "fiscally sound" operation. Any person may file a written complaint alleging that a qualified organization is not fiscally sound or has failed to comply with other federal requirements. Under department regulations, the Secretary of Health and Human Services may investigate to determine whether or not the HMO is in compliance. If it is not in compliance, the Secretary may require corrective action and, if that action is not taken promptly, revoke the federal qualification.

If you are in the process of choosing an HMO, don't sacrifice employee satisfaction for lower cost. Select an HMO with facilities that are convenient to employees and that have office hours compatible with your work schedules. Talk to other companies that are using the HMO you are considering, and see if their employees are happy with the group.

Q. What is deferred pay, and how does it help you save for retirement?

A. There is a form of deferred pay, called a salary reduction plan, that some companies are instituting. A salary reduction plan actually seems to provide a better benefit and more flexibility than an IRA. The concept is simple. If a company decides to set up a plan, a certain percentage of an employee's salary can be set aside for investment for the future. The employee can elect to give up part of a scheduled raise or take a pay cut. In some cases, employers match part or all of the employee's contribution. The benefit is that the amount set aside isn't included in gross income, which means the employee doesn't have to pay taxes on it.

Q. What's the difference between an IRA and a salary reduction plan?

A. The main difference is the amount that can be contributed. With an IRA, you are limited to $2,000 per year, or $2,250 if you include a nonworking spouse.

Under a salary reduction plan, the amount can be much greater, in some instances up to 25 percent of your salary. However, the average for all employees is restricted to 15 percent.

The ceiling is determined by the plan itself and by a complex formula designed by the government to assure balanced participation by both higher-paid and lower-paid employees.

There are other elements of a salary reduction plan that should be reviewed if your company is considering such a plan. The withdrawal clauses of both IRAs and salary reduction plans should be reviewed before a plan is instituted. Here again, a knowledgeable, experienced consultant can give some expert advice.

5.7 THE ACCELERATING COSTS OF BENEFITS

Employee benefits now cost employers 37.1 percent of every dollar paid in wages, according to a benefit survey completed by the U.S. Chamber of Commerce. The survey of 983 companies shows that payments for benefits ranged from less than 18 percent of payroll to more than 65 percent of payroll, and from less than $2,600 to more than $10,000 per year per employee.

Of the 186 companies that have participated in the survey since 1959, there has been a rise in benefit payroll of 41.1 percent over the 21-year period. For more information on the survey, write Employee Benefits 1980, U.S. Chamber of Commerce, 1615 H Street, N.W., Washington, D.C. 20062.

How One Company Fights Medical Inflation

The health-care benefit costs at the Ford Motor Company doubled every five years from 1965 to 1978, and the trend was continuing, so Ford installed several cost-containment approaches.

1. The company has established preventive care programs to assist employees in identifying health problems and learning how to manage them.
2. The United Auto Workers union and Ford worked jointly with their insurance carriers and health-service providers to improve cost efficiency. These efficiencies included second-opinion elective surgery. HMOs were also encouraged.
3. Executives of Ford Motor Company are encouraged to sit on the boards of insurance carriers like Blue Cross and Blue Shield. Executives are also encouraged to sit on hospital boards and to get involved in community service activities.
4. The company has been involved in legislative efforts with other businesses and with labor to encourage private- and public-sector programs dealing with medical cost containment.

Some Key Issues in Medical Cost Containment

1. The high cost of new medical technology.
2. Overcapacity of health-care delivery facilities and excess hospital beds.
3. Overutilization of both consumer and provider services; too much surgery, too many drugs being dispensed, and too little use of outpatient facilities.
4. Many health care institutions not cost-conscious or productivity-oriented.
5. Inflation of medical facility, technology, and manpower costs.
6. Lack of incentives to contain costs.

More companies today, however, are joining together to form community health-care cost-containment coalitions, and this should produce visible results.

Besides the obvious issue of cost containment through monitoring utilization, some other ideas for cost-containment could work:

1. Monitor coordination of benefit provisions to preclude double payment for the same expense.
2. Use careful claims administration, including selective audit controls of hospital bills.
3. Offset expenses by negotiating the release of insurance-carrier-held reserves and managing these funds as part of the company's general reserves.
4. Reduce underwriting costs by entering into minimum premium or administrative-only service contracts.

Health-care cost containment should be a major challenge for innovative personnel managers.

5.8   HOW COMPANY-SPONSORED FITNESS PROGRAMS ARE KEEPING EMPLOYEES ON THE JOB

The escalating costs of health care have prodded companies to change their attitudes about employee health, and many companies are installing fitness programs as a means of cutting costs.

There are many types of fitness programs. Following are some key features:

1. Comprehensive screening process for employees who wish to participate in fitness programs.
2. A medical history form, giving all pertinent information.
3. Lab work and multiphasic screening.
4. Company-paid physical examination.
5. Health counseling.
6. Lifestyle assessment and health program design, which might include exercise, stress management, and recreation programs.

The most important measure of a health program's success is employee acceptance. Programs are voluntary, so the most obvious measure is participation rate. Most companies that sponsor fitness programs measure absenteeism, illness, and the number of medical claims before and after a program is installed.

Health-care utilization could be assessed by comparing overall employee health-care costs in constant dollars before and after the program's inception and comparing health expenses of employees who participate in fitness programs against the expenses of nonparticipants.

These evaluations would require employee permission and cooperation, but the results could justify a reduction in insurance premiums in proportion to the percentage of participating employees.

Personnel managers may obtain more information about industrial fitness programs by contacting the American Association of Fitness Directors in Business and Industry, in care of the President's Council on Fitness and Sports, Washington, D.C. 20201.[3]

5.9   THE PROS AND CONS OF FLEXIBLE BENEFITS

Why all this talk about flexible benefits? The work force has changed dramatically in the past decade. Today, only one out of every five employees is married with a nonworking spouse at home. The problem is that most companies' benefit plans are tailored for the old, "traditional" family unit, which now makes up less than 20 percent of the work force. The benefits being furnished to most employees are expensive and are not necessarily the specific benefits that are needed. There is a growing need to involve the employee in discussion and review of benefit cost containment and in choosing the benefits most needed on an individual basis.

---

[3] American Association of Fitness Directors in Business and Industry, c/o President's Council on Fitness and Sports, Washington, D.C. 20201.

The problem with "cafeteria" benefit programs is the cost of administration. Depending on the number of employees a company has, letting employees elect what benefits they want can become a recordkeeping nightmare in a large organization, but some organizations feel that the benefits to employees and to the company far outweigh the disadvantages.

There are basically three phases of installation of a flexible benefit program, according to Kwasha Lipton, consultants in employee benefits:[4]

- *Communication.* The solicitation and confirmation of each employee's annual election.
- *Payroll.* The application of each employee's credit allowance.
- *Benefit administration.* The recognition of the elections in premium payments to insurance carriers and in claim processing.

A flexible benefit program can be introduced gradually by working with benefit consultants who know the field.

5.10 MENTAL WELLNESS PROGRAMS

Some organizations are setting up mental health programs to assist employees with such problems as alcoholism, drug abuse, and mental illness in an effort to restore employees to full productivity. Employers are spending $10 to $13 billion annually on drug abuse and medical treatment of alcoholism. The loss of productivity in industry because of alcoholism is another $30 billion per year.

Seven Basic Characteristics of a Successful Mental Wellness Program

Following are the key elements that make a mental wellness program effective:

1. Top management commitment and follow-through.
2. A written policy and workable procedures.
3. Manager and supervisor commitment.
4. A coordinated effort among employees, management, and the company's mental wellness coordinator.
5. Privacy guarantees between the troubled employee and the mental wellness coordinator.
6. Professional treatment resources for each type of illness.
7. An effective communication, publicity, and education program.

> HUMAN RESOURCE DIRECTOR'S TIP:
> It's important to determine who will have access to information and treatment records and under what conditions. There is an important privacy issue here, and this should be resolved before you install a program.

---

[4] Kwasha Lipton, Benefit Consultants, 2100 North Central Road, Fort Lee, New Jersey 07024.

5.11   COMMUNICATING THE VALUE OF EMPLOYEE BENEFIT PROGRAMS

Employees tend to take benefits for granted. The only time you hear an employee make disparaging remarks about benefit programs is usually when a specific feature of a plan isn't as good as someone else's.

With the tremendous increases in the costs of benefits, more and more organizations are looking for innovative, visible ways to communicate the benefits of their total compensation and benefits programs.

One of the most commonly used tools for communicating employee benefits is the annual employee benefits letter. Every spring, hundreds of thousands of employees receive a tastefully designed computer-printed statement of their company benefits. The statements report what each employee is receiving and how much. Companies hope that this statement will begin to instill a feeling for the real cost and value of the benefits long taken for granted by employees.

Most companies have ambivalent feelings about communicating all the details of their compensation program but less reticence about benefit communications, because benefits aren't as confidential a subject and because ERISA regulations mandate benefits communication anyway.

Benefits play an extremely important part in attracting and retaining top-level people, and companies miss the boat when they don't communicate the value and cost of their benefits programs.

5.12   SAMPLE EMPLOYEE BENEFITS STATEMENT

- Employee's name, address, and Social Security number.
- Employee's gross wages for the previous year and current salary.
- A cost breakdown of the various benefits the employee has that are paid in W-2 earnings. These might include:

> Regular earnings
> Overtime earnings
> Accident/illness benefits
> Shift premiums
> Allowances
> Military pay
> Jury duty
> Funeral pay
> Holiday pay
> Vacation pay
> Service awards
> Suggestion awards
> Company car
> Relocation expenses
> Club memberships
> Lunch and coffee breaks
> Cash bonus

Stock bonus
Scholarships for employees' children
Social and recreational programs
Health/fitness programs
Physical exams
Paid parking
Food services
Medical facilities
Employee newsletters
Matching donations to colleges and universities

 Translating as many as possible of the benefit costs into a monetary value to the employee is certainly one of the best ways to sell employees on the true worth of your programs.

• Benefits paid but not included in W-2 earnings, including company contributions to:

Pension plan
Hospitalization
Life and accidental death insurance
Dental insurance
Vision insurance
Stock purchase, thrift, or other savings plans
Social Security tax on wages and salaries
Cost of premium on Workers' Compensation
Cost for tax on wages for Unemployment Compensation
Cost of tuition refund program
Cost of safety equipment

Because benefits are linked to salaries that escalate with inflation, pension and insurance payouts are moving up almost 10 percent a year, and benefits specialists say a middle manager can easily have benefits that exceed $500,000.

Benefit Trends

Many companies either have imposed a freeze on current employee health benefit levels or plan to do so, according to a *Business Insurance* survey of eighty-three employee benefit managers.[5] Overall, the study notes, 30 percent of the responding companies decided not to implement planned health benefit improvements. Twenty-three percent already had instituted a freeze within the past year, while 7 percent were planning a moratorium within the next six months on existing health benefit levels. Employers also are taking other cost-containment measures, the survey notes, including:

• *Raising health insurance deductibles.* To make workers more responsible for medical care costs, 8 percent of the surveyed companies increased deductibles within the past year, and another 7 percent planned such action over the next six months.

---

[5] "Employee Wellness Programs," *Business Insurance,* April 12, 1982. Crain Communications, 740 Rush Street, Chicago, Illinois 60611.

- *Increasing employee premium contributions.* In the past year, 6 percent of the respondents boosted the employee share of their health insurance premiums, and 8 percent said they will take this step in the coming months.
- *Establishing new claims-auditing procedures.* Forty-five percent of the employers instituted new auditing programs within the past year, and 13 percent planned to do so within the next six months.
- *Sponsoring employee wellness programs.* One-fourth of the surveyed companies initiated a wellness program during the past year, and 18 percent had such plans on the drawing board for the current year.

HUMAN RESOURCE DIRECTOR'S TIP:

The whole benefits area is complex and so regulated by various laws that few companies have the expertise in-house to manage the benefits function effectively and economically. This is an area where an outside consultant is almost always needed. Some of the most well-known consultants in this field are Towers, Perrin, Forster and Crosby; Hewitt Associates; A. S. Hansen, Inc.; and Arthur Young and Company.

CHAPTER 6

Human Resource Development

The constant acceleration of science and technology makes knowledge increasingly perishable, and this rapid change places an enormous premium on learning efficiency and timeliness and on total human resource development.

One of the most important responsibilities of the human resources director is to create an atmosphere in the organization that is open and responsive to new data and new technology, and to support employees in their efforts to stretch and seek personal challenges as they work to assist the organization in achieving its business objectives.

Because of these rapid changes, human resources development (HRD) is more critical today than it has ever been. The function must cover everything from skills and safety training to management development and retraining of workers whose jobs are made obsolete by fast-changing technology. There are hundreds of books and articles in the wide field of training and development, and they discuss in depth the common practices and procedures in the HRD field.

The American Society for Training and Development keeps its members informed of current HRD practices; their excellent publication, *Training and Development Journal*, tracks current trends in the field.

The aim of this chapter is to highlight some current HRD concerns in areas where there is little material to draw on and to highlight new trends in HRD.

6.1 COMING CHALLENGES IN HRD—THE INFORMATION AGE

Tremendous opportunity exists in one HRD field for innovation and creativity, utilizing significant new electronic telecommunications systems, more sophisticated hardware, and new participative approaches to learning and doing work. In the future, business success will be more closely intertwined with these two elements (telecommunications and participative approaches) than most of us now realize.

Significant changes will occur in the nature of work, the workplace, in the way we produce goods and services, and in the way we learn:

- Training will occur more frequently in remote classrooms, including participation, using telecommunications equipment. Video disc and computer-based instruction now provide remote learning experiences, including immediate feed-back and discussion.

- A new sense of time will emerge, and learning will be available 24 hours a day. In addition, telecommunication-based learning can be interrupted and picked up again later, with little loss in continuity.
- Both learning and work will be done more frequently at home, which will allow companies to cut down on the number of offices, plants, and equipment. The cost saving here has tremendous potential.
- There will be a new HRD emphasis on learning processes rather than merely job content; this will include the process of time management, team building, decision making, and so on.
- The central workplace will look very different. Computers will be as common-place in the office as the calculator is now. Offices will be more functional. All training will be more telecommunication-oriented. People will be freed for deci-sion making and planning. In order for this transition to be successful, advance training and human resource development must take place.

6.2   NINE WAYS TO MEET YOUR TRAINING NEEDS AND SAVE THE COMPANY MONEY

Organizations are always watching for ways to maximize revenues, and they look to the human resource director to carry the major responsibility of development and effective utilization of people at all organizational levels.

It is especially important to look for creative ways to save money and still do a good job of training and development. Following are some ideas for maximizing train-ing dollars:

1. Conduct training programs in-house, using current staff. For example, a com-pensation manager can teach a course on how to do performance reviews, or an employment manager or interviewer can teach a course for managers on interviewing. Allowing your own staff to participate in training and develop-ment activities gives them a growth opportunity and saves the company train-ing dollars.
2. Trade services with training professionals in other companies. For example, if your trainer has expertise in communication skills, and a trainer in another company you know has expertise in time management, it's cost-effective to trade out the training time on an hour-for-hour basis rather than teaching each trainer to present a new program. Maintaining contacts with other companies in order to facilitate trades in expertise makes economic sense.
3. Cut human resources training costs by charging outside seminars and confer-ences back to the department. When department managers know that outside seminar costs will show up in their budget, they are more selective when send-ing employees to outside programs.
4. Develop formal cross-training programs in-house in order to double your on-staff expertise. Include formal shadowing and mentor programs to utilize the expertise you already have.

5. Use local community colleges to provide training programs. They are usually less expensive than the large commercial companies.
6. Use more video and cassette tape programs. They cost less and can be used over and over to maximize initial development costs. A tape course can be taken while on the job or driving to and from work.
7. Set up a system of formal written critiques of all courses or seminars that the company sponsors for any employee. The critique files will tell you which programs are worthwhile and which are not. This file will help you maximize the return on your investment.
8. Check with department managers before you schedule training programs to make sure your programs will be held when the largest number of employees are available, in order to maximize the trainer's time. Classes that are not full are not cost-effective.
9. There are thousands of films, filmstrips, and slide programs that may be borrowed free of charge from companies, associations, governmental agencies, and others. *The Educator's Guide to Free Films,* found in most libraries, lists many sources.

Human Resource Development (HRD) is the new term today in the training and development arena. HRD is more than training. It's not just the administration of training and tuition refund programs, but the development of all the valuable human resources of the organization. The bottom-line return on investment in HRD is tremendous. There are many new elements, some of which you'll readily recognize:

- Computer-based training
- Video-based training
- Organizational development
- Sensitivity training
- Transactional analysis
- Assessment centers
- Quality circles
- Interpersonal skill training
- Career planning
- Media presentation skills
- Self-fulfillment and the new work ethic
- Quality of work life programs
- Organizational development intervention
- Simulation for problem solving
- Behavior modeling

The key to the success of the training and development function is being able to effect positive change in your organization and to show a return on each training dollar invested. Saving the company money is important, but it can't be so important that you forsake the quality of training. Quality and effectiveness are the absolute vital prerequisites of any training or development effort. The credibility of the training function can be lost very quickly if the quality of the training effort is compromised.

6.3 PERFORMING A TRAINING NEEDS ANALYSIS BY INTERVIEWING TOP MANAGEMENT

If the training manager tries to define organizational training and development needs in a vacuum without discussing the needs as defined by vice-presidents and key managers and directors, the overall organizational development will suffer, and top management probably won't buy in to the program.

The key to the success of the training function is frequent communication between the training manager of the human resources director and top management. It's always easier to sell programs that management supports.

If your organization does succession planning and replacement charts on key individuals at several levels, those programs usually provide individual development needs analyses and plans for getting high-potential individuals into programs that will prepare them for bigger jobs.

If discussions with key management personnel take place in the fall, the training plan can be determined in advance and a program established for the coming year.

When interviewing top management on the development needs of the people reporting to them, it's a good idea to have a predetermined list of questions that help you identify needs in a variety of areas. The following is a list of questions that might be used to identify the development needs of a supervisor or manager:

1. What type of training do you feel supervisors and managers need? Why?
2. Are current training programs filling the needs of the organization?
3. What type of training would you like for your people? For yourself?
4. Does your organization effectively use the talents of all of its people?
5. Do managers in your organization integrate their personal goals with the business objectives?
6. Do managers in your organization have opportunities for growth and actualization of their skills and abilities?
7. Do you know how to use meetings to resolve conflict and solve problems?
8. Have your managers had individual development experiences beyond their areas of specialty?
9. What are the major problems your managers face?
10. What do you think are the most common problems of supervisors and managers in your company?
11. What are the positive aspects of the company's training programs?
12. What percentage of your employee population participates in training and development programs? Why?

Scott B. Parry, president of Training House in Princeton, New Jersey, has compiled the checklist in figure 6–1 for use by corporate executives in identifying their training and development priorities.[1]

After the interviews with key executives have been completed, put together a matrix of all of the training needs that have been identified, the timing, the training staff needed to implement the programs, and the budget. Then, get the executives to choose the programs that are the most critical to them, set some priorities, and agree to a

---

[1] *Objectives for Management Development*, Dr. Scott B. Parry, President of Training House, P.O. Box 3090, Princeton, New Jersey 08540.

FIGURE 6-1.

OBJECTIVES FOR MANAGEMENT DEVELOPMENT

Here is a list of ten objectives for management development programs. In the box in front of each, place the number 3, 2, or 1. Very important=3. Somewhat important=2. Not important=1. If an item doesn't apply, put an X in the box.

☐ 1. to provide managers with a *conceptual framework* . . . and a perspective for examining their behavior and its effect on others in the organization. To satisfy this objective, programs include such concepts as: authority and responsibility, leadership, management style, types of organization, the management cycle, Theory X and Y (McGregor), motivation theory (Herzberg, McClelland, Maslow, Gellerman), etc.

☐ 2. to develop *skills for handling people.* These usually involve the application of principles drawn from the fields of communication and behavioral psychology, blended with the organization's policy and procedures. To satisfy this objective, programs include such topics as: conducting employment interviews, giving on-the-job training, conducting performance appraisals, handling discipline, counseling and coaching employees, team building, conducting effective meetings, and others. These topics should be taught as "how-to-do-it" workshops with role playing and other forms of experiential, hands-on learning.

☐ 3. to develop *skills for handling tasks.* This is the administrative side of a manager's or supervisor's responsibility. Programs designed to meet this objective include such topics as: time management, problem solving, project management, report writing, planning and scheduling, methods improvement and work simplification, and the manager's role in administering the organization's policies and procedures in such areas as wage and salary, budgets and finance, and personnel practices.

☐ 4. to impart management's way of thinking . . . a *philosophy of management.* This is sometimes considered important for those who are new to management and whose education has not provided an understanding of the values inherent in free enterprise and private ownership. Topics here include economics (the meaning of profit, long versus short-term goals, return on investment, cost-benefits analysis), the history of management (scientific management and Taylor, human relations and Mayo, motivation theory, MBO), understanding unions and labor relations, women in management, community relations, corporate social responsibility, consumerism, efficiency and waste, the sociology of the work place, organizational climate.

☐ 5. to provide a forum where managers can *exchange experience,* voice concerns, solve problems, and develop better communication with upper management. By regarding the classroom as a "senate" where the participants are "delegates" representing the various operating units of the company, top management has a sounding board and feedback mechanism . . . a two-way street to help in formulating or implementing change (in plans, policies, procedures, product, etc.). In programs where this is an objective, top management must be represented in class — either as part of the instructional team, as co-participants, or as ombudsman.

☐ 6. to build a stronger management by getting separate departments and individuals together. As managers *come to know one another personally,* the informal communication network is strengthened. Back on the job they begin to solve minor problems by directly contacting one another and working out differences rather than the more cumbersome "going through channels" that is often not appropriate (e.g., when it escalates, magnifies, or delays a problem that could have been handled "on the firing line" if only the supervisors involved had known one another). To meet this objective, participants should be seated differently at each meeting and should have many opportunities to interact and share their perceptions with one another in small group exercises.

☐ 7. to *acquaint managers with the resources* and individuals that the organization makes available to them to assist them in accomplishing their goals. Typically, the topics in a management development program relate to the services of certain staff departments (e.g., methods improvement and work simplification relates to the systems-operations-procedures department, performance appraisal to the personnel department, training and coaching of subordinates to the training department, motivation and morale to the staff psychologist or O.D. consultant, alcoholism-drugs-health to the company nurse or doctor, etc.). Where this is an objective of the management development program, staff specialists should be present — as guests to answer questions, or as cotrainers on the instructional team for that particular topic.

☐ 8. to *address specific problems or opportunities* that are now affecting the organization or that may do so in the future. Management development can be directed to current issues (e.g., decline in morale resulting from lay-offs, problems of EEO compliance, preparation for a merger or acquisition, development of a team for new overseas operations, etc.). Management development can thus be used as a tool for producing specific organizational change.

☐ 9. to demonstrate to supervisors and managers that *the organization cares* about their welfare. Top management owes its middle and lower echelons the opportunity to develop to the fullest of their potential. Management development is visible proof of the investment the organization is making in the future of these managers . . . a strong vote of confidence and support.

☐ 10. to *identify the high performing managers* and assess the strengths and weaknesses of all participants. This information is useful to top management and to Personnel in selecting managers for promotions, transfers, and other personnel action. The interactive classroom provides an opportunity for the instructor and/or members of top management to compare performance among the participating managers.

Name:_____Dept./Organization _____

companywide training program for the coming year. In order to budget and plan for training programs, you need a lead time of at least six to eight months, and a year would be even better, especially if you plan to use outside resources.

6.4 TYING THE TRAINING NEEDS ANALYSIS TO THE INDIVIDUAL PERFORMANCE APPRAISAL

One of the best ways for managers to do performance appraisals is to meet with the employee at the beginning of each year to discuss and agree upon the employee's objectives for the coming year. At this time, there is an opportunity to discuss the skills, abilities, and development needs of the employee. Tying the individual training needs analysis to the performance appraisal gives it more emphasis and could elicit a more serious development commitment from the employee.

There are many ways to assess individual development needs, but the quickest and maybe one of the best is to use an assessment form and to ask every manager to complete the form for each employee. Figure 6–2 presents two formats that would work in most companies. You can add to or eliminate data, based on your specific needs. Pick the form that best suits your company, and use it on a trial basis. An initial effort should be made to look at the fundamental concepts of management roles and styles in your organization. Many consultants have forms and methods of assessing development needs, and the American Society for Training and Development, P.O. Box 5307, Madison, Wisconsin 53705, is an excellent resource.

6.5 ETHICAL CONSIDERATIONS IN PERFORMANCE APPRAISAL AND SUCCESSION PLANNING

When completing an individual needs analysis for promotion or doing a succession plan, when individual employees are discussed, there are ethical considerations. Ask yourself the following questions, using the ones that pertain to the specific situation:

1. Do you personally know about the employee's skills and abilities?
2. Are there current performance reviews, or are they outdated? Basing a promotion decision on an outdated appraisal could be a mistake.
   For example, five years ago, the wife of the man you're considering for promotion had a serious illness, and he missed a great deal of work. After the family problem was resolved, the man did not have an absentee problem and was an outstanding employee. You should not let that one incident reflect on a current promotion decision.
3. Are current performance reviews subjective and personality-based, rather than performance-related?
4. If the job does not require a college degree and if the employee has comparable work experience, do you still insist on the college degree?
5. If you have an employee who is marginal, but you can't level with him or her, do you give a good performance review, rather than giving the bad news?
6. Do you keep performance appraisal information confidential? It's unethical to discuss one employee's appraisal information with another employee.

FIGURE 6-2.

INDIVIDUAL DEVELOPMENT NEEDS ANALYSIS

Name	Department	Date		
Development Need		O	M	DN
Gathering and analyzing data				
Planning objectives				
Organizing a function				
Selecting people				
Training people				
Utilizing people				
Delegating				
Coaching, developing people				
Motivating others				
Building credibility				
Interpersonal skills				
Oral expression				
Writing				
Works well with supervisors				
Works well with peers				
Works well with subordinates				
Achieving results through others				
Controlling operations				
Follow-through				
Measuring results				
Reporting feedback				
Controlling costs				
Budgeting				
Promoting the company				
Promoting good morale				
Creative problem-solver				
Gets things done on time				
Develops and promotes his or her people				
Handles discipline problems				
Other skills development:				

_____

_____

_____

O = Outstanding
M = Meets requirements
DN = Development need

7. When you are thinking of promoting or transferring an employee, do you look into an appraisal where there are broad, general statements made, to determine if the information is factual?
8. Do you make a copy of all written appraisals available to the employee?
9. Do you ask the employee for input into the appraisal?
10. Do you provide for an employee appeal of the performance appraisal?

Managers should be encouraged to show respect for their employees by giving feedback, coaching, leveling, and counseling regarding performance. There are special programs to train managers in these skills. One good one is Xerox Learning System's program on Interpersonal Managing Skills.[2]

The questions of ethics and employee privacy are coming under increasing scrutiny.

HUMAN RESOURCE DIRECTOR'S TIP:

Be aware of the ethical considerations of succession planning, promotion, and performance appraisal. Don't judge the worth of an employee on other than performance-based criteria and previously agreed-upon results. In the coming years, there will be more litigation on promotion criteria and promotion decisions, which previously may have been management prerogative and maybe not as performance-based as they could be. Good performance also includes all those characteristics that make an effective, successful employee: good interpersonal skills, self-starter, ability to get things done, good conceptual skills, and so on.

6.6   THE TRAINING PLAN—FORMS FOR USE IN FACILITATING TRAINING PROGRAMS

Whether you use an MBO (management by objectives) approach to training planning or a simpler format setting out a yearly calendar of training events, some form of written plan will facilitate the overall development effort. Figures 6–3, 6–4, 6–5, and 6–6 present formats that can be used effectively.

They include three formats for a training and management development plan, a sample training schedule, a specific training and development plan one company used, and a training program request form.

HUMAN RESOURCE DIRECTOR'S TIP:

It's difficult for the human resource director or training manager to "sell" the programs. There's a self-serving tone implied in the effort. It's a good idea to form an advisory board made up of professional or managerial employees from each major functional area to advise on the effectiveness of training programs and to sell the programs in their respective departments.

---

[2] Xerox Learning Systems, One Pickwick Plaza, Greenwich, Connecticut 06830.

FIGURE 6-3.

XYZ COMPANY
SAMPLE TRAINING AND MANAGEMENT DEVELOPMENT PLAN
Summer and Fall

Date	Course	Time
July 7, 8, 9, 13, 14 (5 half-days)	Management Skills (Planning, Organizing, Controlling)	8:00 A.M.–11:30 A.M.
21, 22 (2 sessions) "A" — 7/21 "B" — 7/22 (6 hours)	How to Conduct a Performance Appraisal	8:00 A.M.–3:00 P.M.
August 12, 13 (2 sessions) "A" — 8/12 "B" — 8/13 (6 hours)	Interviewing Skills	8:00 A.M.–3:00 P.M.
18 (7 hours)	Communications Workshop	7:30 A.M.–3:30 P.M.
September 10, 11 (3 hours)	Conducting Effective Meetings	To be arranged by group or department
23–25 (2½ days)	Functional Business Presentations	8:00 A.M.–4:00 P.M.
October 1, 2, 5, 6, 7 (5 half days)	Management Communication Skills	8:00 A.M.–11:30 A.M.
15, 16, 19 (2½ days)	Writing for Professionals and Managers	8:00 A.M.–4:00 P.M.
29, 30 (2 half-days)	Time Management	8:00 A.M.–12:00 P.M.
November 3 (4 hours)	Introduction to Mining, Part I	8:00 A.M.–12:00 P.M.
12 (4 hours)	Introduction to Mining, Part II	8:00 A.M.–12:00 P.M.
December 8, 9, 11 (2½ days)	Finance for the Nonfinancial Manager	8:00 A.M.–4:00 P.M.
12, 14, 15 (3 days)	Data Processing for the Non-Data Processing Manager	8:00 A.M.–4:00 P.M.

FIGURE 6-4.

XYZ COMPANY   SAMPLE TRAINING SCHEDULE

MARCH	APRIL	MAY	JUNE	JULY
7, 8—Effective Technical Writing Workshop 10, 11—Effective Presentation Skills	12, 13, 14—Interviewing Skills Workshop. In-house. 19, 20—AMA Program. Finance for the Nonfinancial Manager	4, 5, 6—How to Manage by Objectives 23, 24—Project Management	13, 14, 15, 16—The Manager's Job: How to Plan, Organize, and Control Your Function 27—Secretary's Workshop in Communications	11, 12—How to Manage Conflict 26, 27—Motivation and Productivity
AUGUST	**SEPTEMBER**	**OCTOBER**	**NOVEMBER**	**DECEMBER**
18, 19—Train the Trainer. In-house. 25—First Aid for Supervisors and Managers	21, 22—Communication Skills Workshop for Supervisors. In-house.	12, 13—Time Management 17, 18—Safety and Health Workshop	10, 11—Positive Discipline for Supervisors and Managers	7, 8, 9—Creating Productive Work Relationships

FIGURE 6-5.

SWENSON EQUIPMENT COMPANY
Training and Development Plan
January

Programs   Hours   Date Scheduled

Skills Training:

- Blueprint Reading
- Lathe Operation
- Purchasing/Warehousing
- Welding
- Safety and Health
- Safe Driving
- Word Processing

Supervisory Training:

- Supervisory Skills I, II, III
- Interviewing Workshop
- Performance Appraisal Workshop
- Communication Skills Workshop
- Data Processing for the Non-Data-Processing
  User

Management Development:

- Planning, Organizing, and Controlling a Func-
  tion
- Written Communication—Track I
- Technical Writing—Track II
- Coaching and Developing Employees
- Financial Forecasting and Budgeting
- Advanced Communication Skills for Managers
- Middle-Management Development Program

FIGURE 6-6.

<u>TRAINING PROGRAM REQUEST</u>

Program: _____

Department: _____ Date: _____

TO: _____

FROM: _____

REQUEST: _____
                        (Program Name)

     A.   Statement of problem to be addressed.

     B.   Results desired (objectives of program).

     C.   Suggested type of program.

     D.   Department personnel in need of training.

     E.   Scope of training.

     F.   Desired implementation date.

     G.   Budget.

Requesting department: _____

Approved by: _____
(if approvals are
     necessary)

_____
(Date)

6.7 COST–BENEFIT ANALYSIS OF TRAINING—A QUANTITATIVE METHOD

Even though more executives have come to recognize the need for training and development of people and the long-term economic benefit to an organization of a well-trained staff, most top executives still want human resource or training managers to justify the cost of training programs, especially in times of an economic downturn. As a human resource director, you have to use appropriate business techniques to sell your programs and to prove their effectiveness.

Glenn E. Head and Charles C. Buchanan of Instructional Communications, Inc., Denver, Colorado, have developed a cost–benefit analysis model (see figure 6–7), and provide the following information.[3]

The corporate training cost model is an attempt to get you started in the analysis process. For the model to be effective in your individual case, you will have to create your own values and judgments, customizing the model to meet your requirements.

Five elements constitute training cost: student cost, instructor cost, facilities cost, administrative cost, and instructional development cost. Each of these elements, when calculated and totaled for each course or training program, will result in a reasonable estimate of cost.

The first element, student costs, is reflected in table 1 of figure 6–7. Note the lost opportunity cost factor in the formula. This is defined as the value of the productivity being lost because the trainee is not on the job. Several techniques have been used to calculate the value of this factor. In one case, a manufacturing company found that in a supervisor–foreman course, in addition to the salary cost (a substitute was required while the supervisor–foreman was in the course), the production line actually slowed down while the supervisor–foreman was absent. As a result, the company decided that for the course being considered, the lost opportunity factor was equal to the student salary per day multiplied by the course length in days, the number of students, and then by 4 to accommodate the slowdown.

Another company found that when they held a course for operators of expensive heavy equipment, the equipment did not remain idle. Additional operators were on the payroll to fill in during training. As a result, the total cost of training included the salary cost of these replacement operators multiplied by the number of students and the course length.

One other example is the company that decided to calculate lost opportunity cost by determining the amount of dollars each individual in a particular job category contributed to gross corporate revenues. By dividing the gross corporate revenues earned per trainee by the number of productive days in the year, and then multiplying that figure by the number of days in the course, the value of productivity lost while the worker was in training was determined.

Lost opportunity cost is a significant factor that should not be overlooked when determining student cost. The method you use to calculate its value must be realistic for your situation. Just remember that you are after the corporate cost of training. (See tables 2 through 6 of figure 6–7 for the remaining elements of the cost analysis mode.)

---

[3] "Cost–Benefit Analysis of Training," Glenn E. Head and Charles C. Buchanan, Instructional Communications, Inc., Denver, Colorado.

FIGURE 6-7.

COST–BENEFIT ANALYSIS OF TRAINING

Table 1. Student Cost

$$(NS \times L \times SS) + (SPD \times L) + (NS \times STC) + (NS \times LO) = S'$$

NS	=	number of students
L	=	course length in days (including travel time)
SS	=	student salary per day (monthly pay + fringe ÷ 21)
SPD	=	student cost per day (housing + meals + tips)
STC	=	student travel cost (round-trip fare + local travel cost)
CO	=	lost opportunity cost per student
S'	=	total student cost

Table 2. Instructor Cost

$$(NI \times IS) + (L \times IPD) + (NI \times IT) + LO = I'$$

NI	=	number of instructors
IS	=	instructor salary per day (monthly pay + fringe ÷ 21)
L	=	course length in days
IPD	=	instructor cost per day (housing + meals + tips)
IT	=	instructor travel expense (round-trip fare + local travel cost)
LO	=	lost opportunity cost (ability to create new programs)
I'	=	total instructor cost

Table 3. Facilities Cost

$$(AO \div NSD) \times L \times NS = F'$$

AO	=	annual overhead (utilities, space, maintenance, administration of building or rent as applicable)
NSD	=	number of students days per year
L	=	course length in days
NS	=	number of students
F'	=	total facilities cost

FIGURE 6-7 (cont'd)

COST–BENEFIT ANALYSIS OF TRAINING

Table 4. Administrative Cost

$$LM + LC + SM + SC + S = A'$$

LM = line management costs (percentage devoted to employee training administration)
LC = line clerical costs
SM = staff management cost within the training department (annual cost + NSD/year × NSD of training option or precise allocation)
SC = staff clerical—training department
S = supplies
A' = total administration cost

Table 5. Instructional Development Cost

$$(PL \times T) + (ID \times T) + (SME \times T) + P + M + E = D'$$

PL = project leader—salary per day (monthly pay + fringe ÷ 21)
T = time in days on project
ID = instructional designer—salary per day
SME = subject matter expert—salary per day
P = production cost (writers, artists, talent, direct costs)
M = materials cost (books, equipment)
E = evaluation costs
ID' = total instructional development cost

Table 6. Corporate Training Cost

$$S' + I' + F' + A' + ID' = CTC$$

S' = total student cost
I' = total instructor cost
F' = total facilities cost
A' = total administrative cost
ID' = total instructional development cost
CTC = total corporate training cost

You don't need to use such a sophisticated system to identify the costs of training in your company. You can use simpler methods. *The Training and Development Handbook*, sponsored by the American Society for Training and Development, provides a different training cost analysis format.[4] Another good reference book on this subject is *Costs, Benefits, and Productivity in Training Systems* by Greg Kearsley.[5]

6.8 USE OF COMPUTERS IN TRAINING

Computers are rapidly becoming an important training tool. Thousands of corporations and educational institutions are using computers for a wide variety of training and instructional applications. The terms "computer-based training (CBT)" or "computer-based instruction (CBI)" imply the use of a computer to author materials, manage students, and deliver instruction.

The use of a computer to deliver instruction alone is called computer-assisted instruction (CAI). With CAI, the trainee sits at a computer terminal while the computer presents information. The trainee responds to the information and receives further information, based upon his or her responses.

The use of a computer to manage trainees administratively, that is, to record trainee progress, is called computer-managed instruction (CMI). CMI is more valuable within most training situations because it allows the creation of individualized lessons. Each person can be trained according to his or her individual needs, with the CMI system tracking and measuring the learner's performance. More importantly, training materials are available in any medium. Systems can be relatively simple or highly complex, depending upon the needs of the organization.

Glenn Head, president of Instructional Communications, Inc., based in Denver, Colorado, provides the following questions and answers on the use of computers in training.[6]

Q: When is computer-based training most useful?

A: Computer-based training is most valuable when the performance required of trainees is defined and measurable. Generally, effective training materials will be designed following a systems approach, with criterion-referenced measures of trainee performance.

Typical courses include anything of a "how-to" nature: how to install a device or product, how to service a product or maintain a piece of equipment, how to sell, manage, develop, design, organize, or measure.

The critical component of teaching the how-to is the instructional approach. The computer is only the highly valuable tool that will allow the trainer to utilize sound instructional design principles. The tool can be effective within any training setting, provided the instructional developer utilizes it in the proper manner.

Q: How are companies using computers in training?

---

[4] *Training and Development Handbook, Second Edition,* Robert L. Craig, editor. Sponsored by the American Society for Training and Development, published by McGraw-Hill Book Company, New York, New York.

[5] *Costs, Benefits, and Productivity in Training Systems,* by Greg Kearsley. Published by Addison-Wesley, 1982.

[6] "Use of Computers in Training," Glenn E. Head, President, Instructional Communications, Inc. P.O. Box 6312, Cherry Creek Station, Denver, Colorado 80206.

A: Some companies are using computers to deliver training at distant locations. This avoids travel costs and takes training to the trainee, rather than the more traditional approach of bringing the trainee to the training. Other companies are using computers to manage trainees in learning centers.

Training content can cover almost any subject. One organization teaches trainees how to drive special equipment; another uses computers to provide instruction on completing insurance forms. Equipment repair is a frequent topic for courses. Computer simulations are being used in areas where trainee safety and equipment costs are important. Computers also are used to operate video equipment. Computer-controlled videotape and videodisc are becoming popular applications.

Q: What is computer simulation?

A: A computer can be programmed to act like another piece of equipment. Screen displays can look like control panels for almost any device. The trainee can use the computer keyboard, touch screen, or light pen—and, soon, voice input—to make the computer respond just as the device being simulated would respond in an actual situation.

Computer simulations have been used for many years, especially within the military and the airline industry. Today, the lower cost of microcomputers is making simulation affordable for many industrial applications. Computers are being used to simulate real problems and concepts for training in many fields, including medicine, music, and oil field techniques.

In many cases, trainees can learn more from simulation than from actual equipment, because what would be potentially dangerous using real equipment can be experienced without danger through simulation. Additionally, it is easy to insert random faults and problems with the computer that would be very difficult to control using actual equipment.

Q: Do trainees like working on computers?

A: A number of studies have been conducted to analyze trainee attitudes toward computer-based instruction. Virtually all of them indicate high trainee acceptance when adequate preparation has been made. Many of the studies indicate that trainees prefer the computer to the traditional group-paced approach. Instructors, however, often dislike the computer because they feel it is replacing them. Instructors must be provided with additional training to prepare them to function efficiently in a computer-based training environment.

Q: Will computers save money in training?

A: The money saved through the use of computers is the result almost entirely of the instructional approach the computer permits. Individualized, self-paced training has been proven effective in reducing trainee time in class while, in many cases, improving the quality of learning.

Studies have found reductions in training time ranging from 20 to 70 percent. The vast majority of this reduction resulted from the application of a systems approach to training, utilizing criterion-referenced instructional material with defined performance outcomes. While the computer is not directly responsible for this savings, it is the single tool that allows the creation of this more sophisticated training environment.

Q: What kind of instructors are needed for computer-based training?

A: The more sophisticated environment of computer-based training requires a professional, usually called an instructional technologist. This person might have an educational background in psychology, learning theory, computer science, media, or industrial engineering, as well as other skills. This person generally is not a subject matter expert or an instructor.

Utilized properly, an instructional technologist might save hundreds of thousands of dollars in training costs, primarily through cost avoidance. The training created by this person is effective in producing a trainee capable of job–task performance. This person also is capable of working with the structure of the job to ensure that it is designed to allow an employee with a reasonable level of training to accomplish the tasks required.

Q: Can computer specialists provide the training?

A: Data processing people don't design the training materials. That's the job of the training department. The training manager usually controls both subject content and instructional approach.

Q: Has the effectiveness of computer-based training been proven?

A: The use of computers in training has been studied since the early 1960s. One estimate places the investment in CBT at between $500 million and $1 billion. Almost every government agency has projects involving the use of CBT. The U.S. Senate, the Library of Congress, and hundreds of corporations—including IBM, AT&T, EXXON, General Motors, Target Stores, United Airlines, Texas Instruments, and Aetna Life Insurance—have CBT projects ranging from small feasibility studies to full-scale implementations. Thousands of public elementary and secondary schools also have computers in their classrooms.

Q: How should I begin using computer-based training?

A: Most begin with a feasibility study. This study should include an analysis of the existing training program to determine current costs. Only then can one determine the expected benefits of CBT. The feasibility study should identify training areas with the highest payoff potential. It also should identify the expected return on investment.

This study should be done either by a consulting firm with experience in the design, development, and implementation of CBT systems or by someone hired as an employee who has hands-on experience. Vendors of CBT systems may suggest solutions that fit their system, and their system may not be the best one for your company. When dealing with consultants, ask them in detail about their hands-on experience.

The second step is usually a small-scale project designed to demonstrate the potential effectiveness of CBT. This demonstration project generally will lead to the development of a broader functional specification. This document will become the basis for the design of the system that will fit your corporate needs.

A competent consulting firm will find a vendor willing to customize their system to fit your needs. You should find a consultant who will work for you somewhat like an architect, someone who will help design a system to meet your needs. The consultant should assist you in finding an appropriate vendor and provide plans to that vendor for the design of your system; but the consultant works for you, not the vendor.

Maintain a sensitivity to new approaches to training that involve the use of computer technology. Many of the most aggressive companies are turning to instructional technology to improve job performance. The use of individualized, self-paced training has demonstrated capabilities to increase the effectiveness and efficiency of training. The computer has demonstrated capabilities to manage training and to enhance instructional delivery. The challenge is to use computer technology in a way that will benefit both the trainee and the company.

The leading professional society in the area of human performance technology is the National Society for Performance and Instruction (NSPI), 1126 16th Street, N.W., Suite 315, Washington, D.C. 20036.

The ad (shown in figure 6–8) for PLATO, a CBT system, gives a brief review of the diverse capabilities of computer-based training. Control Data's PLATO is one of the most popular CBT systems. In fact, in a move that marks a major development in the computer-assisted instruction industry, Control Data Corporation has agreed to supply educational programs from its PLATO system for use on home computers made by Texas Instruments of Dallas. Under the agreement, 450 programs and 108 educational courseware packages, previously available only on the mainframe-based PLATO system, will be converted for the TI 99–4a home computer.

For two decades, CDC has pioneered computer-based education systems and has developed more than 12,000 programs for the PLATO system.

6.9 QUESTIONS AND ANSWERS ON ASSESSMENT CENTERS, QUALITY CIRCLES, AND QUALITY OF WORK LIFE PROGRAMS

These are three new and rather controversial assessment and work methods areas that require involvement of the human resources director and training manager, and generate numerous questions.

The problem that continues to trouble most companies is why competent executives continue to hire and promote the wrong people. A brief review of common selection problems reveals the following:

1. Misinterpretation of résumé and application data is common among managers and executives who interview. Past performance is a good predictor of future performance, but it takes more than questions about the technical and operations part of the job to get the information you need about the person's behavior. Most people can learn to interview and to tell the story they need to tell in order to get a job. In addition, many people interpret information from a base of their own motives, their own personalities and environment, thinking that others will have similar characteristics.
2. Inexperienced executives, when interviewing, may let one dimension of the individual favorably or unfavorably influence their decision.
3. When an executive is in a hurry to fill the job, a candidate with less than top qualifications may be hired for the sake of expediency.

There are other reasons for using a more objective method of hiring and promoting people; these are only a few. A formal assessment process provides a more objective picture of a person's qualifications and interpersonal and managerial skills.

FIGURE 6-8.

Control Data's PLATO is changing how the world learns.

Business and industry are turning to PLATO® computer-based training to meet the most massive training and retraining challenge in U.S. history. Technology is changing too fast, competition is too keen, and time is too short for anything less than the state-of-the-art answer to training's toughest problems.

Developed by Control Data, PLATO computer-based training is a major advance in self-paced individualized learning.

Because of its proven ability to produce better-trained, more proficient employees, it is the choice of companies respected for their training excellence.

• Leading airlines use PLATO for the quality of flight and maintenance crew training that

is absolutely essential in the airline industry.

• Major utilities rely on PLATO for the critical job of training nuclear plant operators, dispatchers and maintenance personnel in safety procedures.

• Auto makers are turning to PLATO for the tough challenge of retraining people for the advancing technologies needed to build better cars.

PLATO

FIGURE 6-8 (cont'd)

- Large pharmaceutical companies use PLATO to take training to their field sales forces, reducing travel cost.

- A consortium of oil companies use PLATO to help industry personnel master the latest techniques in the search and development of energy.

In finance, manufacturing, research, sales—every sector of business and industry is using PLATO to sharpen its productive edge.

PLATO is unique.
PLATO gives you interactive, individualized training—cost effectively. One-on-one, it manages the *entire* learning process. It tests, grades, evaluates, monitors, counsels *and feeds the results back* to the learner. It responds

to touch—keyboard or screen—with split-second accuracy. It makes complex technology easier to understand and use.

PLATO graphics can simulate virtually any schematic. You can store and retrieve all the information necessary for your process. Most importantly, users tell us that people trained by PLATO retain what they learn longer and perform better on the job.

All this adds up to cost-efficient training—individualized training on a scale that no traditional method can match. *Your employees can learn faster, learn better,* and become more productive without leaving their work location.

Use PLATO to keep pace with changing technologies.
PLATO's more than 7000 hours of standardized courseware is ready to be put to work on your tough training problems. Or we can help you develop specific training programs to help meet your most critical needs.

There are no barriers to PLATO training. You can train your employees wherever and whenever the need exists. PLATO can be used anywhere within your main location, at a branch office or at any of Control Data's 100 Learning Centers.

Ask for an executive briefing. Learn how PLATO computer-based training can help your employees keep pace with technology and increase their productivity. Call 800/328-1109 or write Control Data, HQV003-3, P.O. Box 0, Minneapolis, MN 55440.

ᏩᏋ CONTROL DATA

Addressing society's major unmet needs as profitable business opportunities

Q. What is an assessment center?

A. Rather than calling it an assessment center, we should call it an assessment process. It's a method where employees or prospective employees participate in a series of work-related situations closely resembling those they might be expected to face in that specific work environment. They are tested by participating in situational and simulated exercises. Several trained assessors relate the simulated problems and then process the information and final data in an impartial manner. The assessment process measures critical job-related skills and abilities.

Q. Why should a company have an assessment process?

A. The assessment process is a highly organized way of collecting data on individuals. In addition, it provides a more objective content-valid method for evaluating an individual.

Q. Can you have an assessment center in-house?

A. You can set up your own assessment process in-house, or you can send people to an outside firm that provides assessment evaluations.

Q. Who can design the assessment process? Do you need a psychologist?

A. You don't need a psychologist to design the process, but you do need someone who knows human resource management systems and something about career paths, development, counseling, and selection. In addition, the person should be sensitive to administrative concerns and issues like equal employment opportunity, fair employment practices, and testing procedures.

Q. What should we tell employees about the assessment process?

A. There is probably a certain degree of fear associated with any assessment and evaluation process. People should be put at ease. Tell them exactly how you intend to use the data, where they will ultimately be stored, who will have access to the data, and so on. If the assessment and evaluation process is to have credibility, there must be a feeling of trust regarding use, dissemination, and storage of the results.

Q. How do you measure the validity of the assessment process?

A. Employee selection guidelines that appeared in the *Federal Register 1978* are acceptable measures of validity.[7] When simulated or situational exercises are formulated, they must be based on an actual job analysis.

There have been court rulings on hiring and promotion as a result of the use of assessment centers within the context of fair employment practices; however, the compilation of court rulings and opinions bears out the fact that assessment centers are appropriate when content-valid criteria are applied. A good article on this subject appeared in the June 1982 issue of the *Personnel Administrator.*[8]

Q. What happens after the assessment and evaluation? Are people given the results?

A. Assessees should be given feedback on the results of the evaluation and informed of recommendations made. In addition, the assessee should be told what data were collected and how they're to be used, disseminated, and stored.

Figure 6–9 shows the elements of the assessment process.

---

[7] Equal Employment Opportunity Commission, Civil Service Commission, Department of Labor, Department of Justice, "Uniform Guidelines on Employee Selection Procedures," *Federal Register,* vol. 43, no. 166, August 25, 1978.

[8] "The Validity of the Assessment Center Approach and Related Issues," Fredric D. Frank and James B. Preston, *Personnel Administrator,* June 1982.

FIGURE 6-9.
RELATIONSHIPS THAT SHOW THE
CONTENT VALIDITY OF AN
ASSESSMENT PROCESS

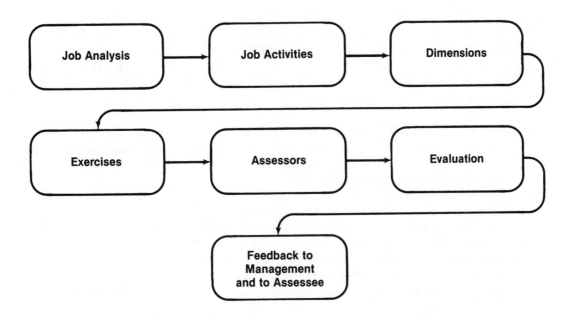

6.10 QUALITY CIRCLES—GIMMICKS OR VALUABLE MORALE BUILDERS?

U.S. industry has rushed to adapt the Japanese productivity-improvement quality circle (QC) idea. A typical QC program includes autonomous groups of employees, usually eight or ten, who meet weekly to discuss product quality and production problems and to make suggestions for improvement.

Some of the benefits are:

• Higher productivity
• Greater teamwork
• Higher motivation
• Greater safety awareness
• A more open worker–manager relationship
• Reduced production costs
• Capitalizing on people's talents

According to an article that appeared in the January 11, 1982, issue of *Business Week,* there are about 1,500 companies that now have quality circles. A new question was raised in 1982 with a marked increase in layoffs. The question is whether a collaborative approach can survive if workers believe that their cooperation in cutting costs and improving quality and output will not result in greater job security. Most companies guarantee that layoffs will not result from work-improvement suggestions.

One company, Allied Tube and Conduit, at its plant in Harvey, Illinois, has had such a good experience in cutting costs through quality circles that it was able to weather a business slowdown in 1982 by going to four-day work weeks rather than scheduling a massive layoff. When business picked up, they went back to the regular five-day work week. Here are some questions and answers regarding quality circles:

Q. How do you establish a quality circle program?

A. An important first step is to become as familiar as you can with the whole subject. Read extensively, attend a seminar or workshop, and contact companies that have QCs, to get the pros and cons of starting your own program. Hewlett-Packard, Honeywell, and Lockheed are three large companies that have QCs.

There are six key elements in most quality circle programs:

1. *Steering committee.* Consists of several managers who represent a cross-section of the company: production, product assurance, personnel, marketing, research and development, finance. They are responsible for establishing overall objectives and operating guidelines.
2. *Facilitator.* Trains team leaders and helps train the members. The facilitator is a resource to the team and serves as process consultant.
3. *Leader.* Usually the immediate supervisor of the members. This individual guides the direction and process of the QC.
4. *Members.* Make up the primary element of the QC.
5. *Nonmembers.* Also involved, they may have chosen not to join a team, but they are still affected by team activities and decisions or actions implemented by the team.
6. *Specialists.* Occasionally brought in to help the team. This usually is done when a team needs additional data. These specialists are usually engineers, statisticians, accounting, or personnel people.

Q. What are some of the characteristics of the successful QC program?

A. There is top-management approval and visible support. There is a participative people-building philosophy. Team efforts are stressed, as opposed to individual efforts. Creativity is encouraged, and there is more freedom to solve problems. Training is provided for both workers and managers. Both quantity and quality improve. QCs are measurement-oriented. There's an interdisciplinary approach that involves many people.

Q. What are some of the concerns of the QC program?

A. The major concern seems to be that some organizations are using them as quick-fix programs for raising productivity without stressing the importance of QCs as long-term programs. Using QCs as gimmicks to increase quality or productivity, and not tying them to a total employee participation program, is shortsighted.

A lack of training and preparation is another reason given for the failure of some QCs. Some managements took up the QC idea as more of a fad, without building the trust and credibility between management and workers that make a QC program a success.

Another reason for failure has been that unionized companies didn't consult with the unions before installing QCs, and did not include union members on the steering committee.

Q. What are the other elements of successful QCs?

A. QCs must have clear goals and objectives. It's easy to meet and discuss problems and lose sight of the time, but time is money, so the team must understand that and use their time productively. Team members should be prepared for the meetings in order to save time.

It's a good idea to rotate the team leader responsibility, perhaps every dozen or so meetings.

QCs are successful when the suggestions and results of the meetings are used. If teams meet and make suggestions, and the suggestions are not utilized, QCs can be a waste of time.

Q. Do QCs work only in blue-collar, production-type environments?

A. No, they also work in clerical jobs and almost any other type of job where there are a lot of people doing the same type of work.

Supermarkets are trying QCs. There are 28,680 supermarkets across the country that take in $171.6 million per year, but they realize a profit only on about 1 percent to 2 percent of gross sales for their net profits. There are approximately 2,000 stores trying QCs, according to the April 18, 1982, issue of the *New York Times*. Broken eggs, spoiled meat, wilted vegetables, and absenteeism are only a few of the problems they are trying to solve.

HUMAN RESOURCE DIRECTOR'S TIP:

The degree of involvement of various levels of management is critical to success. It's essential that middle managers and line supervisors both run part of the program. The staff people or the facilitator get in the habit of going directly to the production workers, bypassing management. You must make sure managers are given a part in the implementation of the program and in making some of the decisions about it. Furthermore, the program must be tied to the goals middle managers are rated on.

6.11 WHAT IS QUALITY OF WORK LIFE, AND IS IT WORKING?

Quality of work life (QWL) involves employees in improving their work and work lives. It provides problem solving, training, and team building, and gives the employee more information about the job and the company's business. Although participation is important, pay tied to performance, work-time flexibility, and lesiure options are also elements of most programs.

QWL uses participatory processes instead of the normal top-down orders and rigid rules and regulations. QWL programs foster a more people-oriented, collaborative organization. Companies that have QWL programs say they are better able to respond to change.

The *New York Times* has called QWL programs the gospel of worker participation. *Business Week* and *Fortune* have featured articles on the new "human side of enterprise."

Human resource issues finally have captured the attention of management after thirty years of behavioral sciences flag-waving. It appears that employee participation programs aren't a fad. Devotees at Harvard and MIT say that employee participation and QWL programs do make organizations more effective. The key to success, however, is in the total commitment of management to programs and to the concept, the follow-through. One of the most publicized QWL programs is the one at the General Motors assembly plant in Tarrytown, New York. Both *Harvard Business Review* and *Newsweek* have published articles on the GM success. GM has asked all 100,000 salaried employees to complete a QWL assessment form. They have designed QWL programs for many of their locations and describe dramatic results: absenteeism reduced by 90 percent and a drop in grievances from 3,000 to less than 70. GM has invested millions in making life better for employees.

HUMAN RESOURCE DIRECTOR'S TIP:

If you want to install a QWL program, talk to some of the human resource directors in companies that have such a program. Don't reinvent the wheel. Then, start with a pilot program and build support.

If management doesn't believe in and support the program, you're better off not installing it.

A few companies who have QWL programs:

General Motors
Honeywell
American Hospital Supply
AT&T
Xerox
Lincoln National Life
Ford Motor Company

Resources on Quality of Work Life Programs

- *Directory of U.S. Productivity and Innovation Centers.* U.S. Chamber of Commerce, 1615 H Street N.W., Washington, D.C. 20062.
- Work in America Institute, 700 White Plains Road, Scarsdale, New York 10583.
- American Center for Quality of Work Life, 3301 New Mexico Avenue, N.W., Washington, D.C. 20016.

At least three universities are conducting studies on QWL programs. They are Harvard, the Wharton School (University of Pennsylvania), and the University of California, at Berkeley.

6.12 IDEAS FOR IMPLEMENTING A TRAINING FUNCTION AT AN OUTLYING LOCATION

There may be several differences between starting a training function at an outlying location and starting one at corporate headquarters. Not everyone agrees on this subject. There seem to be two points of view, so two sides of the question are included here. The two sides give enough data to review and from which to select the best ideas for your particular organization. Both sides agree that there must be:

1. Top management commitment to training and development.
2. A training budget that is sufficient for the needs of the work force at the site location.
3. An assessment of specific training needs based on the jobs to be filled, the technical skills needed, and the skill levels of the people who will fill the jobs.

After these initial elements are considered, the following items may be reviewed:

Side I. There are different needs for startup of a training operation at an outlying location. Some startup traits that are different from those of a headquarters facility might be:

1. If the new operation is in a remote area, you may need to make more use of video equipment in training, especially for skills or safety training.
2. Site employees may have a variety of work schedules and overlapping responsibilities, and video equipment provides a self-paced, diverse training tool.
3. There seem to be more repetitive-type jobs at site locations. Video equipment is particularly cost-effective when used in repetitive situations.
4. Local schools at both the secondary and college levels often can provide training by part-time instructors at your site or at the school. They might be able to provide skills training, office education, and managerial-level training.
5. If the company has more than one outlying location, the training films you produce can be utilized at each site, making them more cost-effective.
6. There may be union considerations at the outlying locations, which may or may not be the case at the corporate headquarters.
7. Travel time to and from the site may dictate the amount of time that can be devoted each day to training. Travel time also might affect work and training schedules.
8. If there is a lengthy commute to and from the work place, you may want to take advantage of tape recorders and cassette tapes. Many outside tape courses are available on a variety of subjects.
9. There may be a need for correspondence-type courses at a remote site. One company successfully used a correspondence course in elementary electronics to help their people learn to do simple repairs to some equipment in the field, and saved thousands of dollars in down time.
10. Another company used vans to transport their people to and from the work site each day. There was an hour of travel time, and the training manager used the time well by putting new recruits in the same van and giving training sessions in the van.

Side II. Initiation of training at satellite locations parallels that at a corporate headquarters or single-site operation. According to Julie B. Aragon, director of employee development at NERCO, Inc., an energy and resources company, certain steps should be followed to ensure a sound program that helps contribute to the overall corporate goals and profit. She maximizes training at existing locations by:

1. Involving existing senior and middle management in determining training priorities, using information gained in the assessment process, because these peo-

ple need to feel a sense of ownership of the training projects to help ensure success of the programs. Having them participate in priority setting is a key way to gain needed ownership. A forced-choice comparison of the determined needs is a good way to have the group set priorities. In this process, each item is compared with every other item to determine ranking of the items.

2. Researching the available resources to meet the prioritized needs; identifying those consultants or programs that will most closely meet the needs.
3. Deciding the cost-effectiveness of identified training programs being held in-house.
4. Scheduling the in-house programs far enough in advance to allow for signup and adequate staff coverage for the participants.
5. Determining the location of the seminar (at the site or in a hotel), consultant's or program's audiovisual needs, participants' needs (breaks, lunch), consultant's travel needs, and arranging to meet those needs.
6. Evaluating the appropriateness and value of the seminar for continued use and impact on the training need. A questionnaire is a convenient tool and can be distributed shortly after the seminar. A sample form follows. Later, the seminar's effect on work or interpersonal capabilities of the participants can be evaluated by the attendees' supervisors.
7. Encouraging the participants' managers to provide opportunities for the individuals to use their recent training. If the new knowledge or skill is not used soon afterward, the training is not as valuable and can be lost. This is a most important step and one that is often ignored, but without this important follow-up initial training costs can't be maximized.
8. Periodically reviewing with senior management the overall effectiveness of training programs. Reassessment of training needs should be done whenever significant organizational or staffing changes occur, or at least every few years, in a stable environment.

Developing Locations

All of the preceding steps should be done at new locations, but according to Aragon, a few additional things need to happen earlier:

1. With as much advance time as possible, develop long-range manpower planning for the new site. Answer such questions as:
   a. Do we want to pull staff from existing sites to staff the developing one?
   b. If yes, which staff?
   c. What are the predetermined skills needed by the staff at the new site?
   d. Do we train them when they are at the new site to ensure a consistency of thought, or do we have them trained in advance to gain earlier productivity upon arrival?
2. Analyze the impact on the existing sites if staff is to transfer to the new site. If significant numbers of people are transferred, this definitely alters the training needs at that site.
3. Decide with the senior management person at the new site who at that site will have responsibility for the implementation of training activities, and help with assessment of needs and the post-training follow-up.

You may decide to wait for six months to a year before conducting an organizational assessment of training needs, particularly if training has been conducted before many individuals have been transferred to the new site.

Figure 6–10 is a workshop evaluation form for satellite locations.

FIGURE 6-10.

WORKSHOP/SEMINAR EVALUATION
FOR SATELLITE LOCATIONS

Title of program:

Location of program:

Cost of program:

Travel and related costs (estimate):

Subject areas covered, by topic:

Personal evaluation:

Would you recommend it to others?

Who else would benefit from the program?

What would you do differently?

Name _____   (If you prefer not to sign your name, please do
                                                show the date you took the course.)
Department _____

Date _____

6.13 CHECKLIST AND IDEAS FOR UTILIZING EXTERNAL RESOURCES FOR TRAINING AND DEVELOPMENT

The American Society for Training and Development reports that the private sector in the United States is currently spending in excess of $40 million annually for training and development. Because the costs of training are accelerating, the human resource director needs to analyze more closely the use of external resources.

Dan Schaeffer, manager of training and development for Rocky Mountain Energy, a subsidiary of the Union Pacific Corporation, provides the following checklists and ideas for the use of external resources.[9]

Consultants

Ask yourself and any potential training consultants the following questions:

1. Why should I go outside the organization for training programs? No expertise in-house to develop or conduct program? Credibility that a neutral party might bring to the problem or program?
2. What about the time issue? How immediate is the need? What are the time limits of your staff or yourself?
3. Budget considerations? Consultants may be less expensive than internal staff. They will concentrate on a specific issue or a specific problem, and some will guarantee results.
4. Sales calls from consultants should not justify hiring someone or altering your training priorities. Be careful of salespersons selling the answers to all your training needs. Such persons are often trained as salespeople, not training professionals.

Assuming that you have decided to look outside the organization for expertise, here are some specific criteria for selection:

1. Prior track record—What organizations were previously served? What topics or services were rendered? When were the services rendered? Whom can you contact at those organizations to verify results? If they can't supply these kinds of specific data, continue your search.
2. Can you see or hear the consultant by previewing a demonstration tape? Would they consider a briefing session for a select group of managers or employees (at minimal or no cost)? What about an executive briefing? What would they charge for a pilot of the program?
3. Most important for persons who will be conducting programs, are they adult-centered in their teaching or seminar leading? How would they describe their presentation style? Are they participative? Do they use audiovisuals? If they can't react to these questions adequately, continue looking.
4. Are your candidates generalists or specialists? Do they have a list of topics they can consult and conduct programs on? Be wary of "can do all" types. They are probably not the people for your program.
5. Ask for a written proposal based on what you see as your needs. Look for training objectives and outcomes in such proposals. If they can't write down what the expected outcomes are, it is doubtful that any will be realized.

---

[9] "Checklist and Ideas for Utilizing External Resources for Training and Development," Daniel L. Schaeffer, Manager, Training and Development, Rocky Mountain Energy, 10 Longs Peak Drive, Broomfield, Colorado 80020.

6.14 PREPACKAGED TRAINING AND DEVELOPMENT PROGRAMS

There are currently hundreds of packaged programs in the marketplace on virtually any topic and in any format you might want. Slides, audio tapes, videotape, films, books, and any combination of such can be purchased to teach everything from welding to management development to stress management.

The cost of these programs ranges from several hundred to several thousand dollars, depending on length, delivery, development, and marketing costs. Dan Schaeffer provides two checklists to help you decide when to buy and what to consider when selecting a program.

When to Buy Instead of Developing Your Own Program

1. When there are limitations on internal resources for developing your own programs, including cost, internal expertise, and time.
2. Consider how wide the usage would be in your department. What's the need for a program in your organization? How many people would be included? Is there a single location, or are there multiple locations that could use the program?
3. Consider costs. Don't reinvent the wheel; development costs for a supervisory training series could be much more than for buying an existing program. An in-house program instead of attendance at public offering can be cheaper for multiple users.

What to Buy

1. Get a list of past participants and talk with other users of the program firsthand. Ask for specific results from users. What other programs did these users consider to fulfill their needs? Would they purchase the program again?
2. Preview the entire program, or attend a public offering.
3. Conduct an in-house pilot program before purchase.
4. Can the program be tailored easily to your organization's needs?
5. Be aware of all costs. Are there lease/purchase options? Costs for individual workbooks or materials? Initial licensing fees? Train-the-trainer fees? Volume discounts on materials? Equipment purchase needs in order to use materials?
6. What about an executive briefing of the program before purchase?

Short Courses and Seminars

Of the $40 million expended annually for training and development, the largest percentage is spent sending employees to workshops, conferences, and seminars on every topic imaginable. Like other external resources, some of these programs are result-oriented, but some can be a waste of time and money. There are things that you or your training specialist can do to ensure that the programs your employees attend are worthwhile.

Before attending a program:

1. Get names of people who have completed the program, and talk with them. When did they attend and where? Seminar leader and effectiveness. Specific results they have realized by attending. Would they attend again?
2. Be aware of "slick" marketing with brochures that promise "all." Direct mail efforts have become highly sophisticated, and some sponsoring organizations spend more on marketing than they do on developing and validating the content.
3. Avoid one-day programs that will do "all," unless you have talked with an attendee who can attest to results.
4. Find out the enrollment maximums in the program. More than 40 may suggest a goal of maximizing profit rather than learning.
5. What is the method of delivery—lecture, discussion, role-play, case problems? Programs that tend to be lecture-based may not provide any real learning.

After attending a program:

1. Ask for a written evaluation from participants. Debrief as time and staff permit. Keep evaluations on file for future reference.
2. Get a copy of handouts for files and sharing with other employees.
3. Follow up on job-related outcomes at a future time, usually a month or more away. Was there any real impact?
4. Is this a program that could or should be brought in-house?

6.15 CURRENT TRENDS IN TRAINING AND DEVELOPMENT

Perhaps the biggest trend is the growing commitment to training and development in organizations today. Organizations are opting to develop internal training specialists who can in turn develop and coordinate internal programs that are result-oriented specific *to the organization's* needs. The catchall term today is *cost–benefit training.* Is the training you are doing going to the bottom line? Outside the skill development areas, outcomes are hard to measure. Identification of assessment procedures in cognitive areas is one of the challenges facing training professionals.

HUMAN RESOURCE DIRECTOR'S TIP:

Build your own critique file on all external programs your employees attend. This is the best reference for future use of such resources and could save big dollars.

Figure 6–11 is a critique form to use in evaluating most types of programs. Change it to suit your particular needs.

FIGURE 6-11.

<u>SEMINAR OR WORKSHOP EVALUATION</u>

Date:

To:

From:

Course:

Date(s) Attended:

Sponsor/Location:

     Please indicate your reaction to this course by responding to the following questions:

1. What was your purpose in attending this course or seminar?

2. Was the purpose achieved?   Yes ____   No ____

    What additions/deletions/changes would you recommend?

    How will you apply the skill(s)/knowledge gained?

3. What improvements would you like to see in the presentation methods? (Consider hands-on time, role-plays, exercises, visual aids, the presenter, discussions, etc.)

4. Overall reaction (check one):

    Highly recommend ____   Recommend ____   Would not recommend ____
    Comments:

CHAPTER 7

Human Resource Policies—Their Purpose and Their Frailties

Policies in the old personnel manual ran the gamut from broad, general statements ("We do not discriminate in employment") to narrow rules ("Sleeping on the job is grounds for immediate dismissal"). The language tended toward stilted sentences that talked down to employees. The current trend is away from narrow, arbitrary policies or dictates, to more positive approaches to specific problem areas.

Human resource directors have the responsibility to write and interpret policies; and because we deal with so many critical and sensitive human issues, we have to be aware of the dangers inherent in interpreting and administering policies and procedures. The dangers are narrow, rigid interpretation, contradiction, inequity, and ambiguity.

Realistically, we need to understand that organizations do not run headlong toward a single purpose or goal such as profitability. The experienced human resource director understands that there are contradictions, short-term objectives, and day-to-day dilemmas that affect our progress, and our decisions must take all of these things into consideration.

Another important area is the constantly changing internal environments of an organization. Effective human resource people have a good sense of timing and recognize change, watching for policies that have become outdated or obsolete. If managers are spending too much time solving the same problems over and over, obsolete policies or procedures may be the reason.

7.1 PERSONNEL POLICIES YOU NEED IN YOUR HUMAN RESOURCE MANUAL

Do you operate by expediency or good business procedure? Are daily decisions made by immediate business pressure or standard operating policy? In today's work environment, written personnel policies are essential.

Some obvious reasons for having effective policies are:

- They free people to take action quickly.
- They provide continuity and fair and even treatment.
- Policies provide control without strangling a company. They set out the conditions of employment.
- Policies reduce the fear of taking action.
- They support the company position in arbitration or litigation.
- They allow decentralization of authority.
- Policies save time.
- They simplify the decision-making process.

The American Management Association recently completed a survey of 600 companies that are users and preparers of manuals. Among other things, a key item was the finding that manuals pay for themselves by making things work better in most companies.

According to Charles L. Hughes, director of the Center for Values Research, however, complex company policies are a major cause of employee dissatisfaction. Therefore, policies should be simple, openly communicated, and fairly administered.

There is no limit to the number of policies a company can have. The key is to have enough to speed the decision-making process and to free managers to act, but not so many that they strangle the organization. Integration of policies is important so that they work together to accomplish the business objective.

Depending on the size and organization of the company, the human resource manual may include policies like mileage allowance, expense account guidelines, and so on, but these items normally are found in administrative manuals.

The important point is that where written personnel polices used to be primarily for large companies, in today's work environment written policies are essential for small, medium, and large organizations, in order to prevent "seat of the pants" decisions.

The key is to provide guidelines for wise, equitable resolution of day-to-day problems.

HUMAN RESOURCE DIRECTOR'S TIP:

Company manuals are becoming legal documents and are being dragged into court in lawsuits. It's a good idea to have your attorney review your manual with an eye to possible litigation. Watch what you say and how you say it. Review your policies at least once a year.

7.2 CHECKLIST OF NINETEEN POLICIES YOU MAY WANT IN YOUR HUMAN RESOURCE MANUAL

1. Absence
     Absenteeism
2. Benefits

3. Civic Duty
   Jury duty
   Voting
   Witness
   National Guard
4. Complaint Procedure
5. Discipline
6. Employment Policies
   Orientation
   Payment of employment fees
   Relocation
7. Equal Employment Opportunity Policy
   Equal employment complaint procedure
8. Expatriate Policy
9. Leaves of Absence
   Maternity leave
   Military leave
   Personal leave
   Funeral leave
10. Pay, Hours of Work, Records
    Workday
    Time records
    Overtime
    Garnishment
    Rest periods
    Severance pay
    Probationary period
11. Performance Appraisal
12. Promotion and Transfer
13. Safety and Health
14. Temporary Employment
15. Terminations
16. Training and Development
    Educational assistance
17. Unemployment Compensation
18. Vacations
19. Workers' Compensation

Layout of the policy manual is usually either alphabetical or by major heading and then alphabetical. Most companies prefer the alphabetical layout, because it's easier and faster to look up one word—"Vacation"—than it is to look at two references such as "Time Off with Pay" and then "Vacation."

There are three important elements of a good policy manual:

1. Statements are short. Each sentence contains one thought. Unnecessary words are eliminated.
2. Jargon and complex terms are eliminated.

3. The style and tone of writing don't talk down, preach, or dictate to the employee.

In order for policies to be effective, there must be a continuous review procedure. At least once a year, you need to review each policy and ask yourself the following questions:

- Does each policy reflect current conditions in the company?
- Has the policy helped or hindered operations?
- Has the policy fostered good morale and productivity?
- Does the company operate in the same way now as it did when the policy was written?
- Does the policy reflect the company's goals and business plans?
- Do supervisors and managers complain about the policy, or do they use it constructively?

It's a good idea to communicate the objectives of your policy manual to supervisors and managers when it's distributed and on an ongoing basis. An objectives statement might include the following.

1. To state the company position to all employees.
2. To provide uniform guidelines for personnel decisions.
3. To provide authority and responsibility for administration of personnel polices and procedures.
4. To establish reference points for auditing the human resource function.
5. To provide a uniform guide for use in employee counseling.
6. To standardize handling of personnel matters across all functions in the organization.
7. To provide a basis for company actions and to support that position in litigation or arbitration.

HUMAN RESOURCE DIRECTOR'S TIP:

If you have a few key managers read the manual and critique it before you have it printed and disseminated, there will be more acceptance on their part. If they have some input, they will also have some ownership.

Copying policies of other organizations or using standard policies from a commercial manual isn't always a good idea. Each company has its own environment and its own problems. If you use someone else's policies, be sure to adjust them to your organization.

The best way to start a new policy manual or revise an old one is to list the policies you feel your organization needs and, for each policy, itemize the key issues involved.

7.3 POLICY STATEMENTS, KEY ISSUES, AND TIPS ON MAJOR HUMAN RESOURCE POLICIES

POLICY	KEY ISSUES
Absence	A policy is needed to serve as a guideline for what may be too much absenteeism. Without guidelines, it's difficult to talk to an employee about an absence problem.

Evenhandedness is the key. One supervisor may be lenient, another too strict.

Set a reasonable guide:

First Absence	*Second Absence*	*Third Absence*
No warning	*Discussion, with supervisor or manager*	*Verbal warning*

Fourth Absence	*Fifth Absence*	*Sixth Absence*
Written warning	Suspension	Discharge

Affirmative Action

Fair employment laws mandate that employers must take positive steps to integrate the work force. Affirmative action is a results-oriented plan for bringing the company into compliance with EEO requirements.

In order to comply, you need the following:

1. Statement of EEO policy.
2. Assignment of responsibility for the affirmative action program.
3. Procedures for issuing information.

Athletic Activities

Many companies have health centers to encourage better health.

Companies also support such activities as softball, volleyball, and bowling teams.

The key issue here is to watch that you don't discriminate by supporting such activities for men only. If you support a team, it must be open to both men and women.

Most companies allow people outside the company to fill out a team, but have a statement in the policy that says, "If an employee decides to join the team, the outside person must drop off the roster in order to allow the employee to participate."

POLICY	KEY ISSUES

Some companies pay a portion of the costs—usually the association and entry fees—and share the cost of uniforms or shirts with the employee. If the employee has something invested, there seems to be more commitment.

Benefits

Benefits usually are set out in a separate handbook, but you may wish to make reference to or list benefits anyway.

In the benefits area, be sure you provide the same disability benefits to all women on maternity leave that you do male employees. Regulations state that maternity is a disability just like any other, and the same benefits must be provided.

Breaks

Companies normally provide two paid breaks a day, one in the morning and one in the afternoon.

Bulletin Boards

Employees should not be allowed to post information on bulletin boards without prior approval from the human resource manager.

Certain posters and notices are required to be posted, and bulletin boards should be provided in central areas where employees can see them easily.

Company Rules

If you find yourself in an arbitration over a company work rule when the rule hasn't been properly explained, put in writing, or otherwise communicated, you know why it is important to put the company's rules in the policy manual and/or employee handbook.

Some of the rules you'll want to include in your handbook involve:

- Drinking or taking drugs on company premises, or reporting to work under the influence of drugs or alcohol.
- Theft of company or employee property.
- Assault on supervisor or another employee.
- Gambling on company property.
- Falsifying company records.
- Possession of illegal weapons or firearms on company premises.
- Intentionally misusing or damaging company property.
- Disregarding safety rules or failure to wear safety equipment.
- Unauthorized absence.

These are a few company rules. You may think of others for your special situation.

Complaint Procedure

Give each employee a full and impartial hearing on any complaint. It's a good idea to have several levels to which the complaint can progress. Start with the employee's immediate supervisor, then the manager, human resource director, appropriate vice-president, and all the way to the president if resolution can't be arranged at a lower level.

POLICY	KEY ISSUES
Discipline	Disciplinary action is taken when there are serious performance problems. There are six basic disciplinary actions that can be taken: 1. Supervisory counseling and coaching 2. Verbal warning 3. Written warning 4. Suspension 5. Probation 6. Discharge The key to effective discipline that protects the company from unnecessary and expensive litigation is the evenhanded administration of the policy.
Dress Code	In the May 1982 issue of *Management World*, the monthly magazine of the Administrative Management Society, information on a survey of 500 companies was reported.[1] Of the 500 responses, there were 366 usable replies: 112, or 31 percent, said they had a dress code; 254 companies did not have a dress code; and 217 of the 366 companies (59 percent) have an informal dress code. Companies that have a dress code usually communicate it to employees during new employee orientation, and after that it is up to each supervisor to enforce the code on an individual basis. It is fairly easy to enforce a grooming or dress code if: • Employees meet the public. • There are safety or health reasons. In other work situations, it can be difficult to enforce a dress code. The key to success here seems to be individual treatment of each particular situation, ensuring evenhanded, fair, and consistent treatment.
Employment Policies	Establish who pays employment agency fees. Present the company's relocation policy, whom it covers, and what items can be paid. Provide guidelines for new employee orientation, which normally include basic work rules, compensation and benefits, company history, products and services, and data on the employee's job and department.
Equal Employment Opportunity	All human resource manuals should include an EEO policy. Following is a sample policy:

[1] *Management World,* May 1982, Administrative Management Society, 2360 Maryland Road, Willow Grove, Pennsylvania 19090.

POLICY	KEY ISSUES

It is the policy of XYZ Company to afford equal employment opportunity to all qualified persons regardless of race, color, religion, national origin, age, or sex, except where age or sex is a bona fide occupational qualification. In keeping with the intent of this policy, the company will adhere strictly to the following personnel practices:

1. Recruitment, hiring, and promotion of individuals in all job classifications will be conducted without regard to race, color, religion, national origin, age, or sex, except where age or sex is a bona fide occupational qualification.
2. Employment decisions will be made in such a manner as to further the principle of equal employment opportunity.
3. Promotional decisions will be made in accordance with the principles of equal employment opportunity by establishing valid (job-related) requirements for promotional opportunities.
4. All other personnel actions, such as compensation, benefits, transfers, training and development, educational assistance, and social and recreational programs, will be administered without regard to race, color, religion, national origin, age, or sex, except where age or sex is a bona fide occupational qualification.
5. Periodically, at least annually, analyses of all personnel actions will be conducted by the human resource director to ensure equal opportunity.

The aforestated policy is implemented by means of the company's affirmative action program, which is updated annually and is available for review in the human resource department.

Equal Opportunity Complaint Procedure

This policy establishes a procedure for employees to follow in order to bring complaints of discrimination or harassment to the attention of management.

Following is a review procedure guideline:

1. If there is a question or complaint with regard to employment practices that an employee has been unable to resolve with the immediate supervisor, the employee is encouraged to make that question or complaint known to the affirmative action coordinator or the director of human resources. The employee will be asked to state in writing the nature and detail of the complaint.
2. The equal opportunity coordinator or the director of human resources will investigate the complaint with the manager of the department and will arrive at a response to be given to the employee.
3. The employee will be advised in writing of the results of the investigation and the company's decision regarding the complaint.

POLICY	KEY ISSUES

4. Should the employee feel that the resolution of the complaint is not satisfactory, the employee may seek a review of the facts by the vice-president of human resources.

5. The vice-president of human resources will call a meeting involving the appropriate vice-president and the employee. Following the investigatory procedure, the vice-president of human resources will advise the employee in writing of the company's decision.

6. A record of the complaint and the findings will become a part of the complaint investigation record, and the file will be maintained separately from the employee's personnel file.

7. It is understood that any person electing to utilize this complaint resolution procedure will be treated courteously and the problem handled swiftly and confidentially, and the registering of a complaint will in no way be used against the employee, nor will it have an adverse impact on the individual's employment status.

The attached summary of this policy/procedure will be posted on all bulletin boards at all locations, operations, and facilities. Additionally, each new employee hired subsequent to the development of this policy will receive a copy.

Expatriate Policy

With an increase in overseas employment, some companies provide guidelines for:

- Base pay
- Expatriate premium
- Hardship allowance
- Living allowance
- Cost-of-living differential
- Shipment of household goods
- Letter of agreement
- Home leave
- Meal allowances
- Automobiles
- Health and physical exams
- Educational assistance for families

Flexitime

Flexitime is an innovative program used in many companies today to improve employee morale and productivity by letting employees set their own hours of work around a set core of work hours.

Main considerations:

- Does the environment lend itself to flexitime?
- Would you consider flexitime by the day, or by the week, where employees could take hours from one day and work them on another?

POLICY	KEY ISSUES

- Will some workers have to be eliminated from flexitime because of support needs? An example might be a telephone operator if you have only one.

Following are some flexitime advantages:

- It improves employee morale.
- It decreases absenteeism and tardiness.
- It assists working parents with school and babysitting problems.
- Traffic problems are cut down.
- Productivity can be increased.
- People are on duty during longer hours in a department if some come in early and others later.

Disadvantages of flexitime:

- A manager, secretary, or other employee might not be at work when needed.
- It is more difficult to plan work schedules and meetings.
- There might be abuse of the system if it isn't properly administered.

Following are some guidelines for instituting a flexitime program:

1. Institute a new flexitime program on a trial basis and make sure you communicate to all employees that it is just a trial.
2. Establish the flexible hours and the core hours.
3. Define the work day, lunch period, breaks, and so on.
4. Establish and communicate a policy on tardiness and overtime.

The success of the program depends in great part on the ability of supervisors and managers to administer it effectively on an ongoing basis.

Some companies find flexible scheduling, gliding time, or simply staggered work hours better suited to their needs.

*Funeral
Leave*

A sample policy might read as follows:

Time off without loss of pay will be granted for up to three regularly scheduled working days to arrange for and attend the funeral of a member of the immediate family. In the event of special or unusual circumstances, such as long distances to travel, multiple deaths, or similar tragedies, additional time off with pay may be granted at the discretion of the employee's manager.

Immediate family is defined as an employee's spouse, child (including grandchild), parent (including grandparent), and sibling; those same relatives of the employee's spouse; or any other relative living within the employee's household.

POLICY	KEY ISSUES

Holidays

Time off without pay to attend the funeral of other relatives or friends may be granted at the discretion of the employee's manager. As much advance notice as is possible under the circumstances should be given in departments where production schedules are a consideration.

The policy should list the regular paid holidays and what day employees will be off when a holiday falls on Saturday or Sunday. In addition, it should state how an employee will be paid if he or she has to work on a holiday.

Jury Duty

The key issue to be resolved here is whether or not the company will give the employee full pay or make up the difference in pay from any jury fees paid. Many companies have found the bookkeeping hassle costly when trying to get proof of jury fees (which are negligible) and determine how much pay is due, so they let the employee keep the jury fees and pay full pay anyway.

Following is a sample guideline:

Employees summoned to jury duty will be paid their full base salary for the period they are required to perform jury duty, in addition to receiving whatever fees may be paid them by the court.

Leaves of Absence

When writing a leave of absence policy, consider the following:

1. For what purposes will you provide a leave of absence? Most companies provide maternity leave, military leave, illness or disability leave, funeral leave, and personal leave.
2. For which leaves will employees receive pay?
3. Who can grant the leaves, and must they be in writing?
4. When is an employee eligible for a leave? For example, most companies require that an employee be a permanent employee who works more than 20 hours per week and has passed the probationary period.
5. What effect will the leave have on the employee's benefits? Will the employee continue to accrue seniority? Will the employee be eligible for benefits during the leave? Will the employee be allowed to pay the medical insurance premium at the group rate or have to convert to an individual policy and pay the premium during the leave in order to continue medical insurance coverage?
6. If the company does not provide a certain amount of paid sick leave, does medical coverage provide for salary continuation or disability pay?
7. Amendments to Title VII of the Civil Rights Act of 1964 require that maternity leave be treated like any other disability or medical condition, and the same benefits, including pay, must be provided to a woman on maternity leave as are provided to an employee on disability or medical leave.

POLICY	KEY ISSUES

Some questions that may arise here are, is a male employee eligible to receive maternity leave to help his wife who is having a baby? Will the company provide maternity leave for an employee who is adopting a child?

8. Will the company require notice from the employee as to date of expected return? Will the company guarantee the employee the same job and rate of pay?

9. What will be the relationship of paid leave time and overtime if both occur in the same week? Following is a sample statement: "Time paid for funeral leave will not be counted as hours worked for the purpose of computing overtime."

10. What will happen if an extension is needed? What if the employee fails to return?

All of these issues should be resolved before the policy is finalized.

Performance Appraisal

Most companies have a policy of reviewing employees' performance at least once a year. Some companies put the performance appraisal policy in a salary manual rather than the personnel policy manual.

The policy should state the frequency of the appraisal process and who is responsible for administering it.

There is a trend toward a more open and honest appraisal process as employees have become more assertive. This means that managers and supervisors must be trained in the art of leveling, coaching, and counseling.

There is also a new emphasis on the ethics of performance appraisal. Employees want to be appraised on the basis of relevant, objective criteria. The employee should receive a copy of the appraisal.

Probationary Period

The probationary period is the time allowed all newly hired permanent employees to demonstrate the qualifications for their job.

A reasonable time guideline is 120 days. Probationary periods used to average six months, but many organizations have shortened that time.

Promotion and Transfer

State the general policy: "It is company policy to promote current employees, rather than hire from outside the organization, whenever possible."

What happens when a vacancy occurs? Do you post the open position on a bulletin board? What part does seniority play? What are the procedures to follow if there is an employee in another department who fits the job? What are the procedures to follow to effect a transfer?

POLICY	KEY ISSUES
Safety and Health	Define company policy: "It is the intent of the company to provide for the safety and health of its employees by maintaining safe and healthful working conditions." Do you have a physical examination program for all employees? Do you have regular safety inspections? Spell out what procedures are in place to carry out the intent of the policy.
Severance Pay	The following severance pay guidelines are provided by the Shore Manufacturing Company in their personnel policy manual: An employee dismissed after the six-month probationary period will receive two weeks' pay for each year of service, to a maximum of 26 weeks, prorated according to the number of months of continuous employment. Severance pay will be issued with the final paycheck. An employee who voluntarily resigns does not qualify for severance pay. No severance allowance normally will be granted for dismissal of an employee within the probationary period. However, a maximum of one week's pay may be granted at the discretion of the manager, with approval of the president. An appropriate reason for doing so might include necessary layoff caused by anticipated organization realignment. A statement outlining applicable severance provisions should be inserted in the "General Comments" section of the termination report form. You might say: "If the requested severance provisions are at variance with the guidelines of this policy, the president's signature is required on the termination report form."
Temporary Help	Establish criteria for use of temporary help, from a temporary agency and with a temporary employee put on the company payroll. Set out the procedure to follow if a manager needs temporary help. Include approval levels. Establish a time limitation for use of temporary help. At the end of six months, for example, the policy might require new approvals. Establish a policy for benefit eligibility and benefit levels.
Terminations	Termination is an area where the company is vulnerable to litigation, so the policy is important and should provide specific guidelines that are administered evenhandedly. Establish what is a voluntary termination and what is involuntary. Establish the grounds for involuntary termination and the amount of notice that will be given. Will exit interviews be conducted? Establish procedures for returning company property and for distributing final pay and benefits. The key issue in the case of disciplinary action is that all

POLICY	KEY ISSUES

procedures must be followed before an involuntary termination can take place. You may want to provide managers with a termination checklist to ensure that all managers handle this vital area in an appropriate and systematic way.

Another key issue is the time element involved in the distribution of the final paycheck. Several states have laws that provide specific time deadlines. Following are the Colorado regulations, as an example:

Voluntary, with notice

Employees terminating voluntarily after giving the company at least 72 hours advance written notice will be paid within three business days after their final shift.

Voluntary, without notice

Employees terminating without giving the company at least 72 hours advance written notice will receive their final check on the next regular payday.

Involuntary, discharged

If an employee is terminated involuntarily (discharged) by the company, every effort will be made to pay the employee immediately upon being terminated. In cases where there is no advance warning, the check must be available the next business day.

Training and Development

State the company position on training and development. If you have a commitment to promote from within, how do you administer development activities to facilitate that objective?

Do you have a tuition reimbursement program? How does it work?

What are the procedures that must be followed if an employee chooses to participate in training and development programs, and what eligibility requirements are there?

Unemployment Compensation

The policy should state whether or not the company is a covered employer and, if so, what procedures a separated employee should follow to collect benefits.

Vacations

State the policy, the eligibility, and the standard vacation year. For example: "The vacation year begins January 1 and continues through December 31."

State who must approve vacations and what the vacation benefit will be. Example:

For permanent full-time employees

1 week after 6 months
2 weeks after 1 year

3 weeks after 5 years
4 weeks after 10 years
5 weeks after 20 years

For permanent part-time employees

Normal Weekly Schedule	Paid Vacation per Week of Eligibility
8 hours or less	4 hours
9 to 16 hours	12 hours
17 to 24 hours	20 hours
25 to 32 hours	28 hours

Workers' Compensation

The policy should state that in accordance with applicable state laws, employees are eligible for Workers' Compensation benefits in the event of illness or accident resulting from an employee's occupation and requiring medical treatment, hospitalization, or loss of time.

State reporting requirements.

There are other policies that can be included in a manual, but these are the ones most companies have. The Prentice-Hall *Personnel Management Service* goes into greater detail and provides a longer list of policies, if you have a specific need that isn't covered here.[2]

The key issue in writing any policy is to avoid the "legalese" approach. Make the manual easy to read, short, and to the point, but be sure you are in regulatory compliance and have not put the company in jeopardy of litigation, either from lack of a needed policy or from having a policy that is incorrectly stated or administered.

7.4 KEYS TO SUCCESSFUL IMPLEMENTATION OR REVISION OF POLICIES AND PROCEDURES

Few organizations are started with a full set of policies and established to meet present and future work conditions. Most organizations periodically revise existing policies and procedures as times and technologies change. Often, changes are met with resistance, and even good ideas fail to be implemented successfully because of the ways in which the new policies or procedures were conceived and implemented. Julie B. Aragon, director of employee development at NERCO, Inc., has listed some ideas that should be helpful when contemplating a policy or procedure design or revision.[3]

Preimplementation

1. Ask potentially affected department heads to choose a representative to aid in the determination of need, shaping, structure, and implementation of the proposed policy or procedure.

[2] *Prentice-Hall Looseleaf Management Service on Personnel Policies*, Prentice-Hall, Inc., Englewood Cliffs, New Jersey 07632.

[3] "Keys to Successful Implementation or Revision of Policies and Procedures," Julie B. Aragon, Director, Employee Development, NERCO, Inc., 111 S.W. Columbia, Portland, Oregon 97201.

2. Involve representatives from affected departments in all phases.
3. Explore the reasons for the change—advantages and disadvantages—with representatives of affected departments.
4. Evaluate potential alternatives in content and structure with representatives.
5. Determine if a trial period and subsequent "fine-tuning" format is appropriate.
6. Plan and organize the implementation or revision to ensure smooth transition through clear advance communication and training, if necessary.

Postimplementation

1. Have the representatives from each affected department oversee and monitor the success of the transition and post-transition phases.
2. Any problem areas that run across departmental lines should be addressed by the committee of representatives.
3. Problems that lie within one department only should be addressed by the representative, department head, and policy initiator.
4. A formal survey throughout affected departments might be conducted six months after implementation in order to assess the workability and success of the newly implemented policy or procedure.

HUMAN RESOURCE DIRECTOR'S TIP:

Ask yourself the following questions:

Does everyone affected clearly know the new policy or procedure?

Is the policy or procedure constructed to produce the desired result?

Are the skills that are necessary for successful administration found or developed in those who will need them?

Does the policy and procedures manual contain the current information?

Involving Employees in Significant Policy Changes

Eric L. Harvey, executive vice-president of Performance Systems Corporation, a management consultancy based in Dallas, provides the following example of a company that involved employees in a significant policy change.[4]

Example. People generally do not resist change. They do, however, resist having change shoved down their throats. If we expect employees to respond as committed adults, we must involve them appropriately in the change process. This doesn't mean that we adopt a totally participatory approach to organization decision making, but it does mean that we take advantage of appropriate opportunities to communicate, involve, and work toward overall acceptance.

One of the more vivid examples of the importance of effectively managing change came as a result of a project with a large manufacturing firm several years ago. The company manufactured electrical components and had more than 2,000 employees. We were helping them install our "Positive Discipline" program (a nonpunitive disciplin-

---

[4] "Involving Employees in Significant Policy Changes," Eric L. Harvey, Executive Vice-President, Performance Systems Corporation, 2925 LBJ Freeway, Suite 281, Dallas, Texas 75234.

ary process) and used a participatory implementation process. A team of employees representing a cross-section of the organization was established to help manage the change process. Because the company was open and honest about their intentions and expectations, and in addition used the participatory process to implement what turned out to be some significant administrative modifications, they reaped the benefits. The trust level throughout the organization was extremely high, which meant that when the new concepts were actually implemented there was also an extremely high degree of acceptance and a smooth transition from the old procedures to the new.

Perhaps the most vivid behavioral indicator of program acceptance came four or five months into the new program when a group of employees approached senior management with a suggestion for program enhancement. Through clear and straightforward communication, management had positioned "Positive Discipline" as a way of helping manage employee performance. The employees not only heard but saw this to be true, and because of their level of commitment, they took it upon themselves to offer a suggestion regarding a second-generation vehicle for managing employee performance. They suggested that the company introduce an employee evaluation program for nonexempt hourly employees, something that senior management had always wanted but had not initiated because of concerns about employee receptivity.

The company's management took the employees up on their offer and helped them form an employee committee to design and implement the performance appraisal system. The result was an intrinsically sound system that was highly supported throughout the organization, proving that commitment, not compliance, makes the difference between an employee system just being there as opposed to working effectively.

7.5 FIFTEEN WAYS TO COMMUNICATE YOUR POLICIES AND PRACTICES

If policies and procedures are not communicated frequently, in a manner that your current work force will accept, they will not be followed or used properly. In addition, any communication program must stay current with the times and with changing business conditions.

Following are fifteen ways to communicate with employees:

1. Conduct one-on-one communication between supervisor and employee at least once a month, quarterly, and at the yearly performance review.
2. Publish employee newsletters, articles, and stories about employees who are actively supporting the company and its business plans.
3. Use the media. Show films and slides on topics of current interest. Use video to train employees and for special programs.
4. Have programs during the lunch period, where speakers come in to speak on a variety of subjects pertinent to your business and industry. The company may donate 30 minutes extra if the program helps employees on their jobs, and the investment may be well worth the cost.
5. Some organizations, like U.S. Homes, have started monthly discussion group programs, aimed at managers and professionals. This is used as a management development tool. A particular book will be chosen, all participants read the

book, and then a vice-president leads a discussion group on the merits of the principles set out in the book.

6. Sometimes, when companies are going through a particularly difficult time, a question box or telephone hotline will encourage dialogue. The employee doesn't have to give a name. Guarantee a response to all reasonable questions within a few days. You can reply through a special newsletter to all employees. If you do have a question box or hotline, it's important to reply in timely fashion, and you and your top management must agree to be open and honest or these avenues won't work well.

7. Create a communications task force to identify communication problems and suggest solutions. The task force should include people from a variety of functions and all levels in the company. People have more ownership in programs they or their peers help create.

8. To communicate policies and procedures in your own department, route the policy book throughout the department and ask each employee to read it.

9. Put an extra copy of the policy manual in your library or in the personnel office, where employees can check it out if they want to.

10. Implement an orientation program for families so they understand the company, its products, its policies, and the office or plant facilities.

11. Publish an annual report to employees and their families, updating them not only on employee benefit statements, but also on the company's business plans and accomplishments.

12. Use athletic activities and health programs as avenues for employee communication.

13. Start an employee speakers' bureau. Give employees training in public speaking, and select topics that would be of benefit to the company as well as topics the employees choose.

14. If you have extra space that can be used occasionally, have an employee crafts fair where employees can sell their crafts.

15. Set up closed circuit TV/VHF programs to inform employees about important management meetings, and pass on specific information employees may read.

How to Communicate with Younger Employees

In Daniel Yankelovich's book, *New Rules—Searching for Self-Fulfillment in a World Turned Upside Down,* he draws our attention to the changing demographics and the new work ethic. "The self-fulfillment motif stands out prominently."[5] He further states, "They [the younger generation] are preoccupied with their inner psychological needs." Workers want more than ever to adapt their lives to their own standards and desires.

There is a danger, however, in generalizing and saying that all younger people have the same desires and goals and trying to manage the whole group in the same manner.

It's essential to manage and to communicate with each employee individually, appealing to the values that motivate that particular individual. The new workers want

---

[5] *New Rules, Searching for Self-Fulfillment in a World Turned Upside Down,* Daniel Yankelovich, Random House, 1981.

communication and feedback, they want to know why something must be done a certain way, and they must see how their individual efforts affect the total organization and the company's business plan.

In order to communicate with today's worker, you need to talk frequently and include discussions on the merits of doing things one way as opposed to another. Ask for suggestions—use them when you can—tell the worker why you can't use them, if that's the case. Participation in decision making is one answer to better communication with today's workers.

7.6   DISCIPLINE AND DISCHARGE IN TODAY'S ENVIRONMENT— HOW TO ADMINISTER THE TOUGHEST POLICY IN YOUR MANUAL

Every human resource director must take a long, serious look at the changing trend in the law relating to "termination at will." Organizations have had a long period where they could run their own show and fire people for any reason other than causes covered by the Civil Rights Act or the Federal Labor Relations Law.

It's a different story today, however, as courts in some states have ruled that statements made to employees and some statements made in employee handbooks (such as the discipline procedure) must be honored and can, in some cases, eliminate termination at will.

The main issue in disciplinary action is "just cause." The company must have just cause for enforcing discipline. Just cause definitions vary, but it's a good idea to ask yourself the following questions before you terminate an employee:

- Did the supervisor, manager, or human resource representative adequately communicate the policy or procedure involved in the disciplinary action?
- Has the employee been warned verbally and/or in writing of the consequences of his or her action?
- Did the supervisor, manager, or human resource representative investigate the misconduct? Was the investigation thorough and fair?
- Has the policy or procedure that was violated been violated by other employees? Was disciplinary action taken in those cases? If so, what action was taken?
- Have you reviewed the employee's personnel record to see if this is the first time discipline has been administered?
- Is the planned discipline too tough or too light? Choose the discipline that fits the crime.
- Use discipline as a corrective, learning experience, not a punitive action.

The key to appropriate discipline is equal treatment and internal consistency.

7.7   SAMPLE DISCIPLINARY ACTION POLICY

A medium-sized manufacturing company provided the following policy in their human resource manual.

I. Policy

Open communications between management and employees and the establishment of a friendly, cooperative work atmosphere go a long way toward eliminating serious disciplinary problems. If, however, disciplinary problems do arise, supervisors and managers should make every effort to ensure that employees have a thorough understanding of company policies and an awareness of what is expected in the area of job performance.

The purpose of this policy is to provide for disciplinary action. Application of these guidelines must be consistent and equitable, so that all employees receive like treatment for similar offenses.

II. Procedure

The procedures described below are meant to assist supervisors and managers in determining a proper course of action when discipline is needed. They are a guideline, not a substitute for common sense. Documentation of all verbal and written warnings is important in order to avoid the situation of an employee being discharged for cause with no written proof of earlier warnings. In most cases, it is advisable to give an employee at least one documented verbal warning and one written warning before termination.

A. Warnings

Supervisors and managers should use their own judgment in determining the length of time between warnings. A minimum of three days and a maximum of sixty days is suggested as a guideline. The warning should be specific in describing what improvement is needed. Copies of the warning should be forwarded to the senior officer of the employee's department and to the affirmative action coordinator in the human resource department for follow-up.

1. *Verbal warning.* Before a written warning is issued, a verbal warning may be given to the employee. This verbal warning should be recorded in the personnel files.
2. *Written warning.* If improvement is not made within the time period granted in earlier warnings, it will be necessary to issue a written warning. This may be done in the form of a memo. In such cases, signature of the employee acknowledges receipt of the written warning but may not indicate concurrence with the information contained in the warning. Copies of written warnings must be furnished to the human resource department and to the employee. If the employee fails to improve by the date given on the warning, other disciplinary action, including termination, may result.
3. *Consultation.* Following the issuance of a written warning, there should be consultations with the employee to check on progress and improvement in the problem area. These consultations should be documented accurately as to the dates and outcomes of the meetings.

III. Retention of Records

Records of verbal and/or written warnings will be removed from an employee's file and destroyed twelve months after the employee has improved behavior in the problem area to the satisfaction of the supervisor or manager. Employees should not be penalized unduly in future years for past difficulties.

The employee relations department will purge the employee's file when the employee's supervisor notifies them that twelve months have elapsed, the employee has improved, and there have been no subsequent warnings necessary.

IV. Consistency of Treatment

If there is one guideline that cannot be stressed enough, it is consistency and equality of treatment of all employees. Your consultation with the employee relations staff will ensure fair and equitable treatment.

Suspension

Some companies employ progressive disciplinary procedures that include suspensions. Suspensions work best when the problem is not serious enough to warrant discharge, but the supervisor needs to take action.

Probation

A probationary period also is utilized by some organizations to give the employee time to change poor behavior.

The key here is to identify the best disciplinary situation for your specific organization and your work force.

HUMAN RESOURCE DIRECTOR'S TIP:

Set up a tracking system (a log works well) to ensure that proper follow-up occurs on any disciplinary action. If the human resource department doesn't follow through, chances are the supervisor won't, either; and then you might have to reinstitute the disciplinary procedures and a new time period.

The key to discipline is to make it as positive as possible, to allow the employee to retain self-respect. The objective is to correct problem behavior and, when the employee has corrected behavior, to wipe the slate clean.

A complete package called "Positive Discipline," mentioned earlier in this chapter, may be reviewed by contacting Performance Systems Corporation in Dallas, Texas. This package is used by many large organizations today. The program throws a more positive light on a tough, emotion-packed management problem.

7.8 SAMPLE EMPLOYEE HANDBOOK

The following sample of an employee handbook includes many of the policies and procedures a company needs; however, each organization is different, and your company may need a policy that is not included.

Refer to the Prentice-Hall *Personnel Management Service* on communications for an in-depth review of other important personnel policies.

XYZ COMPANY
EMPLOYEE'S HANDBOOK

TABLE OF CONTENTS

INTRODUCTION

(An introduction to the company, its business, various locations, management style, and its feelings toward its employees should appear here.)

XYZ ORGANIZATIONAL POLICY

The XYZ Company will make every effort to ensure that your work experience will be desirable and rewarding. All of our policies are devoted to fulfilling this goal.
It is our intent:

- To provide management that is skilled, fair, and concerned about the welfare of employees.
- To competitively compensate each employee in accordance with assigned responsibilities, professional ability, cooperation, and development.
- To fill vacancies or new positions, when possible, by transfer or promotion from within the company.
- To discuss willingly and frankly any problems, complaints, or questions on company policy.
- To keep all employees informed in advance of public notice, whenever possible, of any changes that may affect them or their families.
- To provide equal opportunity to all applicants and employees regardless of race, color, religion, national origin, sex, age, handicap, or veteran status.

YOUR JOB

Hours

The established work week for XYZ is 40 hours. The work week always begins at 12:01 A.M. on Sunday and ends at 11:59 P.M. on the following Saturday.

The usual work week is Monday through Friday. Each day consists of eight paid working hours and one unpaid hour for lunch. The workday is typically scheduled from 8:00 A.M. to 5:00 P.M. but may change at various locations.

Attendance

You are an essential member of the XYZ team, and teamwork is the very heart of our business. It is important that employees be prompt and regular in attendance. If you are unable to report to work on time because of circumstances beyond your control, you should notify your supervisor as soon as possible. We appreciate your cooperation.

When You Are Absent

The company and your co-workers depend on you for certain essential work. When you are absent, it is difficult to fill your shoes. If you need to be away from work, your supervisor should be given advance notice so the vacancy can be filled with a minimum of inconvenience to the company and to your fellow employees.

If your absence will be longer than one day, your supervisor should be given an expected date of return. Should this date change, notify your supervisor at once. When returning to work after an illness of five days or more, a written medical release from your doctor may be requested. If you are given a conditional medical release, the doctor must state what the conditions of the partial release are and specify any job limitations.

In case of serious personal illness or other situations in which advance notice is impossible, notify your supervisor as soon as you can. A member of your immediate family may, if necessary, fulfill this obligation. If your immediate supervisor is unavailable, notify the human resource department, giving your name, your supervisor's name, and the number of days you expect to be absent.

An absence for a period of three consecutive days without contacting your supervisor or the human resource department will be considered justification for termination.

Civic Duties

Employees are encouraged to respond to their civic responsibilities and obligations and to participate in local civic activities and projects. In general, it is the company's policy to allow employees reasonable time off without loss of pay to attend to civic duties such as court appearances, witness or jury duty, and voting.

Leave of Absence

A leave of absence must have the supervisor's recommendation and the department manager's approval. It is necessary to contact the human resource department for assistance in preparation of the application and to review the leave policy, which sets out the duration of leave, benefit status, and so on.

Military Leave of Absence: Any permanent full-time employee of the company who enters active duty in the armed forces of the United States will be granted a military leave of absence without pay and may be rehired upon return under the provisions of our military service policy.

National Guard: Any permanent full-time employee, employed seven months or longer, who is a member of a reserve component of the armed forces of the United States or a member of the National Guard or Air National Guard, will be granted a paid two-week leave of absence for annual training or emergency duty.

Funeral Leave: Time off without loss of straight-time pay will be granted for up to three regularly scheduled working days to arrange for and attend the funeral of a member of the immediate family. Immediate family is defined as an employee's spouse, child (including grandchild), parent (including grandparent), and sibling; those same relatives of the employee's spouse; or any other relative living within the employee's household. Time off without pay to attend the funeral of other relatives or friends may be granted at the discretion of the employee's manager. As much advance notice as is possible under the circumstances should be given.

Personal Leave of Absence: The company may make provisions for a personal leave of absence for an employee who needs more than one month off for a valid reason other than those covered by the above paragraphs. The maximum leave granted is six months.

Personal leaves of absence for reasons other than civic duties, military duty, reserve duty, or work-related injury or illness are granted on an individual basis at the sole discretion of the company, but always taking into consideration the purpose of the leave, the employee's work record, and the need of the company at that particular time.

A personal leave of absence may be granted upon the expiration of salary continuation benefits received under the company disability income plan as a result of illness, accident, pregnancy, or any other reason of a personal nature not specifically covered under other XYZ policies.

You must be classified as permanent full-time and have completed six months of continuous service before the effective date of the leave.

The company cannot guarantee reinstatement to the former position or to a position with like status and pay.

Length of Service

Your length of service with XYZ is computed in years, months, and days from the date of your most recent employment with the company. Please check with the human resource department if you have questions about your length of service.

Probationary Period

A 120-calendar-day probationary period is required for all new employees. This probationary period provides an opportunity for you as a new employee to evaluate your new work situation and, in turn, provides your manager an opportunity to judge your performance and suitability for continued employment. This probationary period does not represent a guarantee or contract for employment for 120 days or any other period of time and does not affect the eligibility requirements for company benefits.

Promotions

Whenever possible, it is the intent of management to promote from within the company. There is an internal placement policy set out in the Personal Policy Manual, and this policy is followed when a vacancy occurs. Your supervisor has a copy of the policy if you wish to review it.

In addition, the company has an open position listing policy, and most open positions will appear on the company bulletin boards. The listing will include basic job qualifications. You may wish to consult with the human resource department if you have an interest in a job vacancy or questions concerning the promotional opportunities associated with the job.

There are occasions when jobs will not be listed. Two such examples might be:

- When a job can be filled best by natural progression or is a logical career path for an employee already in that department.
- Jobs may be created from time to time to provide development opportunities for specific high-performance employees.

In keeping with this policy, managers are encouraged to work with employees in career development.

YOUR PAY

Pay Periods

You will be paid twice a month. Paydays are the fifth and the twentieth. Time worked from the first through the fifteenth is paid on the twentieth of the same month. Time worked during the remainder of the month is paid on the fifth of the following month.

If payday falls on a holiday or weekend, you will be paid on the last working day preceding the holiday or weekend.

Please endorse your check and cash or deposit it within thirty days.

Salaries

XYZ makes every attempt to ensure that you receive a fair and competitive salary based upon the responsibilities of your job and rates paid in our industry or in the area.

Overtime

If you are a nonexempt employee (as defined in the Fair Labor Standards Act), you will be paid one and one-half times your base rate for all hours in excess of 40 worked in a week, or 8 in a workday. If you are asked to work on a company-recognized holiday, you will receive your base pay plus time and one-half for all hours worked on that holiday.

Meal Allowances

If you work at least 3 hours on Saturdays, Sundays, or holidays, you will be given a lunch allowance of $4.00. A supper allowance of $7.00 will be given if you work at least 3 hours overtime and beyond 7:00 P.M. on weekdays, or at least 7 hours, excluding lunch, on Saturdays, Sundays, or holidays. Overtime must have been requested and approved by your supervisor.

Holidays

There will be eleven paid holidays per year as follows: New Year's Day, Washington's Birthday, Good Friday, Memorial Day, Independence Day, Labor Day, Thanksgiving Day, Thanksgiving Friday, Christmas Day, plus two floating holidays that will be determined and announced at the beginning of each year.

When a holiday falls on a Saturday, it is observed on the preceding Friday. When a holiday falls on a Sunday, it is observed on the following Monday. If a paid holiday occurs during your vacation, an additional day may be added to your vacation period to compensate for that holiday.

To be eligible for holiday pay you must be at work on the scheduled workday before and after a holiday, unless you are on a paid leave of absence, salary continuation, long-term disability, or vacation. New permanent full-time or permanent part-time employees will be eligible for holiday pay after the first day worked.

If the manager approves of the employee's being off on a scheduled workday before or after a holiday, the employee will receive holiday pay. Approval by the manager of the exception report is required.

YOUR BENEFITS

Benefits

As an employee of XYZ, you will participate in our many fine benefits, including medical, life and dental insurance, thrift plan, stock purchase plan, pension program, educational assistance, vacations, and more.

These benefits will provide you and your family with a good measure of financial security and protection.

To explain these plans in depth, the company has compiled a benefit handbook that not only gives you the "total picture" but is also designed to serve as a file to keep your personal benefit program papers together and current. If you do not have a copy of this handbook, ask for it in the human resource department.

The company provides internal claims processing, and you are encouraged to discuss any problems concerning medical or dental claims with the human resource benefit technician.

HEALTH AND SAFETY

Safety

Your safety is a major concern, and we make every reasonable effort to provide you with a safe place to work. Learn the safe way to do your work. Please use safety equipment when it is required. Don't take chances. When you think safety, you make things safe for yourself and your fellow employees.

In Case of Injury

Should you become injured on the job and in the normal course of your employment, you are directed to seek medical attention at once and to report to the health unit on the first level.

If, on the day of your work-related injury, you are, in the opinion of your supervisor and the company nurse, unable to work the remainder of the day, you will be compensated. Compensation for this time will be at your straight time.

All XYZ employees are provided Workers' Compensation insurance protection. Appropriate accident report forms should be completed. Forms and physician referral service may be obtained from the company nurse.

Health and Fitness

All employees are eligible and encouraged to take part in the XYZ fitness programs. In the interest of safety, all prospective participants are encouraged to check with the company nurse to obtain a fitness evaluation, especially if the employee is aware of or suspects any physical impairment that might preclude an exercise program. The extent of the evaluation will vary according to the employee's age and health history. Additional testing such as a stress electrocardiogram or pulmonary function may also be necessary for those who might be at high risk.

To encourage use by all interested employees, the Fitness Center will be open Monday through Friday from 7:00 A.M. until 7:00 P.M. Employees may use the exercise room during working hours provided that the work time is made up during the same week. It is expected that supervisory approval be obtained and that the employee's location be known by the department.

PROBLEMS AND HOW TO SOLVE THEM

1. Discuss the problem first with your supervisor. This will clear any misunderstanding and resolve a majority of the issues.
2. If the problem was not handled to your satisfaction by your immediate supervisor or if you fail to receive a response within ten working days, you may discuss the matter with your department manager.
3. If the problem still has not been resolved to your satisfaction, you may direct a formal written complaint to the functional head of your operating unit.
4. If a satisfactory resolution did not occur under step three of this procedure, you may direct a complaint to the director of human resources. The director of human resources will consult with the functional head, the manager, and you, in an attempt to resolve the problem. A written report and final recommendation will be furnished to all participants.
5. If you are still not satisfied with the resolution of the problem, you may submit a written appeal to the president. A final decision on the matter will be made at this level.

It is understood that any employee who elects to utilize the employee complaint procedure will be treated courteously and that the problem will be handled confidentially at all times. Problems or concerns of a personal or equal opportunity nature not resolvable directly between you and your supervisor may be taken to the director of human resources.

WORK RULES

The Rules We Live By

Any group of people working together must honor rules for their common good and safety and maintain a consistent standard of action for all. Therefore, some rules have been established to protect you and your rights against arbitrary actions by others. They are intended to provide a uniform policy upon which to base actions and decisions.

The severity of the problem will determine whether verbal reprimand, written reprimand, suspension, or termination would be appropriate. Before a written warning is issued, a verbal warning is usually given to the employee. If improvement is not made within the time period granted in earlier warnings, it will be necessary to issue a written warning. Copies will be furnished to the human resouce department and to the employee. If the employee fails to improve by the date given on the warning or suspension, termination of employment may result.

Upon notification from the director, the human resouce department will remove records of verbal or written warning from an employee's personnel file twelve months after the employee has improved in the problem area to the satisfaction of the supervisor. We feel employees should not be unduly penalized in future years for past difficulties.

Disciplinary Action

The intent of disciplinary action is to ensure through a progressive process that the employee has knowledge of the specific rule, policy, or performance expectations and is given every opportunity to correct the problem. The sequence of disciplinary actions generally will follow from verbal reprimand to written warning to termination. Where suspension is thought to be an appropriate measure of disciplinary action, it may be used following a written warning.

Work Guidelines

Infraction of one of the following may be grounds for immediate termination of employment without use of the progressive disciplinary action procedure:

1. Theft, vandalism, or careless destruction of company or employee property.
2. Unauthorized possession, consumption, or sale of alcohol or illegal drugs on company property.
3. Unauthorized possession or use of firearms or other weapons.
4. Making fraudulent statements on employment applications or job records.
5. Performing work of a personal nature on company time.
6. Soliciting for any purpose or selling anything during working hours. (See "Solicitation and Distribution" below.)
7. Unauthorized gambling during working time or on company property.
8. Insubordination, willful disregard of supervisor's instructions, or fighting on company property.

The above list of guidelines and rules is not all-inclusive.

Solicitation and Distribution

Out of the respect for the private lives of our employees and our desire to receive the full benefit of your productivity, no person who is not an employee of this company (except for commercial salespeople calling on the company) may come onto the property at any time to solicit for any cause or to distribute material of any kind for any purpose without permission of the human resouce department.

Employees may not engage in solicitation or in the distribution of materials of any type for any purpose during working time on company property, except for that which is necessary to carry out their assigned job duties. However, employees may engage in solicitation during their nonworking time and may participate in the distribution of materials on their nonworking time in nonworking areas as long as standards of neatness are maintained.

An employee is not to enter or remain in the working areas except during scheduled working time and a reasonable time before and after scheduled work. If an employee wants to enter those working areas at any other time for a legitimate reason, permission must be secured from the appropriate supervisor.

TERMINATION

If it is your intent to resign from employment with XYZ, a one-week written notice is necessary. The company will appreciate the opportunity to make arrangements to cover the vacancy created by your leaving.

Upon termination, you will be paid all wages earned, including unused and accrued vacation, to the date of termination. You will also be given information concerning the disposition of other employee benefits.

SERVICES

Cafeteria

Cafeteria serving hours are 7:00 A.M. to 8:00 A.M. for breakfast and 11:30 A.M. to 1:30 P.M. for lunch.

The breakfast menu includes the usual variety of breakfast items; the lunch menu includes hot entrees, salads, sandwiches, soups, beverages, and desserts. Designed for quickness and efficiency, the food service system has six serving points that can be approached independently. At the completion of the meal, dishes should be taken to the dish return area. Dishes are not to be removed from the cafeteria. A "No Smoking" section is provided.

Lunches for meetings in the private dining rooms are obtained through the normal food service systems. Following lunch, dishes in the private dining rooms will be removed by cafeteria personnel. Arrangements should be made with the cafeteria caterer for coffee and/or pastries for meetings in conference rooms or private dining rooms.

For after-hour and weekend workers, a vending area is located at the west end of the first level and contains the following machines: canned soft drinks, snacks, cigarettes, food, and change.

Car Pooling/Van Pools

The XYZ Company has a commitment to encourage van pooling, car pooling, and use of public transportation. Van pools are available from various areas within the city. The coordination of the vans is the responsibility of the human resource department.

XYZ maintains a pool of cars and trucks that are available by reservation. Whenever possible, reservations for a vehicle should be made at least one day in advance. Obtain a pool vehicle use form from your manager, complete the form, and present it to the fleet coordinator. For special details regarding these special-use vehicles, contact the fleet coordinator.

Cashier Services

Cashier services are provided for XYZ employees. The cashier's office is located in the lobby area between the reception desk and the cafeteria. Cashier services are available from 10:00 A.M. to noon and from 2:00 P.M. to 4:00 P.M.

EMPLOYEE COMMUNICATIONS

XYZ has numerous ways to inform its employees about what is happening in and around the company. These include weekly and monthly publications, the use of bulletin boards, and noontime communications programs.

Publications

XYZ News is a weekly publication distributed to employees every Monday. It provides general information about XYZ and employee activities. It also includes want ads, the weekly menu, and announcements of company job openings. All employees are encouraged to contribute information to this capsule form of in-house news.

Each new employee is photographed and featured in the monthly *People* publication. Also included are promotions, new titles, career ladder progressions, and job anniversaries.

Bulletin Boards

Bulletin boards may be found in all coffee rooms, the vending area, and the cafeteria. These boards are for general company-related information, with the exception of the one in the vending area, which is for personal postings by employees who have items for sale or trade, services to offer, or other general announcements. All posted notices must be initialed and dated by the human resource department.

Noontime Programs

Every Monday and Wednesday at 12:30 P.M., a special program is provided for all employees. The programs are varied to include management sessions, XYZ projects and activities, guest speakers, and slide shows and films on a variety of topics such as energy, sports, science, and culture.

WHAT ELSE YOU NEED TO KNOW

Keeping Your Records Up to Date

It is important that you notify your supervisor and the human resource information center in the human resource department of any changes in your home address, telephone number, marital status, dependents, beneficiaries, military reserve status, and education courses or seminars.

Only you can keep your records up to date.

Miscellaneous

Information regarding employee parking, building access, and facilities may be obtained from your supervisor or the human resource department.

WELCOME TO XYZ COMPANY ! ! !

HUMAN RESOURCE DIRECTOR'S TIP:

Because handbooks are being hauled into court, use of the following disclaiming statement is recommended:

"This employee handbook describes only the highlights of XYZ Company's policy, procedures, and employee benefits. In all instances, the official Personnel Policy Manual, Administration Manual, Benefit Plan Texts, Trust Agreements, and/or Master Contracts, as appropriate, are the governing documents. Your employee handbook is not to be interpreted as a legal document or employment contract."

7.9 ORGANIZATION CHARTS—A TOUGH ASSIGNMENT FOR THE HUMAN RESOURCE DIRECTOR

The CEO wants an organization chart quarterly. You start putting one together, and before you can finish it, twenty-three people have transferred or changed jobs. What can you do?

1. Agree on a regular date for issuing new charts, and do the chart on a regular basis as of a specific date, say, quarterly.
2. Have one person responsible for updating and printing charts. That person needs access to personnel change notices in order to stay current.

If you need help—you aren't sure how the company should be structured, and you want to know how other similar organizations are organized—the Conference Board has an organization chart exchange.[6] The Board maintains charts on 1,300 of the largest corporations in the United States.

What can other companies' organization charts be used for?

• To compare your company to a competitor in number of people on staff, ratio of managers to hourly workers, span of control figures, and so on.
• See what job titles other companies use.
• Find new options for structuring key functions.

The Conference Board updates charts yearly, and companies that contribute their organization charts are eligible to participate. There are charges to cover the cost of the exchange.

---

[6] The Conference Board, 845 Third Avenue, New York, New York 10022.

CHAPTER **8**

EEO, Affirmative Action, Age Bias, Equal Pay, Sexual Harassment—Where Are We, and Where Are We Going?

- A growing number of fired employees, many of them barely into their forties, are filing age discrimination suits against their former companies and winning big settlements. Some attorneys feel that companies underestimate age bias claims.
- The question of termination at will is being challenged in courts across the country.
- The September 16, 1982, issue of the *Wall Street Journal* carried an article entitled "Big Fight Looms Over Gap in Pay for Similar 'Male' and 'Female' Jobs." The article stated that some unions have taken up the fight over comparable worth, hoping to enlist more women members.
- In a 1982 article in the *Los Angeles Times*, Cynthia Maduro Ryan, a Los Angeles attorney who specializes in defending employers against charges of sexual harassment, says they have become very costly for employers. No one knows for sure how much private businesses have paid out, but government statistics show that agencies of the federal government paid $180 million between May 1978 and May 1980.

These are just some of the current issues facing human resource directors in the equal employment/affirmative action arenas. In this chapter, we review key issues and suggest some solutions to the more troubling problems.

8.1 PREVENTING, INVESTIGATING, AND AVOIDING CORPORATE LIABILITY FOR SEXUAL HARASSMENT

EEOC guidelines on sexual harassment state that prevention is the best tool for eliminating it. An employer should take all steps necessary to prevent sexual harassment from occurring. Suggested preventive steps are raising the subject affirmatively, expressing strong disapproval, developing appropriate sanctions, informing employees of their right to raise the issue of harassment under Title VII and how to raise it, and developing methods to sensitize all concerned.

Most supervisors are unaware of what sexual harassment really is. EEOC guidelines state that unwelcome sexual advances, requests for sexual favors, and other verbal or physical conducts of a sexual nature constitute harassment when (1) submission to such conduct is made either explicitly or implicitly a term or condition of an individual's employment, (2) submission to or rejection of such conduct by an individual is used as the basis for employment decisions affecting such individual, or (3) such conduct has the purpose or effect of unreasonably interfering with the individual's work performance or creating an intimidating, hostile, or offensive working environment.

In addition, the guidelines state that, with respect to conduct between fellow employees, an employer is responsible for acts of sexual harassment in the work place where the employer (or its agents or supervisory employees) knows or should have known of the conduct unless it can show that it took immediate and appropriate corrective action.

Many managers and supervisors don't understand what types of conduct are offensive to employees, so it's important to have an awareness program. There are some excellent 16-mm films available that explain sexual harassment. Provide examples of harassment that include verbal behavior. Telling dirty stories, asking inappropriate questions (like "How's your sex life?"), circulating sex-related cartoons, hanging nude calendars or pictures in work areas where both males and females must work, jeers and whistles, hugging, patting, and punching are all considered forms of sexual harassment.

Case Example of Sexual Harassment

A male supervisor continually told dirty stories in the presence of his secretary and other females in his department. He took the harassment a step further with his secretary. After she had worked for him for about six months, he told her that he would like to take her to bed and described in detail what he wanted to do to her. She was frightened, and told another (female) supervisor in her department what had been said and how fearful she was of her supervisor. Because she needed her job, she was reluctant to tell anyone else about the problem. The harassment continued and finally the woman went to the company's human resource manager and described the harassment and her fears about losing her job if she complained.

The human resource manager assured the employee that the company did not condone the actions of the supervisor and that action would have to be taken to investigate the alleged harassment. The employee asked the human resource manager not to tell anyone she had complained. The human resource manager said that it was essential to tell the vice-president in charge of her department so that he could take appropriate action, and assured the employee that there would be no retaliation against her for bringing the problem to light.

Other women in the department also went to the human resource manager to complain about the supervisor. The human resource manager had lengthy discussions with the vice-president of the department about the problems and provided dates and specific details that had been relayed by employees in the department. The vice-president still did not believe there was a problem of harassment. The human resource manager tried to make the vice-president understand that the problem was serious, that it was his feeling that the situation did involve sexual harassment, and, further, that not only should there be a thorough investigation but that the supervisor should be told to discontinue such actions immediately.

The vice-president did nothing, and the harassment went on for another six months. The supervisor told the employee during her performance appraisal that she would move up a lot faster in the company if she'd be a little more open to his advances. The employee decided she had no alternative but to file charges with the EEOC and to bring a civil suit in order to keep her job and eliminate the threatening behavior.

After the employee filed charges, the company called in their attorney to work with the human resource manager in investigating the situation. The human resource manager and the attorney found that there was sexual harassment, and the supervisor was fired.

Had the vice-president of the department investigated the situation after the initial complaint, he could have saved the employee unwarranted harassment and the company approximately $6,000 in attorney's fees.

Case Example of Hazing of a Woman on the Job

Hazing is teasing or threatening that is carried on by co-workers rather than a supervisor. The question that arises in hazing is what the employer should do about it. The leading case on hazing involved a female engineer who experienced verbal teasing, which included remarks and questions about her sex life, as well as nonverbal conduct (circulation of lewd cartoons). She was fired when she filed charges to force the company to take action regarding the offensive behavior. In that case, the employer was found liable for damages under Title VII. In addition, her co-workers were required to pay her monetary damages.

A review of this case is instructive. The employer did nothing to stop the abusive behavior. Instead, the female engineer was punished by being transferred to another floor because she couldn't get along with fellow workers. The company did not investigate her charges of harassment. In talking to her about her co-workers, her supervisor told her to disregard the hazing, because it goes on in the man's world all the time. Her supervisor also said that she should be flattered by the attention.

After the woman told her employer that the transfer had not remedied the problem, the employer began to "document" the situation, and the supervisor suggested that she seek psychiatric help. The court discounted the documentation prepared during that period, because it was obviously done in preparation for litigation.

A lesson to be learned here is that documentation of management's actions isn't necessarily in management's best interests if it is done after a problem has escalated to the point of litigation.

The woman was terminated when the company learned she had filed charges with the State Civil Rights Department. The actions of management (and the lack of appropriate action), as well as other conversations with representatives of the company, led the court to conclude that the employer had tacitly approved of the harassment or hazing by disregarding the complaint and failing to take any action to stop the men from hazing the employee. Both compensatory and punitive damages were awarded in this case.

New York's Chief Judge Brietel, quoted by the court in the decision in the case of the female engineer, might be considered seriously:

> It often happens that those who are not supine and fight for their rights will be regarded as troublesome, and those disturbed by the struggle would wish that the troublesome one would just go away.

An employer cannot ignore the problem, hoping it will go away, but must investigate and deal with the problem in a thorough and timely manner.

Preventing Sexual Harassment

It is important to establish a policy regarding sexual harassment and to communicate and enforce the policy.

The policy should state the procedures to be followed by supervisors when harassment is brought to light, the employee complaint procedures, and the avenues for investigation.

Handling Sexual Harassment Complaints

- Obtain information about the alleged harassment from the employee who has complained. Ask for facts and any documentation of the incidents of inappropriate behavior. Assure the employee that there will be no retaliation for bringing the problem to light.
- Notify the employee's immediate supervisor and department head. If the employee is covered by a collective bargaining contract, also notify the union representative.
- Assign the investigation to one specific human resource representative, to ensure timely and effective follow-through of the investigation, assuring that the investigation is handled in a confidential manner that protects the identities of all involved.
- If the investigation reveals that there was sexual harassment, take corrective action immediately. Depending on the seriousness of the harassment, termination of the guilty employee may be indicated.

It's a good idea to train your supervisors to identify and deal with sexual harassment.

Training Is the Key to Avoiding Sexual Harassment Charges

The March–April 1981 issue of *Harvard Business Review* reported that in a survey of over 7,000 of their subscribers, the biggest issue with sexual harassment on the job is not defining it, but recognizing it when it occurs. Pointing out that, according to the EEOC, employers have "an affirmative duty to prevent and eliminate sexual abuse," the magazine states that "the survey clearly shows that management should address the problem which affects the morale, self-confidence, and efficiency of many workers."

To "ensure a uniform corporate response" to the problem of sexual harassment in the workplace, General Motors Corporation has set up an organizationwide training program to teach supervisory personnel the do's and don'ts of sexual harassment. In order to ensure that the program works, all General Motors units in the United States must take the following steps:

- Each unit's personnel director must meet with the unit head, such as the general manager, plant manager, or managing director, and those persons reporting to the unit head to discuss sexual harassment and its implications in the workplace. These discussions are designed to ensure that management understands its responsibility for communicating company policy and for ensuring a workplace free of sexual harassment.
- Information sessions for all supervisors are held, during which the managers are instructed on the nature of sexual harassment, the company's policy in the area, and their role in dealing with sexual harassment incidents. A question-and-answer period follows.
- A bulletin board notice outlining the company's policy for all employees is posted, once the supervisory meetings are concluded.
- The unit personnel director designates persons responsible for counseling employees who report sexual harassment concerns.

As an employer, you are responsible for the actions of your managers and supervisors, whether you know about their actions or should have known about them. The repercussions of this statement are staggering.

It is important to educate your supervisory personnel about their responsibilities in the area of sexual harassment.

- Educate and inform your managers on the subject of sexual harassment and its legal implications.
- Teach them how to cope with the problem in day-to-day situations.
- Outline the liabilities and responsibilities of a supervisor or manager in relation to sexual harassment.
- Provide suggestions for handling a complaint.
- Show a film and include questions for stimulating discussion.
- Answer the most commonly asked questions.
- Train someone on your staff to conduct sexual harassment awareness programs.

8.2 GLOSSARY OF EEO TERMS

The following glossary of terms can be found in the *OFCCP Federal Contract Compliance Manual.* You can order the manual from the Superintendent of Documents, U.S. Government Printing Office, Washington, D.C. 20402. In addition, you may want to order the Equal Employment Advisory Council's *Contract Compliance Under the Reagan Administration: A Practitioner's Guide to Current Use of the OFCCP Compliance Manual,* issued in August 1982.[1]

The book is designed to be used in conjunction with the *OFCCP Compliance Manual,* and it analyzes each section of the manual that no longer is consistent with current enforcement policies, with proposed regulatory changes or with relevant judicial precedent.

These manuals set out in detail the policies and procedures used by OFCCP personnel in investigating organizations and in enforcing the rules and regulations set forth in Title 41 of the *Code of Federal Regulations,* chapter 60. The compliance manual conforms to the requirements of Executive Order 12067.

If you don't want to buy the manual, the following glossary of terms will give you a good idea of the key elements of an affirmative action program.

Accessibility	A handicapped individual's ability to approach, enter, and use a contractor's facilities easily, particularly such areas as personnel office, worksite, and public areas.
Adverse impact	A substantially different rate of selection in hiring, promotion, transfer, training, or in other employment decisions that work to the disadvantage of members of a race, ethnic, or sex group. If such rate is less than 80 percent of the selection rate of the race, sex, or ethnic group with the highest rate of selection, this generally will be regarded as evidence of adverse impact.
Affected class	One or more employees, former employees, or applicants who have been denied employment opportunities or benefits because of discriminatory practices and/or policies by the contractor, its employees, or agents. Evidence of the existence of an affected class requires (1) identification of the discriminatory practices, (2) identification of the effects of discrimination, and (3) identification of those suffering from the effects of discrimination.
Affirmative action	Those results-oriented actions which a contractor by virtue of its contracts must take to ensure equal employment opportunity. Where appropriate, it includes goals to correct underutilization, correction of problem areas, and so on. It also may include relief such as back pay, retroactive seniority, makeup goals, and timetables.

---

[1] *Contract Compliance Under the Reagan Administration—A Practitioner's Guide to Current Use of the OFCCP Compliance Manual,* Jeffrey A. Norris, Published by Equal Employment Advisory Council, 1015 Fifteenth Street, N.W., Washington, D.C., 1982.

Affirmative action clauses	Clauses included in federal contracts and subcontracts detailing the affirmative action requirements for disabled veterans, Vietnam-era veterans, and handicapped workers. "Affirmative action for disabled veterans and veterans of the Vietnam era" is included in all federal contracts and subcontracts of $10,000 or more. "Affirmative action for handicapped workers" is included in all federal contracts and subcontracts in excess of $2,500.
Affirmative action program	A written, results-oriented program, meeting the requirements of 41 CFR Part 60-2, 60-250.5, and 60-741.5, in which a contractor details the steps it will take to ensure equal employment opportunity, including, where appropriate, remedying discrimination against an affected class, and so on.
Aggregate work force	For geographic areas designated by OFCCP under 41 CFR 60-4.6, the total work force of a covered constuction contractor. The term encompasses all of the contractor's work force, including those performing on federally funded or assisted and all nonfederal projects within the designated geographical area.
Annual goal	A yearly target, expressed as both a number and a percentage, for placing minorities or females in a job group for which underutilization exists. It normally should be the maximum rate that can be achieved by making every good-faith effort.
Applicant flow data	A statistical compilation of employment applicants showing the specific numbers of each racial, ethnic, and sex group who applied for each job title (or group of job titles requiring similar qualifications) during a specified time period.
Applicant for employment	A person who files a formal application, or by some other means (résumé, letter, request, etc.) indicates a specific desire to be considered for employment. An applicant log should record requests for employment made in person, whether or not an application form is completed.
Apprentice	A worker who is employed to learn a skilled trade in a structural program of on-the-job training and related instruction.
Availability	The percentage of minorities or women who have the skills required for entry into a specific group, or who are capable of acquiring them.
Back pay	Compensation for past economic losses (such as lost wages, fringe benefits) caused by contractor's discriminatory employment practices, including its failure to remedy the continuing effects of past practices.
Business necessity	Justification for an otherwise prohibitive employment practice based on a contractor's proof that (1) the otherwise prohibited employment practice is essential for the safety and efficiency of the business, and (2) no reasonable alternative with lesser impact exists.

Career counseling	Discussion between a contractor and an employee or group of employees to plan a course of training and advancement for the employee or group.
Compliance	Adherence to the applicable equal opportunity clause or affirmative action clauses. In establishing methods for carrying out its obligations, the contractor shall follow the requirements of the applicable regulations of 41 CFR chapter 60 and Executive Order 11246, as amended, Section 503 of the Rehabilitation Act of 1973, as amended, and/or Section 402 of the Vietnam Era Veterans Readjustment Assistance Act of 1974.
Conciliation	Discussion between OFCCP and a contractor aimed at resolving findings of noncompliance.
Conciliation agreement	A written agreement between a contractor and OFCCP that details specific contractor commitments to resolve identified compliance deficiencies set forth in the agreement.
Construction contract	Any contract for the construction, rehabilitation, alteration, conversion, extension, demolition, or repair of buildings, highways, or other changes or improvements to real property, including facilities providing utility services. The term includes supervision, inspection, and other onsite functions incidental to actual construction.
Continuing discrimination	Where individuals or groups suffer the current effects of past discrimination that have not been remedied. This may include, for example, loss of income or other benefits, lower job seniority, or other injuries.
Contracting agency	Any department, agency, establishment, or instrumentality in the executive branch of the government, including any wholly owned government corporation, that enters into contracts. With respect to federally assisted construction contracts, this term also includes the grant or aid recipient.
Deficiency	Noncompliance with a requirement of Executive Order 11246, Section 503 of the Rehabilitation Act of 1973, Section 402 of the Vietnam Era Veterans Readjustment Assistance Act of 1974, including implementing rules, regulations, or orders.
Dictionary of Occupational Titles	Publication of the Employment and Training Administration, U.S. Department of Labor, which classifies more than 20,000 jobs based on their duties and commonly required qualifications.
Disabled veteran	A person entitled to compensation under laws administered by the Veterans Administration for disability, or a person whose discharge or release from active duty was for a disability incurred or aggravated in the line of duty.
Discrimination	Illegal treatment of a person or group (either intentional or unintentional) based on race, color, national origin, religion, sex, handicap, or veteran status. The term also includes the failure to remedy the effects of past discrimination.

Disparate treatment	Differential treatment of employees or applicants on the basis of their race, color, religion, sex, national origin, handicap, or veteran status (including, for example, the situation where applicants or employees of a particular race or sex are required to pass tests or meet educational requirement which similarly situated contemporary applicants or employees of another race or sex were not required to take or meet).
EEO-1 Report	(Also termed Standard Form 100.) The Equal Employment Opportunity Employment Information Report, an annual report filed with the Joint Reporting Committee (composed of OFCCP and EEOC) by employers subject to the Executive Order or to Title VII of the Civil Rights Act of 1964, as amended. This report details the race, ethnic, and sex composition of an employer's work force by job category.
Employment offer	An employer's offer to an applicant for employment, usually in a specified job.
Equal Opportunity Clause	The seven subparagraphs contained in Section 202 of Executive Order 11246, as amended, and required to be part of all contracts covered by the Executive Order. Pursuant to 41 CFR 60-1.4(e) and 60-4.9, the clause is a part of all covered contracts whether or not it is physically incorporated into the contract and whether or not the contract is written.
Focus job area	A unit of an establishment's work force (such as a seniority unit, department, line of progression, or job title, as appropriate) in which minorities or women are concentrated or underrepresented relative either to their overall representation in the relevant workforce sector or to their availability for the jobs in question. This concept is related to determining the existence of discrimination rather than to the process of finding underutilization for the purpose of setting goals as part of the contractor's affirmative action program.
Fringe benefits	Medical, hospital, accident, life insurance, and/or retirement benefits, profit sharing, bonus plans, leave, and terms and conditions of employment other than wage or salary compensation.
Front pay	Compensation provided to an individual or group which begins when a remedy for alleged discrimination is agreed to and ends when the individual or group attains its "rightful place."
Goals for nonconstruction contractors	A contractor-established employment target for minorities or women where the contractor has identified underutilization of, or other employment problems relating to, minorities or women in certain job categories. The contractor agrees to make a good-faith effort to achieve its goals. Goals are expressed as both numbers and percentages.
Good-faith efforts	Those actions required by 41 CFR chapter 60, and those the contractor may voluntarily develop, to achieve compliance with the contract's equal opportunity and affirmative action clauses.

Government contract	A written or unwritten agreement or modification thereof between a contracting agency and any person or firm for the furnishing of supplies or services, or for the use of real or personal property, including lease arrangements.
Handicapped individual	Any person who (1) has a physical or mental impairment that substantially limits one or more of his or her major life activities, (2) has a record of such impairment, or (3) is regarded as having such an impairment. A handicap is "substantially limiting" if it is likely to cause difficulty in securing, retaining, or advancing in employment.
Impact ratio	For employment decisions that offer people employment opportunities (e.g., hire, promotion, training), the impact ratio for a group is the selection rate for the group divided by the selection rate for the group with the highest selection rate. For any adverse employment decision (e.g., termination, disciplinary action, layoff), the impact ratios is the (termination) rate for the group in question. Impact ratios are compared to the 80 percent rule of thumb to determine adverse impact.
Internal review procedure	A procedure by which an employer can adequately address and resolve a complaint of employment discrimination made by a handicapped individual, a disabled veteran, or a veteran of the Vietnam era (for example, grievance procedures under a collective bargaining agreement, EEO counselors, etc.).
Invitation to self-identity	An invitation by the contractor extended to all employees and applicants for employment who believe they are covered by Section 402 or 503 to identify themselves as handicapped or disabled for purposes of making reasonable accommodations and taking affirmative action on their behalf.
Job area	Any subunit of a blue- or white-collar work-force sector (such as a department, job group, job title).
Job area acceptance range (JAAR)	A sliding scale of minority or female representation in job areas based on their percentages in the contractor's work force. JAAR is a mathematical formula used to identify possible affected classes, and concentration and underrepresentation of minorities and women in the contractor's work force. JAAR is not the same as the process for determining underutilization, nor is it conclusive proof of discrimination.
Job categories	The nine designated categories of the EEO-1 report: officials and managers, professionals, technicians, sales workers, office and clerical, craft workers (skilled), operatives (semiskilled), laborers (unskilled), and service workers.
Job description	A written statement detailing the duties of incumbents in a particular job title.
Job group	One or more positions having similar content, wage rates, and opportunities.

Job specification	Minimum qualifications necessary to perform a job.
Layoff	The process by which workers are removed from the active payroll to the inactive payroll during a reduction in force (RIF).
Life activities	Activities including but not limited to communication, ambulation, vocational training, employment, transportation, or adaptation to housing.
Mandatory job listing	The provision under Section 402 of the Vietnam Era Veterans Readjustment Assistance Act which requires covered employers to list suitable job openings with the local office of the State Employment Service.
Minorities	All persons classified as black (not of Hispanic origin), Hispanic, Asian, Pacific Islander, American Indian, or Alaskan native.
New hire	A worker added to an establishment's payroll for the first time.
Noncompliance	Failure to follow the conditions set out in a contractor's equal opportunity or affirmative action clauses, and the regulations applicable through those clauses.
Organizational unit	A group of closely related jobs or functions (for example, a department, division, branch, or section) functioning as a single unit.
Physical and mental job requirements	Physical and mental health standards established by contractors for determining an applicant's or employee's ability to perform a job.
Placement	Assignment of a person to a job.
Preemployment medical examination	An evaluation by the employer of the health status of applicants or employees made through written questionnaires or examinations by company-designated physicians as part of the hiring process.
Problem job groups	A job group for which a compliance question must be resolved (for example, missed goals).
Progression line charts	Lists of job titles in a broad job family, generally starting with the less difficult, lower-paying jobs, and progressing to the more difficult, higher-paying jobs.
Progression sequences	A hierarchy of job titles through which an employee may progress in following a career path or ladder. Such sequences generally begin with lower-paying job titles and ascend, through intermediate job titles, to higher-paying job titles.
Promotable minorities and women	Minorities and women eligible for promotion on the basis of selection criteria valid under 41 CFR Part 60-3.
Promotion	Any personnel action resulting in movement to a position affording higher pay, or greater rank, and/or providing for greater skill or responsibility or the opportunity to attain such.
Qualified disabled veteran	A disabled veteran as defined in Section 1-60.51, who is capable of performing a particular job with reasonable accommodation to his or her disability.

Qualified handicapped individual	A handicapped individual as defined in 41 CFR 60-741.2, who is capable of performing a particular job with reasonable accommodation to his or her handicap.
Reasonable accommodation (402/503)	Alterations, adjustments, or changes in the job, the workplace, and/or term or condition of employment that will enable an otherwise qualified handicapped individual or disabled veteran to perform a particular job successfully, as determined on a case-by-case basis depending on the individual circumstances.
Recall	Returning workers to active employment from layoff.
Recruiting and training agency	Any agency, firm, or person that refers workers to a contractor or provides or supervises apprenticeship or training for a contractor.
Referral	The process of sending job-seekers to employers by community organizations, employment agencies, labor organizations, or other sources.
Regarded as handicapped	An individual who has no physical or mental impairment, or whose impairment does not substantially limit major life activities, but who is treated by a contractor as having such a limitation.
Rehire	To return a worker to the payroll after a complete break in service.
Relevant labor market area	Geographic area used to determine availability.
Requisite skills	Those skills that make a person eligible for consideration for employment in a job. (The term should not be confused with the total representation of minorities or women in job titles of the contractor under review or with the population of such persons in the relevant labor area.)
Rightful place	The job that an affected class member would now hold had there been no discrimination.
Skills inventory	A list of persons and their skills kept by a contractor to encourage maximum utilization of the skills of applicants or employees.
Standard Industrial Classification Code (SIC)	A numerical coding system, developed under the sponsorship of the Office of Management and Budget, that classifies establishments by principal activity or service.
Substantially limits	Where a handicap affects an individual's employability to such a degree that he or she is likely to have difficulty in securing, retaining, or advancing in employment.
Support data	Statistical data, documentation, and other materials regarding employment practices; generally used in development, support, and/or justification of an affirmative action program.
Systemic discrimination	Employment policies or practices that, though often neutral on their face, serve to differentiate or to perpetuate a differentiation in terms of conditions of employment of applicants or employees because of their race, color, religion, sex, national origin, handicap, or veteran status. Systemic discrimination normally relates to a recur-

	ring practice rather than to an isolated act of discrimination and may include failure to remedy the continuing effects of past discrimination. Intent to discriminate may or may not be involved.
Termination	Separation of an employee from the active and inactive payroll.
Terms and conditions of employment	The entirety of the environment in which an employee works. The term encompasses all aspects of an employee's relationship with his or her employer and fellow employees, including compensation, fringe benefits, physical environment, work-related rules, work assignments, training and education, and opportunities to serve on committees and decision-making bodies.
Training: formal	A structured program, often in a classroom setting, to develop an individual's skills and abilities. Some or all aspects of on-the-job training may fall into this category.
informal	Experience-oriented training to increase an individual's skills and abilities. Typically, most aspects of on-the-job training fall into this category.
on-the-job	The process of learning a job by actually performing it under close supervision or with assistance.
vestibule	Informal orientation provided by the contractor for the benefit of new employees.
Transfer	Movement from one position or function to another.
Underutilization	Employment of members of a race, ethnic, or sex group in a job or job group at a rate below their availability. The concept of underutilization includes any numerical disparity and is not limited by the 80 percent rule applicable to concepts such as adverse impact.
Validation in accordance with OFCCP regulations entitled "Uniform Testing and Selection Guidelines"	The process that a contractor carries out under 41 CFR Part 60-3 to establish that an employee selection device such as a test or an education requirement is an unbiased predictor of performance on the job.
Veteran of the Vietnam era	A person who served on active duty for a period of more than 180 days, any part of which occurred between August 5, 1964, and May 7, 1975, and was discharged or released therefrom with other than a dishonorable discharge; or who was discharged or released from active duty for a service-connected disability if any part of such active duty was performed between August 5, 1964, and May 7, 1975; and who was so discharged or released within 48 months preceding an alleged violation of the Vietnam Era Veterans Readjustment Assistance Act of 1974, the affirmative action clause, or the regulations issued pursuant to the act.

White, not of Hispanic origin	A person with origins in any of the original peoples of Europe, North Africa, or the Middle East, who is not of Hispanic origin.
Willful violation	An act committed by a contractor who could be expected to know its consequences, or failure to act where a reasonable person would be expected to understand the result of such failure (for example, perpetuation of the effects of past discrimination by failure to change a seniority system).

8.3   THREE SAMPLE POLICIES YOU SHOULD HAVE IN YOUR AFFIRMATIVE ACTION MANUAL

Some companies put their affirmative action and equal employment opportunity policies in their human resource or personnel policy manual. It's good to have the policies in a separate affirmative action manual with the actual AA plan. Figures 8–1, 8–2, and 8–3 are samples of three policies you need. You may want to alter them to fit your needs and have your EEO attorney check them before you send them to your supervisors and managers. (See pages 269–271.)

8.4   FIVE CEOs LIST THEIR MAJOR EEO CONCERNS

1. The CEO of a large bank in the western United States has concerns about sexual harassment charges. He's had complaints and isn't sure if he should investigate them or wait and hope they'll go away.

   They won't go away. The bank needs a policy regarding sexual harassment. The policy must be communicated to everyone, and all managers should be told that sexual harassment will not be tolerated. The bank needs a procedure for investigating complaints and communicating the results to the appropriate people.

2. A CEO in charge of a large high-technology company on the West Coast is concerned about back pay awards because a group of women programmers and systems analysts were paid less than male employees in similar positions. The situation has now been corrected.

   The OFCCP has proposed changes to Executive Order 11246 that will limit back pay awards to two years from the date a contractor was notified of the violation or the date the complaint was filed. Back pay would be available only for people identified as victims of discrimination. There also would be a limit to the actual number of job openings. In addition, an arbitrator could be used to resolve a dispute, rather than the courts, which should speed the process.

3. The CEO of a medium-sized engineering firm in the Midwest has concerns about the availability analysis and finding qualified minorities.

   It's been proposed that the availability analysis be reduced from eight factors to four. The four factors are:

- The civilian labor force in your immediate area.
- Number of minorities in the immediate area with the requisite skills.
- Number of minorities in the immediate recruiting area with needed skills.
- Number of minorities transferrable or promotable within the contractor's organization.

The factors that are proposed to be dropped from the analysis are:

- Amount of formal training a contractor may undertake.
- Population of labor area.
- Number of umemployed in the immediate labor area.
- Number of training organizations available in the area capable of training minorities.

The contractor will be able to use civilian labor force data to compute minority availability and will be able to do an availability analysis on job groups of fifty or more.

Finding minorities with the necessary skills, experience, and academic credentials is one of the most difficult problems. Contacting local colleges to find minorities still in school but working on the type of degree needed (such as engineering) and employing the students on a part-time basis is one way to find and tie qualified minorities to your company.

Several prominent organizations in Denver sponsor a minority search firm called Minority Enterprise, Inc., which operates the Rocky Mountain Regional Minority Purchasing Council, one of forty-three such groups around the country. Minority groups spend $80 billion for goods and services.

4. The CEO of an energy company in the Southwest is concerned about a desk audit by the OFCCP because he has just signed a large contract with a local government agency.

An OFCCP desk audit is not a problem or a serious concern if you have your records in order and if you have been meeting at least some of your goals to hire and promote women and minorities. The first thing that happens is that you will receive a letter from the OFCCP announcing the audit. The letter will contain a list of questions and requests for data. The normal list includes the following:

- EEO-1 forms for the previous four years.
- Work-force analysis for the first and second quarters of the current year.
- Progression line charts as of the first of the current year.
- Current year job group and availability analysis.
- Goals and timetable charts for the past year and the current year.
- Data from sections IV A, C, F, VIII, IX, and X of your affirmative action plan.
- Analysis of the selection process.
- Promotion and transfer reports for the past year and the current year.
- Termination reports for the past year and the current year.
- Personnel policies regarding educational assistance program, open position listings, and promotion policy.

FIGURE 8-1.

XYZ COMPANY
Human Resource Policies and Procedures

AFFIRMATIVE ACTION/EQUAL EMPLOYMENT OPPORTUNITY

Objective

To establish by policy our commitment to afford equal employment opportunity to qualified individuals regardless of their race, color, religion, sex, national origin, age, physical or mental handicap, or veteran status, and to conform with the content and spirit of applicable equal opportunity and affirmative action laws and regulations.

Policy

In keeping with the intent of this policy, the company will adhere strictly to the following human resource practices:

- Recruitment, hiring, and promotion of employees in all job classifications will be conducted without regard to race, color, religion, national origin, age, sex, physical or mental handicap, or veteran status, except where a bona fide occupational qualification exists.
- Employment and promotional decisions will be made in such a manner as to further the principle of equal employment opportunity based upon objective selection criteria and relatedness.
- Personnel actions in the areas of compensation, benefits, transfers, training and development, educational assistance, and social and recreational programs, will be administered without regard to race, color, religion, national origin, age, sex, physical or mental handicap, or veteran status, except where a bona fide occupational qualification exists.
- All forms of discrimination with regard to employees or applicants for employment, including any form of racial slurs, religious intimidation, epithets, sexual advances, or harassment, are prohibited; and any charges will be investigated and, if warranted, appropriate disciplinary action taken.

Implementation

Overall responsibility for the development and execution of our affirmative action program and equal opportunity compliance is the responsibility of company managers; however, the day-to-day administration of the program is the responsibility of the human resource director. The human resource director will provide the president of the company with quarterly progress reports. The affirmative action plan is available in the human resource department for review by all employees.

FIGURE 8-2.

XYZ COMPANY
Human Resource Policies and Procedures

EQUAL OPPORTUNITY COMPLAINT RESOLUTION

Objective

To establish by policy a procedure for employees to bring complaints of harassment or discrimination to the attention of management. It is incumbent upon management to mitigate any such charges so that recourse outside the company will be unnecessary.

Policy

By policy and practice, the XYZ Company specifically prohibits any form of discrimination with regard to employees and applicants for employment including any form of racial slurs, religious intimidation, ethnic epithets, or sexual harassment.

- Should there by any question or complaint with regard to our employment practices that any employee has been unable to resolve with the immediate supervisor or others of authority in the employee's department, the employee is encouraged to make that question or complaint known to the affirmative action coordinator or the director of human resources.
- The employee will be asked to state in writing the nature and detail of the complaint.
- The affirmative action coordinator or the director of human resources will investigate the complaint with the manager of the department where the harassment or discrimination is alleged and will respond to the employee.
- The affirmative action coordinator or the human resource director will advise the employee in writing of the results of the investigation and the company's decision regarding the complaint.
- Should the employee feel that the resolution of the complaint is not satisfactory, the employee may seek a review of the facts by the vice-president of human resources.
- The vice-president of human resources will call a meeting involving the appropriate vice-president and the employee. Following the investigatory procedure, the vice-president of human resources will advise the employee in writing of the company's decision.
- A record of the complaint and the findings will become a part of the complaint investigation record and the file maintained separately from the employee's personnel file.
- It is understood that any person electing to utilize this complaint resolution procedure will be treated courteously, the problem handled swiftly and confidentially, and the registering of a complaint will in no way be used against the employee, nor will it have an adverse impact on the individual's employment status.

Policy Dissemination

The attached summary of this policy/procedure will be posted on all bulletin boards at all XYZ locations, operations, and facilities. Additionally, each new employee hired subsequent to the development of this policy will receive a copy.

FIGURE 8-3.

XYZ COMPANY
Human Resource Policies and Procedures

AFFIRMATIVE ACTION PURCHASING PROGRAM
POLICY STATEMENT

The XYZ Company is committed to a policy of nondiscrimination in the conduct of its business, including the employment of women, minorities, and the handicapped, and, where appropriate, the procurement of goods and services from minority-owned businesses. We recognize our responsibility to the communities in which we operate and to the society we serve, and we are dedicated to the development of mutually profitable business relationships with minority-owned business enterprises to ensure their fair share of XYZ's purchases. The use of minority suppliers is a function of our normal purchasing procedures, practiced at all levels and in all areas. In order to carry on our affirmative action purchasing program effectively, we have appointed a coordinator within our purchasing function. At least twice annually, the affirmative action purchasing coordinator will provide a progress report to the director of human resources and the president, setting out our affirmative action purchasing efforts.

- Affirmative action plan for woman and minorities.
- Affirmative action plan for handicapped and veterans.

After the material has been returned to the OFCCP, you will get a call from an investigator to set up an appointment to come to your offices to complete the investigation. The investigator will review your EEO-1 report, your applicant logs, promotion data, and other relevant records, and will ask to speak to some of your minority and female employees. After that investigation, you will receive a letter detailing any problems that were found. The result could be a "show cause" letter enumerating deficiencies and stating that you are not in compliance with Executive Order 11246.

If you receive a letter stating deficiences, you will be asked to sign a conciliation agreement to undertake specific corrective action within a specified period of time.

If you don't have any deficiences, you will receive a letter of compliance.

If the company does not have a qualified human resource director who can handle the audit, an attorney experienced in EEO law should be called in.

5. The CEO of a manufacturing company that has a large government contract is concerned because he doesn't have any handicapped people on the payroll.

He should be concerned. He must take affirmative action to hire the handicapped. Section 503 of the Rehabilitation Act of 1973 established affirmative action for handicapped people, and about half of all businesses in America, almost 3 million, are covered.

There are agencies in most cities that can help you find qualified handicapped job applicants.

8.5 WHAT YOU SHOULD KNOW ABOUT EMPLOYING THE HANDICAPPED

Following are definitions of the handicapped and actions an organization should take in order to affirmatively employ the handicapped.

1. A handicapped person is anyone who has a physical or mental impairment that substantially limits one or more of his or her major life activities; has a record of such an impairment; is regarded as having such an impairment.

2. "Substantially limits" relates to the degree to which the disability affects employability. A handicapped worker having a hard time getting a job or getting ahead on the job because of a disability would be considered "substantially limited."

   "Major life activities" includes communication, ambulation, self-care, socialization, education, vocational training, transportation, housing, and employment. The main emphasis is on those life activities that affect employment. For example, a blind person or a paraplegic person would have "an impairment substantially limiting one or more major life activities." So would a mentally retarded person.

3. Every federal contractor must include an affirmative action clause in each of its contracts or subcontracts. The clause must cover the following points:
   - The contractor agrees not to discriminate against any handicapped person who is qualified to perform the job and also agrees to take affirmative action to hire, advance, and treat handicapped people without discrimination.
   - The contractor agrees to abide by all Department of Labor rules and regulations.
   - In the event of noncompliance, the contractor will be declared in default.
   - The contractor agrees to post notices of affirmative action in conspicuous places around the plant.
   - The contractor agrees to notify all union or worker representatives that they are covered by the affirmative action law.
   - The contractor includes the affirmative action clause in all subcontracts or purchase orders of more than $2,500.

4. Each contractor holding a contract or subcontract of $50,000 or more and having at least fifty employees is required to develop and maintain an affirmative action program that sets forth policies and practices regarding handicapped employees.
   This program may be kept separate from other affirmative action programs, or it may be integrated into the other programs; if this is done, it must be identifiable and retrievable.
   The program must be reviewed and updated each year. Explanations of major changes must be readily available to employees and to applicants for jobs.
   There have been proposals to increase the dollar amounts and the number of employees covered.

5. Handicapped job applicants and employees who want to be covered by affirmative action may be asked to identify themselves. They are told that:
   - The information is to be given voluntarily and will be kept confidential.
   - Refusal to give it will not subject the person to any kind of adverse treatment.

Sample Notice

"If you have a handicap and would like to be considered under the affirmative action program, please tell us. This information is voluntary. It will be kept confidential, except that (1) supervisors and managers may be informed regarding work restrictions or accommodations, and (2) first-aid people will be informed regarding possible emergency treatment."

What Should a Handicap Affirmative Action Program Consist of?

So far, we've shown who is covered by affirmative action programs and how handicapped people can make use of the programs. So that affirmative action might succeed, the Department of Labor has outlined what a program should consist of and what steps a contractor should take to carry out a program.

General. Affirmative action covers all levels of employment, including executive. It also covers all kinds of employment practices such as hiring, upgrading, transfer, demotion, recruitment, layoff, and termination.

Physical and Mental Qualifications. Contractors must look over any physical or mental requirements for jobs to see whether they screen out handicapped people. If by chance they do, they must be clearly job-related and consistent with business necessity and safe performance.

Whenever a contractor looks into a person's physical or mental condition, before hiring or before a change in job status, the query must be based only on the requirements of the job. And the information may be used for purposes of proper job placement.

The information that a contractor gets must be used only for purposes of affirmative action and proper placement. Also, the information must be kept confidential except that:

- Supervisors and managers may be told about work restrictions and necessary accommodations.
- First-aid people may be told if the person's handicapping condition may require emergency treatment.

A contractor may conduct a comprehensive medical exam before hiring, but the results can't be used to exclude or limit opportunities of handicapped people.

Accommodation. A contractor must make "reasonable accommodation" to the physical and mental limitations of handicapped employees or job applicants, unless the contractor can show that the accommodations would create an undue hardship on the business.

Pay. Handicapped people may not have their pay reduced because of any outside disability pension or compensation or payments they may be getting from another source.

Outreach. A contractor must review employment practices to see whether they provide for affirmative action, and outreach efforts should be made. Not all of the following items are required, just those that are appropriate and effective for an individual business. In general, the company should:

1. Build acceptance of handicapped people by managers, supervisors, and all employees through internal communications.
2. Use personnel audits to ensure that affirmative action programs are followed.
3. Use all recruiting sources, such as state employment services, vocational rehabilitation, sheltered workshops, college placement officers, state education agencies, labor organizations, and organizations of and for handicapped people.
4. Recruit candidates at schools for handicapped students—blind, deaf, mentally handicapped, physically handicapped.
5. Get advice on placement, recruitment, training, and accommodations from vocational rehabilitation, voluntary health organizations, handicapped groups, and others.
6. Review employment records of handicapped people to find out whether their full abilities are being used.
7. Try to attract qualified handicapped people from outside the labor force, through organizations to which they belong.

Spreading the Word. To gain full support of affirmative action within the company, it should be publicized in the policy manual; in company publications; by special meetings for executives, managers, and supervisors; in employee orientation programs; in meetings with unions; in nondiscrimination clauses in union contracts; and on company bulletin boards.

Executive Responsibility. An executive of the company should be appointed director of affirmative action activities and should have top-management support. The director's duties should include developing policy statements, affirmative action programs, and communications activities; identifying problem areas and developing solutions; arranging for audit and reporting systems; serving as liaison between the contractor and enforcement agencies and organizations of and for handicapped people; keeping management informed of developments in affirmative action; and arranging for career counseling of handicapped employees.

Carrying Out the Program. To make certain that the greatest possible number of people benefit from affirmative action, the contractor should do things such as:

1. Look over the employee selection process to be sure handicapped people aren't being considered only for certain stereotyped kinds of jobs.
2. Hold briefing sessions for recruiting sources, letting them know about company policies, future job openings, and the like.
3. Carefully select personnel people to ensure that they will implement affirmative action.
4. Include handicapped people in the personnel department.
5. Take part in career days, work–study programs, and other efforts that reach out into the community, as well as other activities that include handicapped people.

Sheltered Workshops. Contracts with sheltered workshops alone do not make an affirmative action program. But they can be part of affirmative action if the workshops train handicapped workers who will be taken on by the company after they complete their training.

Summary. Affirmative action should be positive, not punitive. Its purpose is to encourage employers to hire more qualified handicapped people. An unstated secondary purpose is to encourage more handicapped people to enter the labor market and qualify for jobs.

Note: These are highlights of regulations issued by the Employment Standards Administration of the U.S. Department of Labor. They've been prepared by the President's Committee on Employment of the Handicapped as an aid to understanding the regulations.

For a copy of the official regulations, write to the Employment Standards Administration, U.S. Department of Labor, Washington, D.C. 20210.

Publications similar to this will be issued by the President's Committee, covering the nondiscrimination program of Section 504 of the Rehabilitation Act of 1973, and the affirmative action program for veterans who get special consideration under Section 402 of the Vietnam Era Veterans Readjustment Assistance Act 1974 (Public Law 93-508).

8.6 IDENTIFYING QUESTIONS ASKED IN AN OFCCP COMPLIANCE REVIEW *BEFORE* YOU HAVE ONE

Q. What is the purpose of an OFCCP compliance review?

A. The *Federal Contract Compliance Manual* states that reviews are conducted to determine whether covered contractors and subcontractors are complying and, in the case of preaward reviews, whether potential contractors and subcontractors are complying and are able to comply with relevant provisions of 41 CFR, chapter 60, by not discriminating and by taking affirmative action to ensure equal employment opportunity without regard to race, color, religion, national origin, sex, handicap, or covered veteran status, and by acting in conformance with federal regulations regarding employment of disabled and Vietnam-era veterans.

Q. What is the first thing that occurs when you have a compliance review?

A. The OFCCP sends a letter to the president of the company, asking for specific information and stating that the review will include a desk audit, an onsite review, and, where appropriate, an offsite analysis. The letter will request a copy of your Executive Order 11246 affirmative action program and supporting documentation, prepared in accordance with the requirements set forth in 41 CFR 60-2.10 through 60-2.32. In addition, your Section 402 and 503 affirmative action programs must be submitted for desk audit, normally within thirty days.

Q. What kind of data, other than the affirmative action plan, does the OFCCP request?

A. Following is an itemized listing of information the OFCCP usually requests during a compliance review:

- Copies of your Employer Information Reports EEO-1 (standard form 100 Rev.) for the last four years. (Note: For educational institutions, form EEO-6 is required.)
- Work-force analysis.
- Copies of progression line charts.

- Job group and availability analysis.
- Documentation that areas of underutilization have been identified, and goals and timetables have been established to correct any deficiencies, together with a plan of action to achieve those goals and timetables.
- Summary data and information that indicate the numerical and other results of your affirmative action goals for each job group for the current goal year and the preceding goal year. For each goal not attained, describe the good-faith efforts being made to achieve them.
- An analysis of your selection process, including a determination of whether it eliminates a significantly higher percentage of minorities or women than nonminorities or men. This analysis may consist of a summary of applicant and hire activity identified by race and sex for each job group for (1) the present goal year and (2) the previous goal year, and includes total applicants, total offers of employment, total hires, and total rejections. However, if you do not have the data arranged in that manner, you may choose to submit them in the form available.
- Analysis of your transfer and promotion practices to determine if lateral or vertical movement of minority or female employees is occurring at a lesser rate (compared to work-force mix) than nonminority or male employees. The analysis may consist of a summary of promotion and transfer activity during (1) the present goal year and (2) the previous goal year, identified by race and sex, including the department/job, group/job title into which employees were promoted and each department/job group/title from which promoted. However, if you have performed the analysis under a different arrangement, you may choose to submit it in the manner in which it is available.
- Summary of monitoring reports that reflect the degree to which the nondiscriminatory policy is carried out with respect to terminations of employment. This information may consist of a summary of employee terminations with identification of race and sex and the departments and job titles from which they were terminated. However, if you have not compiled the data in this form, you may choose to submit them in the form in which they are available.

If you don't have experience with OFCCP compliance reviews, and you receive notice that your company is going to have a review, it's a good idea to call in an attorney with EEO or OFCCP compliance review experience.

HUMAN RESOURCE DIRECTOR'S TIP:

The Equal Employment Advisory Council, 1015 Fifteenth Street, N.W., Washington, D.C. 20005, is an excellent resource. The council performs the following activities:

- Assists members in complying with federal EEO requirements.

- Provides members with two days of meetings and workshops on important EEO issues three times each year.

- Presents skill-development seminars on EEO compliance and administration.

- Develops and publishes analytical studies on major EEO issues.

- Monitors court and agency EEO decisions.

- Prepares and files *amicus curiae* briefs in important cases.

- Comments on federal regulatory proposals.

- Analyzes congressional legislation.

- Monitors state-level judicial, legislative, and administrative EEO activity.

- Serves as a clearinghouse on enforcement policies and methods of compliance with federal requirements.

8.7 PRODUCING AN AFFIRMATIVE ACTION PLAN—SAMPLE FORMS AND POSITION STATEMENTS

Forms and position statements for an affirmative action plan are standard and are used in most organizations with little variation. The regulations, Title VII of the Civil Rights Act of 1964, Executive Order 11246, which applies to federal contractors and subcontractors, and Revised Order no. 4 (41CFR Part 60-2) specify requirements of written programs.

It's important for an organization to designate an EEO/AAP coordinator in order to ensure compliance with government regulations and to write and administer the affirmative action plan.

According to Myrna Mourning, EEO coordinator at Rocky Mountain Energy in Denver, Colorado, the EEO coordinator should:[2]

- Develop and update the affirmative action plan annually.
- Implement affirmative action plans to include internal and external communication.
- Design and implement audit and reporting systems that will measure the effectiveness of the AAP, indicate the need for remedial action, and determine the degree to which the company's goals and objectives are being achieved.
- Identify potential and actual problems within particular departments.
- Assist management in the resolution of problems related to EEO/AAP.
- Inform management of the latest developments in the area of equal employment opportunity and on legal issues.
- Serve as a liaison among the company minority, female, and handicapped organizations and governmental compliance agencies.
- Participate in the development of goals and timetables, and assist department managers with efforts to achieve the established goals.

In addition, there are eight key elements to an effective affirmative action program that a human resource director should provide for management review:

[2] "Producing an Affirmative Action Plan, Ensuring Compliance with Government Regulations," Myrna D. Mourning, EEO Coordinator, Rocky Mountain Energy, 10 Longs Peak Drive, Broomfield, Colorado 80020.

1. Corporate policy statement
2. Policy dissemination/communication
3. Assignment of an EEO coordinator
4. Work-force analysis
5. Goals and timetables
6. Development and execution of the program
7. Support of community and outreach programs
8. Effective auditing and reporting systems

In order for an affirmative action program to be effective, there must be an action plan. Mourning provides the following guidelines for an AAP action plan:

- Employees should understand that all charges of discrimination will be investigated by the EEO officer. The employee bringing the charge shall be protected from or not subjected to any form of retaliation.
- All employees should know who the company EEO officer is, so that complaints, concerns, or EEO-related grievances can be directed to him or her.
- The AAP policy statement should be posted in a conspicuous location, so that it is accessible and visible to all employees and applicants.
- The policy should be discussed at new employee orientations and presented to all new employees.
- All publications, pictures, or articles featuring employees should include female, minority, and handicapped employees, along with nonminority men and women.
- All employment agencies and state job service centers should be informed of the company's EEO/AA policy.
- Include the EEO tag line, "Equal Opportunity Affirmative Action Employer," on all advertisements and solicitations for applicants.
- Purchase orders should include the EEO tag line.
- All employees should be informed that they are eligible to participate in company training and development and educational assistance programs.
- All employees (including protected classes) should be encouraged to participate in company-sponsored social and recreational programs.
- The company should communicate to all employees that discriminatory practices in the form of sexual harassment, racial and religious slurs, and other forms of harassment will not be tolerated.
- Encourage female, minority, and handicapped employees to participate in community work and volunteer activities. Write about their involvement in the company newsletters and magazines.
- Ensure that female and minority employees are provided equal opportunity in promotions. To achieve this goal, post all open positions. Have an established career counseling program. Remedial courses in writing, math, and other skills should be offered. Properly and accurately written job descriptions and established salary ranges for each job are on file. Require supervisors and managers to document reasons why an apparently qualified minority or female employee was turned down or passed over for an advancement opportunity.
- The company should appoint top managers and supervisors to serve on community advisory boards and public-sector selection boards.
- The EEO officer and/or other personnel staff should participate in and speak at programs at schools and colleges where greater numbers of minority and female

students are students, actively recruit applicants from these institutions, and use the news media for advertisements, particularly in minority and female publications. Company newsletters and magazines are excellent ways to publicize the achievements of minority, female, and handicapped employees.

- Summer employment programs should include female, minority, and handicapped students. In-service training sessions for minority and female employees should include teachers from the predominantly minority and female schools and colleges.
- Provide tours and orientation sessions for the students and teachers from predominantly minority schools and colleges.
- Ensure that selection procedures and processes comply with the OFCCP Uniform Selection Guidelines of primary importance; train managers and supervisors in the Uniform Selection Guidelines.
- To increase the company's applicant pool, establish ongoing involvement with civil rights groups, such as Urban League, Local Alliance of Business Programs, and colleges in the development and implementation of special employment programs for youths and disadvantaged persons. Provide technical experience and know-how to such programs.
- Encourage referrals from minority and female employees.
- Employees should be encouraged to discuss problems of discrimination or harassment with their supervisors, or if they feel they cannot talk to their supervisor, the EEO coordinator or the human resource director. When you counsel an employee, it's important to keep a record of the meeting. A sample counseling log appears in figure 8–4.

Auditing and Reporting Systems

In order to be effective over time, any program needs built-in auditing and reporting systems. Here are some that are helpful:

- Regular reports of referrals, placements, promotions, transfers, and terminations are essential to ensure that discriminatory practices are not carried out.
- Report results should be reviewed regularly with all managers and supervisory personnel, so they are aware of goal achievement and potential problems within their individual departments.
- Program effectiveness should be reported to top management, along with recommendations to improve or eliminate deficiencies.
- Any company with 500 or more employees would receive substantial benefits from a computerized EEO/AAP planner. All reports can be sorted by job group, race, sex, title, age, handicapped, and veteran status. The primary advantage of a computerized EEO system is that the data can be retrieved instantly.

Pages 281-293 provide sample position statements and a format for packaging your affirmative action program.

FIGURE 8-4.

COUNSELING LOG

EEO COORDINATOR or
HUMAN RESOURCE DEPARTMENT STAFF MEMBER_____

Date	Comments:	Date of Follow-Up (if required)	Minutes/Hours Spent in Session
	Total Minutes/Hours		

XYZ COMPANY

AFFIRMATIVE ACTION PROGRAM

I. AFFIRMATIVE ACTION POLICY STATEMENT

It is the policy of the XYZ Company to afford equal employment opportunity to all qualified persons regardless of race, color, religion, national origin, age, or sex, except where age or sex is a bona fide occupational qualification. In keeping with the intent of this policy, the company will adhere strictly to the following personnel practices:

1. Recruitment, hiring, and promotion of individuals in all job classifications will be conducted without regard to race, color, religion, national origin, age, or sex, except where age or sex is a bona fide occupational qualification.
2. Employment decisions will be made in such a manner as to further the principle of equal employment opportunity.
3. Promotional decisions will be made in accordance with the principles of equal employment opportunity by establishing valid job-related requirements of promotional opportunities.
4. All other personnel actions, such as compensation, benefits, transfers, training and development, educational assistance, and social and recreational programs will be administered without regard to race, color, religion, national origin, age, or sex, except where age or sex is a bona fide occupational qualification.
5. Periodically, and at least annually, analyses of all personnel actions will be conducted to ensure equal opportunity.

The aforestated policy is implemented by means of the company's affirmative action program, which is updated annually and is available in the personnel department for review by all employees.

APPROVED: _____
President

DATE: _____

II. POLICY DISSEMINATION

The XYZ Company desires that its equal employment opportunity policy be well known and understood, both within the company and in the communities in which we are located.

A. *Internal*

In order to ensure that our policy is known and understood internally, XYZ will do the following:

1. The policy will be included in the XYZ Personnel Policy Manual distributed to all management and supervisory personnel, particulary those engaged in recruiting and employment.
2. The affirmative action policy statement will be posted in conspicuous locations, easily accessible and visible to all employees and to applicants for employment.

3. The human resource department will conduct periodic meetings with executive, management, and supervisory personnel to discuss the intent of the policy and individual responsibility for effective implementation.
4. The policy will be mentioned in employee orientation and any management training programs.

B. *External*

In order to ensure that our policy is known and understood in the community, XYZ will do the following:

1. Inform all recruiting sources of company policy, and request that these sources refer qualified minorities and qualified females for job vacancies.
2. Include an equal opportunity clause on all purchase orders, leases, and contracts.
3. Insert in all advertisements, solicitations for applicants for employment, and other materials concerning recruitment and hiring the following: "The XYZ Company is an Affirmative Action/Equal Opportunity Employer."

III. POLICY IMPLEMENTATION

The president and chief executive officer of XYZ has designated responsibility for administration of the company's affirmative action policy to the human resource department under supervision of the human resource director. In this capacity, the human resource director has been delegated the authority to implement the affirmative action program which will be reviewed and updated annually.

The duties and responsibilities of the human resource director include:

1. Developing and implementing affirmative action policy, programs, procedures, and internal and external communication techniques.
2. Designing and implementing audit and reporting systems.
3. Serving as liaison between XYZ and the agency minority organizations and community action groups.
4. Keeping management informed about the latest developments in the area of equal employment opportunity.
5. Assisting all departments in fulfilling their responsibilities relative to the company's affirmative action program.
6. Providing guidance in executing personnel practices embodied within the affirmative action policy statement.

IV. INTERNAL AUDIT AND REPORTING SYSTEMS

In order to evaluate progress toward meeting and maintaining company commitments embodied in the affirmative action policy statement, certain information is assembled on a regular basis. This information is tabulated by the human resource department and includes pertinent data on applicant flow, new hires, promotions, transfers, demotions, and terminations. Copies of these logs are included in the appendix.

V. SUPPORT OF COMMUNITY ACTION PROGRAMS

XYZ reaffirms its support of local and national organizations and programs dealing with equal employment opportunity. XYZ personnel are encouraged to become involved in community programs and projects that can contribute to the success of the company's affirmative action program.

VI. SEX DISCRIMINATION GUIDELINES

XYZ is familiar with and intends to comply with Title 41, chapter 60, Part 60–20 of the Code of Federal Regulations, which contains the sex discrimination guidelines issued by the Secretary of Labor. While it is our intention to comply fully with the spirit and intent of these guidelines, we also will be guided by pertinent judicial decisions that interpret or modify these guidelines.

VII. WORK-FORCE ANALYSIS

A work-force utilization analysis has been prepared for XYZ in compliance with the requirements of Title 41, Part 60-2 of the Code of Federal Regulations. The total analysis has been divided into three subdivisions, which are as follows:

1. *The in-house analysis* enables XYZ to evaluate the composition of its work force. The results show the female and minority composition throughout the company.
2. *The labor area analysis* establishes whether the company is underutilized in a specific job category with respect to minorities and women. Underutilization is defined as "having fewer minorities or women in a particular job group than would reasonably be expected by their availability" (within the labor and recruiting area).
3. *The comparison—goals and timetables* indicates those areas where XYZ does not meet the statistical comparative base established through the Labor Area Analysis and provides for goals and timetables to correct the underutilization. See Table 3.

The results of these analyses will be reviewed with management, and goals and timetables will be established to increase the utilization of minority and female persons within XYZ.

The XYZ affirmative action program is of a continuing nature and will be formally updated and revised annually, building on past plans and results.

APPENDICES FOLLOW—ATTACHMENTS A–F AND TABLES 1–3.

XYZ COMPANY
APPLICANT LOG

QTR. BEG. (MO. DAY. YR.) _____ QTR. END. (MO. DAY. YR.) _____

NAME (FIRST AND LAST)	DATE MO.	DA.	YR.	SEX M	F	MINORITY GROUP N.	SSA	O.	A.I.	Oth.	POSITION TITLE	E E O JOB CATEGORY	SOURCE OF APPLICANT	REFERRED TO (ORG. UNIT)	DISP. (Reasons for Rej.)	INTER- VIEWED BY	REQ. NO.
TOTALS																	

XYZ COMPANY
HIRING LOG

QTR. BEG. (MO. DAY, YR.)   QTR. END. (MO. DAY, YR.)

NAME (FIRST AND LAST)	DATE			SEX		MINORITY GROUP					POSITION TITLE	E E O JOB CATEGORY	SOURCE OF APPLICANT	HIRED BY (ORG. UNIT)	INTERVIEWED BY	REQ. NO.
	MO.	DA.	YR.	M	F	N.	SSA	O.	A.I.	Oth.						
TOTALS																

XYZ COMPANY

PROMOTION LOG

QTR. BEG. (MO. DAY, YR.) ___ QTR. END. (MO. DAY, YR.) ___

NAME (FIRST AND LAST)	DATE		SEX		MINORITY GROUP				E.E.O. JOB CATEGORY		POSITION TITLE		ORGANIZATION UNIT		COMMENTS
	MO.	DA. YR.	M	F	N.	SSA	O.	A.I.	Oth.	FROM	TO	FROM	TO	FROM	TO	
TOTALS																

XYZ COMPANY

DEMOTION LOG

QTR. BEG. (MO. DAY, YR.) _____ QTR. END. (MO. DAY, YR.) _____

NAME (FIRST AND LAST)	DATE			SEX		MINORITY GROUP					E.E.O. JOB CATEGORY		POSITION TITLE		ORGANIZATION UNIT		COMMENTS
	MO.	DA.	YR.	M	F	N.	SSA	O.	A.I.	Oth.	FROM	TO	FROM	TO	FROM	TO	
TOTALS																	

XYZ COMPANY
TRANSFER LOG

QTR. BEG. (MO. DAY, YR.)   QTR. END. (MO. DAY, YR.)

NAME (FIRST AND LAST)	DATE			SEX		MINORITY GROUP					E.E.O. JOB CATEGORY		POSITION TITLE		ORGANIZATION UNIT		REASON FOR TRANSFER
	MO.	DA.	YR.	M	F	N.	SSA	O.	A.I.	Oth.	TO	FROM	TO	FROM	TO	FROM	
TOTALS																	

XYZ COMPANY
TERMINATION LOG

QTR. BEG. (MO. DAY, YR.) ____ QTR. END. (MO. DAY, YR.) ____

NAME (FIRST AND LAST)	DATE			SEX		MINORITY GROUP					E.E.O. JOB CATEGORY		POSITION TITLE	ORGANIZATION UNIT	REASON FOR TERMINATION
	MO.	DA.	YR.	M	F	N.	SSA	O.	A.I.	Oth.	FROM	TO			
TOTALS															

XYZ COMPANY
IN-HOUSE ANALYSIS

ORGANIZATION UNIT & POSITION TITLE	EEOC JOB CLASSIFICATION	SALARY RANGE	TOTAL EMPLOYEES	TOTAL BY SEX		MALE MINORITY BY RACE					FEMALE MINORITY BY RACE					% MINORITY	% FEMALE
				MALE	FEMALE	N	SSA	O	AI	OTH	N	SSA	O	AI	OTH		

XYZ COMPANY
LABOR AREA ANALYSIS

EEOC JOB CLASSIFICATION	BASE	POPULATION	UNEMPLOYMENT	CIVILIAN LABOR FORCE	AVAILABLE WORKFORCE								AREA TRAINING INSTITUTIONS	IN-HOUSE TRAINING PROGRAMS	PROMOTABLES AND TRANSFERABLES
					MINORITY				FEMALE						
					RECRUITING AREA		LABOR AREA		RECRUITING AREA		LABOR AREA				
					NO.	%	NO.	%	NO.	%	NO.	%			
		GRAND TOTAL: ___%	GRAND TOTAL: ___%	GRAND TOTAL: ___%											
		TOTAL FEMALE: ___%	TOTAL FEMALE: ___%	TOTAL FEMALE: ___%											
		NEGRO ___%	NEGRO ___%	NEGRO ___%											
		SSA ___%	SSA ___%	SSA ___%											
		O ___%	O ___%	O ___%											
		AI ___%	AI ___%	AI ___%											
		OTHER ___%	OTHER ___%	OTHER ___%											
		TOT. MINORITY: ___%	TOT. MINORITY: ___%	TOT. MINORITY: ___%											

(12)

XYZ COMPANY
THE COMPARISON ·· GOALS AND TIMETABLES

| EEOC JOB CLASSIFICATION | IN HOUSE ANALYSIS | | LABOR AREA ANALYSIS | | UNDERUTILIZATION | | PROJECTED OPENINGS | AAP YEAR GOALS | | | | Goals | | | | IN HOUSE ANALYSIS IF GOALS ARE MET | |
| | | | | | | | | MINORITY | | FEMALE | | MINORITY | | FEMALE | | | |
	% MINORITY	% FEMALE	% MINORITY	% FEMALE	MINORITY	FEMALE		NO.	%	NO.	%	NO.	%	NO.	%	% MINORITY	% FEMALE

HUMAN RESOURCE DIRECTOR'S TIP:

Consulting firms are springing up around the country to fill a matchmaking need. The consulting company works on behalf of organizations that need to hire females and minorities, and also to find minority firms with which to do business in order to fulfill the minority vendor requirements of federal contracts. In some instances, the organizations that use these services pay an annual fee and donate time and other resources to support the effort. The firm provides information and can be a meeting ground for minority and female vendors and corporate purchasing agents.

CHAPTER 9

Programs That Will Help Attract and Retain Today's Workers

Who is today's worker? In his book, *New Rules Searching for Self-Fulfillment in a World Turned Upside Down,* Daniel Yankelovich provides some new insights.[1] The typical household of the 1950s was comprised of a working father, a stay-at-home mother, and one or more children. Today, fewer than one in five people who work fall into that category. By the late 1970s, 51 percent of the women in America were working outside the home. By 1980, more than two out of five mothers of children aged six or younger worked for pay. In families that earned more than $25,000 per year, the majority depended on two incomes. It's been projected that by 1985 nearly 70 percent of the women in America will work outside the home.

When you look at the jobs in most companies, you find that the pay and benefits are still structured for outdated ways of doing things; and when you look at benefit programs, you find that they are still structured for the 1950s-style family. Benefit programs in the 1980s will need to fit the new worker. Jobs in the 1980s and 1990s will need to appeal to new value systems that include participative management styles and provide for more personal time off, flexible work schedules, and better, more open communication to support corporate objectives.

A trend study by the National Opinion Research Council in Chicago reflects the growth of feelings of frustration and lack of control over one's destiny; and there is a growing need for health, stress, and employee assistance programs in most firms.

Today's worker has been described in various articles and books as expecting a high standard of living, clean air and water, and wanting stringent environmental protection and protection against unemployment, illness, industrial accidents, and old age. In addition, the new worker wants self-fulfillment, wants to participate in management decisions affecting his or her work, and wants more leisure time, a personalized lifestyle, and more promotional opportunity on the job.

How can the human resource director assist management in relating to this new worker? And, more importantly, how can we make corporate goals workers' priorities?

---

[1] *New Rules, Searching for Self-Fulfillment in a World Turned Upside Down,* Daniel Yankelovich, Random House, 1981.

Dr. G. Dale Meyer of the Meyer Group, a consulting organization based in Boulder, Colorado, offers the following suggestion as one way to assist a company in identifying workers' priorities and values:[2]

> Assess the organization climate as it relates to the present work force. One way to do this is through an employee survey. This survey should be systematic and continuous to discover trends in such matters as employee attitudes, total organization climate, expectations, satisfactions, and frustrations. The survey might be completed utilizing a variety of instruments, both published and/or custom-tailored to your organization. Whatever instrument you use, it should address such matters as:
>
> * Organization design
> * Reactions to management groups and styles
> * Conflict identification
> * Employee views of career opportunities
> * Employees' challenges and their sense of security
> * Economic factors (pay, benefits, inflation, retirement, etc.)
> * Communication and participation opportunities
> * The overall company atmosphere
> * Pertinent factors not regularly considered
>
> On the basis of a well-designed audit, the program should be designed to integrate with the human resources charter. The program should be communicated widely, beginning with the supervisors and managers. Management training and development activities, individual goal setting (objectives), and performance evaluation systems should be tied carefully to the program, and the program itself should be monitored, revised, and evaluated on a systematic basis.

There are many pros and cons regarding employee surveys, and if your company decides to conduct a survey, get some help from an expert. Employee surveys can create more problems than they solve if they aren't done right and if the results of the survey are not communicated adequately to employees.

The company that sets about to synchronize company goals with individual goals, and to communicate that objective to management, supervisors, and employees, is the one that will be most successful. If a company can achieve its business plans while helping employees to achieve their personal goals, success should follow.

There is a better educated, more savvy work force out there today, and companies need to adjust to that idea and tap their productivity by being more open and by structuring work and work rules to the current work ethic, not the work ethic of the 1950s, 1960s, or 1970s.

As Yankelovich said, "This shift in the shared meaning of profit-making—from immoral to ethically worthy—took several centuries to complete. But the shift from self-denial to duty to self has taken place within our lifetime, as have the great changes in sexual morality, attitudes toward credit and indebtedness, and toward women working outside the home, divorce, abortion, and so on."

---

[2] G. Dale Meyer, Ph.D., The Meyer Group, Inc., 2885 East Aurora, Suite 17-G, Boulder, Colorado 80303.

To quote Yankelovich further, "The genius of a great social ethic is neither to supress desires indiscriminately nor to endorse them indiscriminately; it is to make certain that desires and social goals are compatible with each other."

The companies that can find that human–corporate compatibility and communicate it will be most successful in the future.

New ways of working, new benefit programs, and new communications programs are at least a beginning.

9.1 EMPLOYEE ASSISTANCE PROGRAMS

The growth of employee assistance programs may be an indication that there has been a need for many years, but it has been just recently that organizations let the problems of alcoholism, drug use, and mental illness out of the closet.

The rate of growth of employee assistance programs is impressive. Two opinion research corporation surveys show that the number of Fortune 500 companies with employee assistance programs has increased from 25 percent in 1972 to more than 57 percent in 1982. Another survey done in 1979 showed that more than 5,000 programs existed in the public and private sectors, covering approximately 10 million workers.

Programs can assist employees with a wide variety of problems: alcohol, drug, mental, family, financial, legal, and emotional. The three key elements of an employee assistance program are:

1. Accurate assessment of the problem
2. Appropriate and timely treatment
3. Regular follow-up

A *Rocky Mountain News* article dated February 15, 1981, stated that alcohol-related problems may cost the U.S. economy $25 billion per year. The trend is to early detection and treatment. A *U.S. News and World Report* article stated that industry has 10 million alcoholic workers and that employers, unions, insurance companies, and distillers are joining forces to do something about detecting problem drinkers and helping them get treatment.

An Employee Assistance Program

An industrial firm in the Midwest published the following policy and procedures for their employee assistance program. The employee will:

• Be given a physical examination, consultation, and follow-up with possible short-term hospitalization if the company doctor finds there is a need.
• Be granted an approved leave of absence and will receive illness benefits equal to those of any other illness.
• Be expected to return to work on the day following discharge from the hospital. Failure to do so will result in termination of pay and benefits.

- Undergo rehabilitation counseling on a mandatory weekly basis for the first six months on program and at the request of the human resource counselor thereafter.
- Be entitled to see the counselor during working hours, if necessary, after getting permission from the immediate supervisor.
- Agree that the counselor discuss the problem frankly with the immediate family as soon as possible after enrollment in the program. The family will be made aware of the company's objectives and will be referred to agencies available to help and guide them through the problem.
- Participate in Alcoholics Anonymous (AA), the most successful organization in helping the alcoholic.
- If a drug abuser, be referred to local drug facilities or clinics in place of AA meetings. The program will be identical, with this exception.
- Agree that failure to make satisfactory progress in the program after a reasonable period will result in either a mandatory leave of absence for rehabilitation or dismissal from our program. In the latter case, the department head will be notified, and the employee will be subjected to the usual disciplinary action and possible termination.

Supervisors' Guidelines for Handling Drug or Alcohol Problems on the Job

Even when a company has good policies and procedures, supervisors must be trained to spot problems and advised about what to do when faced with an alcohol or drug problem. Following are guidelines for supervisors for discussions with employees.

- Make it clear that your responsibility is for job performance, productivity, and attendance, and that your responsibility is a concern to do what you can to help the employee improve job performance.
- Remember that documented evidence of a downward trend in performance or attendance is the best tool to help a valued employee recognize a possible illness or addiction, and motivate the person to seek assistance.
- Behavioral problems that are manifest in declining job performance, which the employee has been unable or unwilling to correct, will only get worse.
- Make it clear to the employee that the employee assistance program (EAP) is a benefit and that assistance is available and recommended.
- Explain that employees must decide for themselves whether or not to seek assistance through EAP. Either way, unless job performance improves, the employee's job is in jeopardy.
- Emphasize that all aspects of EAP are completely confidential.

Don't try to diagnose the problem:

- Listen, but don't offer advice for solving personal problems. An employee's responsibility includes handling these situations so they do not continue to interfere with job performance. The supervisor's responsibility is to see that the employee gets professional help.
- Don't be misled by sympathy-evoking tactics or other seemingly acceptable excuses when they are used excessively. Insist that the employee get help.

- Don't moralize—right or wrong, good or bad—concerning personal behavior. It isn't your responsibility to judge. Restrict criticism to your responsibility of subordinate on-the-job performance and attendance.
- Don't cover up for friends. Your well-meaning but misguided kindness can lead to a delay in the employee receiving needed help, and the situation, without effective intervention, will become more serious.

The key is to take action, to get help for the employee as soon as possible.

There are consultants who help companies set up employee assistance programs. They come into an organization and help human resource directors set up their own programs in-house.

The Union Pacific Railroad has had an alcoholism rehabilitation program for several years. Darrel Sorenson, director of the program, says they have put 4,000 employees and 2,500 members of their families through the program and have experienced an 80 percent rehabilitation rate.

Some other organizations that have programs are Xerox Corporation, Morgan Guaranty Trust, Metropolitan Life, United Technologies, United Airlines, and Mobil Oil.

The American Management Association has published a booklet entitled *Guidelines for Developing an Employee Assistance Program* that provides more information.[3]

9.2 FLEXITIME AND OTHER ALTERNATIVE WORK SCHEDULES

According to the Bureau of Labor Statistics, about 7.6 million working people—or 12 percent of all those in full-time, nonfarm wage and salary jobs—are on flexitime or some similar schedule that allows them to vary the time their workdays begin and end. Another 2.7 million part-time people (schedules of less than 35 hours a week) also are on flexible schedules.

The basic concept of flexitime is simple. People arrive and leave work at any time during the flexible hours at either end of the working day. The two obligations are that the employees be present during certain mandatory hours designated by management as core time, and that they work a fixed number of hours during a specific period. That period can be a day, a week, or a month. A flexible period also may be programmed for the lunch break, providing an added measure of freedom to the system.

The following advantages are just a few of the benefits gained by instituting a flexible work hours program. Problems such as traffic congestion are alleviated by the natural time spacing of employees that occurs under a flexible system. Flexitime is a system that is accepted enthusiastically by both employee and employer if it is understood and effectively administered. There are some disadvantages, and those are listed here.

---

[3] American Management Association, 135 West 50th Street, New York, New York 10020.

Possible Flexitime Advantages for the Company

- Reduction in lost days for illness and personal reasons (mental health days), resulting in improved productivity.
- Improvement in employee morale.
- Improvement of working climate, as individuals become more self-responsible.
- Less utilization of overtime.
- Elimination of punctuality as an issue and a resulting increase of working time for the company.
- Increase in utilization of office machines and equipment.
- Reduction of turnover and associated costs for hiring and training.
- Improvement of intradepartmental communications and greater team spirit fostered through peer influence on the part of those employees who desire the flexitime concept to succeed.
- Improvement in recruiting response and visibility as "preferred place of employment" because of the company's progressiveness.
- Reduction of lost time for dental and doctor appointments scheduled outside working hours.
- Reduction of informal work breaks.

Possible Disadvantages for the Company

- Increase in cost to heat, air condition, and light the building between earlier starting and later finishing times.
- Necessity for some additional scheduling to ensure adequate supervisory coverage—and support—in smaller departments.
- Occasional unavailability of staff when needed for unplanned developments.
- Increase in overtime and associated expenses in the early stages of the new schedule.
- Employee repercussions if it becomes necessary to return to the traditional work week.

Possible Flexitime Advantages for the Employee

- Increase in individual freedom, allowing a balance between personal work demands.
- Improved opportunity for handling both domestic and job responsibilities by employees with children.
- Easier travel outside of rush-hour congestion.
- Enjoyment of more daylight hours for recreational purposes.
- Elimination of the need to request time off for scheduling personal responsibilities on the employee's own time.
- Reduction of tardiness.
- Avoidance of rush-hour traffic on Fridays, for faster starts on weekend trips.

Possible Disadvantages for the Employee

- Additional transportation problems in making arrangements for car pools.
- Loss of accustomed overtime pay.

Installing a Flexitime Program

Human resource personnel should assist management in implementation of a flexitime program. Following is a four-step implementation process:

Step 1. Analyze company procedures and policies, workload variations, accounting practices, personnel classifications, productivity levels, absenteeism rates, and general worker and management attitudes. Based on this analysis, guidelines are established and the new rules and operating procedures defined.

Step 2. Employees working within the system are given a complete explanation of the operating procedures and philosophies, as well as the reasons for each. Management personnel and supervisors receive a briefing on the administrative requirements of the program.

Step 3. Written rules and procedures governing application of the program are introduced and explained to all employees. The mechanics of daily operation are reviewed prior to the designated startup date.

Step 4. To provide the information for each employee to determine start and stop times, and to comply with legal requirements concerning wages and hours, the total hours actually worked must be recorded.

Flexitime Terms

Core time	The designated work periods during which all employees must be present.
Fixed hours	The hours that comprise a fixed work day, such as 7:00 to 3:00 or 9:00 to 5:00.
Fixed work day	A day with fixed starting and finishing times between which an employee undertakes to work a contracted number of hours.
Flexible periods	The designated work periods during which employees may come and go without supervisory approval.
Flexible work day	A workday that allows the employee to choose the start time, duration, and stop time on a daily basis. The day usually contains both flexible time periods and core time periods.
Flexitime	Accepted term for flexible workday, not to be confused with "staggered hours."
Minimum staffing	Number of employees required in a department during flexible periods.
Reporting period	The length of time during which hours worked may be accumulated and reported. A typical reporting period might be one week.
Short work week	Deviation from standard 8-hour day and 40-hour week, but with set hours (e.g., four 10-hour days, or three 12-hour days).

Staggered hours   A fixed-length workday where employees are assigned different start times. The assignment is usually on a departmental basis.

Standard day   The normal workday prior to establishment of flexible working hours.

Other underlying assumptions for a flexitime program are:

- Self-management, an internal control, is a more effective motivator than most external controls, such as financial incentives or lateness penalties.
- In an environment of trust, essential to any flexitime system, most people will meet their responsibilities rather than take advantage of situations like honor systems or nonsupervised periods.
- Given the opportunity and encouragement, most workers will find solutions to problems at work themselves, whether these arise from flexible work schedules or otherwise.

Examples of Flexitime and Core Time

Example 1:

FLEXIBLE BAND	CORE TIME	FLEXIBLE BAND	CORE TIME	FLEXIBLE BAND

8 hours + ½ hour lunch

6:30 A.M.   9:00 A.M.   11:00 A.M.   1:00 P.M.   3:00 P.M.   5:30 P.M.

8 hours + ½ hour lunch

In example 1, the core time has been established at 5 hours, to include a half-hour for lunch to be taken at some time within the established core. Flexible time bands extend 3 hours on either side of the core. An employee, therefore, might come to work at 6:30 A.M. and leave as early as 3:00 P.M., or, alternatively, may begin as late as 9:30 A.M. and leave at 6:00 P.M. He or she may, however, begin at any other time between 6:30 and 9:30 A.M., and the departure time will be 8½ hours later.

Example 2:

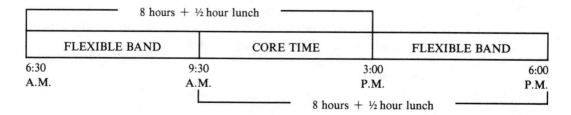

FLEXIBLE BAND	CORE TIME	FLEXIBLE BAND

8 hours + ½ hour lunch

6:30 A.M.   9:30 A.M.   3:00 P.M.   6:00 P.M.

8 hours + ½ hour lunch

In example 2, an analysis of the workload revealed a requirement for the entire work force to be present between the hours of 9:00 and 11:00 A.M., and again between 1:00 and 3:00 P.M.

The major difference between example 1 and example 2 lies in the splitting of the core time. An employee might choose to work straight through 8 hours plus a half-hour for lunch, or may take advantage of the center 2-hour flexible band for personal business, shopping, or a long lunch or luncheon meeting. A half-hour period within this flexible band is allocated for lunch.

HUMAN RESOURCE DIRECTOR'S TIP:

If you want to know if a flexible schedule will work well in your company, try a short-term experiment. Pick a department that has employees who cooperate well with management and are teamwork-oriented. Then, design a flexible schedule to be used in that department for a sixty-day trial period. Discuss the proposal with employees and management, and fully explain the concept. Point out that increased personal freedom will be worth the higher level of productivity predicted.

If they agree to a test, hand out information describing the purpose and rules of the project. Hold meetings with supervisors so they do not feel that you are forcing the project on them without notice. Send letters to those customers affected. For instance, they should know if they can expect difficulty reaching your employees early in the morning or late in the afternoon.

At the end of the trial period, survey the reactions of employees, managers, and customers. General agreement that the test was successful should lead you to try a longer experiment. A short trial period may expose problems that indicate that the concept would be unworkable, but remember that many of the major costs and benefits are long-term. By the end of the year, you should know if the efficiency and morale gains are sufficient to warrant continuation or expansion of flexitime.

Two major organizations that have implemented flexitime programs report the following results. Control Data Corporation had goals of maximizing employees' choice in establishing work hours and ensuring that business needs as well as employee needs would be satisfied.

Research design: There was a pilot study, over a three-year period, measuring attitudes. Also, hard data were monitored for such factors as absenteeism and sick leave. Sample: one hundred managers and 286 nonmanagerial personnel from the aerospace and microcircuit divisions.

Research results:

Hard data: Turnover, productivity, and sick leave showed slightly favorable trends.

Nonsupervisory personnel:

- 85 percent felt morale improved under flexitime.
- 73 percent felt that the pressure of getting to work on time had decreased.

- 57 percent felt that driving time had decreased.
- 66 percent felt that productivity had increased, while 11 percent felt it had decreased.

Managers:

- Felt that flexitime had a positive effect.

Hewlett Packard started with the goal of allowing employees greater flexibility in arranging their personal schedules—giving them time for family, leisure, and personal business; avoiding traffic jams; and satisfying other individual needs.

Research design: An attitude survey was conducted in 1975 as a follow-up to a 1974 study. Sample: forty-five supervisors and 183 employees at the Colorado Springs Division.

Research results:

- 97 percent felt that flexitime was successful—and most successful in alleviating traffic problems for supervisors and employees alike.
- 81 percent of the supervisors and nonsupervisory personnel felt the program had a positive effect on tardiness.
- 20 percent believed that flexitime had a negative effect on customer relations in 1974, but only 16 percent felt this way in 1975.

For more information on companies that have flexitime programs, send for *The Alternative Work Schedule Directory,* published by the National Council for Alternative Work Patterns, Inc.[4]

9.3 CHILD CARE—THE NEW BENEFIT MORE WOMEN ARE REQUESTING

In the December 21, 1981, issue of *Business Week,* an article titled "Child Care Grows As a Benefit" created a great deal of discussion and interest on the part of human resource managers. The article stated that the 46 million women currently in the work force include 49 percent of all mothers of children under six. But only 160 companies, unions, and government agencies—mainly the first group—provide child-care assistance for workers, according to the Health and Human Services Department. That may change in the wake of a tax code revision that frees employees from paying income tax on child-care benefits.

The article further states that women who have climbed to positions of influence in companies are pressuring employers for day-care benefits—backed by the growing number of men who share child-care tasks with their wives. Twenty percent of all families who responded to a Harris Poll that queried executives rated onsite child care first among a list of employer benefits that would best help families balance work and family responsibilities.

---

[4] National Council for Alternative Work Patterns, 1925 K Street, N.W., Washington, D.C. 20006.

Some companies have built their own onsite day-care centers, but that is not necessarily the best or most cost-effective choice. Some alternatives to onsite centers are:

- *Community centers.* There may be child-care centers in the community that need money to expand or upgrade facilities. For example, if you have problems recruiting reliable people to work at night, your funds could be used to expand the hours the center is open. That way, employees who work at night as well as those who work during the day will have dependable supervision for their children.
- *A voucher system.* Under this system, a company pays parents for at least part of the child-care cost. Vouchers also work well under flexible benefit plans, where an employee receives a basic benefit package and then picks, cafeteria-style, from a list of electives. Hewitt Associates, a benefits consulting firm in Lincolnshire, Illinois, reports that several of its clients are considering such plans just to have an equitable way to offer child-care help. The change in the tax law should lead to some creative design.
- *A vendor system.* Companies that use this system pay part or all of the child-care cost to the organization providing the service. At this time, the vendor system is more advantageous than the voucher system, because the vendor system is considered a tax-free benefit.
- *Child-care insurance plan.* Under this plan, an agency outside the company screens employees and determines how much an employee can pay for child care. The company picks up the rest of the cost.
- *Consortiums.* Several companies share the costs of operating centers. One company may pay for lunches, another may pick up transportation expenses, someone else pays for medical fees, and so on.

What One Company Is Doing

Honeywell, Inc., of Minneapolis, Minnesota, found that an onsite center wasn't practical for its particular needs. The company has thirty-two buildings in the vicinity; and homes of employees are scattered over a wide area. So an onsite center could only help a handful of employees.

Under the direction of a working parents' consultant, Honeywell is developing a computerized referral system. Parents will be able to feed the computer information about their needs and find out what facilities are available. It was noted that the referral system also will help the company find out whether more child-care services are needed in the area. In addition, Honeywell is exploring flexitime and parent education programs as possibilities for helping parents.

What's Ahead

Child care is becoming more important to corporations. When a company considers moving to a new area, it automatically investigates housing, schools, and transportation. Many companies also locate child-care facilities in order to offer employees timely referrals.

What to Look For in a Child-Care Center

Following are tips from child-care professionals that employers can use in judging a center's quality:

- *Child–staff ratio.* Most localities have guidelines that must be met for certification. The ratios generally vary according to the age of the children.
- *Staff stability.* Employee turnover is often a problem at centers with a low-paid staff.
- *Legal requirements.* The center should be licensed and have adequate property-liability insurance.
- *Hours of operation.* Some employees may need child care early in the mornings or late in the afternoon.

Other factors involved in the suitability of a child care center are:

- A good supply of equipment and space.
- Adequate menus and cleanliness.
- Policies governing attendance of sick children and availability of medical services.
- Professional training for the director and staff.

9.4 JOB-SHARING—A NEW WORK SYSTEM THAT'S CATCHING ON

Job-sharing refers to a situation where two qualified people who want to work part-time share one full-time job (not to be confused with work-sharing). Work-sharing is a reduction of working hours and pay during a period of economic downturn, so that all workers may be retained on the payroll. Work-sharing has not been very productive in most cases. Job-sharing is productive, however, and is growing more popular with women who:

1. Would like to spend more time at home with small children.
2. Cannot work full-time but need some income.
3. Are older, maybe retired, and need income to augment a pension or annuity.
4. Are handicapped and unable to work a regular 40-hour week.

Job-sharing has been a boon to women professionals with families. It gives them a chance to stay active in fast-changing career fields and still spend time raising children. Like flexitime, job-sharing seems to reduce absenteeism and tardiness.

The main advantages to job sharing seem to be:

- Increased productivity.
- Wider pool of applicants.
- Reduced costs.
- More enthusiasm for the job.
- Working harder.
- Tedium and frustration of menial or repetitive jobs reduced.

- Reduce expense of overtime and training.
- Both employees unlikely to leave at once.
- Reduced training.
- Job covered for vacations, illnesses, etc.

Some disadvantages of job sharing are:

- Increased benefit costs because you now cover two people.
- Two employees increasing the supervisor's job.
- Only one person on the job at a time, but still two different people to work with.
- Scheduling problems if you don't have two workers who agree on schedules.
- Communication problems, with both people having to attend meetings on subjects they both must know about (the same goes for training sessions).

There have been several good articles written on job-sharing. Most articles on the subject are written by those sharing jobs, and they like and promote the concept. Articles against job-sharing are usually written by part-time workers or executives who don't like the concept.

There is sometimes a problem in finding two people who match the job requirements, who can work the hours needed, and who will work well together, but the benefits of job-sharing seem to outweigh the disadvantages.

9.5 HEALTH, FITNESS AND WELLNESS PROGRAMS

Approximately 50,000 business firms in the United States have programs promoting health and fitness; however, less than 0.1 percent have fully staffed facilities. The justification business uses for establishing physical fitness programs is that the employee is helped personally and productivity is improved. Many companies have found a correlation between the installation of health, fitness, and exercise programs and a reduction in medical claims, and stronger personal attachments to the company.

Following are a few companies that are reported to have physical fitness programs: IBM, Xerox, General Foods, Firestone, Chase-Manhatten, Goodyear, Boeing, Metropolitan Life, Rockwell International, Merrill Lynch, Phillips Petroleum, Mobil, Texaco, Weyerhauser, Western Electric, Control Data, Northern National Gas, Rocky Mountain Energy Company (a subsidiary of Union Pacific Corporation), and the Adolph Coors Company.

It's a good idea to visit another company's fitness facility to find out what that company's management has to say about starting a program. No sense in reinventing the wheel. You may want to try a fitness program out on a few people in the company and have them act as a pilot group, to see if a program would work companywide.

In an article that appeared in the *Rocky Mountain News,* August 20, 1982, entitled "The Health-Care Answer: Wellness," W. K. Coors, chairman of the board of Adolph Coors Company, stated that health-care costs are one of the more serious long-range economic concerns. They absorb 10 cents out of every dollar of our gross national product. Coors outlines several guidelines that he feels should be followed by educational institutions and physicians, but, most importantly, he states that employers should include a wellness center or clinic as an essential service to employees.

Elements of an Effective Health and Fitness Program

Most fitness programs have similar components:

- *Commitment.* Top management must be committed and understand that the program is important and will require an investment of both time and money, and that it may be months before the benefits achieved can be measured in dollars.
- *Knowledge.* The program must be matched to fit the organization's employees. This requires an initial assessment of the health of employees.
- *Leadership.* The person who establishes the program's goals should be familiar with setting up wellness programs.
- *Rank-and-file involvement.* While anybody can start a program for the "jocks," the trick is to involve a strong number of rank-and-filers initially and direct their enthusiasm to new recruits.
- *Recruiting.* The program needs an ongoing recruiting effort and periodic boosts for long-term participants.

Guidelines for Establishing a Health and Fitness Program

- Survey management and employees to ascertain interest in such a program, and find out how many people would participate in a program if one were established.
- In the survey, ask what specific types of programs the employees would actually participate in if they were available.
- Find a suitable exercise area. The setting for workouts can be an unused portion of the stockroom, the roof, a yard, or the facilities of nearby churches or schools.
- Ensure the cooperation of managers. Support from the top helps inspire employees.
- Publicize the activity. Company bulletin boards, newsletters, and house organs should be used to provide a steady flow of program news.

Mental Wellness Programs

Employers spend $10 billion on medical treatment of drug abuse and $13 billion on treatment for alcoholism each year. Another $30 billion a year is spent by organizations on nonmedical costs associated with these human resource problems, such as lost productivity, absenteeism, and accidents.

In spite of these staggering costs, only 600 of more than 50,000 U.S. firms with more than 100 employees have established mental wellness programs.

General Motors reports a three-to-one return on dollars invested in their employee assistance program. They report a 29 percent decrease in disability payments, a 56 percent decrease in sick leave costs, and a 49 percent reduction in lost hours.

Five Key Elements of a Mental Wellness Program

- A written policy.
- Top management support.
- Clear guidelines.
- Management and employee orientation.
- Coordinated effort and involvement at all levels of the organization.

9.6 RETRAINING PROGRAMS THAT MATCH SKILLS TO JOBS AS TECHNOLOGY CHANGES

In spite of long unemployment lines, there are shortages of workers with critical skills, and this problem may worsen in coming years as technological change accelerates and workers with specific technological know-how are unavailable.

Companies will have to lead the way in retraining workers to meet the challenge. Many of today's workers are more positively motivated by increased personal challenge and the opportunity to learn new skills.

This country's 300,000 machinists have an average age of fifty-eight and there are many people employed or unemployed who could be trained in this scarce skill area.

An excellent article on this subject by Pat Choate, senior policy analyst for economics at TRW, Inc., and Noel Epstein, former education editor of the *Washington Post,* appeared in the *Washington Post* on May 9, 1982. The article, "Workers of the Future, Retool! Nothing to Lose But Your Jobs," is a review of America's current state of readiness for a great stride into the new technological era just around the corner.

9.7 THE LUMP-SUM SALARY INCREASE IS GAINING POPULARITY

A lump-sum salary increase is basically paying an employee the annual salary increase in one lump sum after appropriate deductions, rather than paying the increase in the normal twelve or twenty-four payments over a year.

There are at least twenty-five life insurance companies in the country currently using lump-sum increase programs, and companies that have tried the method claim that it has enabled them to improve employee motivation and morale at almost no added cost.

There are variables in the administration of the program, and it's important to work out the details to suit your particular organization, but basically most companies administer the program under the following general guidelines.

Eligibility requirements. Some companies offer it only to managers or employees of higher rank. Most offer it to all salaried exempt employees. Some companies require a minimum of three to five years of service.

Types of increases offered. Most companies offer the lump sum only on the annual merit increase. However, some also offer it on promotional increases.

Employees benefit contributions. When an employee contributes to a medical or life insurance plan, if the contributions are based on salary, some companies take the deduction from the regular base salary after calculating it as though the increase were being paid in installments. Others calculate the increase in deductions that will be made for a year, and take that amount out of the lump sum.

Income tax withholding. In some cases, all taxes, including (in most cases) Social Security withholding, are calculated and deducted at the time the lump-sum increase is given. Other companies treat the lump-sum as a loan to be repaid by earning it over twelve months and do not deduct taxes. They take the additional tax out of the regular paycheck. Other companies treat the lump sum as an advance instead of an increase. By considering it an advance, the cost of the program can be lowered.

Discount factor. Because the money to pay the lump-sum increases must be diverted from investment, or maybe even borrowed, the loss of investment income is a factor. Some companies discount the lump-sum increase, resulting in a reduction of the gross increase. Some companies reduce the total merit pool to make up for a decrease in interest income.

Lump-sum increase option. The most popular option for companies is for the employee to take the entire increase as a lump sum; however, some companies allow employees to take part of the increase in a lump sum and part at their regular pay periods.

Payment upon termination. Most companies require an employee to sign a statement promising to repay the unearned portion of the lump sum in the event of termination. Some companies do not require a statement but say they are still, in most cases, successful in recovering the unearned portion of the lump-sum increases.

HUMAN RESOURCE DIRECTOR'S TIP:

One of the most favorable aspects of the lump-sum increase is that the second year the previous year's merit award increases the employee's regular pay, and the second-year lump sum is then viewed almost as a bonus.

As with any program, there are advantages and disadvantages:

Advantages

- Employees can immediately accumulate a fairly substantial sum of money for major purchases, paying debts, vacation, or investment.
- A lump-sum program helps overcome the negligible effects of a small increase on take-home pay. For example, an employee can receive a $1,200 lump sum rather than $100 per month.
- For nonbonus companies, it offers some of the advantages of bonuses without any serious disadvantages.
- It conveys the impression that the company is doing something different and perhaps better than other companies.
- It offsets potential disappointment with a relatively small merit program.

- Employees receive two morale boosts from one increase—the first when the lump payment is made, and the second when it goes into their base salary a year later.

Disadvantages

- The effect diminishes with time. The employee forgets about the lump sum received as the year goes on and base pay has not increased.
- A lump-sum program generates additional administrative work.
- If the lump sum is not discounted, it represents an added cost to the company in lost investment income.

9.8 EMPLOYEE COMMUNICATION HEATS UP AS ONE OF THE MOST IMPORTANT ISSUES IN EFFECTIVE HUMAN RESOURCE MANAGEMENT

"Autocratic, club-wielding organizations need to adopt better ways of communicating with employees if they wish to survive and thrive." So says Roger D'Aprix in the *Journal of Communication Management*. D'Aprix says that the manager is the single most important communicator in any organization.

To be effective, an employee communication program must track along with the organization's business plans. The employee communication program should be an important element of the human resource function, just as important to the organization's success as recruiting or compensation and benefits. Employees must understand what the organization is about, what its long-range plans are, and how their job will help the company achieve its goals.

Ten Steps to an Effective Employee Communication Program

1. Gain commitment from the CEO and other top executives for the need for such a program and the importance that should be placed on the entire employee communication effort.
2. Establish a policy that works at all levels of the organization. Ensure that everyone understands the policy. Build an open, proactive communication style.
3. Assign responsibility for the program and its success to a high-level executive. The human resource director is a good person, because there is already a responsibility for establishing a positive, effective human resource environment.
4. Establish a broad-based task force to help build the program and to interpret it to employees. The committee can work to resolve problems as they arise, and ensure up-and-down communication and feedback.
5. Set yearly objectives for the program, and tie the objectives to the company's business plans. Plan objectives that are practical, attainable, and can be carried out in timely fashion.
6. Establish an effective feedback system that works at all levels of the organization, and include at least one anonymous element such as a suggestion box or hotline.

7. Communicate during good times and bad. When things get tough, you need to put a great deal of time and effort into a communication program.

8. If morale is low and communication stifled, conduct an audit to review internal communications and find out what the problems are. Identify organizational needs, and ask the task force to suggest new ideas and programs.

9. Hold meetings with employees to determine how your communication program is working. Gulf Canada (P.O. Box 460, Station A, Toronto, Canada M5W 1E5) conducts dialogue sessions in which executives and senior management meet with employees to provide a discussion and an exchange of viewpoints.

10. Follow up constantly to ensure that your programs are working. Listen to employees, and don't become complacent. Be sensitive to changes in morale.

CHAPTER 10

How People Communicate in Organizations

So much has been written about the importance of effective organizational communication that a chapter on the subject almost seems redundant; however, in the organizational environment today, with employees seeking self-fulfillment more than ever and management of accelerant change being a key issue, effective organizational communication is extremely important.

Almost thirty years ago, Peter F. Drucker made the following statement: "As soon as you move one step up from the bottom, your effectiveness depends on your ability to reach others through the spoken or written word; and the further away your job is from manual work, the larger the organization of which you are an employee, the more important it will be that you know how to convey your thoughts in writing or speaking."

10.1   FIFTEEN WAYS PEOPLE COMMUNICATE IN ORGANIZATIONS

Let's look at fifteen of the most common avenues of communication found in organizations.

 1. Face-to-face (90 percent of all communication done this way)
 2. Memos and letters
 3. Staff meetings
 4. Organizational charts
 5. Committees, advisory boards, and other ad hoc groups
 6. Newsletters and other employee publications
 7. Employee handbooks
 8. Training programs
 9. New employee orientation programs
10. Bulletin boards
11. Performance appraisals
12. Lunch-hour programs
13. Grapevine

14. Suggestion system
15. Employee meetings

Seven New Communication Programs Seen More Frequently in Organizations Today

1. Managerial reading and discussion programs
2. Annual reports to employees
3. Issues-management brainstorming sessions
4. Speakers bureau, with in-house presentations to employees
5. In-house health and fitness programs
6. Libraries including magazines, books, and tapes on current subjects for employee review
7. In-house lectures by people prominent in fields pertinent to the organization's business

10.2 THE PSYCHOLOGY OF ORGANIZATIONAL COMMUNICATION

Ask yourself the following questions about the importance of written communication and your organization's communication style:

1. Do key executives and managers write a great many memos and letters?
2. How do the memos and letters written by key executives look and sound? Is there a formal style? An informal style?
3. Are memos and letters done meticulously, or is there a rather loose approach to written communication?
4. Is a great deal of attention paid to the grammar, punctuation, type style, and placement on the page of written communications?
5. Does the organization pay for people who must write a lot of reports and documents to go to writing courses, or does the organization have effective in-house writing courses?
6. Does your organization publish a preferred style and spelling pamphlet?

If the answer to most of the above questions is "yes," you work for an organization whose top management pays a great deal of attention to written communication. A wonderful technical education, a thorough job of research, brilliant ideas, and creativity are all useless unless you can put them to paper in a brief, persuasive, clearly written report. If you can't write well, your chances of getting ahead are probably slim.

10.3 EFFECTIVE ORGANIZATIONAL COMMUNICATION

Interviewing several executives regarding their definition of effective organizational communication gives a clearer understanding of the tremendously wide scope of communications within most organizations today. Communication includes both verbal and written forms, and many organizations have become proactive rather than reactive in communicating outside as well as inside their business environments.

The element of communication most executives agree on, however, is that no matter what form communication takes there must be a common understanding of the meaning of the message that is sent. When we communicate, we are dealing in meanings, and the meanings of things to you and the meanings of things to me are different.

Experience and meaning are related, and if there is no commonality of experience or perception between people who are trying to communicate, there is little chance for full communication of ideas.

Speaking and writing in business has a significant impact on human relations. It's not only important to understand how to communicate effectively when speaking and writing, but it's also very important to understand the personality of the organization you work for. It's important to learn how to communicate effectively inside and outside the formal structure.

Each act of communication requires all the persuasive reasoning and skill in human relations that you can gather together. The goal is to communicate, whether verbally or in writing, so that your audience listens, understands, and ultimately remains your friend.

Good human relations come from an appreciation for the feelings of others. This appreciation will result in selecting the most tactful words and phrases to put across a point of view and in saying and writing things in ways that are understandable, reasonable, accurate, and pleasant.

Effective communication contributes significantly to good human relations, with the public and among people working together in an organization. Whether the communication is a letter or a personal greeting, a newspaper advertisement or a telephone conversation, it can be effective only if it recognizes that human beings are involved. If you are insensitive to others' feelings and show a lack of empathy in your communication, you'll drive people away. You'll also have a hard time getting people to cooperate with you in the future.

The use of positive psychology in business communication is an important skill. How do you acquire this skill? One easy way is to ask yourself, before you speak or write, if you would be offended if someone spoke to you in the way you plan to communicate.

Case Example

Even routine memos can be dynamite in terms of human relations. Suppose you want to let members of the human resource committee know that you want them to attend a meeting next Friday afternoon. Doesn't that sound simple? But see how you can lose friends and influence people negatively:

> "There will be a meeting of the Human Resource Committee in Conference Room H on Friday, January 8, at 2:00 P.M. You are expected to be on time."

What is wrong with this memo? The first sentence is fine, but the second sentence is too demanding. It implies that the members have arrived late at previous meetings. (They may have, but demanding promptness isn't likely to foster good will.) If you want to make sure that each person arrives promptly, think about how you would like to be reminded. You might word the memorandum this way:

> "There will be an important meeting of the Human Resource Committee in Conference Room H on Friday, January 8, at 2:00 P.M. I know you all want to start on time, so please arrive as promptly as possible."

See the difference in tone? There is no demand, only a tactful request.

Ask, Don't Demand. If you want to get people to do things, don't demand—ask. "Get me that report from the files" is a demand that will arouse resentment. Try "Would you mind checking those figures again?" "Let's find out where our figures disagree." "May I make a suggestion?" Treat people as you would like to be treated.

Know Company Policy. Company policy reflects the company's attitude toward its employees. Policies are guidelines for doing business. Major policies are sometimes put into writing in employee manuals—policies regarding administration, purchasing procedures, personnel relations, and so on. Other policies are merely understood. When there is an established company policy, follow it.

Here are five rules to remember when interpreting company policies:

1. Be sure you have all the facts.
2. Always be courteous and tactful.
3. Never lose your temper.
4. Give reasons for your actions.
5. In the absence of established rules, do what you believe is best for your organization.

Don't become a corporate casualty through an error in judgment, communication procedures, or style.

An effective communication is one that does the job intended by the communicator. For example, if an advertisement persuades people to buy the product advertised, that advertisement is effective. If a speech prompts listeners to feel that they have profited from the message, that speech is effective. Anyone can transmit a message, but to do so in such a way as to bring about the desired result is an art.

Be Polished. In business communications, polish is a secret ingredient that may make a very important contribution to increased profits. For example, every business message carries with it the company image—an impression of the organization whose name is on the letterhead. A polished communication conveys the image of a top-quality organization.

Be Explicit. One of the marks of an effective communicator is the ability to put down on paper a message that the reader can interpret in only one way, the way intended by the writer. Lack of such ability causes misunderstandings.

Show Empathy. Indirect persuasion involves sensitivity to the needs of others and to the probable effects of a person's words on the reader. Indirect persuasion, as well as direct persuasion, involves empathy. There is an old rhyme sometimes quoted to teach new salespeople the art of selling: "To sell Jane Doe what Jane Doe buys, you must see Jane Doe through Jane Doe's eyes." The rhyme means that if you hope to sell a product to a customer, you must first put yourself in the customer's place. You must look at the situation—and the product—the way the buyer might look at them. It takes empathy.

How Much Do You Know About Your Organization?

If you want to be successful in communicating, both internally and externally, on matters concerning your organization, you must know a great deal about it—how it functions, what its products are, what its assets are, how it compares to other organizations in the same industry, and so on. Take the following quiz and identify your organizational IQ:

1. Who owns your company? Is it privately or publicly held?
2. Do you know your organization's history and accomplishments?
3. Do you know your organization's past goals?
4. Do you know your organization's current and future goals?
5. What has been the rate of growth of your organization in the past five years?
6. Do you know who your organization's main competitors are?
7. How does your organization compare with its competitors in assets, profits, sales, productivity, and so on?
8. If your organization is publicly owned, what is the stock selling for and on what exchange is the stock listed? Does the stock pay regular dividends? Can employees buy stock at a discount or through a company-sponsored program, such as a thrift plan where your contributions are matched by the company?
9. If asked to discuss your organization, can you talk knowledgeably about its business and its success?
10. Does your organization have subsidiaries? If you work at the corporate headquarters, can you discuss the subsidiaries knowledgeably?
11. What is your organization's total income?
12. Does your organization have a formal organizational chart? If so, have you seen and studied it?
13. Do you know your organization's key executives and managers?
14. What employee benefits does your organization provide?
15. Does your organization pay competitive salaries?
16. Does your organization have a good reputation in its field?
17. Do employees generally have a good feeling and a sense of pride in your organization?
18. Do you know your own department's current objectives?

10.4   SAMPLE LETTERS AND MEMOS—WRITING EFFECTIVE HUMAN RESOURCE REPORTS

Here are the kinds of letters human resource managers write:

• Letters in response to résumés and applications
• Letters responding to recruiting firms
• Letters to schools regarding college recruiting
• Letters regarding training programs
• Letters to doctors regarding preemployment and/or yearly physical examination programs
• Memos to compliment an employee on a job well done
• Memos warning an employee of poor performance and detailing what is expected in the way of improvement in performance
• Memos to let employees know about organizational changes and promotions
• Memos telling employees about labor relations activities
• Memos regarding changes in benefits
• Memos regarding office closings

There are many more types of letters and memos, but the following samples are a representative group to review.

May 16, 1985

Richard M. Mooten
4630 Elm Street
Omaha, Nebraska 14999

Dear Mr. Mooten:

Thank you for taking the time to interview with us concerning the marketing position.

Although your experience and accomplishments are excellent, we filled the position with another candidate whose experience and background seemed better matched to our current needs. Your file will remain active for one year, and you will be contacted should an appropriate position become available during that time.

Your interest in our company is appreciated. We wish you success in your job search.

Sincerely,

Lawrence O. Ogden
Human Resource Manager

LOO:rac

March 4, 1985

Mary L. Logan
273 Maple Street
Dallas, Texas 21999

Dear Ms. Logan:

Thank you for your inquiry regarding our advertisement for an accountant.

Unfortunately, this position was filled just prior to the receipt of your résumé, and no other position requiring your experience and background is available at this time. The information you submitted will be retained for one year, and you will be contacted should an appropriate position become available.

Thank you for your interest in our company.

Sincerely,

Donald C. Green
Human Resource Manager

DCG:lcm

February 1, 1985

John R. Brown
1627 R Street
Buffalo Hills, Wyoming 82834

Dear Mr. Brown:

Thank you for your inquiry regarding employment opportunities at XYZ Company.

Unfortunately, we do not anticipate any openings for a geologist at the time you expect to graduate. However, the information you submitted will be retained in our files for one year, and you will be contacted should an appropriate position become available during that time.

Your interest in our company is appreciated. We wish you success in your job search.

Sincerely,

Ralph E. Smith
Human Resource Manager

RES:mfl

July 2, 1985

Alice L. Lane
60 Market Place
Louisville, Kentucky 21477

Dear Ms. Lane:

Thank you for your inquiry regarding employment opportunities at the XYZ Corporation.

Your background has been evaluated carefully in all areas of the company where there would be any possibility of utilizing your skills. Although your qualifications are excellent and directly related to our company's activities, a position commensurate with your background is not available at this time. The information you submitted will be retained in our files, and you will be contacted if an appropriate position becomes available within the next twelve months.

Your interest in our company is appreciated.

Sincerely,

James L. Smith
Human Resource Manager

JLS:col

_____

January 6, 1985

John L. Wood
Vice-President
XYZ Corporation
50 Madison Avenue
New York, New York 10024

Dear John:

I received your letter and copies of the correspondence from the International Association for the Handicapped. We are interested in the opportunity to support this group. Enclosed is a copy of our advertisement, which has been forwarded to IATH in Longview, New York.

During 1981, the International Year of the Disabled, our human resource staff was involved in several handicapped activities. For example, we sponsored a Handicapped Awareness program for all managers and supervisors. The program presenters were employees of local handicapped assistance organizations. Our support and assistance to the handicapped community will be a continuous effort.

Sincerely,

Thomas L. Lincoln
Manager, Human Resources

TLL:mat

August 2, 1985

MEMORANDUM TO: All XYZ Corporate Employees

FROM: Kenneth R. Brown

I am pleased to announce that John H. Doe has accepted the position of Senior Market Analyst, effective August 16, 1985. In this position, John will assume the lead role in our market identification, analysis, and sales support function. Initially, John will be responsible for upgrading our marketing information systems and completing market research assignments for the 1986 long-range business plan.

John comes to the XYZ Company from LMC Coal Company in Pittsburgh, where he was a market analyst for the planning department. His activities at LMC included analyses of domestic and international market demand for the company's strategic and corporate planning groups, and development of a market information system. Before his employment at LMC, John was employed by the Brown Utility Company.

KRB:drs

July 6, 1985

MEMORANDUM TO: Lawrence J. Colvin

FROM: Mary C. Brown

SUBJECT: Delegation of Signature Authority

Please be advised that Ralph P. Pruett has been delegated signature authority at level 3 of the Delegation of Authority memorandum in the Corporate Administrative Manual. This authority includes the signing of:

> Travel requests
> Petty cash vouchers
> Requests for disbursement
> Invoice approvals
> Time cards
> Requisitions for purchases

If you have any questions, please give me a call on ext. 3021.

August 7, 1985

Jane M. Doe
27 Wilton Place
Los Angeles, California 90024

Dear Jane:

Thank you for an outstanding job in running the 1985 United Way Campaign for the XYZ Corporation. Thanks to your good efforts, we achieved our corporate goals, and many less fortunate families in our community will receive the assistance they so badly need.

Sincerely,

Richard M. Lee
President

RML:cod

March 16, 1985

Lawrence D. Logan
Recruiting Chairman
Western College
Spokane, Washington 99204

Dear Mr. Logan:

Our corporate recruiter, Donald T. West, will be at your East Campus on May 27, 1985, to participate in your recruiting activities program. Please provide Mr. West with an agenda of the week's activities and any other information he needs before April 18, 1985.

It is our pleasure to participate once again in your Career Week program.

Sincerely,

Elizabeth R. Jones
Manager, Human Resources

ERJ:cmr

March 9, 1985

Dear Fellow Employee:

On behalf of the Board of Directors, I am pleased to inform you of a significant improvement in the XYZ Merit Scholarship Program. Effective January 1, 1985, the annual scholarship minimum award has been increased from $1,000 to $2,000, while the annual scholarship maximum has been increased from $2,000 to $3,000.

As detailed in the attached brochure, the XYZ Merit Scholarship Program provides financial aid for eligible children of XYZ Corporation employees through the annual National Merit Scholarship Program competition administered by the National Merit Scholarship Corporation.

We are proud of the support XYZ Corporation provides to higher education and continually seek ways to increase that support.

If you have any questions regarding the Merit Scholarship Program, please contact the Human Resource Department.

Sincerely,

Robert M. Wilson
President

RMW:cms
Attachment

July 2, 1985

MEMORANDUM TO: All Denver-Based Employees

FROM: Career Programs Advisory Committee

SUBJECT: Career Planning Week

The week of August 24 has been designated as "Careers Week" at XYZ Corporation. As an introduction to the week's events, the Career Programs Advisory Committee is sponsoring a Poster Coloring Contest for employees and their children.

Various types of jobs at XYZ locations are depicted on the poster. Posters may be obtained from the receptionist in the Human Resource Department on the second floor.

Posters must be colored and turned in to the Human Resource receptionist by August 17 in order to be included in the judging for prizes. See the attached sheet for complete instructions and a list of prizes to be awarded.

Representatives from local colleges will provide presentations during the week and will be available from 11:00 A.M. to 1:30 P.M. each day to answer questions regarding curriculum and course schedules.

Enter the contest and have some fun! Learn about career opportunities at XYZ Corporation!

Attachment

10.5   KEY ELEMENTS OF GOOD LETTERS, MEMOS, AND REPORTS

Fifteen Elements of an Effective Business Letter

You are judged by the letters you write. Do your letters conform to the fifteen elements listed below?

1. Do they create a favorable first impression?
2. Do they appeal to the reader's point of view?
3. Do they catch the reader's interest immediately?
4. Are they correct in every detail? (If not, your credibility will be in question.)
5. Are they courteous and sincere?
6. Do they promote good will?
7. Are they clear and complete?
8. Are they short and concise?
9. Do they hold together well, each idea relating to the others?
10. Are they well paragraphed, including only one idea to a paragraph?
11. Do they avoid jargon?
12. Are they explicit?
13. Are they written in a friendly, conversational tone?
14. Is the presentation appealing? Do your letters look good?
15. Are they sincere?

10.6   MEMOS—AVOID THEM IF YOU CAN. IF YOU CAN'T ELIMINATE THEM, MAKE THEM SHORT AND TO THE POINT

President Ronald Reagan took a rule to Washington that he had enforced during his days as governor of California. If a memo ran over one page, he wouldn't read it.

If a memo stops rather than speeds the flow of information, it's useless. A management study found that top executives spend an average of nine minutes on any one issue. If a memo can't be read quickly, chances are it won't be read at all.

A U.S. Steel Corporation executive complained about memos and reports: "They tell me everything except what I want to know—is the damn bridge going to collapse?"

In an article entitled *Coming to Grips with Memo Mania,* Charles Cleveland reported that Allstate Insurance Company has produced two training books, *Letter-writing* and a follow-up *Letter-talk,* which suggest that memos fall into six categories: stating a fact, asking for facts, stating an opinion, asking for opinions, giving a pep talk, and giving orders.[1] Stick to one objective per memo.

A good memo starts out by telling the recipient what it is all about and how he or she is involved. And good memo writers follow six basic rules:

1. Put your points in logical sequence.
2. Write simply, using words you normally use in talking.
3. Tell the reader what he or she needs to know, but no more.
4. Be sure your facts are accurate and precise.
5. Stick to the point.
6. Check spelling, grammar, and punctuation.

10.7 WRITING EFFECTIVE REPORTS

Written reports are essential to the success of any project. The human resource manager must be able to write effectively in order to report the progress of a project, and to wrap it up, reporting the conclusions.

Eight Key Objectives of Written Reports

1. To report progress and results in an objective, orderly manner, thus allowing more accurate business decisions to be made.
2. To help eliminate duplication of effort and save time.
3. To allow a more timely and effective communication process, both inside and outside the company.
4. To help prepare public relations and media coverage.
5. To provide a record of progress and results for future reference.
6. To provide a history of development possibly needed for patent applications, accounting and tax considerations, or future research efforts, and human resource planning.
7. To help management identify and analyze problems, and assist in the design of policies and programs.
8. To help management choose the best course of action.

---

[1] "Coming to Grips with Memo Mania," Charles B. Cleveland, *Industry Week,* Penton/PC, 1111 Chester Avenue, Cleveland, Ohio 44114, September 1, 1981.

Analysis Is One of the Most Important Steps in Successful Report Writing

Effective analysis includes the following items:

1. Time spent initially thinking about the report.
2. Time spent analyzing the audience.
3. Analyzing the style of writing that will be most effective with that audience.
4. Deciding what style of report will be most effective.
5. Concentrating on timing. Looking for the most opportune time to present the report.
6. Showing how the report will positively affect the business of the organization.

10.8 WHY YOU SHOULD PRODUCE A REGULAR HUMAN RESOURCE REPORT FOR TOP MANAGEMENT

A human resource manager had been with the same company for several years. He did a fine job. His peers in other companies were aware of the many solid programs he instituted in his organization. But two years ago he was fired. He was replaced by a person known to be far less experienced and less professional. Why? It boiled down to two major reasons:

1. He didn't "blow his own horn." He had not done adequate public relations work on his programs. He went quietly about his business, working hard, but not working as smart as he could have.
2. He spent all of his time producing and implementing programs. He should have spent at least one-third of his time selling the programs and building a base of knowledge about them with his boss and other executives of his organization.

A regular report that gives key management the data they need to manage their various functions successfully is a must document and a most effective public relations tool for the human resource manager.

10.9 ORGANIZATION OF DATA FOR A HUMAN RESOURCE REPORT

Something human resource managers sometimes overlook is the very important element of organization of the report.

There are many ways to organize a report. Logical methods build a case step by step, leading to a conclusion and making recommendations. Following are the most frequently used styles:

Chronological   Human resource reports frequently follow a chronological pattern because the human resource manager needs to show a sequence of significant events. This is also one of the easiest ways to arrange data. The chronological approach, however, doesn't lend itself well to complex or involved situations.

Order of importance	Another style of human resource report is the order-of-importance method. Begin with the data most significant to the situation or problem you're describing. Then move on to the next, and the next, and so on. This also allows you to put the most successful elements of a project first, following sequentially to the least successful.
Functional	Another style frequently used in describing the elements of a new program is the functional style, where you are describing each component of the program in a factual, unbiased way.
Geographical	Human resource managers frequently use a geographical presentation. For example, a wage and salary proposal may be best presented by each geographical location.
General to particular	There is a need on occasion to use a general-to-particular style of report, for example, discussing the general principles of a new training program and then moving on to specific benefits attractive to the reader.
Cause and effect	There are times when a cause-and-effect approach might be useful. Start with the facts and proceed to the results that arise from that set of facts.
Pro and con	Some managers prefer the pro-and-con style of report. This style reviews the program or the situation to be discussed and then lists the pros and cons.

Executives are always busy. Time is important, and they want to get the facts immediately. It's a good idea to put the most important information first. State the problem, your answers to the problems, and how you arrived at your recommendations.

- Use a short introductory section to state the problem.
- Follow with a section of conclusions and recommendations and the procedures used to arrive at your recommendation.

Before you prepare your next human resource report, read an excellent book, *The Complete Writing Guide to Preparing Reports, Proposals, Memos, etc.,* by Carolyn J. Mullen, Prentice-Hall, Inc. It's the most current and complete manual for business writing I've found.

HUMAN RESOURCE DIRECTOR'S TIP:

Key executives in operating functions initially may look on the human resource manager's report as a self-serving device, so it's important to review the report personally with the key executive of each functional area when you print the first edition, and assure them that is not the case.

Review the report in advance, and pick an area that has particular significance to each individual executive. Show executives how the report will allow them to do a more efficient job of managing their function with the data in front of them on a regular basis.

10.10   THE HUMAN RESOURCE REPORT

This report should be prepared at least quarterly and may include some or all of the following items:

- Employment—actual vs. authorized/budgeted by major function
- New hires each quarter by major functions
- Promotions each quarter by major functions
- Terminations each quarter by major functions
- Turnover report—broken out by voluntary, involuntary, retirement, death, etc.
- A report of exit interviews, broken out by reason, i.e., dislike the job, dislike the supervisor, another job/higher salary, return to school, perceived lack of promotional opportunity, etc.
- Recruitment costs, including employment agency fees, advertising, etc.
- Recruiting activity report
- Relocation costs, including breakdown of costs such as moving expenses, mortgage differential loans, purchase of residence costs, travel, etc.
- A breakdown of relocation costs by major functions
- Review of compensation and benefits activities, such as wage package approvals for each major location, thrift plan distributions, cost-of-living adjustments by each location, annual merit budget approvals, etc.
- A graph of medical and dental claims filed monthly
- A graph depicting medical and dental claims resolution time by location
- A report of in-house and outside training programs attended by all employees by major functions
- A report of tuition refund program usage
- A report of monthly costs of temporary help by major function
- A report of temporary help costs by agency used
- Equal employment opportunity and affirmative action summary of goal attainment by function by quarter
- Report of minority vending program usage
- Report of handicapped and Vietnam veteran employment
- A report of activities regarding college recruiting and summer student programs

There may be many other measures of human resource usage and development, depending on the type of organization.

Figures 10–1 through 10–15 provide sample formats of human resource reports that could be used.

FIGURE 10-1.

SAMPLE

TABLE OF CONTENTS

*Page
Number*

FIGURE 10-2.

1ST QUARTER 1985
HUMAN RESOURCES QUARTERLY REPORT

XYZ COMPANY
EMPLOYMENT

	12/31/84	3/31/85	Change
Executive Management	11	13	2
Operations	16	6	(10)
Technical Services	82	80	(2)
Marketing	11	13	2
Information Systems	39	45	6
Finance	70	71	1
Human Resources	10	12	2
Public Relations	4	4	—
Subtotal	243	244	1

FIGURE 10-3.

XYZ COMPANY
NEW HIRES BY MAJOR FUNCTION

| | 1985 | | | | Year |
| | First | Second | Third | Fourth | to |
Function	Quarter	Quarter	Quarter	Quarter	Date
Production	8				8
Marketing	9				9
Technical Services	1				1
Operations	—				—
Land	3				3
Finance	7				7
Human Resources	1				1
Executive	1				1
Total	30				30

FIGURE 10-4.

XYZ COMPANY
TURNOVER REPORT
(Exempt/Nonexempt)
1985

Source of Turnover	Jan.	Feb.	Mar.	Apr.	May	June	July	Aug.	Sept.	Oct.	Nov.	Dec.	CUM. YTD
VOLUNTARY:													
Exempt	1.53												1.53
Nonexempt	3.16												3.16
INVOLUNTARY:													
Exempt	0.38												0.38
Nonexempt													
RETIREMENT:													
Exempt													
Nonexempt													
DEATH:													
Exempt													
Nonexempt													
Total Monthly Turnover:													
Exempt	1.91												1.91
Nonexempt	3.16												3.16
Total Number Employees:													
Exempt	262												262
Nonexempt	158												158

Cumulative   EX   1.91
Annual Total: NEX   3.16

FIGURE 10-5.

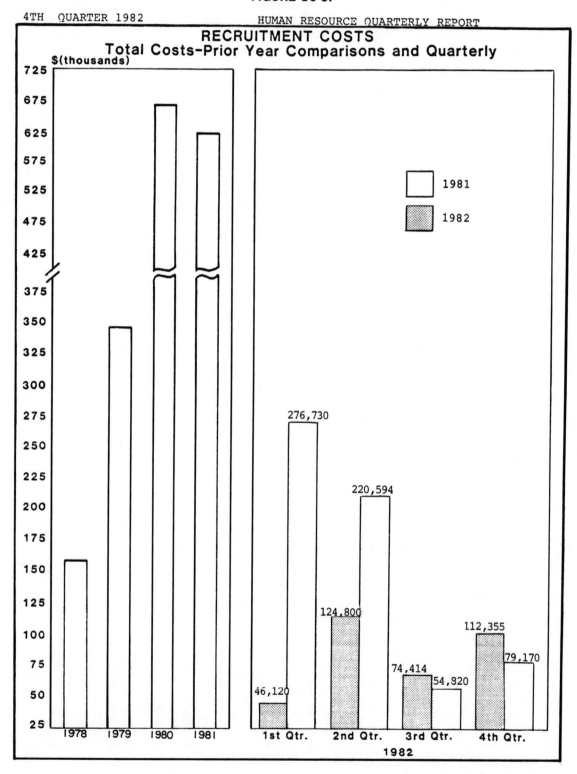

4TH   QUARTER 1982   HUMAN RESOURCE QUARTERLY REPORT

FIGURE 10-6.

XYZ COMPANY
RECRUITING COST DATA
EMPLOYMENT AGENCY AND EXECUTIVE SEARCH COSTS

	1st Qtr.	2nd Qtr.	3rd Qtr.	4th Qtr.	1985 TOTALS
Agency Costs	$25,628.60				$25,628.60
Executive Search Costs	10,600.00				10,600.00
Total	$36,228.60				$36,228.60

		Other Recruitment Costs			
	1st Qtr.	2nd Qtr.	3rd Qtr.	4th Qtr.	1985 TOTALS
Relocations	$17,564.43				$17,564.43
Advertising	1,200.62				1,200.62
Interview Expenses	6,325.00				6,325.00
Physical Exams	2,100.00				2,100.00
Total	$27,190.05				$27,190.05

FIGURE 10-7.

XYZ COMPANY
RELOCATION COSTS

Type of Expense	1st Qtr.	2nd Qtr.	3rd Qtr.	4th Qtr.	Year to Date
Transportation of household goods	$18,600.74				$18,600.74
Storage of household goods	—				—
Travel/lodging to new location	320.00				320.00
Househunting trip	3,530.09				3,530.09
Temp. living at new location	4,350.00				4,350.00
Sale of residence costs	—				—
Purchase of residence costs	2,320.00				2,320.00
Incidental expense payments	7,200.00				7,200.00
Temporary living at old location	572.35				572.35
Travel between old/new location	1,667.60				1,667.60
Miscellaneous	89.70				89.70
Tax adjustments	—				—
MIDA and points reimbursement	—				—
Transcontinental costs	52,100.00				52,100.00
Total	$90,750.48				$90,750.48

FIGURE 10-8.

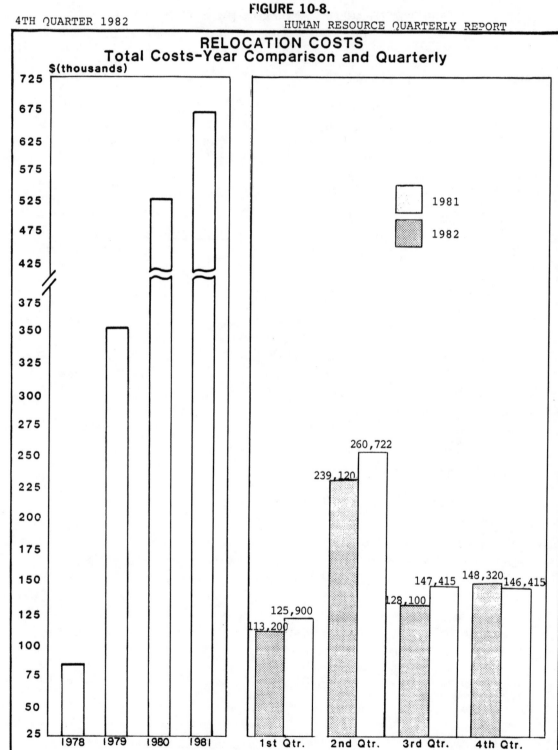

RELOCATION COSTS
Total Costs-Year Comparison and Quarterly

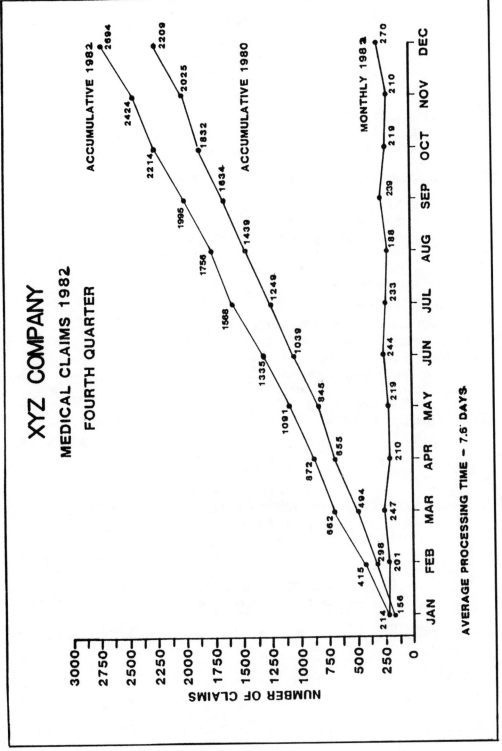

FIGURE 10-9.

XYZ COMPANY
MEDICAL CLAIMS 1982
FOURTH QUARTER

FIGURE 10-10.

XYZ COMPANY
KEY TRAINING AND DEVELOPMENT PROGRAMS

TECHNICAL AND SCIENTIFIC
    The Fluvial System with Applications to Economic Geology
    Symposium on Tectonics and Ore Deposits
    Institute on Mineral Resources Permitting
    Geostatistical Ore Reserve Estimation

MANAGEMENT DEVELOPMENT
    the Management of Exploration
    Fundamentals of Management
    Taxation and Financial Reporting in the Mining Industry
    Human Resource Planning
    Performance Appraisal Workshop

OTHER DEVELOPMENT
    North American Natural Resources Conference
    University of Arizona Field Conference
    Mergers and Acquisitions
    Time Management Seminar
    Government Affairs Seminar
    Colorado School of Mines
    Introduction to Mining

FIGURE 10-11.

XYZ COMPANY
CONSOLIDATED TRAINING/DEVELOPMENT COST REPORT
COST SUMMARY BY FUNCTION

First Quarter 1985

	Technical Scientific	Management Development	Other Development	TOTAL
Production	$3,450.00	$ 75.00	$ 600.00	$ 4,125.00
Marketing	—	—	—	—
Technical Services	2,207.00	3,200.00	—	5,407.00
Finance	—	570.00	—	570.00
Human Resources	2,700.00	532.00	65.00	3,297.00
Public Relations	—	—	1,200.00	1,200.00
Executive	—	—	—	—
Total	$8,357.00	$4,377.00	$1,865.00	$14.599.00

FIGURE 10-12.

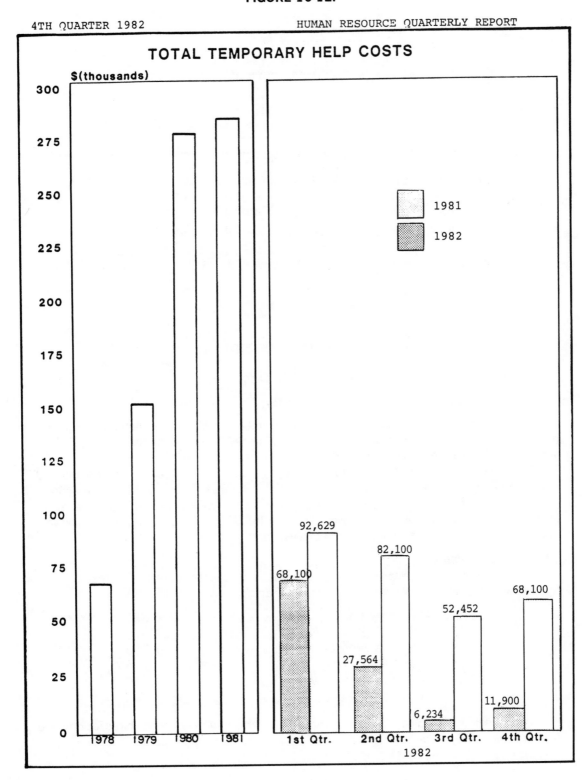

4TH QUARTER 1982   HUMAN RESOURCE QUARTERLY REPORT

TOTAL TEMPORARY HELP COSTS

FIGURE 10-13.

XYZ COMPANY
AGENCY TEMPORARY HELP
MONTHLY COST REVIEW

Department	1985 First Quarter			Total 1st Quarter
	Jan.	Feb.	Mar.	
Executive Management	$4,271	$ —	$1,000	$ 5,271
Business Development	—	5,000	3,300	8,300
Production	8,000	4,928	1,857	14,785
Technical Services	4,350	2,800	5,902	13,052
Finance	4,280	2,160	6,402	12,842
Total—	$20,901	$14,888	$18,461	$54,250

FIGURE 10-14.

EQUAL EMPLOYMENT OPPORTUNITY
AND
AFFIRMATIVE ACTION REPORT

XYZ COMPANY

Affirmative Action planning began in January, when the Affirmative Action Coordinator met with each of the vice-presidents to discuss the AAP commitments for 1985. Last year's progress was reviewed by management.

The Affirmative Action Coordinator invited a group of 62 students from Adams and Lincoln High schools to participate in an educational tour of the company. These schools have a significant minority population. The students visited various departments. Managers in each of these areas gave short presentations to the group. Specific jobs were reviewed, and requirements for obtaining jobs were discussed.

Other EEO/AAP Items

The minority vendor program continues to make excellent progress. The first quarter, the following orders were placed with minority vendors:

KLM Drilling Co.	$26,337
North Drilling Co.	21,079
Metro Data Services	1,382
Gomez Flower Box	244
Sanchez Office Supplies	1,520
Total	$50,562

Two additional handicapped people and one Vietnam veteran were hired during the first quarter 1985. Fifty-three Vietnam-era veterans are now employed, for 12 percent utilization rate.

FIGURE 10-15.

XYZ COMPANY
1985 AFFIRMATIVE ACTION PLAN
CONSOLIDATED

JOB GROUP	EEOC JOB CLASS.	AS OF JANUARY 1, 1985							GOALS FOR DECEMBER 31, 1985			
		TOTAL EMPL.	TOTAL MALES	TOTAL FEMALES		TOTAL MINORITY			TOTAL FEMALES		TOTAL MINORITY	
				NO.	%	NO.	%		NO.	%	NO.	%
Senior Mgt.	A01	8	8	—	—	—	—		—	—	—	—
Middle Mgt.	A05	52	43	5	10	—	—		6	9	1	2
Supervisory	A10	19	13	6	32	1	6		6	28	1	5
Engineering	B15	33	30	3	9	—	—		3	8	1	3
Geology	B20	35	29	6	17	—	—		6	17	1	3
Professionals	B25	72	54	21	29	6	7		24	24	7	7
Upper Level Tech.	C30	26	15	11	42	2	8		11	39	3	7
Lower Level Tech.	C35	20	9	11	55	4	20		13	47	4	17
Sales	D37	—	—	—	—	—	—		—	—	—	—
Upper Level Cler.	E40	83	1	82	99	11	13		83	89	11	12
Lower Level Cler.	E45	13	5	8	62	1	8		8	50	2	13
Craft Workers	F50	15	11	4	27	2	14		4	22	3	13
TOTAL		375	218	157	42	27	7		164	36	34	8

10.11   HOW TO START AND PRODUCE AN EMPLOYEE NEWSLETTER

Starting a new employee newsletter or revamping a current newsletter is a challenging assignment. In order for any publication to be successful, it must be written to attract today's employees—the self-fulfillment-seekers, the more highly educated, savvy work force.

Readership surveys show that internal publications are the primary source of information for most employees and that the contents of most company newsletters are reliable, accurate, and believable. A 1980 survey conducted by the International Association of Business Communicators and Towers, Perrin, Forster and Crosby of 45,000 personnel at forty organizations in the United States and Canada indicates that a high percentage of people (89 percent) find employee publications believable.[2]

More companies are hiring qualified communicators with training in communications, journalism, and English. These people most frequently report either to the human resource function with employee communications responsibilities, or to the public relations manager. The fact that the newsletter editors seem to have more education and background in the discipline may explain the fact that the IABC/TPFC survey indicates that 91 percent of readers find employee publications easy to read and 79 percent find them interesting.

The first thing to do is to meet with the executive who will be responsible for managing the publication, to define the scope and the format and to establish a budget and a time line for publication. It's important to agree on all of the basic issues before you proceed.

A Newsletter Startup Checklist

- Establish the scope of the newsletter. (Is it a total company informational tool, or merely an anniversary, birthday, safety award type of publication?)
- Establish format. (Tabloid, newsletter, etc.)
- Decide on frequency of publication. (Monthly, quarterly, etc.)
- Decide on basic contents.
- Establish a budget.
- Decide what function will be responsible for the newsletter. (Human resources, public relations, etc.)
- Evaluate and decide on the time restrictions of current staff. Will a new person be promoted or hired to produce the newsletter?
- What outside sources will you utilize? (Writers, graphic artists, printers, etc.)
- If outside printers are to be used, get three or four quotes on production costs, and ask for samples of printing to check quality of output.
- Will the publication have to appeal to local employees only, or is there a national and/or international readership?
- Who will have editorial control of the contents?
- What will be the distribution and who has distribution control?
- How will you measure the newsletter's effectiveness over time?

---

[2] "Survey of 45,000 Business Communicators," International Association of Business Communicators, 870 Market Street, Suite 928, San Francisco, California 94102.

Other Areas of Concern

1. It's a good idea to set up a news-gathering network from key areas of the organization. Ask for volunteers to be reporters and field editors, and locate people who have good writing skills to contribute to the newsletter. Build a backlog of articles and fillers to have on hand for times when current events are slow.
2. It's important for the editor to understand design, photography, graphics, and reproduction. If you have a graphics and reproduction group in-house, the processes can be learned. Otherwise, it's best to hire a person experienced in these areas.
3. Review the editor's role. How will readability be measured? How will the editor determine what employees want to read? Who will establish the style and class of the publication? And who will have the editorial and distribution control?

10.12 WRITING FOR YOUR AUDIENCE

Case in Point. Janet Wooley got a job editing a company newsletter and launched the publication quickly and efficiently, publishing the first issue within her first three weeks on the job. Using the experiences she gained with her previous employer, Janet did not take the time to assess her new readership, and instead of her first issue being a hit, it flopped. Her previous employer had an older employee population that appreciated a formal style. Her writing was almost Victorian, and the photography and graphics followed the more formal format she had chosen.

What was accepted and appreciated in her previous company was not accepted at all by her new organization. It is difficult to regroup and gain credibility for a publication if you start off on the wrong foot.

Up-front audience identification would have given Janet a clearer picture of what her readers wanted to see.

HUMAN RESOURCE DIRECTOR'S TIP:

So much writing in company newsletters seems to be from one pattern, one voice—monolithic. Write from various points of view; use quotes, interviews, and a relaxed, informal style. Humorize stories and use photography to get more human interest. Illustrate facts with lively examples, similes, and metaphors. Paint a picture in the mind.

10.13 SEVEN KEY ITEMS TO HELP YOU IDENTIFY YOUR AUDIENCE

1. Identify the average age of your readers. This will tell you what type of articles you should write. It will also give you a good idea of the style that will be most widely accepted (formal or informal).

2. Find out if there is a health and fitness orientation in the company, as there is in most organizations today. If so, include action pictures of employees involved in fitness or sports programs. Photography will take on an action-oriented flavor, rather than a posed, formal style.

3. Include articles that tell employees what the company is doing—what's going on in various departments. But don't write the articles in a self-serving style. Be careful to report the facts and let employees draw their own conclusions.

4. Use humor in many ways. Humor allows people to relax, and it cuts through rigidities and biases.

5. Use a conversational style that people can relate to in a relaxed way. You are more believable when you eliminate trite, stilted words and phrases.

6. You may need two different publications if you have one audience that is site-oriented and another that is corporate-headquarters-oriented. Two publications—one with a folksy and hometown flavor and another with a more sophisticated business orientation—may be best.

7. Quizzes and crossword puzzles are a unique way to communicate in an organizational newsletter.

HUMAN RESOURCE DIRECTOR'S TIP:

The Employee Information Council, 300 North State Street, Chicago, Illinois 60610, conducts a two-day seminar on "How to Start, Organize, and Produce House Publications."

The seminar includes the following key issues:

- How to manage a company publication
- How to get news and information
- How to be a better writer and editor
- How to fulfill your editor's role
- How to speak the language of design
- How to handle graphic reproduction
- How to handle the photos and the photography
- How to design the publication and specify graphics

A prepress kit and a designer's layout kit are provided as part of the cost of the seminar.

10.14   USING QUIZZES AND CROSSWORD PUZZLES

If you're interested in clearing up a misconception, introducing a new idea, or explaining company policy, a quiz in your company publication is an easy-to-understand way of communicating information. It attracts attention and often holds employee interest better than normal reporting techniques. It's also especially helpful in introducing employees to subject matter about which they may have little factual knowledge.

If you are having problems getting information across to employees in some specific areas (benefits, safety, equal employment policies, etc.), a quiz—or a question-and-answer article—could help solve your communications problem. And to enhance your presentation, make use of visual aids.

Crossword Puzzles. Crossword puzzles have been created to educate employees about a host of subjects, and now two publications have used these intriguing word games to explain two major subjects. Security was the theme for a puzzle in *On Target* (Loral Electronics Systems, 999 Central Park Avenue, Yonkers, New York 10704), while general company information was featured in a puzzle imprinted on a telephone in *New Jersey Bell* (New Jersey Bell, 540 Broad Street, Newark, New Jersey 07101).

HUMAN RESOURCE DIRECTOR'S TIP:

Identify companies in a similar industry or business and call or write to them asking if they have a newsletter or in-house publication. If so, ask if you can get copies and offer to share your newsletter with them. See what other people are doing. Subscribe to the *Editor's Newsletter,* a monthly report on trends and techniques in business, published by the Anderson Press, P.O. Box 774, Madison Square Station, New York, New York 10010. It has lots of good tips for business communications.

10.15   NEW IDEAS IN EMPLOYEE COMMUNICATIONS

The objective of any form of communication that reaches employees is to communicate. Organizations are constantly looking for creative, new ideas that work. One such program is used effectively by an international firm in the paper industry.

The International Paper Company is attempting to gain employee commitment to corporate and plant-level goals by providing timely, relevant, and honest information.[3] This is not an easy task with some 50,000 employees in mills, logging camps, and forests scattered throughout the country.

IP has many avenues of communication, but one new and timely approach is a company newswire for disseminating basic timely information. The company has set up what is in effect a private syndicated news service called "Newslink." News about the company or news that could affect the company is sent by telex at 9:00 every morning to the communicator at each of 105 IP facilities.

So, when the company chairman meets the head of the Environmental Protection Agency in Washington, say, to discuss the impact of proposed environmental regulations on IP and the forest products industry, IP's employees get the highlights of the discussions by 10:00 the next morning.

Equally important, the communicator at each facility is expected to link any relevant information to specific issues facing his or her respective facility.

---

[3] *Newslink,* International Paper Company. *Management Review,* AMACOM, a Division of American Management Associations, 1980.

10.16 SEXUAL BIAS AND RACIAL STEREOTYPES IN ORGANIZATIONAL COMMUNICATION

Equal opportunity has been around for a long time. It is a basic human right, and organizational communicators have a special responsibility to fulfill affirmative action requirements by writing in a nonsexist, nondiscriminatory manner. Equally important is an ability to use their unique roles in business to counsel management and to help set the tone for the whole organization.

Today's workers are more aware and more knowledgeable regarding stereotypes and bias, and the human resource manager needs a keen awareness of writing style.

The International Association of Business Communicators has published an excellent guidebook entitled *Without Bias: A Guidebook for Nondiscriminatory Communication*.[4] It provides an excellent review of racial and ethnic stereotypes and myths and how to avoid them in writing. The book also provides information on sexual bias in communication and how to eliminate it.

For example, the guidebook provides the following test for racial stereotypes:

Avoid Using Qualifiers That Reinforce Racial and Ethnic Stereotypes. A qualifier is information added that suggests an exception to the rule. Example: An account of a company event read, "The intelligent black students were guests as part of an orientation program." Under what circumstances would someone write, "The intelligent white students"?

To determine whether or not a qualifier has been used, try this test: Imagine the sentence with the word "white" in place of "black," or substitute an Anglo surname for a Chicano or Asian one. Bias is subtle. The more deeply it has been assimilated, the more difficult it is to uncover.

The guidebook also provides the following tests for sexual bias.

The most subtle form of sexism is the omission of women in references that take in humanity at large. The word "man" has been used in describing the male gender and in describing humanity as a whole, a practice potentially offensive to the communicator's audience.

Include all people in general references by substituting asexual words and phrases for man-words.

No	Yes
mankind	people, humanity, human beings, human race
man-made	synthetic, artificial, constructed, manufactured, of human origin
manpower	human resources, human energy, workers, work force
gentlemen's agreement	informal agreement or contract

---

[4] *Without Bias: A Guidebook for Nondiscriminatory Communication*, 1st Edition, International Association of Business Communicators, 870 Market Street, Suite 928, San Francisco, California 94102.

The lack of a generic singular pronoun in the English language causes many editorial headaches. The continued use of the phrase "he or she" can make writing difficult to read. Stubborn insistence that the pronouns "he," "him," and "his" stand for all people also can create problems. Consider this sentence taken from a group insurance brochure: "If the employee becomes pregnant while covered under this policy, he will be entitled to. . . . "

Consider various alternatives when using pronouns:

1. Reword the sentence to eliminate unnecessary gender pronouns.
2. Recase into the plural.

Some organizations have hurt the sales of their products by unconsciously building racial or sexual bias into their media ads. Women and minorities are powerful, growing consumer groups, able to significantly affect the profits of organizations that count on sales of their products for their success.

10.17　GAINING APPROVAL FOR HUMAN RESOURCE COMMUNICATIONS

One of the toughest jobs you have as a human resource communicator is to get the necessary approvals for newsletters, bulletins, organizational memos, and so on. By the time you obtain the necessary approvals, the copy can be bland and overprocessed.

Six Ideas for Speeding Up the Approval Process

1. Write a short paragraph identifying your audience and another paragraph identifying your approvers. This will help you choose the language and slant you need to gain attention and approval. Put these paragraphs where you can see them as you write, and keep your audience in mind.
2. If you build credibility in your organization for material that is well written and factually accurate, approvals should move quickly through the process. Frequent errors will make approvers suspicious and prolong the process while they try to check your facts.
3. Don't use a shotgun approach to approvals. Make a list of names in order of importance in the organization, and work your way up to the top. That way, you can show that others have approved. By the time you get to the key person, he or she will be more comfortable knowing that others have reviewed and approved your material.
4. Clip a note to the front of the document and state clearly in a few words the purpose of the document. It saves a great deal of time if the reader can grasp the purpose quickly.
5. The document should look good as it makes the rounds, but fresh paper and clean copy asks for editing and correction. Depending on the nature and extent of the changes, an already corrected copy may keep others up the chain of command from overprocessing your material.
6. Routing material for approvals can take a great deal of time. You can minimize the delays by stating your deadline in the routing memo and following up as the material progresses through the approval process, answering pertinent questions quickly and moving the material along.

10.18   THE HUMAN RESOURCE MANAGER AS PRESENTER AND COMPANY REPRESENTATIVE TO THE MEDIA

Human resource managers have come into their own in the 1980s. They must be knowledgeable, articulate managers of a complex, highly regulated function; and those managers who are successful are the ones who have highly developed interpersonal skills and can think and speak on their feet. One executive we know says a successful human resource manager has organizational and media "smarts" like wise kids on the streets of New York have "street smarts."

Here are thirteen occasions when human resource managers are called upon to make presentations:

1. Benefits, presentations to employees.
2. Briefings for executive management on proposed programs.
3. Presentations to the board of directors on strategic and/or long-range human resource plans.
4. Presentations to employees on labor relations activities.
5. Briefings for the human resource department on current activities.
6. Briefings of employees and the media on plant closings or layoffs.
7. Briefings for the media on industrial accidents.
8. Presenting management development programs and participating in functional training programs for management.
9. Presentation to community leaders and the media when opening a new plant, office building, mine, etc.
10. Presentations to employees on charity functions, such as United Way fund drives.
11. Conducting meetings and making presentations to associations such as the American Society for Personnel Administration and local human resource groups.
12. Presenting the company's side of a community relations problem to the community and possibly to the media.
13. Giving interviews or writing articles on human resource management for local newspapers, magazines, radio, and TV.

Five years ago, human resource managers had a low media profile. Today we may be called upon to make television presentations on matters pertaining to employee relations, safety, community relations, and other social issues.

On Television: A Survival Guide for Media Interviews, by Jack Hilton and Mary Knoblauch, published by AMACOM, a division of the American Management Association, provides a checklist to review if you are planning a television appearance. The checklist can be useful if you find yourself in any situation where you will be questioned. Not only a television appearance, but a sensitive community or special-interest group confrontation requires the same preparation and presentation skill.

CHAPTER 11

When to Use Outside Consultants in Human Resource Management

At a recent seminar in New York City, several top human resource professionals were polled regarding their use of outside consultants. In the past, personnel managers didn't use consultants as frequently as we do today. The personnel function was simpler and less complex. There was less legislation, and emotional issues like sexual harassment were still in the closet.

The growing complexity of business, the fast-changing operating environment, the hundreds of government regulations, the new technology in information processing, the contemporary worker with a self-fulfillment urge, and the need for American companies to find new markets overseas have created this increased need for consulting services.

The consulting business has its ups and downs, boom and bust cycles that follow the American economy, but consulting is now so ingrained in our business culture that it's important for human resource directors to keep abreast of the fast-changing consulting field.

Problems do arise on occasion. This is an unlicensed, unregulated profession, one in which anyone can hang out a shingle and take the label of consultant. Because consulting has come on so strong in the past five years, however, there have been renewed efforts on the part of some groups to set basic standards. The Institute of Management Consultants is developing bodies of knowledge that they feel individual consultants should know. The IMC has for years offered the title of Certified Management Consultant (CMC) to people who have five years of experience. Now, the IMC is planning to require a course and perhaps a test on consulting knowledge before granting certification.

Two consultants in key human resource areas have provided a few guidelines for this book concerning when consultants can be effective in assisting human resource directors and what they would look for if they were hiring a consultant.

In the area of executive search, George L. Reisinger, with Korn/Ferry International, provides these guidelines.[1]

---

[1] George L. Reisinger, Korn/Ferry International, Denver Division, 5555 DTC Parkway, Suite 3205, Englewood, Colorado 80111.

Use an Executive Search firm when:

- The job pays at least $40,000 or more per year.
- It's felt that third-party objectivity is vital to the success of attracting just the right individual.
- You feel that the right individual is not looking or out in the job market seeking another opportunity, and therefore is more difficult to find.
- Confidentiality is important for competitive reasons.
- There is a performance problem with the incumbent.
- The organization is going through a transition or reorganization period.
- There is a scarcity of critical skills or of females, minorities, or handicapped executives.
- There is a need for high-level, multiple-technical, or professional disciplines that are difficult to locate.

What should you look for in an executive search firm? According to Reisinger, you should look at:

- The firm's track record through a client representation.
- The practical business credentials of officers and associates.
- Conflicts of interest.
- The firm's code of ethics.

The usual cost of an executive search is approximately 30 percent of the first years's salary, plus expenses, and it normally takes about 120 days to fill a position.

The human resource director's role in executive search is to:

- Seek out the best consulting firm for the job.
- Act as liaison between the chosen firm and the company executive who has a position to fill.
- Interpret and administer company policy.
- Implement the employment process, relocation, and orientation.

Most human resource professionals—at least the most successful ones—realize that we cannot be everything to everyone all the time. We cannot know all and see all, and there is an increase in the use of consultants for special projects or specialized needs, for training and development of people, for expert advice on issues that are expected to affect an organization. When you have a special need for expertise, there are so many consulting firms and so many "experts," you suddenly find yourself inundated with pamphlets, sales literature, and phone calls from all over the country. How do you sort all of this out and find the best consultant for your job?

From time to time, *Business Week* magazine publishes a list of the top American consultants. The list may change from year to year, but the following companies usually make it. The list is alphabetical:

- Arthur Anderson
- Arthur D. Little
- Booz, Allen and Hamilton
- Boston Consulting Group

- Coopers and Lybrand
- Ernst and Ernst
- Hay Associates
- A. T. Kearney
- McKinsey
- Peat, Marwick, Mitchell
- Price Waterhouse
- Reliance Consulting Group
- Touche Ross
- Towers, Perrin, Forster, and Crosby
- Arthur Young

Donald E. Kern, vice-president of Towers, Perrin, Forster, and Crosby, provides the following question-and-answer guide for smaller companies to use when choosing an employee benefits consulting firm:[2]

Q: What are the reasons for using an employee benefits consulting firm?

A: A smaller organization may not have enough staff members to have expertise in all of the major employee benefits issues arising today. The human resource director's only choice may be to use outside expertise. Aside from this question of staffing, however, the reasons for using an employee benefits consultant are the same for any employer, regardless of size:

- Assistance in defining employee benefit program objectives or providing an independent view on those that exist.
- Assistance in solving specific problems, such as designing a new pension plan or analyzing the financial stewardship of a group insurance program.
- Assistance in implementing benefit program revisions (e.g., establishing procedures for pension plan administration).

Q: What are the qualities to look for in an employee benefits consulting firm?

A: • *Independence.* It is important to know whether a consulting firm represents a particular point of view (for example, because it is an insurance agent or broker). In such a case, its advice may still be sound, but the human resource manager should know whether the firm has an economic interest in promoting a particular approach to an assignment.
- *Reputation.* Because the employee benefit consulting practice is well established, the reputations of many major consulting firms are well known. One of the best ways to develop a list of firms is to ask other human resource managers for their recommendations. The local banker or law firm can also be helpful.
- *Local presence.* It is often desirable, from the standpoints of convenience and cost-efficiency, to use a consulting firm that has an office nearby. Provided that the consulting firm is qualified to begin with, its staff may have special knowledge of local benefit practices and competitive practices. But a human resource

---

[2] Donald E. Kern, Vice-President, Towers, Perrin, Forster, and Crosby, 600 Third Avenue, New York, New York 10016.

manager considering the local office of a regional or nationwide consulting firm should make certain of two points—that the local office staff has expertise in the area of current concern and that there are sufficient resources to devote to the assignment.

- *Size of the consulting firm.* Employee benefit consultants must deal with a myriad of technical issues, new legislation, actuarial matters, and an ever-changing regulatory climate. To keep current on these issues requires a commitment to sizable research efforts and expenditures, which can be met most effectively by consulting firms with revenues sufficient to provide the resources and technical support required.
- *Depth of services.* Although an individual consulting project may be limited in scope, the manager also may need a consulting firm for ongoing services, such as performing actuarial valuations for the pension plan or recordkeeping services for a savings plan. Because of this potential for an ongoing relationship, the human resource director should be satisfied that the depth of services of the employee benefit consulting firm is sufficient to satisfy the company's ongoing needs if the relationship develops well. These additional services might include communications consulting, health-care cost-containment studies, welfare plan design and financing, and benefit plan administrative and systems services.
- *Quality of staff.* The most important ingredient in selecting an employee benefits consulting firm is the quality of the staff. A consulting firm can be only as effective as the collective abilities of the individuals that compose its staff.

Q: How should the initial interview with a consulting firm go?

A: After identifying a few consulting firms that seem qualified for the project, the human resource director should arrange separate meetings with them, to gain some idea of each firm's capabilities and qualifications to handle the assignment. The director should ask the consulting firm to have present at the meeting the individuals who will have primary responsibility for conducting the assignment. Any other representatives of the consulting firm at the meeting will be there to sell the firm and, while they may be charming and even informative, will have little if anything to do with the assignment itself. Another equally important reason for the initial meeting is the opportunity for the manager to describe, as precisely and as clearly as possible, the problem he or she needs resolved. The initial meeting should conclude with an understanding that the consulting firm will prepare a written proposal to be presented by an agreed-upon date.

Q: What information should the written proposal contain?

A: Consulting firms' written proposals may take the form of a brief letter summarizing the agreement reached between the consultant and the manager at their meeting, a lengthy formal memorandum, or anything in between. The complexity of the document should reflect the complexity of the proposed consulting assignment. Whatever the form, the proposal should:

- Demonstrate the consultant's understanding of the human resource director's situation and the circumstances leading to the decision to sponsor a consulting project.
- Define the objective of the assignment, the product to be delivered, and its impact on the client's situation.

- Indicate the critical limits of the assignment in terms of the breadth and depth of coverage the consultant intends to provide.
- Delineate the steps the consultant proposes to take, together with his or her own and the client's roles in the process.
- Give a work schedule, an anticipated completion date, and an estimate of professional fees and other costs that may be incurred.
- Name the individuals who will work on the project and briefly indicate their professional qualifications and those of the firm, with specific reference to the assignment under consideration.

11.1 ADDITIONAL GUIDELINES FOR CHOOSING A CONSULTANT

- Did you hear about the consultant from a source you consider ethical and knowledgeable in the field?
- Have you asked how long the firm has been in business?
- Have you asked for a client list?
- Can you call previous clients for references?
- Have you asked how much of the consultant's business is repeat business?
- Have you checked their standards of professional conduct and practice?
- Is there a guarantee of satisfaction?
- Have you checked the backgrounds and credentials of the firm's principals?
- Have you asked how much time the principals of the firm will spend on your project?
- Has the firm had experience with other clients in a similar assignment? If so, can you call those firms to ask about the job that was done for them?
- Have you had a sufficiently thorough discussion with the consultant to feel comfortable with the idea that the consultant understands your problems and objectives and can stimulate new thinking and bring a new perspective to your organization?
- Has the consultant made a proposal in writing, and does the proposal include an estimate of fees for each element of the project if there is more than one? Are the proposal and the fee schedule reasonable?
- Every organization has a personality, an environment all its own within which people must operate to be successful. If you know your organization and you've learned all you can about the consultant, you should be able to match the corporate and the consultant personalities. Since this is an important element for success, have you considered it?

11.2 HOW TO FIND A COMPUTER CONSULTANT

Because computer technology and office automation are so expensive, many companies seek computer consultants. The two key advantages of using a consultant in this field are the need for objectivity and the need for current relevant experience.

For example, John Lowe, former president of a $20-million-dollar-a-year outerwear manufacturer, recalls that a consultant saved his company thousands of dollars by advising him to postpone purchase of a computer system because of anticipated technological developments. Eighteen months later, the same consultant recommended a newly introduced $50,000 minicomputer system that was far more cost-effective than the huge computer system he was thinking of purchasing earlier.

As is the case in choosing any consultant, ask about the charges for each service you are requesting, and request a letter of agreement about what work is to be done for what charge.

There is no central licensing organization for computer consultants, but you can obtain the names of computer consultants by writing to the following professional associations:

Association of Data Processing Service Organizations, Inc.
1925 North Lynn Street
Arlington, VA 22209
(703) 522–5055
Data Processing Management Association
505 Busse Highway
Park Ridge, Ill. 60068
(312) 825–8124
Independent Computer Consultants Association
P.O. Box 27412
St. Louis, Mo. 63141
(314) 567–9708

CHAPTER 12

Labor Relations and the Union

Unions are struggling against a tough economy and other ills like industry moves to the sun belt, the growth of robotics, and the new high-technology industry composed primarily of professional and white-collar workers. This is a move away from production-oriented blue-collar workers that unions have historically been able to organize.

The decline of heavily organized industries is forcing unions to seek more members among office workers, who constitute 57 percent of nonagricultural employees. The pressures on business to avoid unions is also strong.

The human resource director facing a union-organizing campaign with little specific expertise in labor relations may want to hire a labor consultant. Following are three key items to look for:

1. *Experience.* Look for good labor experience and a high-win ratio in previous campaigns. Ask for a client list and permission to check with clients.
2. *Integrity.* Don't just look for a "union-buster"; look for the person who will review all of your options and suggest the best alternatives. Then, you make the decisions.
3. *Personal exposure.* A variety of exposures to all facets of labor relations, administration, and employee relations is needed in order to be effective in fully understanding the human resource function.

It's a good idea to review your labor relations environment periodically to ensure that you have a positive, motivated work force.

12.1 AUDITING THE HEALTH OF YOUR LABOR RELATIONS PROGRAM

William L. Becker, an attorney with the firm of Dorfman, Cohen, Laner, and Muchin in Chicago, provides the following guidelines for reviewing your current labor relations climate:[1]

---

[1] William L. Becker, Attorney, Dorfman, Cohen, Laner, and Muchin, One IBM Plaza, Suite 3301, Chicago, Illinois 60611.

Whether your work force is large or small, unionized or nonunion, clerical or production, its effectiveness and productivity will be enhanced by a healthy labor relations program. Moreover, healthy labor relations programs reduce the likelihood of legal challenges such as fair employment practice charges, unfair labor practice complaints, arbitrations, and so on.

How does a human resource director judge the health of a labor relations program? The secret is to determine how the employees themselves perceive the quality of their working life. For example, you may have the most expensive wage and benefit package in your industry, but if your employees perceive it as being second-rate, poorly administered, or discriminatory in its impact, your company's labor relations program is unhealthy. The underlying problem may be poor communication practices, untrained supervisors, improper insurance claims administration—the list is endless. To diagnose and correct the problem, though, a necessary first step is to determine where the unhealthy symptoms lie.

There are many ways to gather information concerning employee perceptions. Here are a few:

1. Analyze the grievances filed by your employees (if your work force is unionized) or the complaints submitted through your internal complaint procedure. If you do not have such a procedure, institute one.
2. Analyze the results of exit interviews of employees who resign or are terminated. The exit interview should be conducted by a personnel professional, not by the employee's supervisor. If the supervisor is part of the problem, you might never learn the facts. If your turnover is high, an exit interview procedure is important.
3. Encourage supervisors to talk regularly with all of their employees. Some companies insist that supervisors have at least one such off-the-record conversation with each employee under their supervision once a month, to encourage feedback.
4. Institute a system of speak-up meetings with small groups of employees. The composition of the groups should be random, neither appointed by management nor elected by employees, and rotating, so all employees have the opportunity to attend such a meeting once every six months, for example. In order to make the meetings more fruitful, consider an agenda for each one, such as: "Can overtime assignments be handled better in your department?" or "Do our plant rules need revision?" Avoid making promises to change existing procedures unless you are prepared to keep your promise.
5. If your performance evaluation procedure is flexible, it should allow for employee feedback, and a well-trained supervisor can use the feedback aspect of the procedure to gather valuable employee perceptions.
6. Some companies consider the use of employee attitude surveys. If you choose this approach, be aware of the risk that employees who tell you directly through such a survey that they have a problem will expect a timely correction of that problem. Thus, the attitude survey, while furnishing valuable information concerning employee perceptions, could create a new problem if you are not prepared to correct immediately the problems you uncover.

Typically, employee complaints and negative perceptions fall into one or more of the following categories.

Wages/Salaries

- There is no established timetable for reviewing compensation. Employees do not know when they will receive a raise or whether the company has a procedure in place for reviewing wages or salaries to determine whether a raise is warranted.
- The dollar amount of recent increases is perceived as being inadequate, either because the increases compare poorly with cost of living figures or the increases are not keeping pace with those granted by other employers in your geographical area. A thorough survey of compensation policies in area companies and an analysis of various economic factors such as cost of living or federal and state minimum wage increases, can correct this.
- Perceived inequities exist within your work force concerning the compensation received by skilled versus unskilled employees; supervisors versus non-supervisors, especially if nonsupervisors work so much overtime that their gross earnings exceed those of supervisors; senior versus junior employees; males versus females; and so on.
- The wage or salary progression for new hires is unrealistically long compared with their training cycle, so that a six-month employee who is just as skilled and productive as a two-year employee is still earning significantly less.
- Merit increases or bonuses are perceived as being barometers of favoritism.

Hours/Work Scheduling

- Workdays or work weeks are seen as being too long.
- Overtime distribution is perceived as being haphazard or unfair (in some facilities, employees dislike overtime; in others, it is viewed as a benefit).
- Lunch or break periods are not scheduled in accordance with the perceived needs of employees (e.g., a night-shift employee may not want to eat lunch in the middle of the shift).
- Shift differentials are perceived as being inadequate or unfairly administered.

Benefits

- Benefit levels, such as number of paid holidays, vacation amounts, and insurance benefits, are perceived as being inadequate, as compared with those offered by other employers in your geographical area.
- Benefit administration or eligibility requirements are viewed negatively. For example, a holiday is lost if it falls on an employee's scheduled day off or during the employee's vacation; vacation cannot be split up or taken a day at a time; insurance reimbursements are too slow; sick pay cannot be accumulated or will not be paid out if unearned. There may be good business justifications for these policies, but if they are the source of significant employee discontent, you

should consider whether the business justification outweighs the labor relations problem or whether better communication concerning the underlying business justification needs to be implemented.

- Employees do not know how good your benefit program is. Do you have an employee handbook outlining the program? Is there a vehicle, such as letters to the home, through which you can communicate how well your insurance program protected a hardship case, or how much a retired employee appreciates the pension?

Safety/Health

- The work area is perceived as being unsafe or unhealthy.
- Employee accidents are receiving more emphasis than preventive safety programs.
- There is no internal method of resolving or investigating employee safety complaints.

Discipline

- Your work rules or performance standards are not published.
- Employees do not know what discipline to expect from various work rule violations.
- Supervisors in different departments apply the work rules differently.
- There are perceived inequities in the administration of discipline. For example, supervisors play favorites. Female or minority group members perceive discrimination in the application of your discipline policies.
- There is no internal appeal procedure from the decision of a supervisor who chooses harsh discipline.
- Employees do not receive copies of documentation of work rule violations.
- Discipline is not perceived as being progressive and constructive.

Promotion Procedures

- Employees see no chance for advancement. Job vacancies are not published, or new employees are hired "off the street" before current employees have a chance to apply for the job.
- If vacancies are published internally, employees do not understand the standards used to choose the successful candidate. Is length of service considered? Does a poor attendance record affect advancement opportunity? If special training is needed, will it be funded by the company through a tuition-reimbursement program? Are these factors known?

Job Security

- Reduction-in-force procedures are viewed as being unfair, based on favoritism, without regard to length of service. Standards applied by the company when

layoffs become necessary are not published or, if they are, they are inconsistently applied.
- When a layoff does occur, benefit administration is haphazard. How long are employees covered by insurance programs during forced layoffs? Who pays the premiums? Do they continue to earn vacation credits? If there is a formal seniority program, does seniority accumulate, or is it frozen or lost? Is all of this information well communicated?
- Recalls from layoff appear to be administered differently from the layoff procedure itself. What standards are used?

Management Techniques

- Supervisors are not respected. They are perceived as being overbearing, unfriendly, uncommunicative, prejudiced, poor leaders, and poor instructors.
- The company's image is negative. It is seen as profitable without being generous, or unprofitable without being open to employee input for change, uncaring, managed by individuals who are not respected.
- If there is absentee management, those individuals fail to make a good impression because they never visit, or, if they do, they fail to communicate.

If your organization has learned to listen to employee perceptions and to respond in a credible fashion, you probably have a healthy labor relations climate, which is every human resource director's goal.

12.2 SOME QUESTIONS AND ANSWERS ON RETAINING UNION-FREE STATUS

Q: What does it really mean to a company to remain union-free?

A: It means the company maintains full control of its operations. It means the human resource function can be administered in an open environment, with direct communication with employees, without third-party intervention.

Q: What is the key element in remaining union-free?

A: There are many things that foster a union-free environment, but probably the most important is competitive pay. We've all seen the articles that say pay is way down on the list of priorities for employees, but pay is very important. There are naturally other things that make an employee happy in the job, including:

- Good communications up and down in the company
- Job enrichment
- Participative management
- A fair and impartial supervisor
- Pleasant work
- Good benefits

Q: How far can a company go in saying a union could do more harm than good?

A: It used to be that you walked a fine line between what was permissible and what was not permissible. You needed to be as strong as you could be in saying that a union may not do employees as much good as it claimed, but on the other hand, if you went too far, you ran the risk of having your statements viewed by the National Labor Relations Board as threats, and the company could be ordered to bargain on the grounds that a fair election could not be held. In June 1982, the Board began to announce policy-changing decisions that have affected basic rules of labor law. For example, the National Labor Relations Board will not rule at all now on whether campaign statements made by either side were accurate or inaccurate. The NLRB will continue, however, to set elections aside if:

- Either side uses threats, promises, or the like, which interfere with employees' free choice.
- Either side uses a forgery that leaves voting employees unable to tell whether what they are reading is propaganda.
- Official NLRB documents are altered so it appears the board itself is endorsing one side or the other.

The decision that brought about this NLRB change was *The Midland National Life Insurance Company* decision on August 4, 1982.

Another significant decision of the NLRB in 1982 was the *Materials Research* decision, which held that all employees, union or nonunion, have the right to bring help to a meeting or interview that the employee fears may end in discipline. It is incumbent on the employee to ask permission to bring someone to the meeting; however, management has no obligation to advise the employee of the right to help.

There appears to be a trend in these decisions of more rights for employees and for management and less for unions. The *Materials Research* decision, for example, gives employees a right they previously could have had only by joining a union.

Q: What do you do when a union organizer demands recognition?

A: The Mountain States Employers Council, a nonprofit organization located in Denver, represents more than 600 local companies in the area of labor relations and provides the following guidelines to their member companies.[2]

What to Do and What Not to Do When the Union Organizer Demands Recognition

A union gains the right to represent your employees:

1. By a secret ballot election conducted by the labor board
2. By voluntary recognition
3. By board-ordered recognition

In any case, you are required to bargain in good faith with the union over wages, hours, and other terms and conditions of employment.

The union has a right to demand recognition in an appropriate bargaining unit, so long as a majority of your employees have signed authorization cards. You have a

---

[2] Mountain States Employers Council, 1790 Logan Street, P.O. Box 539, Denver, Colorado 80201.

right to demand a labor board election if you have a good-faith doubt that the union represents a majority of your employees in a unit appropriate for bargaining.

Even when a union does represent a majority of your employees and even when you have a good-faith doubt of its majority, the union can file a refusal to bargain charges against you, and the board will order you to bargain without an election if management takes steps to undermine or destroy the union majority by threats or promises to your employees or by committing unfair labor practices that tend to undermine the union's majority.

A union that wants to organize or unionize a group of employees usually tries to persuade the employees to sign authorization cards or a petition. If 30 percent of the employees in an appropriate bargaining unit sign such cards or petitions, the union may petition the National Labor Relations Board for a secret-ballot election in which all eligible employees in the group or unit may vote on whether they want to be represented by the union. However, if more than 50 percent of the employees sign cards or a petition, the union may demand immediate recognition and bargaining from the employer without having to file a petition and prove its majority status in the secret-ballot election. The employer may be forced to accede to this demand and to bargain with the union without an election if the employer makes the wrong move and commits unfair labor practices when the first union contact is made.

A union that has obtained signed authorization cards or a petition from a majority of the employees sometimes demands both recognition and bargaining from the employer and files a petition for an election. Even if the union loses the election, it then may seek an order from the NLRB requiring the employer to recognize and bargain with the union. Thus, the employer's actions after receiving a demand for bargaining must be carefully planned even if the union has also filed a petition for an election.

Once a union has obtained signed authorization cards or a petition from a majority of the employees in an appropriate unit, it almost always will make a demand on the employer for immediate recognition and bargaining. This demand may or may not be a prelude to or be accompanied by the filing of a petition for an election with the NLRB. However, in either case, the manner in which the demand is presented to the employer may vary. It may be by (1) letter, (2) telegram, (3) telephone, (4) personal visit by union representatives, or (5) a combination of these methods.

If and when a demand for recognition is made in person by a union organizer, do *not*:

- Ask to see the cards.
- Look at any lists of employees.
- Discuss, look at, review, count, or accept any cards or even flip through them if they are handed to you or deposited on your desk.
- Review or comment upon any offered document that may be or purports to be a labor agreement.
- Look at, discuss, or review any writing or paper they may attempt to hand you or deposit on your desk.
- Refuse to talk to or meet with union representatives if they are already in your presence.
- Poll or interview your employees to ascertain whether or not they signed cards.

- Engage in objectionable conduct that may tend to undermine the union's majority.
- Threaten employees, directly or by implication.
- Make promises, directly or by implication.
- Interrogate employees about union activities or the union campaign.

When a demand is made, *do*:

- Arrange to have a witness with you if at all possible. There is no need to have a secretary present to record or transcribe what was said during the visit.
- Remain calm and dignified. Keep your cool.
- Ask questions. You run the show, and if you have difficulty, ask them to leave and not return until they can act courteously and in a businesslike manner. Be a good listener! Do not engage in small talk about matters having nothing to do with the purpose of the visit. Do not talk about children, sports, hunting, fishing, the weather, or the state of the nation. The less said, the better. Keep the meeting short.
- When the union representatives identify themselves, either get their calling cards or, carefully and specifically, in their presence, put down their names, addresses, and exactly who it is they claim to represent.
- Ask them to state their business. Obtain, but do not give, information. If and when they claim in any form to represent your employees, state clearly, "I have good-faith doubt that your union does, in fact, represent an uncoerced majority of our employees in an appropriate bargaining unit."

If the union organizers suggest that you agree on a professor, federal mediator, or someone like that to check the cards for the purpose of verifying the union's majority, stand firm on the ground that you believe justice would be better served by utilizing the orderly processes of the governmental agency set up to handle them and to make the necessary determinations.

Should the cards be put on your desk or thrown at you in leaving, you should have a witness that you put them in an envelope at the moment and sealed them without looking at them.

On receipt of any letter, answer the letter in a reasonable period of time. The letter should state your "good-faith doubt that the union does, in fact, represent an uncoerced majority of the employees in a unit appropriate for bargaining."

Q. What are employee, management, and union rights?
A. Employee rights include:

- The right to form and join a union.
- The right to vote the way you want.
- The right to vote no or join a union.

Management rights include:

- The right to wage a campaign and to talk about union negatives.
- The right to run your own business.
- The right of free speech.
- The right to answer false and misleading charges.

Union rights include:

* The right to organize and make promises.
* The right to bring charges against the employer.
* The right to picket for a certain period of time.

12.3 LABOR RELATIONS CHECKLIST WHEN PREPARING FOR A LAYOFF

There have been so many layoffs in industry during the past couple of years that most companies have written layoff and recall policies and have well-defined layoff procedures. The organized layoff builds confidence in employees that they will be treated fairly. The way to handle a layoff in a fair, effective way is to plan it out ahead of time and cover all bases. Use a layoff checklist.

It's important to plan for layoff, taking all eventualities into consideration, ahead of time. Here are some key questions to consider:

* How many people will be involved?
* What departments are involved?
* What will be the layoff criteria? Performance, seniority, job elimination? If it's a job elimination, it may be a reduction in force, rather than a layoff, which means there may be no recall rights involved.
* Prepare a layoff policy, stating criteria decided upon and what regular pay, severance, and vacation pay will be paid.
* Determine how much advance notice will be given.
* Before a layoff or reduction in force, some companies poll employees to determine if anyone wishes to quit voluntarily. If any employees do, the company gives them severance, even though it really is a voluntary termination.
* Ask employees who are old enough to retire if they wish to take early retirement.
* When the layoff notice is given, will employees be allowed time to look for a job before the layoff date?
* Develop a seniority list.
* Review the layoff list to see how your affirmative action plan will be affected. What percentages of minorities, women, handicapped, and people over forty are there?
* Review lists of company property held by employees who will be laid off.
* Draft letters from management to employees regarding the layoff.
* Prepare a press release. Send it to the newspapers *after* employees have been notified.
* Notify corporate people if you have a corporate relationship.
* Have appropriate benefits people make arrangements regarding medical and life insurance coverage. Review pension and thrift plans if you have such benefits. Provide insurance conversion forms.
* Prepare an information sheet to hand out to employees regarding what benefits they will have and for how long.

- Decide on the amount of severance and unused vacation that will be paid to each employee.
- Prepare an outplacement program that includes workshops on writing a résumé and interviewing.
- Provide employees with information on how to collect unemployment insurance.
- Provide a counseling service for employees with special problems.
- Contact employers in the area to find out if there are any employment opportunities.
- If you can afford it, provide offices offsite for laid-off employees to use as a base while they are launching their job search.

A layoff or reduction in force is never pleasant, but if you have a game plan it makes the whole outplacement effort much easier.

12.4 LABOR RELATIONS AND THE SMALL COMPANY

- When does a company need labor relations assistance?
- When should a small company formalize personnel policies?
- When does a small company need someone assigned full-time to personnel administration?

There's no simple answer to these questions, according to Wallace Snyder, a Denver consultant with T. K. Cobb Associates, a firm that installs personnel systems in small companies.[3] He provides the following checklist for a small company to use when reviewing the need for labor relations assistance:

- Systematically review the current policies (written or unwritten) that are followed in the organization. Are there frequent problems with any of the policies?
- Review the cost of carrying out your policies and procedures. Are the costs reasonable?
- The largest costs of doing business for most small organizations (150 people or less) are employee costs. Review the costs of hiring, retaining, and replacing employees.
- Can existing policies be modified or strengthened by putting them in writing and distributing them to the employees? If they were in writing, should they save managers time from constantly interpreting policy?
- Are policies and current practices consistent with federal, state, and local laws and regulations?
- Are processes available so that employees clearly understand what is expected of them and how they are doing in meeting those expectations?
- What are the lines of up-and-down communication in the organization? Are they open and working? How do you know?
- Do you have a healthy labor relations climate, or do you have ongoing problems?

---

[3] Wallace Snyder, Consultant, T. K. Cobb Associates, 4155 East Jewell Avenue, Suite 908, Denver, Colorado 80222.

If you have problems in a majority of these areas, Snyder says it's probably time to install a full human resource function, including (1) personnel administration, and (2) human resource counseling and development programs.

All human resource directors have their own ideas about the best time to add a personnel administration function. The company needs a personnel manager when it gets to the size where personnel activities take executives considerable time on an ongoing basis. Some questions to ask are:

1. Is human resource leadership needed?
2. Is authority to make personnel decisions so diffused that it is perceived as unfair and unequal across the company?
3. Are personnel decisions either too inflexible or too loose?
4. Is effective manpower planning done? Do you have the people you need when you need them?
5. Are people receiving the training they need?
6. Are jobs filled from within, including promotions? Is there effective succession planning? Are open jobs posted, or does the company always go outside to fill jobs? If so, employee morale could be affected.
7. Do you have a lot of EEO charges? If so, in which departments and in which jobs? EEO charges can be an indication of human resource problems that should be resolved before they go too far.
8. Are you complying with all state and federal regulations?

These are just some of the questions that should be answered when considering whether or not to install a full human resource department and to hire a human resource professional.

12.5 SAFETY—MAINTAINING A SAFE WORKPLACE

The human resource director has a responsibility for maintaining a safe work environment for employees, and the first area of a good safety program is hazard identification and prevention. Accident prevention occurs through proper engineering controls, preventive maintenance, and safety training on the proper use of equipment. Following are some basic safety procedures:

- Management should encourage employees to report hazards.
- Offices and plants should be clean, well designed, and controlled for noise, heat, dust, and fumes.
- Plants need good preventive maintenance programs for production equipment.
- Supervisors should inspect work areas informally every day.
- Worker–management teams using checklists should inspect monthly or quarterly.
- Annual plant and office safety audits should be completed annually.
- Base safety training programs and safety checklists on specific hazard information.
- Make refresher safety training available on a continuing basis for all employees, including supervisors.

There are some new guides at OSHA these days. Employers with better than average safety records may be exempted from routine OSHA inspections by participating in one of three voluntary compliance programs that took effect July 6, 1982. If accepted into one of the voluntary programs, which were announced in the July 2, 1982, *Federal Register*, an employer's worksite would be removed from OSHA's general schedule inspection list, although the agency would continue to respond to employee complaints, accidents, and fatalities.

There is also a uniform policy to guide safety and health compliance officers in determining when to cite employers for repeated violations of standards. In fixed establishments, such as a company's manufacturing plants, violations must occur at the same plant for the repeat violation citation to be issued. For nonfixed establishments, such as construction sites or oil and gas well-drilling operations, repeat citations may be issued at any location of a company's operations within the local OSHA area office jurisdiction.

General compliance assistance will be given to employers by OSHA inspectors under the guidelines of a new agency directive. Compliance officers are directed to assist employers in identifying methods for correcting alleged safety and health violations, with the type of help rendered dependent on "the needs of the employer and the complexity of the hazard," but this advice will not replace the agency's statutory requirement to issue citations for violations.

12.6 OCCUPATIONAL SAFETY AND HEALTH ADMINISTRATION'S LEADING VIOLATIONS

The ten most common workplace OSHA violations (132,000 violations with proposed penalties exceeding $25 million), according to the Department of Labor Statistics, were:

1. No posting of the OSHA notice of employer obligations.
2. No grounding of electrical equipment connected by cord and plug.
3. No machinery guards at point of operation.
4. No guards for pulleys.
5. No guards for live parts of electrical equipment.
6. No enclosures for blades of fans in use less than 7 feet above floor of working level.
7. No guards for belt, rope, and chain drives.
8. Disorderliness in aisles and passageways.
9. No guards for vertical and inclined belts.
10. Not maintaining a log and summary of job injuries and illnesses.

12.7 FUNDAMENTAL CHANGES IN OSHA

In 1982, a new emphasis was placed on OSHA. Policies specifically:

- Require the agency to perform a cost–benefit analysis before promulgating new standards, measuring potential benefits to workers' health against the cost to business.
- Allow business more options for meeting standards. This could mean the use of protective devices, such as hearing protection, rather than requiring engineering modification in workplace equipment.

Industry has advocated the cost–benefit approach for years, arguing that worker health and protection actually would improve as business would be better able to allocate its resources to health priorities. This was not the case in the past, however, and that is why there is an OSHA today.

OSHA has repealed 200 regulations considered unenforceable, and the agency is no longer calling on employers with ten or fewer workers if their lost-time case rate is below the national average.

OSHA Recordkeeping

Contact the U.S. Department of Labor, Occupational Safety and Health Administration, for a copy of their recordkeeping requirements and copies of the OSHA log and other necessary forms.

12.8 HOW INVOLVED SHOULD THE HUMAN RESOURCE DIRECTOR BE IN SAFETY?

The depth of involvement of the human resource director in workplace safety usually occurs as a result of the need of that particular organization for safety programs. If the organization is medium to large in size and has several locations, the human resource director may need an experienced safety manager on staff.

Many organizations establish a safety function separate from the human resource function. Workplace safety has become a field all its own, mainly because of the huge body of laws and regulations that have come along in the last ten years.

These are the key steps to take in implementing an effective safety program.

- Assign a safety coordinator for your company. If it's a large organization, assign a person in each major area.
- Teach managers and supervisors the basics of safety for your industry.
- Prepare a safety manual and/or handbook for all employees regarding safety and health procedures.
- Inspect company locations for possible safety hazards.
- Keep complete accident records and investigation reports.
- Provide safety training programs for management and employees.
- Keep emergency numbers at all key locations, including reception areas and switchboards.
- Retain emergency notification phone numbers for every employee.

12.9 CHECKLIST OF SECURITY ACTIVITIES

The Bureau of National Affairs reported in their February 3, 1983, *Bulletin to Management* that in a survey of personnel and industrial relations executives conducted by the American Society for Personnel Administration, the official with most responsibility for company security is the security director in 33 percent of the firms and the personnel director in 27 percent of the companies. The responsibility falls within the personnel department in 34 percent of the firms and rests with the general administration in 29 percent.

Even though the human resource director is not usually responsible for the security function, you may find yourself suddenly in charge, one of the 27 percent of the companies ASPA surveyed who assign the security function to the personnel department. If you do find yourself in charge, and maybe in the dark as to what your key security concerns should be, use the following checklist to familiarize yourself with the most common security activities:

- Screen applicants for potential security risks.
- Provide policies and procedures for terminating any employee caught stealing company property.
- Employ security guards on staff or on a contract basis if your organization is of a size where need for guards is indicated.
- Install an alarm system to protect facilities.
- Mark company equipment for theft prevention and recovery purposes.
- Keep an up-to-date inventory of company equipment.
- Depending on company size, value of equipment, and building access, require employee identification badges.
- Provide procedures for monitoring visitors to facilities. Require visitors to sign in and out, and require that they wear identification badges while on the premises.
- Establish a formal evacuation plan for fire, bomb threats, and so on.
- Develop written security guidelines for bomb threats.
- Develop a community relations program. Work with local community leaders and create a "good citizen" public image in the immediate area of the facility.
- Provide emergency first aid in several locations, and post first aid information in accessible areas. Include fire, police, and ambulance numbers.
- Communicate company security policies and procedures to employees.
- If there is a high incidence of theft, some companies employ an undercover detective service.
- Analyze computer security.
- Audit cash flow and other monetary procedures.
- If there is an area of significant loss, form a risk management committee to review the problem.

Security is a responsibility that becomes more important as an organization grows, and more time and effort must be invested as the need becomes evident. However, there are very basic good business reasons for even moderate security practices in every company, no matter what size.

Index